SNAKES OF NEW ENGLAND

PHOTOGRAPHIC AND NATURAL HISTORY STUDY

LINDA KRULIKOWSKI   **AUTHOR AND PHOTOGRAPHER**

*Young Black Rat Snakes after emergence from eggs, specimens contributed by
John Morrell and children John Wyatte and Maranda, Haddam Ct.*

Printed by Lebon Press
Hartford, Ct. www.lebonpress.com

Published by LuvLife Publishing
Old Lyme, Ct

Krulikowski, Linda, 1943-

Photographs by Linda Krulikowski

ISBN 0-9764316-0-2

"THE IMPOSSIBLE DREAM"

"To dream the impossible dream
To fight the unbeatable foe
To bear with unbearable sorrow
To run where the brave dare not go
To right the unrightable wrong
To love pure and chaste from above
To try when your arms are too weary
To reach the unreachable star
This is my quest
To follow that star
No matter how hopeless
No matter how far
To fight for the right
Without question or pause
To be willing to march anywhere
      for a heavenly cause
And I know, if I only be true
      to this glorious quest
Then my heart will lie peaceful and calm
      when I'm laid to my rest
And the world will be better for this
That one 'man', scorned and covered with scars
Sees him stroll with his last ounce of courage
To reach the unreachable star."

              M. Leigh/J. Darion

DEDICATION:

This book is dedicated to

My son Ernie, whose love of snakes converted my terror to compassion

To

My husband, Ernest, who transformed from " the only good snake is a dead snake", to helping me pose snakes in the wild.

To

Amy, and my grandchildren Kyle and
Savannah Marie to educate and pass on the passion.

To

Steve Berube, without whose charismatic, mystical powers this book never would have been realized, and finally

To

Loving the unloved, and passing on understanding and passion to children everywhere, to follow your dream.

TABLE OF CONTENTS

AUTHORS PREFACE

(Why Me, Why Snakes)

The history of this book represents a "Circle of Life" that can be described only as miraculous. As a child in a family with four brothers, I was raised in a beautiful unpolluted forest in the 1950s, when water and air were still pure, and the woodlands were pristine with natures beauty. My fear of snakes developed early in life. Brothers tend to chase sisters with 'slithery, slimy serpents' and put snakes and frogs in their beds, and think nothing of the long-term terror this inflicts.

There were dens of copperheads in the trap-rock mountain at Hubbard Park, in Meriden Connecticut, and our parents warned us constantly about their possible presence, and how dangerous they were. Back then every snake was considered deadly and evil, and should be destroyed for the safety of all concerned. A bounty on copperheads was even offered by the town in an attempt to reduce the threat to visitors of the park. Fortunately in the past 40 years, although our environment has become polluted, our minds have been cleared of the old erroneous teachings about snakes and their supposed evil aspects. *Evil* spelled backwards is *Live*!

The need to live a life without this fear became paramount, when my son and his young friends started bringing snakes home, and asking all kinds of questions to which I had no answers. We could not distinguish the difference between a copperhead, milk snake, hognose snake, baby black rat and racers, or baby water snakes. The young snakes looked nothing like their parents. We assumed they were totally different species of snakes! A crisis developed when my 12-year old son, and his best friend, Steve Berube, were hiking in the hills behind our home. None of us knew, at least the parents had no clue that an active copperhead den existed in the neighborhood. One day my son Ernie came racing home screaming that Steve had been bitten by a copperhead! 911 was called, and Steve was rushed to the hospital, treated and survived his ordeal as king of the hill, and a hero to his peers. The story at the time was that he was bitten while climbing the ledges. Needless to say, panic pervaded our homes. I became concerned that no one in the area, except the children, seemed to have any knowledge of the snakes in the neighborhood. The books we referred to in the early 1980s were not much help, for they were mostly in black and white, with scientific terms and descriptions, which only increased our confusion. I became adamant about creating a book that would identify and describe the snakes in Connecticut, in such a manner, that any distraught mother or father could pick up this book, and within a few minutes identify the snake that their child had just brought home, or that their family cat had playfully dragged into their living room.

My son and his friends Steve Berube, Billy Ross, and Al Corey were serious snake enthusiasts. I did not want to discourage their outdoor adventures, but desperately wanted to learn all there was to know about the snakes in the area. It was imperative that I over come my paranoid fear of snakes. The fear was so extreme, that if I saw a picture of a snake, or watched a movie that had snakes in it, I would have panic attacks, my hands would get all sweaty, and I would feel sick to my stomach. My dreams were often filled with nightmares after having encounters with the snakes the kids would bring home. The most recurrent one was of my running down a hill covered with snakes that were biting me!

After recovering from the copperhead bite, with no ill effects, Steve began helping me learn how to handle snakes, and remove my fear. With knowledge, fear disappears, knowing this, I became more receptive as Steve taught me how to handle a snake in a nonthreatening manner. His attempts began with, "…ah come on Mrs. "K." it is just a beautiful 6' Black Rat Snake, friendly and tame, and I promise it will not hurt you." He placed it in my sweaty hands, and described how to hold it. Keeping my hands open, putting no restraining hold on the snake, I was instructed to allow it to crawl over my fingers and hands freely. It was important to support the snakes body as it moved from hand to hand, with its tail wrapped securely around my left arm for support as it explored my right arm, shoulder and neck. After several days of handling this sleek black beauty with no ill effects, my paranoia was gradually replaced by the euphoric high that comes with conquering a life-long, crippling fear.

With new respect and love for snakes, I began photographing every snake the kids and I could find. I wanted to photograph them in their natural habitat, and at ground level. The photographs of snakes that I had seen to date were all taken looking down upon them, and if the photos were close-ups, only part of the snake would be in focus. A snake is so long and usually in poor lighting that it is difficult to get the entire animal in focus. I had to develop a technique that would allow enough light to enter the lens, but at the same time have a setting that allowed for a depth of field to give clear, unblurred pictures. After this technique was developed, I was able to focus my attention on close-up photography of all the snakes in Connecticut, using a macro lens, a manual Pentax camera and Sunpak flash unit. No telephoto equipment was ever used. I wanted to lie on the ground with my subjects, and see the world from their viewpoint. The dream of creating a photographic and natural history study was always in the forefront of my mind, as I posed and photographed the snakes. The dream was to create all the images, so that they fit together in a perfect puzzle when it came time to put the book together. This unity of images has allowed for the creation of a unique study.

For several years I traveled and lectured all over the state, taking photographs and accumulating an abundant fund of data from children, residents, teachers and researchers. Life changes caused a break in my active lecture circuit, and I was forced to work outside my home in the retail world, limiting my opportunity to follow my dream of writing this book.

Divine destiny intervened in 2001 when my friend Steve Berube approached me about getting some of my photographs published in a book that he was illustrating for Ed Riccutti. I was thrilled about the prospect, but also apprehensive, for many dreams of being published had gone unfulfilled in the past. My slides were not well organized, but Ed was enthusiastic about the quality of the work, and said he wanted to use some in his book. When we met, we recognized each other from a previous encounter with snakes. Ed had been executive editor of WF (Wrestling Federation) magazine, and had published some of my photos in an article on the wrestler "Jake the Snake" Roberts. The book, *The Snake Almanac* came out in the spring of 2001 with abundant photos by Linda Krulikowski. The circle of life continued. Steve had begun to share in my quest when he removed my fear of snakes, and helped me locate and photograph most of the snakes in this book. He later used my slides in education programs that I could no longer do. He arranged for my photos to be published in a book he illustrated, and now his drawings appear in this book that we dreamed about for 25 years. This is a perfect example of synchronicity, and surrendering to the powers responsible for the continuing circle of life.

The four musketeers! The reason this book was created. From right to left, my son Ernie Krulikowski, Billy Ross, Steve Berube and Al Corey. Photo of the kids hanging out in front of the fire, warming up after a snake hunt in the spring of 1983. They were the inspiration to write this book, and were responsible for locating most of the snakes in this book. This is a tribute to them, and all children.

ACKNOWLEDGMENTS

During the 25 years that it took to create this book, there have been fathoms of friends and enthusiastic children encouraging and stimulating me along my path to creating a book on snakes of Connecticut and New England. It seems a monumental task to acknowledge all the people involved in this adventure, but a loving attempt is now attempted.

The first and foremost thanks are offered to Stephen Berube. Steve has been a catalyst in the production of this book since his childhood. He has always exhibited an uncanny mystical power over the serpents in his life. He could charm a frightened defensive snake into a soft pliable friend with one touch. He tamed the fear in them by simply cupping his large warm hands, and slowly lowered them over the snake, until it disappeared beneath the safe gentle cover of warmth and darkness. After a few minutes, he would lift his hands, and a perfect poised animal was ready for a portrait. Steve has always had a fascination for snakes, and started collecting them when he was eight years old. During the 25-year relationship with Steve, he has removed my fear of snakes, introduced me to exciting habitat hikes, and worked with hundreds of specimens in the wild, locating, posing and calming them for photographs. My son Ernie Krulikowski and Steve were childhood friends, and their constant snake hunting expeditions inspired the creation of this book.

Thanks go to James Morgan, an award-winning photographer, for his patience in teaching me many photographic techniques. Jim has been a close friend for years, and for a few years in the early 1980s, helped my husband, Ernest Krulikowski, create some extremely beautiful woodworking projects. One of those projects was the remodeling of an old porch into a warm-wooded study, overlooking Rogers Lake. The Circle of Life continues, as this book was written in that room.

The actual writing and formatting of this book could not have been accomplished without the loving support and help from my long time friend Thomas Geisler. When the actual writing phase of this project became imperative, Tom donated a beautiful Dell computer for my use. He was upgrading, and asked if I might not like his "old" computer to write my book on! It took a few months to become computer literate, and learn formatting and scanning skills, but without Toms patient guidance through this tedious stage of book preparation, my impossible dream would never have come to fruition.

Before I developed the technique of scanning my own slides, I needed to have prints of my slides made to incorporate into the text. I owe a debt of gratitude to Joe Lambert, owner of Village Photolabs in Old Saybrook, Connecticut, and Christy Cohen, Production Manager for the beautiful prints that were developed from my slides.

I would like to thank all the home owners in Old Lyme and surrounding towns for their conscientious calls to me to remove snakes from their residents, rather than killing them. Many families also contributed snakes that were captured in their home surroundings, and brought to me for photographs. Among the adult friends of the misunderstood snake, I thank Alan and Helen Aroh, Sue Roberts, Marsha Kobutovic, Steve Kuriansky, Paul Maturo, Larry Burke, Ben Kegley, Mike Naumowitz, Paul Nager, Emerson Sartain, John Morrell, and Linda and Bob Claps.

Special thanks are given to all the friends in the Laysville community that encouraged me every day, as they visited me at country stores where I worked. Many devoted friends that have never stopped encouraging me in this impossible dream include; Steve and Dale Malcarne, Carl Kotzan, Chuck Smith, Mark Kus, Ken and Teressa Coffee, Ken and Eileen Coffee, John, Sue and Calli Coffee, Wayne, Evan and Tish Kirk, Everett and Cheryl Lee, Judy Friday, Hank Golet, Ned Pfeiffer, Frank Disbrow, Bob Patterson, Bill Plyler, Erin O'Hare, Jim and Sandra Tripp, Liz Gillette, Bob Mariani, Mary and Hal Hunter, Barbara Matt and Vaughn Allard, Peggy, Al, Patrick, Grace and Charlie Ames, Meg, John and Emma McCulloch, Lynn and Jim Boos, Roz Christison, Mac Godley, all the girls at Citizens Bank in Old Lyme, the wonderful patient and helpful staff at Staples in Old Saybrook, Ginny Allen of Guppies to Puppies, John and Dana Evans, and especially Bob Ballard, the maker of dreams for children everywhere.

Bob Mariani, often known locally as the "man who got bit by that copperhead" has been willing to relive his experience with a severe Northern Copperhead bite which he received in 1979. It was an incredible experience, and I am honored that Bob had the courage and desire to share this traumatic experience with me. Its educational benefits are immeasurable.

Ken Coffee, deserves a bouquet of thanks for allowing me to leave work at Coffees Corner Market in Old Lyme, and go out on snake calls. He also was undaunted by the presence of snakes in various containers, being hidden under the counter during the days work, after some enthusiastic child had dropped off the snake for identification and rescue. "Just keep them out of sight so the customers will not be traumatized!"

Many snakes were also brought to Coffees Market and Deli by Phil Trowbridge. Phil is an accomplished stone mason, and in the course of his work, he and his men often find snakes in the old works that they are reconstructing, or in previously undisturbed habitat. It would be so easy for these men to just do the macho manly thing so often bragged about at after work jam sessions, and kill the innocent animals. Instead, Phil and his men have been dedicated contributors to saving the lives of these snakes, and donating them for this photographic study. I think everyone sleeps better knowing that they have saved a life, and preserved a species that might otherwise be one more dead snake towards extinction.

I want to thank all the children that helped me, through the two generation long journey of preparing this book, for their enthusiastic participation. Acknowledging them as field assistants and field associates in each chapter of this book has been an exciting gift for all of us. The friends of my son, Ernie began the adventure in the early 1980s. This first generation of children of the Snakes of New England include Steve Berube, Al Corey, Billy Ross, Gary Hall, Mark Kus and Chris Guiles, all now successful adults in their 30's. The second generation of young field assistants includes Wyatt Lee Frantz, Evan Kirk, Chris Tompkins, John Stearns, Morey and Grey Tripp, John Wyatte and Maranda Morrell, Tyler Malcarne, Ethan Makuck, and my grandchildren Kyle and Savannah Marie Krulikowski.

The following teachers encouraged their students in the study of "herps" and shared their classrooms with me in the beginning phase of my study: Mrs. Henry, Mrs. McKee and Carl Kotzan. The Southern Library Council sponsored lectures, and The Connecticut State Museum of Natural History encouraged me to participate in their preliminary developmental stages. Working with Maryon M. Attwood, I was included on their speakers bureau, and my work, Poisonous Snakes and their Look-A-likes, was one of the first travelling photographic exhibits (1980s) on their now extensive education program. Thank you Carl Rettenmeyer, founder of the Museum, and now Professor Emeritus, Ecology & Evolutionary Biology, University of Connecticut. Carl has been a great friend and critic, and never diminished in his encouragement.

Family support from Aunt Kathleen and Uncle Fran, Uncle Chester, and Cousin John have contributed so much support that tears of gratitude wash down my face at the thought of them. My sister Aleta Gudelski has kept the sisterhood of spirit alive, caressing both our dreams of leaving something of special beauty behind to nourish the children that follow in our destiny. My brother Art, who though distant in miles, remains constant in his support of my impossible dream. Aunt Betty graciously acknowledged my existence with financial endowment, which helped the final production of this dream.

Friend, chiropractor and neighbors, Dori and Bob Recor, kept my spirits elevated and my body aligned to the tune of cracking joints and renewed life. .

C. F. Smith, Department of Ecology and Evolutionary Biology, The University of Connecticut, has been a friend and advisor in the final stages of the preparation of this book. Chuck has been doing an extensive radiotelemetry study on a population of Northern Copperheads in Central Connecticut. My camera and I have been honored to accompany Chuck and his assistant Steve Berube, on radio-tracking field trips, and in his lab and operating room. His encouragement has been a strong motivating factor in the completion of this book.

Property owner, builder, architect and dear friend, Bob Chapman of Old Lyme, allowed me unobstructed access to his acres of land for photographic purposes. Bob is a conscientious man who owns a herpetological paradise. Sixty five percent of the photographs in this book, taken over a period of 25 years, were taken on Bob's property. The only snakes not found on this quaking bog, granite-ledge sanctuary were the Timber Rattlesnake (now extirpated from this area, but present 50 years ago), Northern Brown Snake, Eastern Milk Snake, Eastern Hognose Snake, Eastern Smooth Green Snake, and the Northern Red-Bellied Snake.

During the years of research for this book, I have been honored to have communicated with many experts in the field, especially Michael W. Klemens, Donald J. Borror, Chuck Smith, Hank Grunner, R. W. Fritsch, Toby Louis Ernst, Rulon Clark and special thanks to Harvey Lillywhite.

The most elusive snakes to locate in the state were the Northern Red-bellied Snake, and the Timber Rattlesnake. Although the friends who helped me locate these two animals are acknowledged in the species chapters on these snakes, I would like to give very special thanks to them now.

A young man from Ashford Connecticut had attended a lecture I gave at UCONN in August 1987. During the lecture, I mentioned that I needed photos of the Red-Bellied Snake. At the close of the lecture, during the question and answer period, this young man, 10-year old Christopher Guiles, excitedly announced that he had Red-Bellies in his back yard! We made plans to meet at his home the next day. It was a hot August day, making snake hunting a questionable success, for the heat would drive them under cover. Chris knew exactly where to go, and found a beautiful animal in the cool moss on the edge of his wooded backyard. Within fifteen minutes, he made a quick dive into another clump of moss, and picked up a baby red-belly! This was absolutely miraculous. We had a wonderful hot hike, and came out with ruby-red treasures. I am deeply indebted to

Chris. The animals were photographed, taken home for further study, and a week later, were returned to their home. Chris had beautiful photos to hang up on his wall, with the dream of eventually having the same pictures in a book on Snake of New England. Well Chris, it took 17 years, but we made it!

The Timber Rattlesnake was another impossible snake to find. I have two friends to thank for their help in finding this extra special endangered animal. My husband and I were taxidermists for many years, and became acquainted with many sportsman and hunters during those years. Most of them reported seeing or hearing rattlesnakes on their deer hunting treks. Checking out their claims was exciting but never produced a rattlesnake. Lots of black rat snakes, racers and hognose snakes were found, but no rattlers. The exception came one June day in Portland Connecticut. A sportsman and friend, Sam Del Russo, whom we had mounted many deer heads for, owned property in Portland Connecticut with his dad. I was given permission to go rattlesnake hunting on this property. Everett Lee, a good friend, and expert amateur herpetologist, accompanied me on a snake hunt on Sam;s property. After hours of hiking, we finally found one beautiful young animal. Many wonderful photos were taken of it, and we left the forest exhilarated and humbled by the gift.

Two years later, a fellow lecturer and herpetologist, Al Bagley, agreed to take me on a rattlesnake hunt. We had previously explored copperhead sites in my "back yard", and on a warm September day in 1986, Al took me hiking up some incredibly beautiful mountain trails in the State Forest. I cannot describe the feelings that raced non-stop through my body as my senses heightened to a state of insurmountable exhilaration and expectation. Every step through knee-high ferns, and glacial rock ledges was like walking on the moon. As we approached the crest of the mountain, in an area with wind-swept dwarfed pines and blueberry bushes, I stepped upon a large flat rock. It came alive with the sound of a thousand buzzing bees. For the next 3 hours we located and photographed over 18 magnificent timbers. Most of them were gravid or recently postpartum females with their babies. I will never again experience anything so exciting and awe-inspiring, of such humbling magnitude in my life. To be lying on the hallowed ground with these beautiful, docile animals, feeling the warm sun, inhaling the scents of pine, blueberry and lichen covered earth was the most spiritual experience of my life. The gorgeous serpents seemed to sense that no danger was present, and that my visit was going to somehow help preserve their now endangered presence in our state. By being allowed to photograph their beauty, and share their most intimate moments of birthing and basking, they seemed to sense a friend. They felt unthreatened by my presence, as seen in Fig. 22.1. The animal in this photo seemed to be the dominant force on the mountain, as he appeared to be watching over all the activity, with a cool calmness that filled the atmosphere. It was such a privilege to be allowed to share in his kingdom, and be present at this most private birthing place. The spiritual soul wrenching experience confirmed my constant belief that this book was meant to be finished some day. I never gave up on the dream to write this book, although many people told me it was just too massive a task, with too many photographs. It would just not happen. Well, thanks to people like Steve, Sam, Al, and Chris, the dream has come true, to be shared with hundreds of children.

The most recent dynamo of power to forge the writing of this book has been friend and cohort, Ed Ricciuti. Ed recently wrote *The Snake Almanac*, 2001, one of over

70 books that he has written in his illustrious career. Ed used many of my photographs in his book. Because of his book, I was propelled into finally organizing over 2000 slides, of Connecticut snakes, into chapters of research that I had accumulated over the past 25 years. The miraculous synchronicity continued, as I was given a window of 8 months of free time, while the local Coffees Market and Hardware store where I worked, were being rebuilt, by Bob Chapman. Steve Berube, who was the major catalyst in the photographic production of this book for the first 15 years of work, also illustrated *The Snake Almanac* and suggested that Ed use my photographs in his book. Steve granted his permission to use some of his drawings in this book. The Circle of Life continued as the *Spirit* gave me the strength, dedication, devotion and power to write endlessly for the past 18 months, between working 40-60 hours a week setting up a new Laysville Hardware store, I spent hundreds of hours writing in the wee hours of the morning, when sleep beckoned, but the book called more loudly.

Deep thanks go to my life-long friend and husband, Ern, for his encouragement in this monumental endeavor and dream. He changed his attitude towards snakes from one of "the only good snake is a dead one", to helping me work the snakes for photographs, and holding captives as I cleaned their homes. He has patiently read and reread drafts of the book with poignant comments, and encouraged my midnight to dawn writing. We desperately wanted to produce a book that parents, teachers and children could use and learn from, but at the same time did not want to alienate the scientific world. As a trained biologist, naturalist and photographer, I often tended to get too technical and scientific with my writing, and Ern was always quick to get me back on track. My deadline was to have this book finished for our 40th wedding anniversary, and we did it! Thanks Love.

I need to express my deepest and sincere appreciation to President Andy Lerner and his amazing staff at Lebon Press; Bruce Hourigan, Debbie Lee and Joe Waggoner for their incredible dedication to the production of this photographic study. Thank you so much for exhibiting a devotion to excellence above and beyond the call of duty. Your work ethic is so rewarding and refreshing. It is a rare commodity in this sometimes impersonal and fast-paced world. I am deeply indebted to you all.

Finally, thanks to a friend, herpetologist and mysterious character that only wants to be known as Richard.

INTRODUCTION

This book was produced in answer to a life long interest in snakes. My curiosity began with stories of the temptress snake in the Garden of Eden, who enticed Adam to eat the apple of knowledge. From curiosity, my relationship with snakes advanced to the days of total fear and paranoia. Once knowledge replaced this fear, I became determined to prepare a book on snakes of New England that would help future generations appreciate, love and admire these beautiful and often misunderstood animals.

Roger Tory Peterson, an unbelievably sensitive artist and writer, has always been my hero. I was blessed with being able to see and talk with him occasionally in our favorite Nehantic State Forest wilderness, early in the spring, listening for the mating sounds of the Ruffed Grouse. I can remember, when I worked at the Old Lyme Pharmacy in the early 1990s, Roger would come into the store and pick up a prescription. I was so enthralled to be near him. He seemed like a god, his photographs, prints and paintings of every bird in the universe are awe-inspiring. Looking into the eyes of his creations, is an experience of sharing his soul, for he transferred his soul into everything he painted. When you entire a room filled with his birds of raptor, you are overwhelmed with the magnitude of peaceful power emanating from each painting. The feeling is so uplifting, you feel almost able to soar with his eagles. After becoming a seasoned photographer, developing techniques to convey the beauty of reptiles and amphibians into my photographs, I early on was determined to become the Roger Tory Peterson of the reptile world. I wanted to present the light of love in every photograph, depicting the animals sensuality, beauty, majesty and character. In creating this book, my main motivation has been to portray the snake as a beautiful animal that deserves to live an unmolested life, and to be respected as a fellow living creature, admired for its incredible powers of survival against immeasurable odds.

When I first started trying to identify all the snakes I encountered on my hunts, I was amazed at how few photographs were available for identification purposes. It was difficult to find pictures of baby and juvenile snakes, which most of the time do not look anything like their parents. A lot of research is available, but it is written so scientifically that translating it into "layman's" terms took hundreds of hours of concentrated effort. A lot of the technical terminology is not defined in *Webster's Dictionary*. Searching out definitions was quite a challenge. Harvey Lillywhite is in the process of compiling an updated dictionary of herpetology, but it is not yet available. Peters *Dictionary of Herpetology*, 1964 was a great help, but does not include a lot of updated terminology. I have included an extensive glossary at the back of this book, in an attempt to help my readers have easy access to some of the more common terminology.

In addition to extensive photographic profiles, I have prepared introductory chapters on the general biology and behavior of snakes. These behaviors include feeding, body temperature regulation, hibernation, reproduction, locomotion and defensive responses. Snakes are simply fascinating creatures that have survived for millions of years with, until recently, very little help from man. It is a marvel to just watch them move, gliding across the ground with no apparent effort, no visible means of propulsion, but within a split second, a graceful slow meandering pace can change to the speed of a bullet.

Part One also includes chapters on venomous snakes and snakebite. The properties and toxicity of venom is discussed, along with fang structure and venom delivery systems. I have included chapters on the history of snakebite first aid, and recommended modern treatments and updated antivenin preparations. I was also fortunate to have a friend, Bob Mariani, relate his experience with a severe copperhead bite in 1979.

A book on snakes is incomplete without an extensive discussion about the mythology and folklore, which surrounds their history. Wild stories are a part of any gathering at which the subject of snakes arises, be it children in the tree house, men at the local hang out, or teachers trying to put truth where fiction abounds. I have included a section on American Indians and their relationship with the rattlesnake, and a discussion of the importance of the rattlesnake symbol in the history of the United States. There is a brief discussion on how scientists classify snakes and a list of the 14 Connecticut Snakes with their scientific names. The snakes of other New England states are listed in Appendix IV, with brief discussions on the two subspecies of ribbon snake and garter snake that are not found in Connecticut.

How to Use This Book: In addition to being an encyclopedia on snakes in general, this book is designed primarily to be used as a guide for the identification of the snakes that you encounter in your back yard, or hikes into the abundant forested areas of our state, and the New England area in general. The quickest way to find the identity of the unknown snake is to turn to Chapter 6, and look at the photographs of the 14 adult and young snakes found in Connecticut. From these 28 photographs, you should be able to make a choice of a few snakes that come close to your mystery snake. Once you have narrowed your choice to one or two species, go to the Table of Contents and find the chapters on the species of choice.

A key to New England Snakes is provided for identification of a snake-in-hand, which may be either alive, dead, or a preserved specimen. All the important diagnostic characters are illustrated in line drawings, and technical terms are defined in the glossary at the end of the book. The key appears as a series of couplets, which use major diagnostic characters to separate groups of snakes. As you make your identification choices, you will eventually get to the name of the snake, which may be looked up in the Table of Contents or index. From there you can read the chapter, and learn about the beautiful animal in your hand. Do not handle Connecticut's two venomous snakes, the Northern Copperhead, or the Timber Rattlesnake. Their identification must be made in the field, at a safe distance, without disrupting their habitat or injuring them in any way.

Description of habitats where each species commonly occurs in New England is based largely on 25 years of personal observation. Where information was lacking, I researched old and new books on snakes, and conferred with any herpetologist that would take the time to discuss my work. An extensive bibliography can be found at the end of the book.

Part Two includes a brief discussion of Colubrids, the typical snakes, and Crotalids, the pit vipers, after which follow the chapters on each individual species of snake found in New Englandt. The chapters include extensive photographic profiles of adult and young snakes. When available, photos of birthing, and/or hatching, feeding, defensive postures, and courtship are included. Close-up photos of different defining characteristics such as head scales, and heat sensing pits are also included.

Each species chapter includes the description, sexual dimorphism, head scale identification, range, habitat, behavior, reproduction, feeding, predators, defensive responses, common names, and a photographic finale of similar snakes that are commonly confused with the one in the chapter. Adults and young are represented in the comparison photos.

Special topics are treated in the Appendixes. These topics include radiotelemetry studies, captive care, and rehabilitation of reptiles and amphibians. A special section on range maps of the snakes of News England, with a brief description of the 2 subspecies of snakes not found in Connecticut, but present in extreme northern New England, and a list of snakes present in each of the other 5 New England states is presented. The Glossary, Bibliography and index follow.

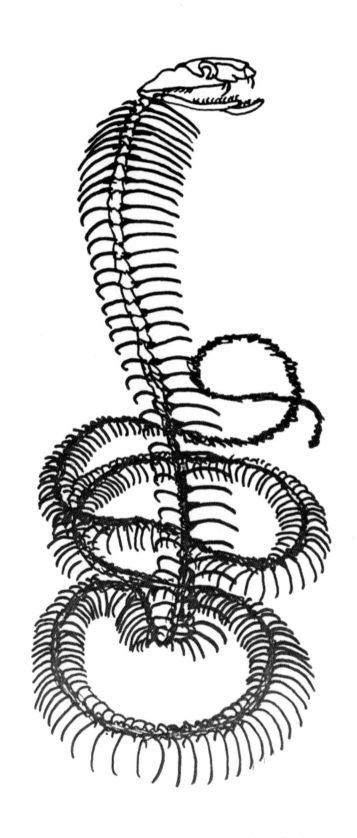

TYPICAL SNAKE SKELETON

CHAPTER ONE
GENERAL BIOLOGY

Anatomy:

While discussing the biology of snakes, it is important to explore the beauty and mystic qualities that make them such sensually alluring, captivating creatures. Snakes are related to turtles, crocodilians, birds and lizards. They are vertebrates with a divided bony spinal column, or backbone. The vertebrae are connected by a strong ball-and-socket joint and connecting ligaments. Each neck and body vertebra, except for the first

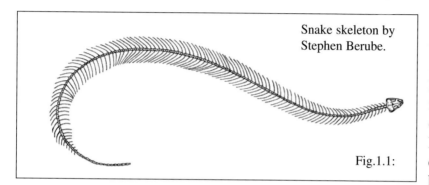

Snake skeleton by Stephen Berube.

Fig.1.1:

two, has a pair of ribs. The first two vertebrae, the atlas and axis, attach the skull to the head. There is no sternum, and because none of the ribs join ventrally, the sides may more easily expand for breathing, feeding, reproduction, and defense. The ribs wrap around the body to the underside of the snake, at the edge of the large ventral scales. Most snakes have a pair of ribs associated with each ventral scale, so that the number of ventral scales usually equals the number of neck and body vertebrae. The ventral scale count can vary from a little over 100 to more than 500 in some seasnakes. Ribs generally only occur on the first few caudal or tail vertebrae. Most snakes have an enlarged anal scale, which covers the cloacal opening, or vent, which marks the boundary between the body and tail. The scales past the vent are called subcaudal scales, and they are either single, or paired, or a combination of both.

Snakes have a sheath or covering of tough, fibrous scales made from a protein called keratin. These scales are formed from folded and thickened portions of the outer layers of skin, called the dermis and epidermis. Each scale has an outer surface, an inner surface and hinge zone where folding occurs, and a thin free area of skin that usually overlaps the next scale. Snakes have smooth or keeled scales, which have longitudinal ridges. The arrangement and numbers of these scales, is important in the classification and

Fig.1.2: Smooth scales of Eastern Smooth Green Snake

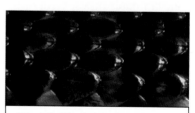

Fig.1.3: Keeled scales of Northern Water Snake

identification of different species. The scales on the heads of most snakes are enlarged and referred to as plates (See Fig. 6.2). The names of these plates, moving from front to back over the head are the rostral, which covers the snout, the internasals, which ar usually paired behind the rostral, the frontal, which is between the supraoculars, and the parietals which are paired and behind the frontals. The scales that line the lips are called labials. Around the nostril are the nasal scales, and behind them are the loreal and/or the preocular scales, in front of the eye. Between the upper lip scales, the supralabials, and the parietal plates are the postocular and temporal scales. On the throat area, there is a

Fig.1.4: Chin scales, Northern Black Racer.

mental scale immediately below the rostral, followed by large paired chin shields and smaller throat or gular scales. Most snakes have expansion grooves between the rows of chin scales to allow for stretching during swallowing large prey. The scales on the side of the head are reduced in size, and the scales around the mouth, the pit, in pit vipers, and the throat are generally small. The scales on the body usually are arranged in regular diagonal rows. Each row has a fixed number of scales, which is species-specific, which means that all snakes of that species have the same number of scales. The accepted counts that are used to identify separate species occur at the neck, immediately behind the head, at midbody (See Fig. 6.1), and in front of the tail. The figures can be identical, such as 13-13-13, which appears in a cylindrical snake such as the Eastern Worm Snake, or appears in a cylindrical snake such as the Eastern Worm Snake, or they may decrease in a regular pattern such as 25-23-17, which appears in the Black Rat Snake. The scale number does not change with the age of the snake. The arrangement and number of scales is the same from hatchling, or birth to adulthood. Thin-bodied snakes usually have fewer scales per row than thick-bodied snakes.

On the underside or belly of most snakes, the scales are large and rectangular. They are called ventral scales, and are arranged in a single row from the throat to the vent. These scales are very important in locomotion by providing the contact points for pushing the sides and top of the body forward. The skin between the ventral scales allows for a small amount of stretch, but the scales on the sides of the body expand the most.

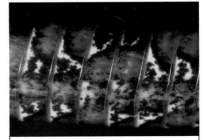

Fig.1.5: Ventral scales of Northern Water Snake.

The skin is loosely attached to the muscles of the body. This soft skin has a large degree of expandability, being able to stretch forward, backward, and up and down on the body. Scales usually overlap each other, with skin between each scale, creating an accordion effect, thus providing for an even higher degree of stretch. This allows for swallowing large prey, and for adjustment to the growth of eggs or fetal snakes in female snakes. Muscles lie between the skeleton and the skin. Because the snakes are without limbs, the body movement is produced by a complex muscular linkage with the ribs and vertebrae. Muscles link the backbone to the ribs, and the ribs to the ventral scales. In the tail, where few if any ribs occur, the muscles link the vertebrae to each other. This anatomy allows the snake a great deal of flexibility, a large choice of modes of locomotion, and in some snakes, the ability to constrict prey.

The typical snake skull consists of a bony braincase, which protects the brain, and provides a surface for attachment of various jawbones and muscles. The jaw is made up of the upper and lower jawbones. Each one can move independently, or in coordination with each other. This gives the skull an incredible

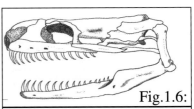

Fig.1.6: Typical snake skull: Steve Berube

flexibility, which is unmatched in any other animal group, allowing snakes to catch and swallow large prey. Because snakes have no arms, legs or cutting teeth, they cannot hold and tear apart their food, so they must swallow it whole.

The internal anatomy of snakes resembles other vertebrates, except that the organs need to fit into a long tubular body (Fig. 1.7), with expandable parts. The organs are staggered in a straight line, and are more elongated than in other animals. The left lung is greatly reduced in size in the typical snake. The right lung extends through most of the body cavity, and ends in a saclike air storage area. The esophagus extends from the mouth almost to the middle of the body, where it gradually increases in diameter to form the stomach. The stomach is separated from the coiled small intestine by a pyloric valve, which empties into the short, straight large intestine. The liver has 2 lobes and is

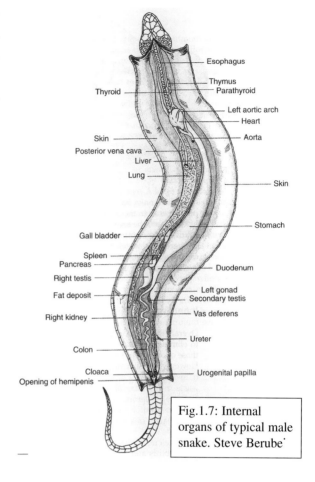

Fig.1.7: Internal organs of typical male snake. Steve Berube'

elongate. Paired kidneys and reproductive organs are in the later part, or posterior portion, of the body. There is no urinary bladder. The mouths function, with its many backward slanted teeth, is to catch, hold and move the food items forward. The teeth also puncture the prey, which allows the introduction of digestive enzymes from their saliva to enter the food. Salivary glands then empty saliva and mucus into the mouth cavity, which gives the food a slippery coat so that it moves down the esophagus and into the stomach more easily. The enzymes and acid in the stomach begin to break down the food, which is enhanced by muscular crushing activity. The food then passes from the stomach into a short coiled small intestine for further chemical breakdown and absorption of nutrients. It then moves into the large straight intestine for reabsorption of water, and the undigested parts of the prey, usually only hair, exits through the anus into the cloaca and finally to the outside through the vent in the tail. The cloaca is a cavity into which the digestive, excretory and reproductive systems all empty.

Male snakes have paired sexual organs. Each organ is called a hemipenis, meaning "half penis", as seen in Fig. 1.8. This term relates to ancient times, when the belief was that the two organs were pressed together to form a single organ. Each organs is a blind, inverted cylinder that can be turned inside out, or everted through the snakes vent by a combination of hydraulic pressure, from blood sinuses in the organ, and muscular action. Semen does not flow through the organ, but travels along a surface channel, or sperm

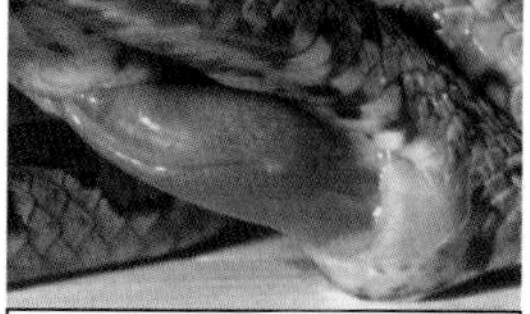

Fig.1.8: Illustration of hemipenes.

3

groove, into the females cloaca. A retractor muscle and reduced blood pressure invert the organ after mating, at which time it is stored in the base of the tail. This gives the tail of the male snake a more stout shape and greater length than the female.

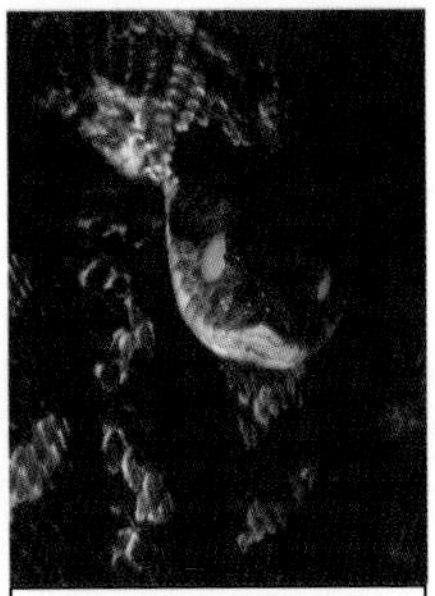

Ecdysis, shedding or molting results from changes in the underlying skin structure. Snakes typically shed their skins in one piece. The time between sheds may vary from a few weeks to several months depending upon food consumption, temperature, health and growth. About 4-5 days before molting begins, the eyes are clouded gray or blue by fluid that is caught between the old and the newly formed spectacles, or eye caps (Fig. 1.9). Snakes in this condition are usually inactive and remain in a moist hideaway.

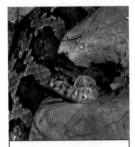

Fig.1.10: Florida Corn Snake beginning shed cycle, freeing snout skin.

Fig.1.9: Opaque eyes of Hognose 4 days before shed

When the snake is ready to remove the old skin, it rubs its snout on any firm, surface until the scales from the upper and lower lips become freed from the margin of the mouth (Fig.1.10). The snake begins crawling out of its old skin as its damp inner surface adheres to the surface upon which the snake is moving. As the skin becomes well anchored, the snake crawls forward, out of its old skin, one fraction of an inch at a time, in a caterpillar crawl. Notice that in Fig. 1.11, beneath the shed skin or cast is a revealed a polished new creation. It is similar to peeling a pair of surgical gloves off inside out. Because of this inside-out process, the tail of the old skin is pointing in the direction of the snakes departure. The end result is a shiny new skin, a longer snake, with new tissue replacing any old abrasions. If the animal had parasites on its skin, called ectoparasites, they are removed with the casting of the old skin.

Fig.1.11: Northern Red-Bellied Snakes Cast.

Senses
Vision and the Pit Organ:

Most snakes rely on vision to gather sensory information with well-developed eyes. In snakes that spend their lives underground, the eyes are simplified and small. Vision with such eyes is probably restricted to light and dark. A few species of snakes, such as blindsnakes, have no externally visible eyes, for head scales completely cover the eyes. However, snakes with well-developed eyes register images, not just light and dark. The eye is usually protected by a convex shaped spectacle, brille or eye cap. The amount of light entering the lens of the eye is controlled by the iris, which expands in low-light situations and contracts in bright light. When the light falls on the retina, behind the eyeball, an image is registered and sent to the brain along the

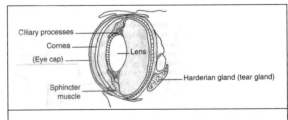

Fig.1.12: Structure of snake eye: Steve Berube.

optic nerve. The lens of a snakes eye does not change shape to allow for distance vision as ours does, but moves back and forth; forward to see close objects, and backwards to focus on distant objects.

Fig.1.13: Green Snake with large eyes forward placed

Fig.1.14: Small eyes of burrowing Worm snake.

The size and position of the eyes and shape of the pupils are associated with habit and habitat. Burrowing snakes have smaller eyes than terrestrial and arboreal, or tree foraging, snakes. Notice the difference in eye size of the Green Snake (Fig. 1.13) who actively hunts for prey above ground and in bushes, versus the worm snake (Fig. 1.14), which is a burrower who hunts earthworms under ground. Diurnal snakes that use sight to hunt their prey often have eyes that are aimed forward, as seen in Fig. 1.13. Eyes positioned in this way produces a wide overlapping field of vision directly in front of the head, creating good depth perception. Ambush hunters and snakes that live in dense habitat have more laterally or side placement of their eyes, such as the rattlesnake in Fig. 1.15. This placement produces a broad field of vision with less overlap.

There is no evidence to date that snakes have color vision. Vertebrate eyes have two basic types of light-receptor cells called rods and cones. Rods are rod-shaped cells in the retina that are sensitive to dim light, but do not yield sharp images. Cones are flask-shaped cells in the retina which are sensitive to bright light and color. More research is needed to study the number of cones and visual pigments associated with those cones, to understand color vision in snakes.

Fig.1.15: Vertical pupil of Timber Rattlesnake.

Diurnal snakes, active during the day, typically have round pupils and moderate sized eyes. Nocturnal snakes that forage at night typically have large eyes, and many also have vertical elliptical pupils, as seen in Fig. 1.15 of the Timber Rattlesnake. Large eyes can gather more light in conditions of low illumination. A round pupil is able to close tightly to a pinpoint opening, permitting a minimum of light to enter the eye on very bright days. In contrast, a vertical pupil can open wider than a round pupil to allow more light to enter the eye. This is a very important feature for nocturnal snakes that must see at night.

Pit Organs:
Eyes perceive light in the visible spectrum, in light frequencies that are visible to the human eye. Some snakes are able to see in the infrared spectrum. These rays are invisible rays just beyond the red end of the visible spectrum. Their wavelengths are longer than those of the color spectrum visible to humans, but shorter than radio waves. They also have a penetrating heating effect. Snakes are able to "see" in this infrared spectrum by using heat receptors called pit organs. Heat radiates from all objects as infrared frequencies, and the intensity changes with the mass and temperature of the

object. Infrared vision detects a temperature difference between an object and its surroundings. Infrared vision is ideal for hunting warm-blooded, or endothermic, prey such as mammals and birds at night.

Fig.1.16: Northern Copperhead

The infrared receptors are usually located in pockets or pits. Pitvipers, Crotalinae, including the Timber Rattlesnake and Northern Copperhead (Fig. 1.16), have a deep pit on each side of the face between the nostril and the eye. The pit contains a membrane, which is suspended above the bottom of the pit. This membrane bears heat receptors, somewhat similar to the function of the retina of the eye. Some rattlesnakes can detect a temperature change as slight as 0.003 degrees centigrade in 0.1 seconds.

Pit organs are positioned facing forward as seen in Fig. 1.16. Each pit is connected to the brain by branches of the fifth cranial nerve, the trigeminal nerve. The left and right field of infrared vision overlap and provide accurate directional information for aiming a strike. Pits might provide information about the size and shape of predators. This could be crucial for a nocturnal pitviper faced with striking at, or fleeing from a large animal. The pits could be useful in searching for warm spots to bask, especially valuable for gravid or pregnant females. More research on the neurobiology of pit organs is need-ed to explain their functions and useful-ness to the snakes equipped with them.

Fig.1.17:Emerald Tree Boa from the Amazon Basin with numerous heat sensing pits. NOT A NEW ENGLAND SNAKE.

Many pythons and boas feed predominantly on birds and mammals that they hunt at night. They have numerous shallow pit organs along their upper lips, and often on the lower lips. The Emerald Tree Boa (*Corallus canina*) in Fig. 1.17, lives in the Amazon Basin, and is a nocturnal, night, feeder. It spends most of its time in trees, sleeping during the day, and catching small mammals and birds at night. It has well-developed labial, lip, thermoreceptors or pits. They are sensitive to minute temperature changes. The numerous pits are clearly visible between the scales around the mouth in Fig. 1.17.

Sense of Smell and the Jacobsons Organ:
Detection of chemical cues, or odor detection, is very important in the lives of all snakes. It is used to find and identify the type of food, for many species of snakes are very food-specific such as the Eastern Hognose Snake who specializes in toad consumption. Detecting the direction of movement and closeness of potential mates, prey and enemies, is determined by chemical cues. Finding habitat sites, and stimulating courtship are also associated with chemical or odor detection in snakes.

Snakes tongues play an important role in odor sensations. The tongue does not smell. It does not actually sense the presence of odors, it carries the odor molecules or particles from the air, to an organ inside the mouth that acts as a sensory device. The snakes also smell through their noses. Airborne odors are breathed in through the

6

nostrils, through the nasal passages, into the olfactory chambers, the organs of smell. The

Fig.1.18: Deply forked tongue of Eastern Hognose

forked tongue flicks in and out through a notch between the rostrum scale on the upper lip and the mental plate on the lower lip, as seen in Fig. 1.18. When the tongue is extended, the tip waves up and down, and odor particles adhere to it. When the tongue is withdrawn into the mouth, the odor molecules are transferred to the roof of the mouth, near a pair of duct openings. The ducts lead into a special olfactory chamber called the Jacobson's organ.   It is also called a vomeronasal organ.   This is a descriptive term relating to the placement of the organ next to the vomer bone in the

Fig.1.19: Opening ducts to Jacobsons organ of Northern Copperhead.

roof of the mouth, and near the nasal chamber leading from the nostril. It is named after a Danish surgeon, Ludwig Levin Jacobson, who was the first man to describe it, in 1811. The organ is lined with sensory and ciliated epithelial cells. The cilia, or tiny hair-like outgrowths, help move the particles through the fluid-filled organ. The tongue tip is not inserted into the organ as was previously thought. It is now believed that particles are transferred from the tongue onto a tissue pad on the floor of the mouth. This pad is then pressed against the roof of the mouth, transferring the odor particles to the sensory organ. The sensory cells in the Jacobson's organ, and in the olfactory chambers react with the odor molecules. The chemical reactions created by this contact are recorded as nerve impulses, or signals, which are sent to the brain for analysis. It is enervated by a branch of the olfactory nerve and appears to be a modified part of the nasal chamber. A coiled, blind sac opens into the mouth. The duct from the organ opens in the roof of the mouth, in front of the internal openings of the nasal passage. The combination of tongue and nose greatly enhances the level of odor detection available.

The deeply forked tongue (Fig. 1.18) gathers odor particles on both tines of the tongue. The different concentrations of chemical odors on the right and left tine tell the snake how close, and in what direction the potential mate, prey or enemy will be. As a snake moves, it pushes against objects, which have odor signatures on only one side, the side pushed against. When the pursuing snake passes the same path, one of its tongue tips or tines picks up more odor particles than the other tip, indicating whether the left or right surface was touched by the earlier snake. This allows the tracking snake to identify the first snakes direction.

Snakes apparently do not have taste buds on their tongues. The taste buds are concentrated in tissue along the rows of teeth. These buds are activated after prey objects have been grasped in the mouth, so snakes do taste their food. Some snakes are very food-specific, such as the Eastern Hognose Snake, which specializes in eating toads. If a hungry hognose snake is offered a mouse for dinner, after tongue scanning, it is refused. It was important to keep one of these animals for several months for study, and the need to keep it fed became a dilemma, as it was difficult to find enough toads to feed it. As a test of this food specific-diet, a frozen toad was puréed in a blender. A frozen

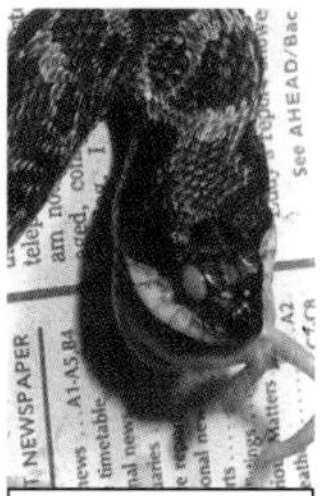

Fig.1.20: Hognose eating a mouse, not its food of choice.

mouse was thawed in warm water, and was dipped in the purée-of-toad. This delicacy was offered to "Hoggie", and immediately eaten after a short time of tongue flicking (Fig. 1.20). After 2 years of captivity, the charming child-loving snake was reintroduced to its diet of toads and this healthy, happy herp was released at its site of capture.

Hearing:

Snakes are very sensitive to tactile or touch stimulation. Snakes do not have external ears or eardrums, but have a modified inner ear. They are able to perceive low-frequency airborne vibrations. Sound waves hitting the surface of the skin in the temporal area of the head are transmitted through the jaw muscle to the quadrate bone. The quadrate bone is a connection between the lower jaw and the skull. The vibrations are then passed on to the columella (Fig. 1.21), which is the inner ear bone, then to the inner ear where sound sensitive cells react with the sound waves and transfer the messages to the brain. This kind of transmission is most effective for low-frequency seismic, ground vibrations. Snakes hear best in the 200-500 hertz range. Hertz is a basic unit of frequency equal to one cycle per second. Vibrational cues may also be detected by receptors on the venter, or belly, of snakes.

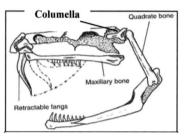

Fig.1.21: Quadrate bone joining cup-shaped columella in pit viper: Stephen Berube.

Breathing in Snakes:

All snakes have a right lung, and many have a left lung, which is usually markedly smaller than the right lung. The right lung is large, and extends to the middle of the body in some species, and almost the entire length of the body in others. Some snakes have developed a new lung-like structure, which develops from the wall of the trachea in front of the heart. Both lungs, the tracheal and conventional lungs, are simple vascular sacs rich in blood vessels and capillaries. Air moves in through the tracheae, into the lungs, and out again, by expansion and contraction of the rib cage. Snakes do not have diaphragms.

When a snake is swallowing large prey, the mouth cavity is filled, and the air passage could easily be blocked. During this process of engulfing prey, a protrusible glottis (Fig. 1.22), which is the opening to the trachea, can extend outward to the edge of the mouth, and off to the side, beneath the food. So even with a full mouth, breathing is not interrupted.

Breathing is a two-stage process consisting of a brief inhalation of air flow, or the ventilation cycle. This is followed by a longer pause period. Constricting the trunk by muscular action forces the air out of the lungs, in the exhalation cycle. Expansion of the trunk creates a semivacuum, which draws air into the lungs. This phase is called inhalation, after which breathing

Fig.1.22: Open mouth of **CAPTIVE** Black Pine Snake, *Pituophis melanoleucus lodingi* from Louisiana, illustrating large trachea and open glottis. **NOT A NEW ENGLAND SNAKE.**

stops for a period of time. This breathing pause, or apnea, may last for a few seconds, or several minutes in a resting, undisturbed snake. Some diving snakes, such as the Northern Water Snake, are able to prolong this state of apnea for 5 to 30 minutes.

CHAPTER TWO
BEHAVIOR

Feeding:

Some snakes hunt for their food, while others sit and wait to ambush their prey. The Timber Rattlesnake typically uses this ambush position next to a fallen log. Extensively studied by H.K. Reinert, this form of ambush is called "Reinert posture." The snake will coil on the forest floor and snug itself against a chosen log. The snake will then rest its lower jaw on the side of the log, poised to strike a rodent traveling along this runway. Both types of hunters use sight, smell, hearing, and touch to locate recognize and capture their prey. Snakes develop food preferences as young hatchlings. If a newborn garter snakes first meal is an earthworm, that snake will prefer an earthworm diet, and if its first meal is a fish, it will prefer to eat fish for a life time diet.

Some snakes use a venomous bite to capture prey. It slows or stops a preys escape by disrupting normal body functions. Many types of venom, especially in vipers such as the Northern Copperhead and Timber Rattlesnake, also begin digestion of the prey before it is swallowed. These snakes usually strike-bite, simultaneously injecting venom into their prey, and then releasing it. The stricken animal will stagger a short distance, collapse, and thus becomes easy to track and eat. If the prey is a lively frog, or bird, the snake will not release its hold after striking. Fixed or rear-fanged snakes such as the Eastern Hognose Snake, hold their captive after striking, and begin chewing almost immediately. This chewing action injects the venom into the muscles and body cavity of the prey. Both methods reduce the amount of struggle between the snake and its prey, reducing the possibility of injury to the snake.

Constricting snakes tighten their coils around the prey with each exhalation of the prey (Fig. 2.1). Each time the struggling prey releases a breath, the snake tightens its coil a few more degrees. There are two theories as to the cause of death from this constricting action. One suggests suffocation, in which case the constriction prevents the prey from breathing, causing asphyxiation and death. However, some researchers after careful observations of this process, indicate that the prey has not been constricted long enough to cause death by suffocation. The theory is that the constricting coils collapse the chest cavity deflating the lungs and compressing the heart. This compression prevents normal heart pumping and leads to immediate

Fig.2.1: Black Rat Snake constricting mouse.

circulatory failure. Constriction may crack a rib or other small bones, but such cracks are rare and the preys skeleton is usually not broken, or crushed. Constricting snakes usually specialize in a diet of mammals and birds.

Snakes do not feed on live large prey, which could inflict injury on the snake during the feeding process. It is killed first. If the prey is small and harmless, there is no need to kill the prey before consuming it. The snakes strike and bite brings the prey into its mouth. Once in the mouth, the jaws move over the prey and it is swallowed alive.

The jaws and mouth skeleton are very flexible, allowing snakes to swallow large food items. The left and right sides of the jaws move independently, and the junction at the angle of the jaw is not fixed as in humans, so the mouth can open very wide. This diagram of the bones in a typical snakes jaw will help in understanding how a snake eats. The diagram shows the right side of the snakes head, which is the same on the left side.

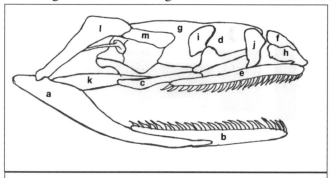

Fig.2.2: Diagram showing the bones of the upper and lower jaw of typical snake skull.

The four bones in the upper jaw are free-floating (Fig. 2.2), in other words, not fused as in a human skull. Two of them, the palatine (not seen in this lateral view) and the pterygoid (k), lie tip to tip on the roof of the mouth, extending the full length of the mouth. The third bone, the maxillary (e), extends from the snout to behind the eye. All three of these bones have teeth. The fourth toothless bone, the ectopterygoid (c), connects the arch formed by the palatine and pterygoid bones to the maxillary bone.

On the lower jaw, only the dentary (b) bone has teeth. At the rear of the jaw, the compound bone (a) joins the quadrate (l) bone with a hinged joint, which in turn joins the skull at the supratemporal (m) bone with another hinged joint. This allows the jaws to move backward, forward, and side to side. The union of the right jaw and the left jaw also forms a flexible moveable attachment. This permits the prey to be moved forward by the jaws "walking" over it. As one side bites down, the other side disengages its teeth, and shifts forward. The teeth are curved inward, which makes them good grasping tools. The rear-facing curve also allows for easy disengagement of the teeth as the food is moved toward the rear of the mouth to the esophagus.

The snake senses it prey before striking. When it strikes, the mouth is fully open, with upper and lower jaws forming almost a 180-degree angle. The accompanying

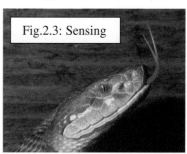

Fig.2.3: Sensing

photos (Figs. 2.3-2.6) show a Northern Copperhead from Connecticut, going through the motions of sensing, gathering and eating a mouse meal. The dead mouse, is grasped by the head, and swallowed

Fig.2.4: Striking

headfirst. Once it has passed beyond the teeth, the neck and trunk muscles twist the mouse towards the esophagus and into the stomach. The impressive skin stretching is well documented in the photos. When the prey is filling the mouth, it is still

Fig.2.5: Engulfing

Fig.2.6: Swallowing

10

imperative that the snake continues to breath. The snake, as mentioned earlier in the sec-

Fig.2.7: Protruding trachea-glottis.

tion on breathing, is able to protrude its trachea and glottis to the side of the mouth in order to continue breathing while consuming large prey. Once the mouse is in the esophagus, the snake goes through a series of yawn-like motions. These yawns manipulate the jaws in such a

Fig.2.8 Yawning.

way as to realign and reset the floating bones of the mouth and jaw to prepare for the next feast. The Northern Brown and Northern Red-Bellied Snakes of Connecticut, love slugs and snails. These snakes bite the soft fleshy part of the snail and push the snail forward until the snail becomes wedged and lodged against something. The snake then rolls and twists, for sometimes 15 minutes, until the snail fatigues, and its muscles relax, at which time the snake pulls the body from the shell, and enjoys its gourmet meal (Fig. 11.10).

The North American Hognose snakes are toad-eating specialists. They are resistant to the toxins released by glands on the toads skin. Hognose snakes have enlarged sword-like teeth on the rear maxillary bones. The swallowing techniques are the same as with other snakes, but are complicated by the fact that the toad puffs up its body in self-defense and becomes difficult to swallow (Fig. 2.9). The enlarged rear teeth were once thought to puncture the toads body cavity and deflate the lungs. Researchers have since determined that the rear teeth are too short to deflate the toad. Instead venom, specific for toads, is released from the Duvenoys gland, and flows into the

Fig.2.9: Hognose with inflated toad.

bite. The envenomation relaxes the toad, which in turn causes deflation of the body.

Body Temperature Regulation (Thermoregulation):

Snakes are "cold-blooded" which is a common way of saying ectothermic, which is a term that describes how an animal obtains body heat. An ectotherm or cold blooded animal gets its body temperature from outside sources of heat, such as the sun, air, water or ground. Another term often used is poikilothermic. This term refers to the constant fluctuations in body temperature as a result of being ectothermic. The snakes temperature does not remain constant as in mammals. Therefore, ectotherm refers to an animal that gets its body heat from outside sources, and poikilotherm refers to the changes in body temperature caused by this outside

Fig.2.10: Copper-head basking

temperature. Some snakes, such as the pregnant female Northern Copperhead (Fig. 2.10), will expose the portion of her body containing the developing embryos to the warming stones, while remaining hidden and safe from predators. Other live-bearing females have favorite basking sites and maintain remarkably uniform elevated temperatures for their

11

developing young. By moving between sunny and shady spots, a pregnant Eastern Garter Snake can keep her temperature between 84 and 90 degrees F. for most of the day. Most snakes bask often to raise their body temperature. Snakes can rapidly raise their body temperature by stretching themselves in the sun or on a hot substratum. Once warm, they may conserve this heat by coiling. Heat is absorbed directly from the suns radiation, from the heated stones surfaces and from the air. When a snake coils its body, it reduces it surface area and slows heat loss. If the surroundings become either too hot or cold, the snake retreats to its resting site, which usually has a stable temperature both day and night. The preferred body temperature for snakes such as ratsnakes and racers ranges from about 75-97 degrees F.

Snakes lose water through respiration and through their skin, due to its high surface area. They conserve water by excreting uric acid, which is a white, semisolid slurry with the feces, instead of urine. Snakes need moist shelters during dry periods and prior to shedding, when they are particularly sensitive to water loss.

Hibernation:
Snakes become less active with the arrival of colder temperatures. They are unable to travel long distances to find a warmer climate, so it is important to find over-wintering sites close to their summer ranges. They survive the winter by becoming inactive and hibernating. They need to find den areas where the temperatures remain low, but above freezing. During hibernation, physiological changes occur. Metabolic rate is lowered, the heart beats slower, and the chemistry of the blood changes. The behavioral changes that occur are: ceasing to eat (aphagia) and sluggishness, followed by torpidity, which is the loss of the power of motion, and dormancy which is the stopping of all   activity, or suspended animation. Many snakes in Connecticut and New England and other colder areas of the country will not reproduce unless they hibernate. The metabolic changes that occur during the cooling down period seem to be linked with annual rhythms. Breeding usually occurs in the spring, when reproductive zeal accompanies rising temperatures.

The low metabolic rate in hibernating snakes is fueled by glycogen, which is a stored form of glucose, in the liver. Liver glycogen levels are high in the fall before hibernation and decrease over the winter. The blood-sugar levels increase, as the glycogen is converted to sugar, which is burned as fuel in the winter. Snakes emerging from hibernation have lost weight, from water loss and the reduced energy stores in the liver.

Picking a hibernation site is critical for the snakes survival. The hibernaculum needs to provide shelter from freezing temperature and from predators. It must have enough moisture to prevent excessive body water loss, or desiccation, during hibernation. Some snakes hibernate singly, and some hibernate in groups or aggregations. Some snakes such as the hognose snakes burrow into loose soil during the winter.   Nevertheless, most snakes do not have this burrowing ability and must find preexisting cavities as hiber-nacula. Small snakes may often crawl under large rocks, logs, stumps, or into the root cav-ities of fallen trees. Other preexisting cavities are rodent burrows,   crayfish burrows, turtle burrows, and ant mounds. Red-bellied snakes, smooth green snakes and garter snakes have all been found sharing an anthill. Rock crevices, old wells, and cracks in rock walls, and building foundations are often used.

Some snakes use communal historic den sites. Northern Copperheads share these sites with Black Rat Snakes, and Northern Black Racers. Timber Rattlesnakes also share their sites with these snakes, and sometimes with copperheads. Aggregation at the hibernation site usually peaks in mid-autumn and slowly declines as the snakes enter the hibernaculum. As long as the weather remains mild, basking near the den will continue. As temperatures drop, the snakes move deeper and deeper into the den. Another important benefit for snakes aggregating for the winter is that males and females are brought together for either fall or spring mating. In a den site in Canada over 10,000 Garter Snakes were found sharing one hibernation site.

Reproduction:

Some snakes lay eggs, a process which is called oviparity, and some give live birth, which is referred to as viviparity. Some oviparous snakes such as the Black Rat Snake lay eggs, which have a long incubation time because the embryo has just begun to develop. Others such as the Smooth Green snake keep the eggs in their bodies until they

Fig.2.11: Black Rat Snake egg with emerging hatchling.

are almost ready to hatch, and upon being laid, hatch within days. Viviparous snakes such as the Northern Water Snake, have embryos with completely functional placentas through which nourishment and oxygen are received, and waste products removed

Fig.2.12: Newborn Water Snakes in embryonic sac.

from the mother all during their development, and are born alive.

Snakes rely on chemical cues picked up by their tongues and analyzed by the vomeronasal organs discussed earlier under *Sense of Smell, Jacobsons Organ*, to find mates and stimulate courtship. These odors are produced by tiny skin glands located on the backs of snakes, and by paired cloacal glands, which produce odors that are different for each species of snake. The cloacal secretions, combinations of musk and fecal matter, have long been known to have defensive functions. Only recently have biologists discussed the relationship of these pheromones with courtship.

When male snakes are sexually ready, their movements become wide-ranging, unless they are at a communal den site, at which time females are readily available. Even with females close by, the male needs to find the females pheromone trail. He is able to determine the direction of her movements and to discover whether she is "in heat" and sexually ready by the concentrations of pheromone laid down in the trail. When he finds her, he begins the courtship ritual, which is similar in most snakes. Courtship involves a lot of body contact. The male crawls over, around and beside the female, often rubbing or gently bouncing his chin against the females back and head. This contact stimulates the female to become receptive, and has shown to stimulate ovulation in some species. When the female is ready to receive the male, she lifts her tail. The male then twists his tail under hers so that their vents meet.

Male snakes have two sexual or copulatory organs called the hemipenes as discussed earlier (p.3). Only snakes and lizards have these unique organs. When not in use they are stored, folded inward, one on each side of the body at the base of the tail. The outside surface of the hemipenis is folded inside upon itself. Think of placing your hands together with fingers pointed upward as in a prayer pose. Bend your fingers toward each other, and down toward your palm. Thus your fingernails, which represent the outer surface of the male organs, are stored inside your palms, which represent the cloacal chamber of the snake. This causes a bulge in the tail of male snakes that is not present in females. When the male is ready to mate, he everts one or both organs into the female's receptive gaping cloaca, as seen in Fig. 2.13). The base of the hemipenis enters the cloaca first. Once inside, the tip, which is the surface that is rough, irregular, pleated, or spiny, depending upon the species of snake, emerges. The irregular shapes of the male organs are distinctive for each species. Mating usually lasts less than an hour, but may persist for more than a day. When mating is over, the hemipenis is again inverted, and withdrawn to settle back inside the male.

Fig.2.13: Illustration of copulation.

In some snakes, such as kingsnakes, copperheads, and rattlesnakes, males compete aggressively when they both find the same receptive female. The snakes face off and hold their heads and fore-bodies erect while each tries to force the others body downward. This behavior is called a *combat dance*. The pushing and shoving continues for several   minutes, until one male establishes his dominance over the other, and the losing male departs.

Most snakes mate and reproduce every year. Mating may occur in late summer, fall or in the spring. Some females may mate more than once with the same male, or with different males. This insures that she has sufficient sperm to fertilize her eggs, and insures stronger offspring from the diversified genetic pooling.

Not all species reproduce each year. Live-bearing females do not eat as much as non-gravid females, during their pregnancy. The larger the species, such as the Timber Rattlesnake, the less they eat. This is especially true towards the end of gestation, because the large developing young take up most of the space in the body cavity. The female survives on her depleting fat storage, and is emaciated after giving birth. Birth usually occurs in late summer or early fall, so that the female has very little time before hibernation to feed. It may take a year or more before she is strong enough to have young again. Smaller species such as the Eastern Ribbon Snake have been observed eating small fish up to one week before delivering 18 young snakes.

Females of some species are able to store sperm for future use, in microscopic sacs in the walls of their oviducts. The sperm may absorb nourishment from secretions produced in these glandular sacs, and stay alive for several years. A captive Indigo Snake (*Drymarchon corais*) from Florida laid fertile eggs four years after her last mating. Some snakes in colder temperate-zones, such as the Timber Rattlesnake, store sperm for several months. This insures species propagation.

Some Snakes such as the Black Rat Snake, have been observed basking on the top of a sawdust pile absorbing heat from the sun, and then tunneling into the pile only to appear later to resume basking in the sun. This was repeated many times. It was later discovered that a clutch of eggs was incubating in this pile, and the snake appeared to be bringing additional warmth to the incubation site.

Locomotion:

It has always been fascinating to watch a snake flowing over the ground with seemingly effortless grace as the wind whispers the wondrous secrets to this gliding serpent. The slither of the snake, which seems to glide across the ground as a fluid movement leaves bystanders in awe. From Proverbs xxx: 18-19, Klauber quotes "There are three things which are too wonderful for me, yea, four which I know not: The way of an eagle in the air; the way of a serpent upon a rock; the way of a ship in the midst of the sea; and the way of a man with a maid." He also quotes John Ruskin (1869, p. 83): "That rivulet of smooth silver-how does it flow…Watch it, when it moves slowly: A wave, but without wind! A current, but with no fall! All the body moving at the same instant, yet some of it to one side, some to another, or some forward, and the rest of the coil backwards; but all with the same calm will and equal way—no contraction, no extension; one soundless, causeless, march of sequent rings, and spectral procession of spotted dust, with dissolution in its fangs, dislocation in its coils." *Poetry in motion.*

The mystery of serpentine motion lies in the lack of any apparent visible force exerted on the ground. There is no evidence of its pushing itself forward. This slender body moving in waves, seemingly without effort, flows evenly forward with each new wave. The mystery is to show how the muscular source of this effort is converted into such even flowing of the entire body.

Snakes use four different kinds of propulsion, or locomotion to which the following names have been applied: Horizontal undulatory locomotion; rectilinear; sidewinding; and concertina. A snake simultaneously uses one method of locomotion anteriorly, while using a different method toward the tail. The only form not demonstrated in New England snakes is sidewinding locomotion.

Horizontal Undulatory Locomotion or Lateral progression: This form of locomotion is also referred to as lateral undulation and undulatory locomotion. Most snakes normally crawl by using the horizontal undulatory method. This is sometimes called the serpentine or sinusoidal, (curving), method of movement. It is the most common, but the most difficult to describe. The simplest way to explain this motion is to describe undulatory movement in swimming. Muscular contractions, passing rearward, create a traveling body wave whose degree of curvature increases as the body becomes narrower toward the tip of the tail. The forces of locomotion come from the outside rear edge of each curve pushing against the water. This lateral (sideward) and rear-ward push against the water propels the snake forward. Snakes do not move

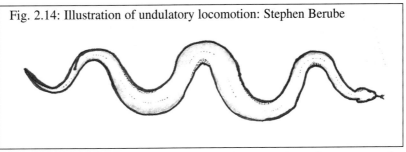
Fig. 2.14: Illustration of undulatory locomotion: Stephen Berube

as fast forward in the water because the water does not offer much resistance to the snakes pushing motion. Snakes that spend all their time in the water, such as sea snakes

(*Hydrophiinae*), have evolved bodies that are laterally compressed or flattened, and have a vertically compressed oar-like tail. *Sea snakes do not occur in the Atlantic Ocean.* Most live in the coastal waters of Australia and southern Asia.

This method of movement is accomplished by the snake lashing its body back and forth, causing lateral waves that force longitudinal motion. They move forward by moving sideways. The snakes head pushes off an uneven part of the ground, and each part of its body follows the head. The snake appears to flow over the ground as water flows. A snakes undulatory movement on land differs from swimming undulatory locomotion. Land surfaces are irregular, and give many points of friction and resistance. When moving on land, the curves of the snakes body are not regular, but match the irregularities of the surface upon which the snake is pushing forward against. The forward thrust originates from the outside rear edge of each body curve. The snake curves portions of its body to the side, in the shape of an **S.** In so doing it uses whatever is beneath it to push itself forward. It is an extremely efficient use of force. Pressure full-force ahead takes more energy than using leverage to the side, so as the snake moves forward, the body push arises continuously from the outer rear edges of each body curve. This allows the entire body to move forward at the same time. Each part of the body on one side of the snake pushes against the same resistant points.

Fig.2.15: Eastern Hognose Snake exhibiting lateral undulation.

Slide-Pushing Locomotion:

When a snake is on a slippery surface such as smooth pavement, the undulatory movement becomes an almost panicky thrashing action as the snake tries to get out of the way of a looming predator or a motor vehicle. This kind of motion wastes a lot of energy and produces very little forward headway, one reason why so many snakes are killed on the roads. They often use the heat from the black top to warm up during the cooler spring and fall evenings, and to forage for prey at night. It is very difficult for a snake to move rapidly on such a slick surface, especially when it is wet, as on warm drizzling summer nights. This form of locomotion, a coordinated thrashing, can be considered a subclass of undulatory locomotion. It is sometimes referred to as slide-pushing. This activity allows for forward movement across slippery frictionless surfaces. The body curves pass backward, twisting the sides of the body and using the ventral scale edges to push against the slippery surface. The constant rapid widespread, seemingly uncoordinated twisting and pushing generates enough friction to move the snake slowly forward. This high-speed pushing of rapid undulation uses a lot of energy and provides for very little forward motion.

Fig.2.16: Northern Water Snake exhibiting slide-pushing on slippery rock.

16

Concertina locomotion:

Concertina locomotion involves alternately pulling up the body into bends and then straightening out the body in a forward motion from the bends. The front part of the body then comes to rest on the surface and the back part of the body is pulled up into bends again. The bends may push laterally against the sides of a tunnel or vertically against the ground to keep the body from slipping. This friction is critical to concertina locomotion.

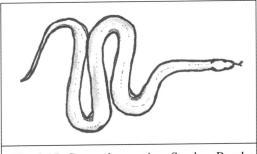

Fig. 2.17: Concertina motion. Stephen Berube

Concertina locomotion is used in crawling through tunnels or narrow passages and in climbing. The head when straight, or tail when curled, are anchored onto the substratum, and the body is shot forward until the whole body is straightened. Then the snake anchors its head and brings its tail together again. This movement has little if any momentum and is used by curious snakes investigating a potential threat, or by snakes stalking or checking out the homes of potential prey. It is used a lot by snakes on tree limbs. By having one part of the body firmly anchored at all times the snake is able to securely move through tree branches. The beautiful Red-Bellied Snake in Fig. 2.18, demonstrates this locomotion in trees. This climbing, and moving from branch to branch is perfectly carried out by the stop-and-go mechanism of concertina locomotion. When branches are numerous and reasonably horizontal, snakes can use undulatory locomotion as rapidly in trees as on the ground. Where branches are widely spaced or include weak support points, stop-and-go concertina locomotion is preferred. First the snake anchors its hind end and slowly extends its head and upper body across the gap (Fig. 2.18). When it establishes a new anchor point, it draws its rear part across the gap.

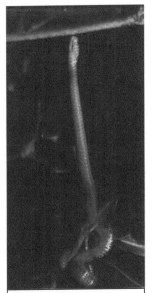

Fig.2.18: Northern Red-Bellied Snake exhibiting concertina locomotion in shrub.

Rectilinear (Caterpillar) Locomotion:

Rectilinear locomotion is movement in a straight line. It is used mainly by large snakes, such as boas and pythons, and stoutly built New England snakes such as the Eastern Hognose, Northern Copperhead and Timber Rattlesnake. In rectilinear locomotion, the belly scales are alternately lifted slightly from the ground, pulled forward, and then pulled downward and backward. However, because the scales are anchored against the ground, the body is actually pulled forward over them. Once the body has moved far enough forwards to stretch the scales, the cycle repeats. This cycle occurs simultaneously at several points

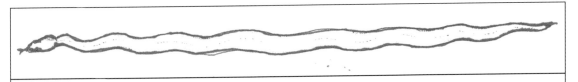

Fig. 2.19: Illustration of reectilinear Locomotion by Stephen Berube.

17

along the body. Rectilinear locomotion involves bilateral activity of the muscles that connect the skin to the skeleton. One set of these muscles lifts the belly scales up and pulls them forward, and another set of muscles pulls the belly scales downward and backward. This process is often called "rib-walking". Each rib and scale are drawn forward by the contraction of muscles on the vertebrae immediately in front of the rib. Because the scales have free rear edges, each rearward-contracted scale catches on surface irregularities. Body weight also provides adequate friction to aid in the movement forward. This is all strictly muscular activity, and the forward movement is made possible both by the strength of the muscles and the good condition of the belly scales. *It involves shifting the body forward within the skin.* Rectilinear progression is the slowest and most methodical locomotion pattern of movement and has two speeds, slow and very slow. It allows the snake to move forward in a straight line, which allows it to stay hidden. It is also useful in stalking prey, or just calmly moving along. It is very fluid looking as the waves of contraction pass along the trunk, and makes the snake look almost as if it is gliding effortlessly through its beautiful world of lichen covered rocks, and soft emerald green moss.

Undulatory movements are the most rapid, moving a snake along at 3.75 mph. Over short distances, some snakes may reach 6.8 mph. Rectilinear locomotion is the opposite, being extraordinarily slow and controlled.

Striking is similar to concertina locomotion but very fast. The snakes

Fig.2.20: Beautiful large 43 inch Northern Copperhead demonstrating Rectilinear Locomotion.

front end extends while the posterior back portion remains anchored to the substrate. Most North American snakes coil and strike in a roughly horizontal plane, and project less than half their body length in a typical feeding or defensive strike.

Climbing:

Gravity has an effect on the circulation of blood in snakes when they spend extended periods in a vertical position. The pooling of blood is a potentially serious problem. The snakes of Connecticut and surrounding New England states are not true arboreal snakes that spend more than 50% of their time in trees and shrubs. However, many species spend 50% or less time in trees and shrubs, such as the Black Rat, Northern Black Racer, Northern Water Snake, Northern Ribbon Snake and Timber Rattlesnake, and may be considered *partially arboreal*. Of these, the Black Rat spends the most time above the ground. This presents an interesting problem of how this very long, (adults may reach 9 feet), and moderately stout animal, is able to remain vertical for long periods of time, without loosing blood pressure in the head region. A similar experience occurs when humans rapidly change from a prone, horizontal position to an upright standing position. A feeling of light-headedness and sometime fainting may occur due to the reduced hydrostatic pressure. Because snakes have elongate bodies, they have the problem of long fluid columns inside their vessels being susceptible to the extreme pressure changes during heads-up vertical postures. Because they lack valves in their veins, blood tends to pool in the lower part of their body when in an upright position. This reduces blood flow to the head and could eventually cause death. True arboreal snakes have evolved special body shapes and structure that allows for this specialized habitat selection. Specialized features of the cardiovascular system have also undergone modification to allow for extended periods of vertical posture.

The force of gravity is especially important to elongate animals that assume vertical postures. The body fluids are subject to significant changes in pressure, called hydrostatic pressure. The pulmonary artery (P) and pulmonary veins (PV) extend the entire length of the lungs and may become a liability that compromises lung function in long snakes that climb or crawl vertically. When a snake is vertical, the effect of gravity on the blood increases the hydrostatic or gravitational pressure in the pulmonary artery and pulmonary vein. This drastically raises pressures within the thin-walled tiny veins called pulmonary capillaries, which causes increased plasma movement into the lung tissue.

Even small increases in lung capillary pressure may cause large accumulation of lung fluid in the snake and stop the gas exchange of oxygen and carbon dioxide.

Describing the circulation of blood through the heart of a snake will help to understand the effects of the climbing position on a snakes blood pressure. The diagram presented here depicts a "generalized" illustration of a "typical" snake heart. Each family of snakes has evolved slight modifications to this generalized scheme.

In general, the snake has two atria (A), and one ventricle (V). Nonoxygenated, or deoxygenated venous blood (DB illustrated in *blue*) from the body enters the right atrium. The right and left jugular veins (RJ & LJ) bring venous blood from the head region, and the inferior vena cava (VC) brings blood from the lower body, and liver. When the ventricle contracts, the deoxygenated blood is forced through the pulmonary artery (PA), which branches (L) upward to the anterior right lung or tracheal lung, and backward to the more posterior left lung sac. Some of the deoxygenated blood also enters the left and right aorta, which become the left and right systemic

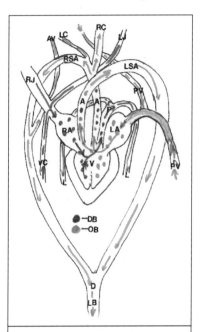

Fig.2.21: Illustration of 'typical', generalized, snake heart.

aortic arches (LSA & RSA), which in turn merge into the dorsal aorta (D). This system is less efficient than the two-chambered ventricle of birds and mammals, which does not allow the venous and arterial blood to mix. This mixing reduces the efficiency of the snakes circulatory system. The pulmonary vein (PV) brings oxygenated blood from the lungs to the left atrium. The head region receives oxygenated blood (OB illustrated in *red*) from the left and right carotid arteries. (LC & RC), which arise from the right systemic aortic arch. The lower body (LB) receives oxygenated blood from the dorsal aorta (Lillywhite, 1992). Truly arboreal snakes that spend more than 50% if their time in trees, pool much less blood during vertical posture than terrestrial snakes. Their slender body shape, tight skin, and increased nerve supply to the posterior arteries and veins to control blood flow all contribute to this adaptation. Their arterial blood pressure is higher (40-70 mm Hg) than in nonclimbing snakes (20-35 mmHg). The heart position in arboreal and climbing terrestrial snakes is closer to the head than in nonclimbing species. Their heart position averages 20% of their total body length, whereas non-climbers average over 35% of their total body length from the head. This helps ensure adequate blood supply to the head regardless of position. Head tilting in climbing terrestrial species also improves blood flow to the head (Lillywhite, 1987c).

Snakes offer a diverse range of adaptation to gravitational influence on the cardiovascular system. Regulatory responses of tree-climbing snakes to vertical posture resemble those of humans to the upright standing position, while the gravitational problems experienced by non-climbing species of snakes resemble problems of humans with cardiovascular deconditioning such as bed rest and space flight. The Space Physiology Laboratory at NASA Ames Research Center in collaboration with Dr. Harvey Lillywhite, performed studies on snakes from various habitats to evaluate the tolerance of different snake species to hypergravity. Aquatic, semi-aquatic, non-climbing and tree-climbing snakes were tested. It was found that semi-arboreal snakes, such as the rat snake had increased capacity to maintain cardiovascular function with increased gravitational force. These species have firm muscle tone and tight skin similar to an antigravity suit, while aquatic, semi-aquatic and non-climbing snakes have more flaccid or limp bodies with looser skin. Tests were also performed on rat snakes to determine if, once acclimated to a higher gravitational force, would the snake be more able to withstand even higher gravitational forces, that in earlier tests proved to reduce blood flow to the head to zero. The snakes responded to the higher gravitational forces with increased heart rate, and blood pressure, and lower plasma and whole blood volumes. These studies in snakes are significant because of the sensitivity of these animals to the effects of gravity on blood pressure and circulation, and the potential application of these models to human space flight.

Defensive Behaviors:

Pope wrote in 1958 the following evaluation of snake behavior. "Snakes are first cowards, next bluffers, and last of all warriors." Most snakes will quickly retreat to a safe hiding place, or rapidly move in the opposite direction of a potential threatening situation. Other snakes prefer to freeze and not make a move, relying on their coloration and patterns to hide them from both predators and prey. Avoidance is the safest behavior, and requires the least expenditure of energy against predators. Contrasting patterns, irregular blotches, spots, stripes and cross bands of alternating colors obscure the outline of a snake. This allows it to blend in with an irregularly colored background such as leaf and stick debris on the forest floor. This visual disruption of the snakes presence is successful whether the snake is stationary or moving.

Fig.2.22: Camouflaged copperhead.

The Northern Copperhead (Fig. 2.22) is remarkably patterned, and spends most of its time in leaf litter, under the canopy-layered forest. The beige, chestnut and pinkish colors, along with irregularities of the snakes pattern, make them almost invisible while lying quietly among the old decaying leaves. Their camouflage not only protects them from predators, but also hides them from prospective prey animals. The copperhead, as well as the Timber Rattlesnake use ambush to capture prey. The snakes successful concealing coloration is equally useful as a protection against enemies as it is in enabling it to ambush its prey. The Timber Rattlesnake (Fig. 2.23) is procryptic or enhanced with protective coloration. Its first line of defense is also to remain motionless, and blend into the background. The principle of disruptive coloration, having colored patterns that blend into the irregular ground colors of the forest and rock crevices, is obviously involved in the dark dorsal blotches, which are so characteristic of the Timber Rattlesnake. According to Klauber, 1931b, heavy-bodied and slow-moving snakes are usually blotched, and rattlesnakes fall into that category. Even the patterns of the head and the color of the iris (Fig.1.15), are successful in making the eye less conspicuous. The Timber Rattlesnake is mild-mannered and prefers retreat to combat. This quiet temperament suits their retreat and hide behavior when threatened. Notice in Fig. 2.23 that the cryptic concealing color of the female beneath the rock blends in with the fallen leaves. The yellowish and rusty hues are from the recent early autumn leaves of September falling down to make a comfortable bed for the mother rattlesnake. The 3 newborn rattlesnakes are gray with black cross-bands, which blend in almost totally with the rocks and fallen twigs at the birthing stone. If concealment fails, an escaping rattler will move away as rapidly as possible, to the closest cover. If it is threatened or closely pursued it will adopt a defensive coil with the head and fore part of the body raised above the ground and poised in an **S**-shaped loop. From this poise it can lunge forward and strike if the enemy approaches within reach. When molested further, the rattlesnake will sound its warning rattle. Klauber states that the primary function of the rattle is to warn away or frighten animals that might be injurious to the snake. "The buzz of a rattler whirling its appendage of segmented, heavily cornified epidermis is a startling sound that can induce a brief spasm within even a seasoned snake hunter (Brennan, 1995)."

Fig.2.23: Mother Timber Rattlesnake with babies.

Another defensive mechanism used by the rattler and other snakes, is the *hiss.* Brennan describes the hiss of a rattlesnake: "When I stopped for a breather, I heard a sound that I only instinctively recognized; although I couldn't visualize its source, my neck hackles stood on end. It sounded like a combination of a stiff breeze swirling through a pine thicket, and an inflating balloon." A hiss is produced by filling the lungs, and then rapidly constricting the body wall to force the air out through the glottis, usually with the mouth open. The startling hiss of the Timber Rattlesnake is produced instead, by a sudden inhalation of air, with an accompanying inflation and enlargement of the snakes body. A hiss can sound like a slowly leaking punctured tire or it can be much louder, like the rapid escape of steam from heating pipes, or the release of air brakes on a semi! Hissing often precedes other forms of bluffing behavior.

This bluffing behavior can take on several forms. Most involve making the snake appear larger or more aggressive than it really is. Appearing larger is often accomplished by inflating the lungs, which enlarges the bodies girth. Hognose snakes are well known for this behavior, which is accompanied by a loud hiss and feigned strike. The mouth is never opened during this bluff act of aggression. During this bluffing display, the hognose snake will flatten its ribs to appear broader. It will also spread its neck to form a hood similar to the cobra's hood (Fig. 2.24). The cervical ribs are spread, which flatten the throat. If the bluffing behavior does not work, the hognose will play dead. When unable to escape its tormentor, it contorts its body and writhes spasmodically, vomits up food,

Fig.2.24: Eastern Hognose Snake with inflated body and spreading neck cape.

defecates, rolls over on its back and plays dead (Fig. 2.25) with its tongue extended, and blood often seeping from its mouth (autohemorrhage). If the snake is turned over again, the seemingly dead snake immediately rolls upside down again.

Most snakes will release a foul-smelling mixture of musk and feces from their cloacal glands if picked up. It is a repulsive and very unpleasant experience, with the odor penetration of the skin and nasal passages lasting for hours. The Northern Water Snake has an extremely unpleasant smelling musk, and can expel it with such force, that it seems to spray from its body.

Fig.2.25: Hognose playing dead.

The best-known snake sound is the rattling of American rattlesnakes. The term rattling is not really appropriate to the high-pitched buzz of a rattlesnake. In most rattlesnakes, the rattle has a peak frequency of 5,000 to 8,000 hertz, which is roughly equivalent to that of an ambulance siren. A hertz is equal to one cycle per second. The

Fig.2.26: Timber Rattlesnake "rattling" its tail as see by the blurring of the rattle.

rattling sound is produced by the rapid vibration of a series of loose-fitting, interlocking, cone-shaped scales on the tip of the tail. The pitch and loudness vary between species and among individual snakes. Larger snakes produce louder, lower-pitched sounds. A snakes body temperature affects the rate of vibration. A cold snake's sound is quieter and lower-pitched. As the snakes body temperature increases so does the frequency and pitch of its rattling.

At birth, a rattlesnake has a single rattle segment, called the prebutton. This prebutton is lost when the snake sheds for the first time. It is replaced by the button, which becomes the first rattle. Each time the snake sheds its skin, another rattle segment is added to the base of the rattle. The original button is at the end of the rattle. If the button has not been broken off, the number of rattle segments, plus the button, indicates the number of times the rattlesnake has shed, but does not tell the age of the snake, because a snake sheds more than once a year. The snake in Fig. 2.26 has 9 segments, so it has shed 9 times. Many snakes, not just rattlesnakes, nervously shake their tails when frightened or threatened. If the snake is in dry grass or leaves, the tail vibration produces a sound similar to the rattlers buzz. This sound alerts the intruder that the snake is alarmed and ready to defend itself.

CHAPTER THREE
VENOMOUS SNAKES AND SNAKEBITE

Venom Definition:

What is the difference between venom and poison. So often venomous snakes are referred to as poisonous snakes. The word poison is a general term used to describe a substance that causes irritation, illness or death when eaten, drunk or absorbed through the skin, eyes or nose. Amanita mushrooms when eaten by humans can cause death. Poison oak irritates the skin and causes inflammation and itching. These plants are said to be poisonous. Venom is a poison that one animal, spider, bee or snake injects into another animal. Therefore, a snake that injects venom by biting is called venomous. A more specific word used to describe venom is a biological toxin. Toxins are substances related to proteins, which cause chemical damage to living tissues when injected into another organism. Snake venom is also rich in substances, which have beneficial medical uses.

Properties of Venom:

Venom is an evolutionary adaptation in snakes used to immobilize their prey. It is also used as a defense mechanism. Venom is a highly toxic chemical produced in special glands in the mouth. These oral glands are closely related to salivary glands, which secrete fluids that aid in swallowing, and digestion. Venom is often described as modified saliva. Venom has been shown to start the digestive process of captured prey, by beginning the breakdown of the preys tissues, as well as immobilizing the prey when injected into its body. Each species of venomous snake has a unique venom with different ingredients, and the more closely two species of snakes are related, the more similar their venom.

The chemical make up of venom is complicated. When venom has all the water removed, it is about 90% protein. Most of the proteins are enzymes. An enzyme is a protein that speeds up a chemical reaction. The enzymes that speed up the breakdown of tissue proteins are called proteolytic enzymes. The enzymes responsible for accelerating the breakdown of muscle and nerve tissue are called phospholipases. The enzymes that speed up the dissolving of cellular materials, thus speeding up the spread of venom through the preys tissues are called hyaluronidases. Enzymes that cause the breakdown of connective tissue in the body are called collagenases, because they are responsible for the break down of the protein called collagen. Many enzymes disrupt normal cellular function, which causes the collapse of cell metabolism shock and death.

Every snake has venom with more than one toxin. In general venoms are described as hemotoxic, affecting the circulatory system or neurotoxic, which affects the nervous system. Most venom contains both, in different concentrations. Cardiotoxins have damaging effects on the heart muscles, causing changes in heart contractions, which can lead to heart failure. Hemorrhagins destroy capillary walls, which causes internal bleeding near the bite, and throughout the body, far from the bite site. Coagulation-retarding compounds that are found in some elapids (cobras, mambas and coral snakes) prevent blood from clotting. Some vipers have thromboses in their venom, which encourages clot formation throughout the circulatory system. Hemolysins are compounds that destroy red blood cells, and cytolysins destroy white blood cells.

Neurotoxins block the sending of nerve impulses to muscles, especially those to the diaphragm, so breathing is drastically impaired. Venom composition may vary among individuals of the same species that inhabit different geographic areas.

Toxicity of Venom:

Of the 2700 species of snakes in the world, only about 450 species are dangerous to humans. Even mildly toxic venom is lethal if the snake injects enough of it. Some snakes with very toxic venom are not dangerous because they are small and incapable of breaking the skin or just are never in contact with humans. In very rare cases, the saliva of some nonvenomous snakes has caused mild to moderate poisoning in humans. People in the United States have had reactions to garter, ringneck and hognose snakes. These snakes have Duvenoys glands, which produce saliva with properties that cause reactions in sensitive people. These humans need to be handling the snakes in order to be bitten, for the snake must chew for a while in order to introduce the saliva.

The answer to which snakes have the most potent venom can be answered in two ways. One way estimates deadliness based on the possible amount of venom that a snake could deliver with a single bite. Most snakes do not deliver all their venom in one bite, and sometimes deliver no venom at all when they strike. This is called a dry bite. The other way to test a lethal dose is to test venom's killing power on mice.

Measured amounts of venom are injected into mice, and the dose that kills 50% of the mice within 24 hours is recorded. This dose, called the LD_{50} is measured in milligrams of venom per kilogram of body weight of the mouse. LD stands for lethal dose. If the injection sites of the venom are in the muscle (intramuscular), or under the skin (subcutaneous), lethal dosages will vary. It is a matter of degree of toxicity and amount of venom capable of being delivered that actually determines the level of danger that a snake presents to humans. In other words, a snake with extremely toxic venom, that is not exposed to humans, has a small venom holding capacity, and has a poor delivery system, is less dangerous than a snake with lower toxicity, high exposure to humans and high venom-hold capacity (Ernst, Zug. 1996).

New England has two venomous snakes. The larger and more rare of the two species, the Timber Rattlesnake (*Crotalus horridus*) has fangs up to 1/2 inch long in larger individuals. On the toxicity level, they register 61 out of the 81 species listed, but on the amount of venom available for a bite they register at 15, making them a formidable adversary if they decide to deliver all their venom at once. They are potentially but rarely lethal. The smaller species, the Northern Copperhead (*Agkistrodon contortrix mokeson*) has shorter fangs, less body mass and length and registered 81 on the list of 81 species. Given the amount of venom available for injection, the copperhead registered 29, so if provoked to deliver a full venom pack, they are able to cause a lot of tissue damage, but are not life threatening to the average adult. Many factors other than the toxicity level influence the seriousness of a bite. In humans, these factors include the size, age, health and psychological state of mind. A frightened panicking individual will cause an increase in heart and respiration rate, causing a faster spread of the venom. The bite itself is also a factor. These factors include penetration of one or both fangs, the location of the bite, whether the bite was close to or penetrated a major blood vessel, and the amount of venom injected. These factors make every snake bite unique, and explain how a bite from a mildly venomous snake may be more life threatening than that of a strongly venomous snake.

Fang Structure:

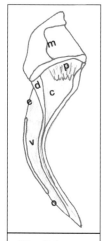

Fig. 3.1: typical fang.

A fang is a tooth that has been modified through evolution to inject venom into prey. They work together with other structures to form a venom delivery apparatus (Fig. 3.3), which works like a hypodermic needle and syringe. The syringe has a barrel, or storage vessel for the fluid to be injected, which can be compared to the venom glands of the snake, that produce and stores the venom. The pump or plunger of the syringe can be compared to the jaw muscles, which supply the pressure for injection. The needle of the syringe is the delivery channel, which compares with the fang of the snake. A fang is an elongate cone shaped curved tooth, which contains a lumen, or tubular passage, which runs its entire length, with openings near the point of attachment and the tip of the fang (Fig. 3.1). A fang is wide at its base, which gradually tapers to a needlelike point. There is a large pulp cavity (c), containing a soft spongy material with vessels and nerves at the base of the fang. The cavity decreases in size towards the tip until it seems to disappear at the angle of curvature. The pedestal (p), or pedicel forms the union with the maxillary bone (m), and is usually left on the bone when a fang is broken off. All snakes fangs are curved, and the amount of curvature is specific for each species. The wide base of each fang is set in the socket of the maxillary bone. This base also contains an opening next to the venom canal. The venom flows into the fang's venom canal (v), from the entrance (e) orifice. The canal extends downward through the fang to the discharge orifice, (o) which is on the front surface of the fang, just above the solid tip. The size and shape of the discharge orifice varies with each species. The outer surface of the fang and the venom canal are covered with enamel (d). The presence of enamel on both of these surfaces suggests how fangs evolved. The fangs seem to have evolved from solid maxillary teeth that had developed a groove on the outer surface. The grooved teeth, over time, became enlarged and the grooves deepened. The walls of the grooves eventually closed over, forming a closed canal.

Fangs are periodically shed, and replaced by new fangs. On either side of the head, in each maxillary bone, there are two sockets, an inner and outer one, which seem to flow together. The sockets are so close together that their edges touch. The inner and outer sockets take turns holding the active fang during fang replacement due to breakage, normal wear and tear, and growth. Future fangs are contained in a staggered row or magazine of immature teeth behind the two sockets. The most mature of the reserve fangs is behind the vacant socket. When the time for change arrives, the mature fang advances to the vacant socket and becomes rigidly seated. The replaced fang drops out, leaving a vacant socket, which will receive the next replacement fang when the time comes. The active fangs alternate between the inside and outside positions. Fig. 3.2 shows an active fang and the replacement fang behind it.

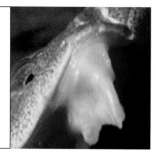

Fig. 3.2: Northern Copperhead with active and replacement fangs surrounded by sheath, which collects the venom from the duct.

25

Venom Apparatus:

Venom is produced by a pair of large venom glands, one on each side of the head. They are located above the upper rear corner of the angle of the jaw, below and behind the eye. The gland is composed of cells that secrete the venom into the hollow center of the gland called the lumen. The lumen tapers to form a narrower venom duct. The duct carries the venom forward to the base of the fang. The duct does not extend into the fang. It opens next to the fang, within a sheath of connective tissue that surrounds the fang's base. This sheath (S) forms a seal around the fang, which directs the flow of venom into the fang's venom canal (C), and outward into the prey. This sheath is well demonstrated in Figure 3.2. The venom duct (V) is surrounded by small accessory glands (A). The accessory glands may act as valves that regulate the amount of venom flow to the fang. The secretions produced by these glands are not toxic, but may serve to activate some of the components of the venom. To support this theory, researchers have found that the venom withdrawn from the lumen of the venom gland (g) is less toxic than the venom taken from the fang!

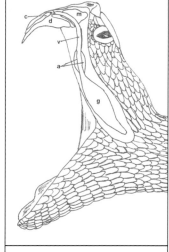

Fig. 3.3: Venom apparatus

Venom-Delivery System:

Biologists have identified three different venom-delivery systems. All three systems evolved from the basic aglyphous snake's tooth, which is cone shaped and slightly curved. Aglyphous is derived from the Greek "without a groove", and refers to a tooth without a groove. Most snakes have only these ungrooved teeth. The only teeth that evolved into grooved and hollow teeth occurred on the upper maxillary bone.

Opisthoglyphous (Rear-fanged):

Some snakes have one or two enlarged rear teeth on each of their maxillary bones, through which flow Duvernoy's gland secretions. These enlarged teeth are separated from the front maxillary teeth by a gap with no teeth called a diastema. These snakes with enlarged rear maxillary teeth are called opisthoglyphous, which is derived from the Greek *opistho*, which means "a groove at the back". Most of the colubrids, the largest family of snakes, with enlarged rear teeth have grooves on either the face or the side of the enlarged tooth. These enlarged teeth probably originally served to hold prey, a function that persists today in garter snakes and ringneck snakes. Garter snakes have Duvernoy's glands, which are advanced salivary glands that produce proteins, which are considered mildly toxic. There have been a few reactions to garter snake bites that have resulted in some bleeding, swelling and bruising, but no systemic symptoms were apparent.

Mucous producing glands in the upper lips called supralabial glands are found on either side of the head of most snakes. Secretions from these modified salivary glands are introduced into the mouth through ducts that open at the base of the maxillary teeth. The Duvernoy's gland is larger and more structured than the supralabial glands. It is composed of branched tubules and can produce mucous and serous secretions. The Devernoy's gland is located under the skin, above and near the angle of the jaw. A duct opens from the gland at the base of one or more of the rear enlarged, sometimes grooved teeth, or "fangs."

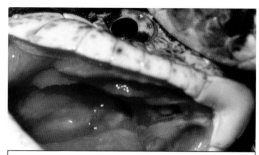

Fig.3.4: Eastern Hognose from Connecticut showing rows of teeth and enlarged rear "fangs."

The secretions vary in toxicity with different species of snakes. The Eastern Hognose Snake of New England possesses enlarged rear teeth (Fig. 3.4), which are connected to the Duvernoy's gland. Bites from hognose snakes, though rare, have caused negative reactions. A few colubrids such as the Boomslang (*Dispholidus typus*) have Duvernoy's glands that are encased in a thin capsule that is attached to a portion of the jaw-closing muscles. Several deaths and serious bites from Boomslangs have been reported. The death of a prominent and highly respected herpetologist brought the dangers of this previously "harmless" snake to the forefront. At age 68, Karl P. Schmidt was bitten on the thumb with only one fang penetration. He became nauseated and had some internal bleeding. He felt better the next morning, but by midafternoon he was dead of a brain hemorrhage and respiratory collapse. The main symptom was chronic bleeding throughout the body.

Proteroglyphous (Fixed Front Fangs):

Proteroglyphous snakes, from the Greek meaning "A groove at the front," have enlarged anterior fangs, which are deeply grooved, or tubular depending upon the species. There are no fixed front fanged snakes in Connecticut or New England, so no detailed description is warranted at this time.

Solenoglyphous (Hinged Fangs):

Solenoglyphous snakes, from the Greek, meaning "a channel or pipe," have a single enlarged tubular fang on the front end of each highly movable maxillary bone. The bones connected with this highly developed biting mechanism are thin and delicate, yet magnificently formed to withstand the stresses of forceful strike-bites, and feeding (Fig.3.6). The hinged fangs represent a more intricately advanced system than the fixed front fangs of other snakes (proteroglyphous) which are limited by the shortened length of their fangs. The fixed front fanged snake must bite, grasp, and hold on to their prey, in order to deliver the venom by a chewing action. This increases the chance of injury to the snake from the struggling prey. The hinged fanged snakes can strike, inject venom, and withdraw from the struggling prey, thereby avoiding injury.

Fig.3.5: Fangs of Northern Copperhead folded in resting position.

The short maxillary bone to which the fang is connected is able to rotate forward and backward. This allows the enlarged fangs to be rotated from a resting position to an active erect position. In the resting position, they are folded back against the upper jaw, as seen in Fig. 3.5 of a Northern Copperhead. The bulge of the folded fangs fits into a hollow in the lower jaw. The advantage of the folding fangs is that long fangs can comfortably set in the mouth without perforating the floor of the snakes mouth. The Timber Rattlesnake may have fangs up to 0.50 inches, and the smaller copperhead's fangs may reach 0.27 inches in a moderately sized adult. Larger snakes have the power to drive in a longer and heavier fang. The measurement of fangs is taken as a straight line from the base to the tip. It is not measured along the curvature of the fang. In the striking active state, the fangs are rotated downward in an arc of about 90 degrees, until the fangs are approximately perpendicular to the upper jaw.

The linkage of the delicate bones involved in the operation of the hinged fangs is illustrated in Fig. 3.6, diagramming the upper head portion of a typical solenoglyhphous snake in an active strike position. Each movable maxillary bone (M) pivots on a hinge with the prefrontal bone ((PF). The prefrontal bone is hinged with the frontal (F) bone. Muscles attached to the pterygoid (P) bones pull the ectopterygoid (E) bones forward, which pushes the maxillary bones forward, and erects the fangs. The snake is able to pull prey into its mouth without erecting the fang, or it can erect the fangs completely for venom injection. The right and left fangs can be rotated independently. A viper often

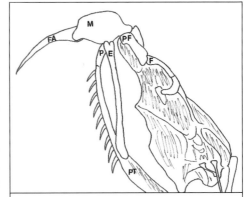

Fig.3.6: Diagram of upper jaw of typical hinged fanged snake showing linkage of bones.

works its fangs back into their resting sheaths one at a time after swallowing its prey (Fig. 2.8). With the fangs fully extended the mouth is open almost 180° as seen in (Fig. 2.4). This allows the snake to quickly stab and recoil from the prey. The viper then tracts the prey, relocates it, and consumes its meal. The venom gland is surrounded by large muscles, which force venom through the venom duct on each side of the head to the base of the fangs. The fang sheath, which surrounds both the fang and the venom duct (Fig. 3.2) serves the very important function of collecting and directing the venom flow from the venom duct (V) to the venom canal in the fang (C), as seen in (Fig. 3.3). There is no permanent connection between the venom duct from the venom gland, and the venom canal of the fang. Because the fangs are constantly being replaced, a permanent connection is impossible.

Pitviper Snakebite:
History:

Practically every portion of the United States is inhabited by venomous serpents. With the exception of the copperhead, water moccasin and a few small coral snakes in the southern latitudes, North America's most numerous venomous snakes are rattlesnakes. Texas alone has 10 different species of rattlesnakes.

Since the dawn of human thought, snakes have had a powerful hold on man's imagination. Our fear of snakes is based on knowledge that a few snakes are venomous and capable of causing serious bodily injury and sometimes, death. Some people have such an overwhelming fear that it is almost impossible for them to discuss the topic. This fear of snakes is called *ophidiophobia.* It is a very difficult phobia to overcome. It is estimated that about 50% of U.S. citizens experience some anxiety in the presence of snakes, and another 20% are absolutely terrified of them. Some examples of this terror even extend to seeing pictures of a snake in a book, or on television. It is difficult to overcome these anxieties. Education about the lives and habits of snakes dramatically helps reduce, and in many cases eliminate the fear. In truth, snakes, even the dangerous ones, are fundamentally shy, and more likely to avoid a confrontation with man by fleeing, when given the opportunity. They will bite only as a last resort in self-defense. The snake has always been an object of fear and worship. The history of snakebite treatment has been surrounded by dread, misunderstanding and confusion. When a snake bites a man, the effects are amazingly variable and unpredictable. The symptoms may range from local discomfort to collapse and death within a few minutes. This unpredictability has confused the thinking of medical men and biologists alike, to say nothing of ordinary citizens, and encouraged a great deal of folklore and magic. The fact that one-third to one-half of all snakebites result in little or no poisoning has made the treatments of snakebites very ambiguous. If a person has been bitten, but received a "dry bite", with little or no poisoning, any treatment given, whether by a snake charmer, or doctor, no matter how bizarre, would appear to be the future treatment of choice. Until the late 1900's, treatment of snakebite has not changed much in over 4000 years, when Egyptian priests incised snakebites of their patients, to let evil spirits out. The Greeks and Romans over 2,000 years ago described a pitviper, probably the puff adder (*Bitis arietans*) as the *Spectaficus* , a snake whose bite consumed the entire body with swelling and putrefaction. Pit viper envenomation was and still is considered a life threatening issue. In the 1800's and early 1900's simple survival from snakebite was considered fortunate. Treatments at the time were seemingly more dangerous than the bite itself.

Early historic treatments included alcohol, consumed orally and by injection; strychnine, quinine, bromine compounds, carbolic acid, enemas, and cauterization. Reports from these early treatments suggest that more people, especially children, died from alcohol poisoning from consumption of large amounts of "medicinal" alcohol.

Between 1960 and 1970 the prognosis of victims of snakebite dramatically improved. Rapid transport to a hospital facility became an important immediate requirement for a snakebite victim. Emergency medical treatment outpost centers became more numerous, which allowed victims to reach professional health care within minutes to hours, instead of hours to days. Critical care medicine with intensive care units provided support for critically ill patients. The most important adaptation was the development of specific antivenom, which reduced the damage done by the venom.

Snakebite from pitvipers is rarely a life threatening issue in the late 1900's and early 2000. Educating the public to seek immediate medical care after snakebite is paramount in eliminating fear of snakes and their bites. Although surviving snakebites is almost guaranteed, loss of fingers, toes, and diminished use of affected arms and legs with scaring and tissue erosion, is still an issue of great importance.

Symptoms of Pitviper Snakebite:

At least a third of the snakebites in the United States involve some sort of deliberate contact with the snakes such as catching, killing, handling or otherwise manipulating them. These bites are referred to as 'illegitimate.' Many such bites involve the victim also being under the influence of drugs and/or alcohol.

Fear of snakes is a learned behavior, which has been made more intense by such things as myths and media misrepresentation. Stories of dramatic and terrifying magnitude about severely poisoned victims of snakebite in Africa and Australia have caused a generalized fear of all snakebites. The symptom involves hemorrhage, which results in an impairment of the normal blood-clotting mechanism, plus damage to the walls of small blood vessels. Victims poisoned by these Old World vipers, ooze blood from all their body orifices, urine and saliva are bloodstained, and red or purplish patches appear on the skin. Death may come suddenly, or occur up to two weeks after the bite, from   internal bleeding. According to Minton, these symptoms can follow rattlesnake bites, if the victim receives a lot of venom and it enters a main vein. Minton, (1980, p.59) states that in a western state, a rancher's son was bitten on the leg by a prairie rattler. He was hospitalized in a nearby small town and seemed to be doing well for about three days. He then developed a nosebleed, hemorrhagic spots appeared on his skin, and his lungs filled with fluid. He was transferred to a large medical center but died within a few hours after his arrival.

A similar reaction was reported by C. H, Brennan, in 1995. A friend and timber rattler adventurer and enthusiast, Burdette Brewer, was snake hunting on a warm June day, in the early 1970's, for that elusive "big one" and received a severe bite. Brewer loved teaching children about the timbers, and was a conscientious hunter who respected the snakes territory and right to life. He enjoyed getting out there in the mountains and seeing the dogwoods in blossom. "You see flowers there in May that people never see. How about the laurel! I mean most people don't see such beautiful laurel, nothing like the blankets you see in the wild. The rattlers fascinate me." While handling a timber rattler about a "forty-incher," the snake got one fang in a vein in Brewer's leg. As soon as it happened, he felt a burning at the bite site. Within about three minutes, his throat and tongue were tingling, and he and his friend headed for the hospital. By the time Brewer arrived at the hospital, his entire body tingled all over, "…like when your arm goes to sleep." Because the bite was atypical, and no tissue swelling had yet occurred, he was sent home from the hospital without antivenin treatment. Shortly after arriving at home, his leg began to swell, and burn intensely. He was taken back to the hospital, and a blood sample was taken. It did not coagulate or clot, as it should have. The venom was destroying Brewer's platelets. Normal cell counts can range from 150,000 to 450,000, and his had dropped to 3,000. He was lucky to be alive. The doctors pumped him full of platelets and antivenin. After four days, he was sent home, alive and wiser.

Pitviper snakebite usually causes discomfort within five minutes. A burning sensation or pulsations of pain increase in intensity rather rapidly. Sometimes the area around the fang punctures is temporarily numb, indicating a large injection of venom and a serious bite. A sensation of yellow vision is another early indication of severe poisoning. Discoloration (ecchymoses) and swelling of tissues (edema) surrounding the wound increase. Other symptoms include muscle twitching (fasciculations), unusual metallic taste, weakness, increased pulse rate, numbness or tingling (paresthesias) around the mouth and dizziness or faintness. Lymph nodes may become painful and tender. Vomiting, and seizures, violent spasms that shake the entire body, may follow.
Major venom poisoning may have either life threatening systemic effects, involving the entire body, or local effects at and around the bite site. The most important systemic effect is hypotension (low arterial blood pressure, or shock), that can lead to major organ damage, renal failure and even death if not corrected. If the snakebite victim collapses and appears to have a fall in blood pressure with a thready and/or rapid pulse, the victim should be placed in a lying down position, and rushed to a hospital. Bleeding from many sites throughout the body, and generalized muscle damage (myonecrosis) are other serious systemic effects, which can be fatal. Significantly low concentrations of fibrinogen, a blood clotting factor, throughout the body (hypofibrinogenemia), and an abnormally low

number of platelets in the circulating blood (thrombocytopenia), can persist up to 2 weeks after the bite.

Viper bites are often followed by the death of tissue, or necrosis, around the bitten area. This is caused by digestive enzymes in the venom and by damage to the local blood supply. It is often made worse by improper us of tourniquets in first aid treatment. Some bites result in nothing worse than a scar, while with others, the entire finger or limb becomes gangrenous and must be amputated. Minton, 1980, stated that in 1963 a Florida surgeon, Dr. Newton C. McCollough, had reported that 17% of all surgical amputations performed on children in his state were done because of snakebites. Today, amputations are rare. At herpetologists' meetings, it is usually possible to tell the museum men, who handle dead specimens, from the zoo men who handle live snakes, by counting fingers. Few of the live handlers have a complete set. When necrosis does occur, tissue contracture, which is permanent contraction of tissue due to scar tissue formation and joint immobility, may result in serious and permanent disability, especially when fingers and toes are involved. Recent animal research suggests that necrosis occurs within 15 minutes of injection, and that antivenom was not effective in preventing local necrosis when given 15-60 minutes following venom injection (Hardy, D.L.1992).

First Aid for Snakebite:
History:

The unpredictable course of snakebite outcomes, gives almost any remedy a chance to become the cure of choice. Many snakebites are not caused by venomous snakes, and at least 33% of bites by venomous snakes are dry bites with no venom injection at the bite site. It is understandable that any treatment applied to bites in these categories will result in complete recovery of the "snakebite" victim, thus establishing a "cure" for snakebite. In the old days, many harmless snakes were thought to be dangerously venomous. Therefore, when an application of radishes or goat's milk cheese, cured the bite of a reputedly fatal but actually harmless snake, they became accepted remedies. Remedies gain their reputations by saving people from dangers that never existed. The mere fact that so many diversified remedies persist for rattlesnake bite indicates that they did not work, for a truly effective cure would have displaced all the others.

Incision and Suction:

The history of incision and suction goes back to ancient times in the second century BC. Galen, the great Greek physician of the second century AD prescribed to the treatment and it carried into every period in history, right into the New World, with the discovery of rattlesnakes. Cupping glasses were used as suction devices. A small bell-shaped glass was heated and applied to the bite and incision. As it cooled, the reduced air volume exerted a suction effect. Leeches were also used to draw out the blood and venom. These were replaced with rubber-bulb operated suction devices, of field use snakebite kits, in the 1950's through the 1980's. In 1984, Sawyer Products Inc. secured a license under a 1982 French patent and began marketing the Extractor vacuum pump in the United States as part of the Sawyer's First Aid Kit. If a Sawyer extractor is available within 5 minutes of the patient's being bitten, it is now recommended to apply it over the bite site and leave it in place for 30 minutes. Suction by mouth has a long history in this country. *Mouth suction is not recommended in modern first aid* because of the chance of *infection at the wound site,* and because of the chance that any venom sucked into the mouth could be absorbed into mouth lesions, cracked lips, or ulcerated teeth. Application of a tourniquet above the bite accompanied the incision-suction first aid. Incision at the bite site accompanied suction. Suction and bleeding were a part of the treatment of many diseases in ancient and medieval times. The bleeding was believed to locally withdraw the venom, and to systemically remove the evil spirits that entered the body with the bite. In the 1920's, Dr. Dudley Jackson introduced the use of multiple cruciform, x-shaped incisions at the bite site, with accompanying tourniquet and suction at each site. Deep incisions involving the fang punctures was advocated by Staley in 1939, but in 1950, Pope pointed out the dangers of deep field incisions, such as severing nerves, tendons and blood vessels. *Incision at the bite site is not recommended as a modern form of first aid in the field.*

Cauterization:

Cauterizing snakebite with either heat or chemicals was a drastic and painfully damaging remedy. The hot iron treatment was first mentioned by Nicander who lived about 150 BC. Chemical caustics were indicated among the remedies reported by Pliny in 1855, especially the use of 'nitrum,' with lime and vinegar. Cauterization with a hot iron was recommended for rattlesnake bites as early as 1648. The cowboys often treated wounds with a hot branding iron, but hot coals were also used. Another method of cauterization used on the western frontier was to sear the wound, by lighting a patch of black powder placed over it. Brymer, 1928, described a small brass or iron ring which was carried by miners, stockmen, herders and Indians that was used to contain the gun powder around the snake bite, to make cauterization easier. Unexploded gunpowder mixed with salt was also used as a poultice to draw out the venom. *Cauterization is not recommended in modern first aid treatment for snakebite.*

Tourniquet or Ligature (Binding): (Fig. 3.7).

A tourniquet is any device used for putting pressure on a blood vessel to stop bleeding or control the circulation of blood to some part of the body. A quick field tourniquet could be any kind of bandaging material wrapped around an appendage, with pressure released at intervals. The tourniquet is a means of delaying venom absorption. It is an accessory to incision and suction, since it may hold venom in tissues close to the bite where it may be withdrawn by suction. The use of a tourniquet for impeding circulation is very old. The Indian tribes and colonists used it in company with suction. It seemed a natural assumption that so long as the venom from a bite could be restricted to some local area, the patient's life would be safeguarded. But the danger of gangrene and subsequent

amputation of the affected appendage, was recognized early in this treatment. The *tight tourniquet is not only dangerous but also unnecessary, because the venom is not diffused through the body via blood vessels but is carried by the lymphatic system.* Only a moderate pressure is required to restrict lymph flow. Many modern first aid advocates in the field recommend a constriction band, 3-6 inches wide, such as an ace bandage, be applied proximal to, or between the bite and the heart. This would block lymphatic flow, not blood flow. It should be loose enough to slip one or two fingers beneath the band. This is a standard worldwide-accepted first aid treatment for bites by snakes such as the cobra, coral and many Australian species. It delays the onset of serious

Fig.3.7: Field tourniquet."

systemic snakebite symptoms when victims are miles away from medical help. The controversy over its use in pitviper bites is that containing the venom at the site will increase local tissue damage. The choice is left in the hands of the victim. If unable to get to a medical facility within an hour, and a life-threatening situation seems to be present, the victim may chose to apply the wide-area, low-pressure wraps to prevent the spread of venom. Thus reducing the widespread damage to nearby limbs and tissues, as well as preventing systemic symptoms until arrival at a medical facility, at which time the systemic issues can be addressed professionally.

Freezing and Cold Packs:

Crum in 1906 was among the first to suggest the use of ethyl-chloride spray, a refrigerant, to freeze tissue at the bite site. In 1908 Wilson suggested that freezing might be used when a bite on the head or body made a tourniquet impossible. In 1953, H. L. Stahnke in Arizona, revived interest in the technique of treatment by chilling. The treatment involved a temporary tight tourniquet on the nearest one-bone site above or proximal to the bite. A piece of ice was then to be placed on the bite. Once at the medical facility the affected limb was immersed in a bath of crushed ice and water for at least 12 hours. This procedure was referred to as the ligature-cryotherapy method, L-C. He did not recommend direct application of ethyl-chloride spray in the field, but suggested spraying a wet cloth with the refrigerant, which could be applied to the bite. This procedure was adamantly opposed by Shannon in 1953. He felt that any external applications at the bite site should not be too hot or too cold. Iced water is not only immediately painful, but the combination of tissue damage from the venom and freezing, could lead to amputation or a permanently crippled extremity. *Application of hot or cold packs is not recommend in modern first aid treatment for snakebite.*

Remedies Derived from the Snake:

A basic philosophy in primitive medicine expressed the idea that suitable remedies for curing a snakebite could be obtained by using parts of the offending animal as part of the cure. In the 1600's Brazilian natives mashed the head of the offending snake, mixed it with the saliva of a fasting man, and applied it to the bite as a plaster to draw out the poison. Another reported recommendation was to swallow the live heart of the snake. Later treatment involved drinking a concoction of pulverized dried snake heart and wine or beer. The Native Indians thought that rattler fat rubbed into the bite would neutralize the poison. Some tribes kept dried snakeskin or powdered rattle in pouches for field treatment. Other tribes would collect the blood from the offending snake, and apply it to the bite. Many Native tribes believed that the person bitten by a rattler should kill the snake, or it would continue to send poison into him. Snake oil often sold as a cure-all in colonial times, applied to the snakebite, was said to draw the poison out of the flesh. Binding the heart of the snake to the bite, or applying any part of the snakes body to the wound, was supposed to reabsorb the venom. Often, either the fresh skin or flesh from the snake was applied to the bite with the belief that the raw rattler flesh would suck out or reabsorb the venom. This theory, of the ability of raw flesh to draw out poison, relates to the world wide split-chicken remedy, a folk cure that is still applied in primitive areas.

Split-Chicken Treatment:

One of the most widespread folklore cures for snakebite is the split-chicken remedy. In this treatment, a live chicken is split in half and the bleeding flesh is immediately applied to the snakebite as a poultice. A poultice is usually prepared from powders or dried leaves, which are moistened with oily or watery fluids and usually applied warm to the wound. It exerts soothing, relaxing counterirritant effects upon inflamed skin and tissue. The use of raw meat for this purpose can also act as a poultice. According to popular belief, the chicken's flesh would turn green from the venom that it draws from the wound. Another chicken would then be applied until the abnormal color no longer appeared after which the patient was assumed to be cured. Not the slightest benefit has ever been shown to result from this cruel method, yet it is still practiced in some backwoods areas. Its use can dangerously delay the application of effective first aid measures.

Plant Cures:

Native Indians and colonists used various plant cures for rattlesnake bites. The plant cures were the most popular and most generally used of all treatments. Extracts or teas made from leaves or roots were given internally. Sometimes poultices, or warm moist lotions or compresses were applied. Often both internal and external methods were used together. Plant cures for snakebite had an extensive place in ancient and medieval pharmacology. The value that the plants contributed was their incidental value as stimulants, narcotics or antiseptics. Like all folklore treatments, their reputations were gained in the cure of cases in which there never was any danger to the patient, either because he had been bitten by a harmless snake, or because no venom had been injected. Chinese practitioners often described remedies using plants closely related to plants used by American Indians. For more than 200 years, plant researchers have recognized striking similarities between the plants of eastern Asia and North America. Most of these similar plants are thought to be remnants of an ancient forest that covered the Northern Hemisphere more than 70 million years ago. Over 140 groups or genera of these medicinal plants share similar ranges in eastern Asia and North America. This explains why the Chinese experience is relevant to North American species, and vice versa. Some of the plants included in this classical pattern of plant separations are various species of Ginseng, Witch-hazel, Sassafras, Magnolia and Spicebush.

A concept known as the 'doctrine of signatures" is sometimes mentioned in discussing the history of medicinal plants. This refers to an ancient idea that if a plant part was shaped like a human organ, or resembled a disease, or illness in anyway, then the plant would be useful in curing that particular ailment or organ. One plant often discussed with American Indian snakebite folklore and the "doctrine of signatures" is the Downy Rattlesnake-Plantain (*Goodyera pubescens*) (Fig. 3.8). The distinctive bluish green leaves with prominent white veins in a 'rattlesnake' pattern gave this plant its name. The leaves so closely resembled snakeskin, that it was one

Fig.3.8: Rattlesnake-Plantain folk remedy for snakebite and "doctrine of signature."

of the more popular treatments of choice. American Indians also used tea made from its roots for snakebites. This plant is now rare. When found it shares the habitat of the

Northern Copperhead and Timber Rattlesnake.

The most common usage of plants for snakebites involved the use of a poultice made from roots, bark, leaves, flowers, or seeds. A poultice is a commonly used term for an external application of herbs. An herb is different from a tree or shrub whose woody stem lives from year to year. Herb refers to any seed plant whose stem withers away to the ground after each growing season. A poultice is a moist paste made from plant parts. If the herbs are fresh, they are beaten to pulp in a mortar and pestle or similar tool. If the herbs are dried, they are pulverized and soaked in warm water to make a paste. The poultice is spread over the snakebite.

Some plants roots that were used as poultices for snakebite by American Indians were from the Wild Calla *(Calla palustris)*, Rattlesnake-Master *(Eryngium yuccifolium)*, Black Sanicle or Snakeroot *(Sanicula marilandica)*, Flowering Spurge *(Euphorbia corollata)*, White Snakeroot *(Ageratina altissima)*, White Lettuce, *Rattlesnake Root (Prenanthes alba)*, Canada Lily *(Lilium* canadense), Red Trillium, (Fig. 3.9) Wakerobin, or Bethroot (*Trillium erectum*), Cypress-Vine *(Ipomoea quamoclit)* a Morning Glory, Feverwort, *(Triosteum perfoliatum)* a Honeysuckle,

Fig.3.9: Trillium root as folk treatment for snakebite.

Fig.3.10: Jack-In-The-Pulpit root used for folk snakebite remedy.

Rough Blazing-Star *(Liatris aspera)*, Jack-In-The-Pulpit *(Arisaema triphyllus)* (Fig. 3.10), Wild Ipecac *(Euphorbia ipecacuanhae)*, and Rattlesnake Fern *(Botrychium virginianum)*. Some plant leaves that were used as a poultice for snakebite were from the White Lettuce, or Rattlesnake Root, Plantain-Leaved Pussytoes *(Antennaria plantaginifolia)*, Tobacco *(Nicotiana tabacum)*, and Venus Maidenhair Fern *(Adiantum capillus-veneris)*. Poultice from the seeds of Fennel *(Foeniculum vulgare)*, and the berries from the Common Juniper *(Juniperus communis)*, were used for snakebite by American Indians. Teas made from plants were also used by the American Indians for snakebite treatment. Teas made from leaves and flowers are called *infusions*. They are made by soaking the leaves or flowers in hot water for 10 to 20 minutes. A cold tea or infusion was made by soaking the leaves or flowers in cold water from 2 hours to overnight. Teas made from roots, bark, or seeds are called *decoctions*. They are made by simmering the roots, bark and seeds under low heat.

Some plant roots that were used to make teas were Downy Rattlesnake-Plantain, Greek Valerian (*Polemonium reptans*), Narrow-Leaved Purple Coneflower (*Echinacea angustifolia*), Virginia Snakeroot (*Aristolochia serpentaria*), New Jersey Tea, or Red Root *(Ceanothus americanus)*, Perfoliate Bellwort *(Uvularia perfoliata)*, and Dutchman's Pipe *(Aristolochia tomentosa)*. The Common Catalpa *(Catalpa bignonioides)* tree's bark was used to make tea for a snakebite antidote. Tea made from the powdered leaves and roots of the Rattlesnake-Weed *(Hieracium venosum)*, were also used as a snakebite remedy. The leaves of the American Dittany *(Cunila origanoides)*, flowers from Canada Goldenrod *(Solidago canadensis)*, and seeds from Great Burdock *(Arcitium lappa)*, were also used to make teas for treating snakebite.

Raw garlic cloves *(Allium sativum)* have been used as a snakebite remedy. The roots of St. Andrew's Cross *(Hypericum hypericoides)*, and Narrow-Leafed Purple Coneflower have been chewed for a treatment for snakebite.

Often a cooled tea made from the roots of False Aloe *(Manfreda virginica)*, Black-Eyed Susan *(Rudbeckia hirta)*, the inner bark from the White or American Ash tree *(Fraxinus americana)*, and the TulipTree *(Liriodendron tulipifera)*, were used as external washes, which were applied to the skin at the snakebite site. Syrup from the Marsh-Marigold or Cowslip *(Caltha palustris)*, was used as a folk antidote to snake venom. Plant juices from the Eclipta *(Eclipta prostrata)* have been used as an external rub to treat snakebite. In a laboratory study, it was found to neutralize the venom of the South American Rattlesnake *(Crotalus durissus terrificus)*.

Steven Foster and James A Duke have recently published (2000) an incredible Peterson Field Guide to Medicinal Plants and Herbs which describes the above folklore snakebite remedies, and discusses pharmaceutical applications of these plants in modern medicine. For further study of this exciting field of research, this book is highly recommended.

New England Pitvipers:

The two venomous snakes of Connecticut and neighboring New England states are the Northern Copperhead *(Agkistrodon contortrix)* and the Timber Rattlesnake *(Crotalus horridus)*. The adult copperhead ranges from 24 to 36 inches in length. When

Fig.3.11: Northern Copperhead Old Lyme CT.

Fig.3.12: Timber Rattlesnake Marlborough CT.

the snake is milked, the total amount of venom obtained is from 40 to 75 mg. of dried weight. The LD_{50} (the amount of venom in milligrams that it takes to kill 50% of the mice tested) is 10.90 mg. of venom per kilogram of mouse mass. An average mouse weighs 0.02 kg, so it would take about 0.218 mg of venom to kill and average mouse. An average man weighs 150 pounds, or about 68 kg. Assuming the lethal dose is similar pound for pound, it would take 741 mg of venom to kill a man. Fatalities from copperhead bites are almost unknown. The adult Timber Rattlesnake is between 35 and 55 inches. The average venom yield is 75.0 to 210.0 mg of dried weight. The LD_{50} for this rattlesnake is 1.64 mg. of venom per kg. of mouse mass. Making a comparison of the hypothetical LD (lethal dose) for an average human weighing 150 pounds, it might take about 111 mg of venom to kill and average human. On this basis, the Timber Rattlesnake could conceivably be about 6.5 times more dangerous than the Northern Copperhead. Combine the higher LD_{50} to the increased amount of available venom for injection, which is about 3 times the amount for copperheads, and the Timber comes out ahead on the danger list. The fangs of the average adult copperhead are about 0.25 inches, compared to the average adult Timber Rattlesnake, which has a fang length of about 0.5 inches. The Timber Rattlesnake is also heavier than the copperhead, so it is able to exert more force behind its strike-bite. The venom composition of both pit vipers is similar but the effects of the bites are magnified by the increased severity of the bite from the rattlesnake. In the past 50 years, only two people have been bitten by the Timber Rattlesnake in Connecticut, and both people were handling the snakes. There have been no deaths in Connecticut from Timber Rattlesnake or Northern Copperhead bites in the last 100 years. Although more people are bitten by copperheads, averaging 5 per year, few cases involve the extensive medical treatment that the rattlesnake bites receive. It is listed as the least toxic snake on a list of 81 selected species for degrees of toxicity (Ernst and Zug, 1996). All bites are potentially life threatening, for each bite is unique, and must always be treated as a medical emergency. All venomous snakebites should be reported to the Poison Information Center in Farmington Connecticut.

Deaths in the United States from Pitviper Envenomation:

Every state except Maine, Alaska, Rhode Island, and Hawaii is home to at least 1 of the 20 venomous snakes found in the United States. In the 1950's, Dr. Henry M. Parrish conducted a survey on snakebite in the United States. About 6.700 cases were treated by physicians, with an average of fifteen deaths a year. Minton, 1980, estimated that at least a third of snakebites in the United States involve some sort of deliberate contact with the snake, such as catching, killing, handling or otherwise manipulating them. Such bites are referred to as "illegitimate." Studies have shown that 16 to 28 % of snakebites occur when the victim has been using alcohol. One of the difficulties in assessing deaths due to snakebites until recent years was the death classification used. Deaths from all venomous animals were listed under one category. This conformed to the International List of Causes of Death, under category E-927 that listed annual deaths in the United States from the bites and stings of venomous animals. An example of this generalization was discussed by Klauber, 1956, in reference to deaths in Arizona between 1929 to 1951. The data covered 22 years, and listed a total of deaths at 102 for that period. When an actual breakdown of causes was researched, 69 bites were from scorpions, of which Arizona has two very dangerous species, which are particularly dangerous to children. Rattlesnakes caused 18 deaths, or only 18%. A similar survey in California, between 1931 to 1944, showed 70 deaths by venomous animals. Of these, only 19 deaths were from rattlesnake bites. Deaths have declined since the early 1930's after the arrival of antivenin in 1927. As the quality, availability, and distribution of antivenin improved, along with the use of antibiotics, more and better hospitals with emergency treatment centers, and faster transportation to the improved medical facilities, deaths from snakebites has steadily declined. Death from pitviper envenomation occurs in 10-20% of victims when medical care is not available, but less than 1% when it is available. Death from pitviper envenomation appears related to delays in providing medical care, or inappropriate care, allowing for development of shock. The treatment of pitviper "poisoning" has improved so dramatically in the past 200 years, that death is now a rare occurrence, although disability, particularly after upper extremity bites, is still common. Since most bites today are nonaccidental, or illegitimate, the simplest strategy would be to simply avoid handling pitvipers. It is important to realize that injury that occurs before antivenin can be administered is probably not reversible. (Dart et al 1992).

Recommended First Aid in Pitviper Bites:

Victim and helper should remain calm.

Remove rings, watches and bracelets from affected hand.

Immobilize the bitten extremity, using a splint if possible, in a dependent position, that is at heart level or below.

Avoid excessive activity. Muscular activity hastens the spread of venom through the lymphatic channels.

The Sawyer Extractor (Sawyer Products, Long Beach, California), a small, lightweight venom extractor kit may be beneficial in extracting some of the snake's venom if applied within five minutes of the bite and left in place for 30 minutes.

A wide constriction band of 3 to 6 inches may be applied proximal to the bite, to block superficial venous and lymphatic flow, and should be left in place until antivenin therapy, if indicated. One or two fingers should easily slide beneath this band, since any impairment of arterial blood flow could increase tissue death. (*This is still a controversial application,* and suggested only if unable to get to a medical facility within an hour of the snake bite. Conant and Collins, 1998, only recommend this band for coral snake bite, not bites from pitvipers. The coral snake venom attacks the nervous system. Keeping the poison localized will reduce the onset of life-threatening symptoms, until medical help can be obtained. However localizing the highly tissue-damaging venom of pitvipers could lead to increased localized tissue damage. The choice of whether to use a wide restricting bandage remains in the hands of the stricken individual, and his assessment of the severity of the bite).

Move the victim to a medical facility as soon as possible.

If a cell-phone is available, call 911, give all-important information about geographic location, severity of the bite, and call ahead to the medical facility so antivenin will be waiting to be administered if deemed necessary. It has often been quoted, that the most effective snakebite first aid kit consists of car keys, a cell-phone, or some coins with which to call a hospital.

What NOT to do if bitten by a Venomous Snake:

Do not cut into or incise bite marks with a blade. Lacerations preformed by untrained people may sever nerves or major blood vessels. This leads to complications that may result in amputation of toes or fingers.

Do not apply oral (mouth) suction to bite.

Do not apply a narrow, constrictive tourniquet such as a belt, necktie or cord.

Do not apply either hot or cold packs.

Do not drink any alcohol or use any medication.

Do not eat or drink anything.

Do not engage in strenuous physical activity.

Do not use a stun gun or electric shock of any kind.

Do not waste time or take any risks trying to kill, bag or bring in offending snake.

Do not administer antivenin in the field because of the high risk of severe allergic reaction.

Prevention of Snakebite:

Do not keep dangerous snakes as pets.

When walking in areas where venomous snakes may be present, protective clothing and boots should always be worn.

Traveling with a companion is always safer than travelling alone when hiking in areas inhabited by venomous snakes.

Drugs and alcohol should never be used while traveling outdoors.

Do not walk through tall grass, fern fields, and underbrush.

Be particularly alert when climbing rocky ledges. Also, be wary when walking near old logs and decaying tree stumps. These are places often favored by copperheads and rattlesnakes.

When crossing a log, first step onto it, in order to see what is behind it, then step down on the other side when it appears safe to do so.

Never reach into mammal burrows.

One of the leading causes of snakebite is the practice of lifting or turning surface objects with the bare hands. It is best to move these items such as rocks, boards, logs, brush, and construction debris with a long-handled tool such as a hoe, shovel, axe or broomstick.

Be wary around stone walls, and piles of wood.

Keep hands and feet out of areas you cannot see.

Keep garage doors closed if sharing habitat space with the Northern Copperhead during hot summer days, for they will seek out cool retreats during the day, and do their hunting at night.

If a snake is encountered, stand still, slowly back up, and find a path around the snake. Leave the snake alone, respect its right to life and freedom, you are privileged to share its wilderness home, enjoy and bask in the spirit.

Avoid dead venomous snakes, for they often can bite reflexively for periods lasting up to an hour after death, as can its decapitated head.

To discourage snakes from making a home near your home, it is advisable to keep the area around the house and outbuildings free of debris. Rock piles, trash piles, stacked lumber, and firewood piles provide snakes with shelter. They also serve as homes to rats and mice that are the chief food of most venomous snakes.

Antivenin:

Antivenin is a serum that is commercially produced to neutralize the effects of envenomation by venomous snakes. The fresh snake venom used to produce antivenin is obtained either by manually milking a snake, or by electrical stimulation. Venom is extracted from captive snakes every twenty to thirty days. The venom is freeze-dried.

Healthy horses, usually 7 to 8 years old, are injected at regular intervals with nonlethal doses of a solution prepared from the freeze-dried venom, until they build up immunity to the venom. The dosage is slowly increased over time to create greater immunity. The horse's immune system neutralizes the venom by producing antibodies, which are specialized proteins. The horse antibodies in turn neutralize the same venom when injected into humans. A similar procedure is now preformed with sheep, which has replaced the horse serum.

To obtain the antibodies, blood is regularly removed from the horse's (sheep's) jugular vein. The blood is combined with a sodium-citrate solution, which prevents coagulation and degradation. The globulin (a group of proteins soluble in salt solutions), to which the antibodies are attached, is separated out and purified.

This equine (horse)-derived antivenin has been the mainstay of hospital treatment for venomous snakebite since 1954. For rattlesnake, cottonmouth, and copperhead bites, Antivenin (Crotalidae) Polyvalent (ACP), manufactured by Wyeth-Ayerst, has been the standard available treatment. ACP is known to cause sever allergic reactions to people. Because it is associated with a large incidence of hypersensitivity reactions including anaphylaxis, a test dose is administered prior to antivenin treatment. In the past, if a snakebite was life threatening, a hypersensitive patient received the antivenin in small incremental doses along with treatment for hypersensitivity reactions. This product, however, will no longer be manufactured after 2001.

Crotalidae polyvalent immune Fab, bovine (CroFab) was approved by the FDA on October 2, 2000. It is the only alternative to the Wyeth antivenin approved for treatment of crotalid envenomation in the U.S. The Fab antivenin is a combination of immunoglobulin fragments from the venom of *Crotalus atrox* (Western Diamondback Rattlesnake), *Crotalus adamanteur* (Eastern DiamondbackRattlesnake), *Crotalus scutulatus* (Mojave Rattlesnake) and *Agkistrodon piscivorus* (Cottonmouth). The Fab antivenin binds and neutralizes the venom once in the blood. The risk of hypersensitivity is decreased.

Compared to the original whole antivenin, the fragmented Fab antivenin has a more favorable side effect profile. Up to 80% of patients who received the original ACP antivenin experienced serum sickness, 7-14 days after administration. None of 11 test patients with progressive symptoms from a pitviper bite, who had received the Fab antivenin, experienced serum sickness. To date, there have been no reported incidences of anaphylaxis with the use of the Fab antivenin. The antivenin should be administered at a medical facility, within 6 hours of the snakebite if possible. The cost of CroFab is approximately $1550 per carton of 2 vials! CroFab offers a new treatment for snakebites requiring antivenin, with less risk of a hypersensitivity reaction, and better safety overall for the patient. However, the best way to treat a snakebite is by prevention (Bartels, Dauenhauer and Osburn, 2001).

Stun Gun Electroshock Controversy:
In July 1986, The Lancet medical journal published a letter to the editor entitled "High voltage shock treatment for snake bite" (Guderian et al., 1986). Ronald Guderian, a missionary physician working in the lowland forest of Ecuador, reported the electric shock treatment of 34 native people having suffered snakebites. Treatment involved 5 one-second shocks with high voltage (20kV), low amperage current delivered within 30 minutes or less after the bite. The shocks were applied to the bite using an insulated probe connected to the spark plug cable connection of a running outboard motor. A second wire grounded the patient to the motor. Patients treated with this electroshock showed no local venom effects. A more available treatment devise was developed by modifying a stun gun to the above requirements.

The news media sensationalized the treatment in the New York Times, Time magazine, American Medical News and Outdoor Life Magazine. Some suggestions as to the biological basis of the treatment referred to the local confinement of the venom by electrospasm of the local vessels so the venom did not spread. Another proposal was that the shock had direct affect on breaking down the structured protein in the venom.

Guderian feels that electroshock treatment should be considered experimental and that it is premature to advocate its use in North American pitviper bites. He believes that electroshock treatment is promising and hopes that other researchers stimulated by his work will conduct well-planned clinical studies on electroshock. Due to the lack of availability of antivenin, and the remoteness of the geographic areas of snakebite occurrences, Dr. Guderian continues to use electroshock in his country. A Washington corporation, Venomex Inc., is dedicated to the development of electroshock for use in snakebite and other conditions. The company is gathering clinical data and conducting basic research on the effects of electroshock. The results will eventually be made available for evaluation by others (Hardy, 1992).

Hardy, 1992, in *Biology of the Pitvipers* states: "Nearly four years have passed since the Guderian's original letter concerning electroshock and snakebite, and no other series of clinical cases have been reported. There are a number of testimonials claiming good results, but animal experiments have been unable to demonstrate favorable effects. Guderian continues to use electroshock in Ecuador, and is convinced of its effectiveness. However, until his findings are reported in detail, and other clinical trials corroborate his findings, with supporting laboratory data, general acceptance must be withheld."

The Arizona Poison and Drug Information Center in Tucson, Arizona, is a national clearinghouse for information on snakebite. It maintains an up-to-date list of which types of foreign antivenins are available in different zoos in this country. They can advise a doctor which zoo to call in case of a bite from an exotic venomous snake. The Center's telephone number is (520) 626-6016 (Conant, and Collins, 1998).

Special Topic:

Severe Copperhead bite in Lyme Connecticut: On a hot summer morning at about 9:00 on July 11, 1979, Bob Mariani, a resident of Lyme Connecticut entered his garage to retrieve a screwdriver from his tool chest. The summer had been hot, reaching 100 degrees for several days. Bob had left his garage door open during the recent heat wave to cool it down. He had his tools in a wooden cabinet, which was four drawers high. The top drawer had the screwdriver that he wanted, so he opened it with this left hand and reached into the drawer with his right hand, only to feel an immediate shooting needle-like pain. He pulled his hand away, and saw two small red spots on the palm of his hand, in the fleshy, muscular area between his thumb and forefinger (right thenar eminence). Towards the center of the palm, there were faint scratch marks from the lower jaw of the offending snake. The fang punctures were about 5/8-inch apart and oozing blood.

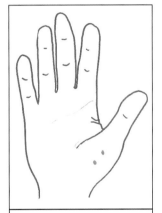

Fig.1.13: Fang marks from Copperhead bite

Bob pulled open the drawer and saw a large copperhead, which later measured 33 inches, coiled for another strike. He grabbed a hammer and disabled the snake. The burning pain in his right hand intensified rapidly, feeling like a burning hot razor blade was cutting through his flesh. A panicky feeling began to take over as he realized that he had a severe bite from a poisonous snake, and having no idea how life-threatening it was, he began to panic and started running to the house. It did not take long for Bob to regain his composure and stop to try to think about what to do for first aid. Tourniquets were recommended in the 1970's as first aid in treatment for snakebite, so Bob grabbed the closest ligature available, which was an extension cord. He wrapped the cord tightly around his lower arm, half way between his wrist and elbow. The pain was intensifying, and his hand began to swell. Within 5-10 minutes Bob felt pain in his armpit, in his lymph nodes. This symptom was indicative of a severe bite. The severity of the symptoms seemed to be developing rapidly to a severe level.

Bob got to a telephone and called the operator. The emergency code number 911 had not been activated at that time. The operator called the local hospital in New London. Worried that he might pass out before help got to him, Bob went out to the driveway, near the road, to be easily seen by the ambulance attendants. A neighbor Trudy Emerson, Sam Harding's sister, was walking by. She noticed Bob waiting, leaning against a tree, and examined his wound. She immediately remarked that he had been bitten by the *'red snake.'* The ambulance, which had been dispatched from Hadlyme Four Corners, arrived in about 20 minutes and took Bob to a local hospital, where he was rushed to emergency care.

Snakebite was a rare emergency in the area, but fortunately, antivenin was on site and available. His arm was immobilized, a tourniquet was applied to his wrist, oxygen was administered, and an ice pack was applied to his forearm and hand. Bobs hand was markedly swollen up to the mid forearm. Due to the apparent severity of the bite, administration of the antivenin began immediately. Bob received 18 units of antivenin over the first 24-36 hours on admission to counteract the affects of the snakebite. The swelling in his arm rapidly progressed to his elbow, and eventually involved his entire arm to his shoulder. His arm was twice its normal size. Bob said it looked more like his leg than his arm. His fingers were so swollen that they blended into one image. His hand resembled a rubber glove blown up, with each finger indistinguishable from the next. When his arm was extended, the top of his hand was so swollen that he could not see his fingers. Bob was experiencing intense pain in his hand. A surgeon was on call in case fasciotomy or tracheotomy was deemed necessary. Supportive treatment continued for about 2 weeks. The pain was so intense, especially on the back of his hand that Bob could not sleep for days. After two weeks, the swelling had gone down. No serious tissue damage or necrosis had developed in his fingers, hand or arm. There was tissue damage at the bite site, with a "caving in of the skin," as Bob described it, but no permanent disability developed. Bob makes his living as an illustrator, artist, and intricate pin stripping detail work, so was grateful for not having lost the use of his fingers. The bite had been so severe, that rumors had circulated to the effect that some of his fingers had been amputated!

Bob broke out with severe hives on 7/16 while still at the hospital. He began to notice extreme weakness and developed a skin rash and intense itching. Bob's discharge was postponed, his wound was healing well, but he was experiencing a systemic reaction to the horse-serum-based antivenon. Later that day he experienced a fainting spell, and was placed in the Trandelenburgh (feet higher than head) position for several hours. Instead of feeling stronger each day, he became weaker, had trouble eating, the skin rash intensified and his body was covered with hives. The itching was almost unbearable. With time and medication, the symptoms diminished, and Bob was discharged on 7/19.

He continued to feel weak, and lost a lot of weight. Bobs skin rash developed into severe dermatitis, similar to eczema, especially on his scalp. His joints began to ache and swell, developing into arthritic symptoms. Annoying food allergies developed, and he must be very careful what he eats, but he is grateful to have survived. Each day is a private miracle for Bob, filled with peace, and determination to make every moment a full experience.

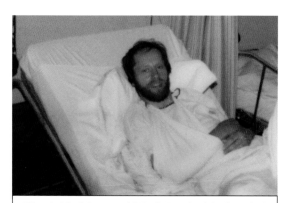

Fig. 3.14: 36-year old Bob Mariani in hospital shortly before discharge after an eight day hospital stay for treatment of a severe Northern Copperhead bite on 7/11/79 in Lyme Connecticut.

The trauma of the bite was such that in an interview 25 years later, the above information was recalled as though it had happened yesterday!

The symptoms that Bob experienced upon arriving at home were classic serum sickness symptoms. Onset of symptoms occurs 1-2 weeks after administration of the antivenin. Fever, malaise, a vague feeling of discomfort and headache are the earliest symptoms. Rash, joint pain, edema, and gastrointestinal symptoms soon follow.

The area where Bob lived abounds with rock ledge, oak forest, a beautiful lake with streams and adjacent wetlands. This is not the typical traprock habitat of the Northern Copperhead in Connecticut, but none the less, there are several active dens sites in the area, to this day. The snakes are docile, quite, and so well camouflaged in their natural habitat that they pose very little danger to the human inhabitants of the area.

Dave Nelson, a neighbor of Bob's had seen one copperhead on his property at about the same time that Bob had been bitten. Just this past year in the spring of 2003, Dave had been moving lobster pots in his garage, when he found the flattened dehydrated body of a large copperhead, estimated to be about 30 inches, underneath one of the pots. The advice to residents who share the habitat with copperheads is to close all doors to outside sheds during the active foraging months of the copperheads activity period. This is especially important during the summer months, when the hot temperatures drive the snake to seek cool cover during the day. The snakes become nocturnal at this time and hunt for mice at night. Care should be taken walking at night, and in moving cluttered accumulations of 'garage treasures' at this time. Avoid working around wood and stone piles or decaying debris during the snakes active time between June and October.

Modern treatment of copperhead bites is more conservative than in the 1970's. Tourniquets and ice packs are no longer recommended forms of treatment. New antivenin prepared from sheep serum is used to reduce allergic reactions and serum sickness. Antivenin is usually not administered for copperhead bites, unless severe symptoms develop, and even then the number of units administered is usually less than 5, but the patient is kept under careful observation for several days.

CHAPTER FOUR:
MYTHOLOGY AND FOLKLORE:

Myths and folklore about snakes strongly influence the attitudes of people toward snakes. The myths become established through repetition. No other animal has been the subject of as many myths and half-truths as the snake. In some cultures, snakes are symbols of healing or fertility, and in others, they are associated with evil and sin. Snakes do not have magical or spiritual powers, man attributes these symbolic and emotional meanings to them.

Many of the stories of snakes develop around actual incidents of human violence associated with war and snakes. Minton, 1980, discusses snakes and human violence as a prelude to folklore. The annals of military campaigns are filled with legends involving snakes. During the fourth century BC, Macedonian legionnaires came home from campaigns in India with tales of snakes with eyes as large as shields. Right up to the recent veterans of Vietnam, telling of snakes that could drop a man to the ground in six paces after he had been bitten. During the Punic Wars, approximately 264-146 BC, the Romans brought stories home from Africa about the legendary basilisk, with its deadly stare and poisonous breath. The basilisk is a mythical snake-like monster with supposedly fatal breath, and the power to kill by a look, fabled to have been hatched by a serpent from a cock's egg. This fable probably originated from encounters with the spitting cobra. Snakes were used as instruments of psychological and physical torture during war, to make prisoners more cooperative. The Incas Indians used rattlesnakes, and the Indian rajas used cobras. The Viet Cong left snakes in caves and bunkers, making snakebite enough of a concern during the Vietnam War, that four snakebite treatment centers were established to care for both military and civilian patients. The fear of snakes surpassed the fear of enemy troops, malaria and intestinal diseases. North American Indians used snake venom, or the pulped heads of venomous snakes on their poisoned arrows. If the venom was not fatal, the tainted arrows had the effect of inducing gas gangrene, tetanus and other severe infections.

A lot of American and European folklore comes from the biblical story of the temptation of Eve by the serpent. The serpent tricks Eve into eating fruit from the forbidden tree, and she persuades her mate Adam to do the same. When God learned of the serpent's role, he placed a curse on the serpent: "You will be punished for this; you alone of all the animals will crawl on your belly, and you will have to eat dust as long as you live. I will make you and woman hate each other; her offspring and yours will always be enemies. Her offspring will crush your head, and you will bite their heel" (Genesis 3:1-13). This association with snakes and women, fear, and death, was intensified in myths about snakes bites. Some snakebites caused such poisoning in men that it caused bleeding from the victim's eyes nose and genitals. These bites signified that some snakes possessed immensely powerful magic. The relationship between the genital bleeding in men caused by the magical power of the snakebite, and the regular menstrual bleeding of women, made the men believe that the women were consorting with snakes, sharing their magic secrets. A deep fear of menstrual blood, and the magic powers of women during their cycle, filled folklore history. Folklore states that a menstruating woman must quickly burn the combings of her hair before they turned into poisonous snakes. If a man bitten by a snake sees a pregnant woman, he will die from the snakebite.

Chinese folklore recognized the snake as a symbol of longevity, wisdom, and flexibility. It had a close kinship with the benevolent dragon. Snakes live in underground burrows, close to the secrets of the earth, and they protect its treasures. In the Chinese calendar, which has a twelve-year cycle, the Year of the Snake follows the Year of the Dragon. Chinese astrologers characterize individuals born in snake years as cerebral, seductive, cultivated, vain and unfaithful, with a talent for making money and a reluctance to share it. Interestingly enough, Aristotle Onassis and Howard Hughes were born under this sign.

The snakes symbol of religious power is portrayed in the story of Moses casting down his staff at the feet of the pharaoh. The staff turns into a large snake that devours the snakes created by the pharaohs magicians. The ancient Greeks revered snakes. The modern symbol of the medical profession's gift of healing, the staff of Asclepius, shows a snake intertwined around a shaft. Quetzalcoatl, a principal god of the Aztecs, symbolized by a feathered serpent was worshipped as the Master of Life by ancient Aztecs of Central America. Some African cultures worshipped the rock python and considered the killing of one to be a serious crime. The Aborigines of Australia associated a giant rainbow serpent with the creation of life. Shamans, or medicine men, of the Hopi Indian tribe of Arizona perform an elaborate ritual snake dance to bring rain and ensure crop fertility. In Appalachia, some Christians handle venomous snakes as part of ritual ceremonies, relying on faith to protect them from bites. The cobra is considered the live representation of India's fertility god, Shiva.

One of the gentlest stories told about a snake concerns the cobra Muchilinda, who spread his hood to protect the Buddha from the sun while he meditated in the desert. The Buddha was so grateful to the animal whose kindly concern had saved him from heat stroke, that he laid his hand on the serpents spread hood and blessed him, leaving behind the familiar spectacle mark.

The snakes periodic shedding of its skin led to the belief that snakes were immortal. Each time a snake shed its skin, it was reborn. Some early Christians believed that snakes shed their skin in an attempt to remove the evil mantle placed on it by God. Among Catholics, who believe in the snake as a representative of sin, Saint Patrick is credited with driving snakes out of Ireland. The truth about the absence of snakes in Ireland lies in the fact that none ever reached its shores. About 15,000 years ago, Ireland lay beneath a Pleistocene ice sheet. As the ice melted, the sea level rose and isolated Ireland from Britain before Ireland was warm enough to support snakes.

Truth Verses Fiction:
Folklore about snakes is handed down from generation to generation. They could be just amusing tales, except that many people still believe them. It is important to learn more about the truth of the nature and life of snakes, so that reality replaces mythology, and wisdom replaces fear and ignorance.

Hoop Snakes with Stingers:
Myth: A hoop snake in the southern United States, chases its victims by rolling down a hill after them. The snake takes its tail in its mouth, forming a rigid hoop. As the snake builds up speed on the downhill chase, it flings itself like a spear, felling its victim with its poisonous spine-tipped tail.

Reality: No reliable records of this amazing feat have ever been recorded. How is a snake able to force itself into a circular upright position from being flat on the ground, turn itself on edge and begin to roll? Once on a roll, so to speak, how is the snake able to steer itself in pursuit of its victim. The hoop snake myth may have been associated originally with the wormsnakes *(Carphophis)* and mudsnakes *(Farancia)* which have pointed scales on the tips of their tails. These spines, though sharp, have no venom and are not dangerous.

Snakes are Cold and Slimy:

Myth: When a snake is picked up and handled it is cold and slimy.

Reality: A snake will be cold to the touch if caught in cool damp weather, or beside a cool stream, but if caught in a warm sunny spot while basking, it will feel as warm as a mammal. Snakes are exothermic, and their body temperatures are determined by their immediate surroundings. A snake will never be slimy. They have dry protective scales formed from keratin, the same material that forms human fingernails, hair of mammals, and bird feathers. The sliminess myth probably arose from confusion between snakes and eels.

Charming Prey:

Myth: Snakes have the ability to charm prey, especially birds, so they cannot flee.

Reality: A mother bird, approached by a slowly moving snake, hops along the branch in an agitated state, but does not fly away. The snake's steady, unblinking gaze (snakes have no eyelids), appears hypnotic. The birds reluctance to fly suggests that the snake's stare has a hypnotizing effect on the bird. But the birds refusal to fly is a mothers instinct to save her offspring, for behind the mother bird is a nest full of eggs and young nestlings. Some animals may freeze their movements around snakes due to fear or curiosity, see Fig 4.1.

Fig. 4.1: Eastern Hognose "charming Spring Peeper."

Triangular Heads:

Myth: All venomous or poisonous snakes have triangular-shaped heads.

Reality: In the United States, a triangular head shape alerts people to the presence of a venomous snake. All pitvipers, rattlesnakes, copperheads, cottonmouths, have broad triangular head and narrow necks. Many nonvenomous species such as the watersnake and juvenile black rats snakes, also have broad triangular heads and narrow necks. On the other hand, venomous snakes such as the coral snakes have slender heads with little distinction between the head and neck. In other countries, the nonvenomous anacondas, pythons and boas have broad triangular heads. The shape of the head alone cannot determine whether a snake is venomous or nonvenomous.

Hooded Snakes:

Myth: All hooded snakes are deadly:

Reality: Spreading necks which result in hood formation are a defense mechanism. The venomous cobras *(Naja, Ophiophagus),* have hoods. Some nonvenomous snakes typically spread their neck ribs to form hoods when they are disturbed or threatened. One such example is the Eastern Hognose Snake (Fig 4.2).

Fig. 4.2:Harmless hooded Eastern Hognose Snake.

All Injured Snakes Die before Sundown:

Myth: An injured snake dies before sundown of the same day.

Reality: There is no evidence to support this myth. Nerve reflexes may cause muscle twitching for several hours after death. These reflexes result in spasmodic movements of the trunk and jaws. These writhing motions usually subside quickly, but if nightfall comes soon after the death of the snake, the cool temperatures will cause the nerve reflexes to cease, thus reinforcing the notion that the snakes die at sundown. Because of the lingering nerve reflexes, even a dead venomous snake is dangerous.

Snakes have Special Odors:

Myth: Copperheads smell like cucumbers.

Reality: The belief in eastern Unites States that copperheads are associated with the smell of cucumbers cannot be explained. The story is prevalent in the late summer and early fall, and it has been suggested that some plant blossoms at that time of year may have a cucumber smell. All snakes have odors, but they are so subtle that detection is almost impossible. The very unpleasant musk odor is unmistakable, and occurs when the snake sprays its attacker with musk and feces. This odor smells more like skunk than cucumbers!

Snakes Chase People:

Myth: People are chased and/or stalked by venomous and nonvenomous snakes. The coachwhip *(Masticophis)* snake chases its human victim, then wraps the forepart of its body around the victim's legs. Once tripped, the victim is whipped to death with the coachwhip's long tail.

Reality: Coachwhips, like their close relatives the racers *(Coluber),* actively defend themselves, and will at times advance toward an intruder if an escape route is not available. Any snake, when provoked, will advance on an adversary when there is no means of escape. Often an intruder will happen upon a snake, unaware that he is between the snake and its refuge. The snake may dash right by the person to reach its shelter, making it appear to the startled human, that the snake is attacking.

Swallowing Young:

Myth: When confronted with danger, mother snakes swallow their young to protect them.

Reality: Swallowing young snakes would not be protective. Snakes have strong digestive juices, and anything that is swallowed would be subjected to a strong bath of acid and digestive enzymes. Any small snake entering the digestive tract of a larger snake would be killed quickly through suffocation and digestion. This myth probably developed from watching large snakes eating smaller snakes. Some snakes give live birth, and if these young snakes are found in a dead female, it could be assumed that the uterus was the stomach, and that the young snakes had been swallowed.

Sucking Milk:

Myth: Snakes suck the milk from cows and goats. In many farming societies around the world, it is a common superstition that snakes suck the milk from cows and goats. In North America, the milksnake *(Lampropeltis trinagulum)* received its common name from the myth that it could drain a cow dry of its milk. In the Old World folklore, the milksnake would enter homes of a newborn, and suck the milk from the nursing mother during the night.

Reality: Although milksnakes are common around barns, they completely lack the anatomy necessary to suck milk. The snakes sharp teeth, and inflexible lips makes it impossible to seal its mouth around the sensitive udder of a cow or goat. A snake drinks by immersing its mouth in water, and then sucks it in by expanding its body wall. A snakes capacity for water would not allow it to drain a cow dry of milk. In experiments on captive snakes, milk is spurned as a drink of choice. American milksnakes and other species are common in pastures, barns and cattle sheds where small rats and mice are abundant. It is this association with cows and goats that led to the myth of snakes drinking milk.

Venomous Snakes Breeding with Nonvenomous Snakes:

Myth: In the late 1960's a story began to circulate throughout the eastern United States that black snakes, either the black racer *(Coluber constrictor)* or the black rat snake *(Elaphe ocsoleta)*, mated with copperheads *(Agistrodon contortrix)*, or rattlesnakes *(Crotalus horridus)*. This mating produced young venomous snakes that looked like their nonvenomous parents.

Reality: Young Northern Black Racers and Black Rat Snakes have spotted and blotched patterns that, to an untrained observer, resemble the patterns of the Northern Copperhead and the Timber Rattlesnake. These young snakes will often vibrate their tails when frightened or threatened, and this buzzing in the leaves sounds like a rattlesnake tail vibrations. The facts that these snakes often share communal dens sites, and are found together in the fall and spring, enhances the idea that they are related.

The laws of genetics prevent this ever from happening. These snakes are all of different species, and they are unable to interbreed. It is as impossible as a cat and dog interbreeding to produce a litter of *catogs,* or a jackrabbit and antelope breeding to produce a *jack-a-lope!* It simply cannot happen.

First Spring Thunderstorm Wakes up Sleeping Snakes:

Myth: The Amish community of eastern North America believe that snakes will not emerge from their winter sleep until the first thunderstorm of the year.

Reality: Thunderstorms occur in all months of the year. It is the slowly rising spring temperatures that cause the snakes to begin moving from their hibernaculum, and the falling autumn temperatures that drive them underground in the fall.

Number of Rattles Tell the Age of Rattlesnake:

Myth: Rattlesnakes add a rattle each year of their life.

Reality: Rattlesnakes add a rattle each time they shed. They can shed several times a year, depending upon their diet and health. An older individual may lose rattles as they break off. Therefore counting rattles on a rattlesnake will not tell the age of the rattlesnake.

The Buddy System:

Myth: Snakes always travel in pairs, and if one snake is killed, the other snake will seek revenge.

Reality: During the breeding season, usually in the spring, male and female snakes of the same species can be found together. After mating, the male and mated female snakes forage in different areas of their home ranges. According to this myth, a snake whose mate is killed while they are together, will avenge its partner, and attack the intruder. The Northern Black Racer *(Coluber constrictor constrictor)*, when interrupted during courtship or mating, will sometimes aggressively attack a human intruder. This behavior could reinforce this myth.

Fang-In-Boot Tale:

Myth: This legend dates back to the early 1700's. It describes the death of a man who was struck through one of his boots by a rattlesnake. The same boot was later worn by the victims son, who was pricked by the fang still embedded in the leather, and died. After his death, a second son eventually put on the same boot, only to also die a mysterious death. When the boots were examined, a fang was found embedded in the leather.

Reality: This is a good campfire story, but not likely to happen. It is true that if venom is quickly dried and properly stored, it will maintain its potency for many years. The amount of venom that could have been stored in the detached fang, under the unsterile conditions, over the extended period of time encompassing this myth, would not be enough to cause death in even one person, let alone three! Moreover, in an actual rattlesnake bite, the venom is forced into the victim by pressure from the muscles surrounding the venom gland, to force it out through the orifice into the victim. However, there is a real danger in handling the recently severed head of a venomous snake, for it can still inflict a bite for several hours after having been separated from its body.

Snakes in Sleeping Bags:

Myth: Snakes crawl into sleeping bags to get warm.

Reality: Campfire stories tell of sleeping campers being awaked by a snake curling around them to get warm. A snake may crawl into, or under a sleeping bag that is left at the campsite during the day to escape the heat of the day. It is extremely unlikely to enter the sleeping bag once a human body is already inside the bag. Simple camp activities and ground vibrations would alert the snake to leave the area. If the snake is already in the bag, and the human enters the bag, it can certainly be a startling experience.

To avoid this happening, it is advisable while camping in snake country, to always zip the sleeping bag closed, place the sleeping bag on a cot above the ground, or in a tightly zipped tent.

Protective Hair Rope:

Myth: This belief, once a widespread myth of the Southwest states, that a rattlesnake will not crawl over a horsehair rope placed around a campsite or sleeping bag. The stiff protruding hairs of the rope would stick and scratch the snakes belly, causing it to turn away.

Reality: The belly scales of a rattlesnake are so tough it would hardly feel the hairs on a horsehair lariat, or rope, especially since some rattlesnakes are accustomed to crawling among and over cactus plants.

Snakes Tongue is Dangerous:

Myth: The forked tongue of a snake is a venomous stinger. It is still a frequently heard belief today. Often when a child sees a snake's tongue flicking, the comment usually heard is "did you see its stinger?"

Reality: The delicate forked tongue of snakes is associated with the snake's senses of taste and smell. It provides the snake with information about its surroundings. The fork in the tongue allows the snake to determine direction of odors, such as the direction that a prey has moved.

Striking versus Biting:

Myth: Snakes can strike only from a coiled position:

Reality: Snakes can bite from any position, and do not need to be in a coil to bite. The belief that the terms bite and strike are synonymous causes confusion. The strike is not an essential part of the bite. A snake strikes from a coiled position, even if the formation of the coil from a stretched-out position into a striking posture is so fast as to be almost invisible. Therefore, a snake strikes from a coil, yet is able to bite from any position.

Venomous Breath:

Myth: A hognose snake, sometimes called a puff adder, can mix poison with its breath. It becomes flat, and opens its mouth hissing. At the same time, it blows from its mouth with great force. If inhaled by an unwary traveler, it will kill the person.

Reality: Hognose snakes do not produce poisonous breath. They will usually hiss loudly when threatened. However, they are harmless bluffers, who would rather roll over and play dead, than attack anyone.

Water Moccasins:

Myth: Water Moccasins live in Connecticut.

Reality: **There are no Water Moccasins in New England.** Their closest northern range is southeastern Virginia. The Northern Water Snake lives in New England, and may look somewhat like a Water Moccasin. Although aggressive, it is not venomous.

Removing Snakes Fangs:

Myth: Removing snakes fangs will make them harmless.

Reality: Removing the fangs of a venomous snake does not make the snake harmless. A new fang soon replaces the lost fang. The fangs are constantly being replaced as part of the snakes natural life-process.

Glass Snakes:

Myth: Snakes called Glass Snakes, will break off their tails to get away from an enemy that has grabbed its tail.

Reality: A Glass Snake *(Ophisaurus)* is really a lizard with no legs, which looks like a snake. As with most lizards, the tail can be broken off or broken into many pieces. These pieces wiggle for several minutes, drawing the attention of the potential predator away from the legless glass lizards head and body. The lizard can use this distraction to flee to safety.

Immunity to Snakebite:

Myth: Repeated bites from venomous snakes cause immunity.

Reality: Repeated bites can create a buildup of antibodies. However, this can also lead to an allergic reaction, with increased sensitivity to bites. This sensitivity greatly increases the chances of a bite being fatal. Repeated bites are not to be considered beneficial.

Spitting Snakes:

Myth: Clumps of foam found on shrubs and vines in areas of the United States, including Connecticut are left by snakes as *snake spit.*

Reality: Some species of African and Asian cobras can propel or spit venom from their fangs but **NO** American snakes are able to spit venom. The snake spit seen on plants is made and deposited by spittlebugs.

Nest of Snakes:

Myth: If one snake is found in the basement of a house, or attic, there will be a nest of snakes somewhere close by.

Reality: Snakes lay eggs in warm, damp areas, such as within rotten logs and old sawdust and compost piles. Live-bearing snakes give birth in secluded spots within the home range of the female. Once the young are born or hatched, they are independent and usually disperse within a few hours or days. Snakes may also congregate in hibernation sites, but these also are out of site, in cavities in embankments, old foundations, rock ledges and walls of abandoned buildings. It is rare that anyone would encounter these groups of snakes. Most *snake nest* stories are the result of several snakes being seen together, which is an infrequent event.

Medusa:

One of the most well known legends, which still persists in the minds of people to this day, is the tale from Greek mythology about a beautiful maiden with snakes in her hair, whose stare could turn men to stone. The myth incorporates all the struggles of male and female dominance from the beginning of recorded time. It is often difficult to separate mythology from real history, especially in the Greek and Roman ancient histories. The Gods and government were so entwined, it is often an intellectual challenge to differentiate the two.

According to Greek legend, Cecrops, the first king of Attica, a peninsula in the southeastern part ancient Greece, founded the city of Athens about 1556 BC. He was represented as half-human, half-serpent, and contributed to civilizing the state by issuing the first laws. He rejected blood sacrifices in the worship of Zeus, and introduced the idea of monogamy, being married to only one person at a time, the invention of writing, and the practice of burying the dead. During Cecrops reign, the gods competed with each other to gain the patronage of the city. This competition took place between Poseidon, the god of the sea and horses, and Athena, the goddess of wisdom and warfare. Athena won over the people by creating the olive tree, the most prized tree in all of Greece. A temple to Athena was erected, with a statue of the goddess and her attending serpent. A living snake was kept near her shrine as the guardian spirit of the city.

Poseidon never forgot that the goddess Athena had won out over him in becoming the patron god of the city. A beautiful virgin maiden, Medusa, whose beauty surpassed even that of Athena, worked as a priestess in Athena's temple. One day Poseidon surprised Medusa while she was praying at Athena's shrine. Being smitten by her beauty, he ravishes her, and flees from the temple. Athena was enraged by the sacrilegious act, and desecration of her temple. Since Poseidon had escaped, she vented her anger on Medusa. She blamed her for attracting the lusty god of the sea, and turned the unfortunate priestess, into a monster. Medusa's hair became a cluster of live vipers, her neck was covered with scales, and she had tusks like a boar's, golden hands and bronze wings. From then on, if a man looked directly into her eyes, he would be turned to stone and instant death.

The legend continues with Athena persuading the hero warrior Perseus to locate the fleeing Medussa and kill her. Not content with turning the beautiful maiden into a monster, Athena sent Perseus on a quest to kill, decapitate and retrieve the head of Medusa. This would require heroic male courage and skill, for Medusa's power over men was not just over life and death, but the power to cause impotence, symbolized by turning the male to stone with just a glance. Athena gave him her sacred shield to protect him from

Medusa's stare, so that he could safely look at Medusa's reflection in it, and decapitate her as she slept. As Athena watched, Perseus cut off the monster's head. Medusa's dying shrieks so delighted the goddesses that she invented the flute, so that the shrill tones might never be lost, and remain music to her ears. Athena collected the rest of Medusa's blood from the headless corpse, and took it home with her to Athens. As Perseus tucked the head into his pouch, a marvelous winged horse, Pegasus, rose from Medusa's body. Perseus mounted the flying horse and escaped toward Africa. Drops of blood seeping through the pouch fell to earth and bred a race of especially virulent vipers. Perseus finds his way back to Athena and turns the head of Medusa over to her. The head of Medusa is fashioned and hammered into shape on the center of Athena's shield, or aegis. The face of Medusa maintains its power to protect the goddess from enemies by turning them to stone.

Asclepius, the god of healing and medicine, visited Athena with his father Apollo, to receive her blessing. Apollo was the Greek god of music, poetry, and medicine. He exemplified manly youth and beauty. Athena gave Asclepius Medusa's blood as part of the blessing. He healed the sick and raised the dead with blood that had been collected from Medusa's body. Temples to Asclepius were built and used as hospitals and sanatoriums. Snakes were kept in the temples for their ability to touch the eyes of the blind with their tongues and restore sight.

In his human form, Asclepius carried a staff entwined with a single snake. It was his emblem and symbol of healing, which was referred to as the caduceus. It became the trademark of healing. It was the precursor of the modern emblematic staff entwined with one or two serpents, used as a symbol of the medical profession.

Although the times have changed since Medusa first brought fear into the hearts of men, her image still lives on. The face of Medusa has changed over the years as well, but the meaning of her terrible gaze has not changed, and she can still strike fear into the hearts of many. Just as snakes represented wisdom and fertility, only to be followed by representatives of evil and deception, so has Medusa's image changed. The struggle between female and male dominance and submission ran the full gambit with the myths of Medusa, and the struggle will continue through eternity.

The Belled-Vipers:

One of the earliest published descriptions of a rattlesnake was in a Spanish work, which described the rattle as a *cascabel*. Bernal Diaz del Castillo's described the snake while writing about the conquest of Mexico. The zoological gardens of Montezuma contained a snake house, which held many vipers. The poisonous snakes carried on their tails, things that sounded like bells. The snake with the bells, or castanets in its tail, became notorious in Europe as a formidable viper, which would courteously warn that it would strike if annoyed, by ringing its belled-tail. It became a symbol for colonial America. Several rattlesnake flags were carried by rebel troops during the American Revolution. The two best know are the Navy jack, which shows a rattlesnake stretched out diagonally across thirteen alternating red and white stripes, and the Gadsden flag, with a coiled rattler on a yellow field. Both include the motto "Don't tread on me!"

Indians and Rattlesnakes:

Among the American Indians, from coast to coast, there was a taboo against killing rattlesnakes. They were afraid to kill rattlers incase the snakes' relatives returned to bring vengeance. The Indians considered the rattler to be the king of snakes, and if one was injured, other snakes would avenge it. The Indian attitude was probably one of reverence or respect rather than worship. They believed that all animals and natural phenomena had souls, which were independent of their physical beings. In this respect, killing a rattlesnake could cause a great battle between the snakes and Indians, for the souls of the dead rattlers would communicate with the other rattlesnakes, and vengeance would follow. It was believed that if one of their tribe were bitten, it was in revenge for his having killed a rattlesnake. The idea was to leave the rattlesnakes alone, and the snakes would leave the Indians alone. If it became necessary to kill a rattlesnake, an Indian would ask the snakes pardon for fear that another rattler would quickly come to avenge its death.

The association of rattlesnakes and rain was common across North America. The Shawnees heard thunder as the voice of a celestial rattlesnake. The Sioux saw lightening as a rattler striking its prey. The Shoshone believed the sky was a dome of ice around which a huge serpent was coiled. As the snake moved, his scales shaved the ice and it fell to earth. It fell as rain in the summer and as snow in the winter. When the snake was angry, it fell as hail. Sometimes the serpent showed itself in the sky as a rainbow.

Hopi Snake Dance:

The Hopi Snake Dance is the best known of all Indian rituals. It has survived from prehistoric times to our present day, and involves a nine-day celebration. Its purpose is to ensure fertility and produce rain. The widespread publicity it has received results from the spectacular dance that occupies only half an hour of the nine day ritual. In this fantastic episode, some priests execute a form of dance around a ring, while each one holds a live snake in his mouth, gripping the snake at the neck with his teeth and lips. Some of the snakes are rattlers. The dance is held annually, during the third or fourth week of August, at the Hopi pueblos in central Navajo County, Arizona. A pueblo is the descriptive word for the communal village built by the Indians. It consists of one or more flat-roofed structures of stone or abode (sun-dried clay bricks), arranged in terraces, which house a number of families. Most of the ceremony is not open to the public. Of the ceremonials that are seen, is the Antelope race in the morning and the Corn dance in the evening of the eighth day, followed by the Snake race early on the morning of the ninth day. The Snake dance itself occurs in the late afternoon of the ninth day.

Rattlesnakes and other snakes are gathered and placed in sacred clay jars that are stored in the *kiva*, of the Snake priests. From a quarter to half of the snakes are reported to be rattlers, the others are harmless snakes such as bull snakes *(Pituophis melanoleucus)* who are masters of the typical defense stance producing sounds of snorts and grunts. They commonly reach a length of nine feet. The kivas are underground vaults, which are entered by means of a ladder through a hatchway in the roof. The hunt continues for up to four days. During these hunts the novices, who may be only boys, are initiated in the capture and handling of snakes. While the hunters are gathering snakes, the priests are making prayer wands *(pahos)* and snake-whips or snake-wands. They consist of a wooden shaft about eight inches long, to which a pair of eagle feathers is attached. Eagle feathers are used because eagles are the masters of the snakes. During the hunts and dances, these wands are used to soothe and herd the snakes.

While the snake hunt is in progress, the Antelope clan is preparing an altar in their kiva to the rain gods. It consists of a beautiful colored-sand mosaic, symbolic of a rainstorm, with clouds and four snake-like lightning strokes. On the morning of the eighth, day young men of the village compete in the Antelope race. On the evening of the eighth day, the Antelope or Corn dance occurs. This ceremony represents a prayer for the growth of corn and other crops upon which the Hopi rely for survival. Early on the morning of the ninth day occurs the Snake race, in which young men participate. At noon of the ninth day, the snakes are ceremoniously washed by the chief Snake priest. After the washing, the snakes are dried by allowing them to crawl on sand freely for a couple of hours. During their time of freedom, they are guarded by boy priests. The snake dance itself occurs at sundown on the ninth day. The snakes are then collected by the priests and carried in cloth sacks to a temporary shrine, the *kisi* at the dancing area. It is constructed of cottonwood branches shaped like an Indian teepee, but smaller. The entrance to the kisi is covered with a blanket. In front of the kisi a hole, or hollow is dug, over which is placed a board, the *sipapu*. This is the entrance to the underworld, which houses the rain god.

The dance begins with the entrance of the Antelope priests, dressed in symbolic costumes holding rattles made of buckskin, and carrying pouches filled with sacred corn meal. They slowly make four circuits of the dance area, scattering cornmeal on the *bahoki,* a permanent stone shrine, and on the sipapu, the board covering the entrance to the underworld. With each pass, they stamp their right foot on the board as part of the dance. After the Antelope dance, the Snake priests enter the area and make four circuits of the central area. Their dance is faster and more aggressively intensive than the Antelope dancers. As the dancing begins, one or two priests enter the kisi, the temporary shrine holding the snakes. Each time a dancer passes the kisi, he stamps violently on the board with his right foot, which creates a loud hollow sound representing thunder. This alerts the rain gods below of the impending ceremony. After a long slow weaving dance by both the Snake and Antelope priests, the Snake priests break up into trios. The trios consist of a carrier, a hugger and a gatherer. As the first carrier passes before the kisi, he stoops and is handed a snake by one of the priests within the temporary shrine. He puts the snake into his mouth, holding it with his teeth and lips from six to twelve inches behind the head. The hugger then puts his left hand on the carriers right shoulder, and together, they slowly dance around the circular area. Each pair is followed by a gatherer. After about one and a half times around the circle, the carrier puts the snake on the ground and in passing the kisi, receives another snake. Other trios have followed the first, and the circle of dancing priests becomes larger. The hugger often brushes the snakes head with the eagle feathers of the snake-wand. This engages the snakes attention, to keep it from biting the carrier. Meanwhile the gatherer picks up the discarded snake after sprinkling it with sacred corn meal. If it has coiled, he brushes it with the snake-wand until it straightens out to escape, at which time he seizes it. After gathering several snakes, some are handed to the Antelope priests who hold them until the end of the dance. The Antelope priests continue to furnish the rhythm for the Snake priests with chants and rattles. Women scatter white cornmeal on the snakes and dancers. After all the snakes have been danced with, one of the priests draws a circle on the ground with corn meal. All the snakes are piled into this circle. The women scatter the rest of their sacred meal on the snakes.

The Snake priests rush to the squirming pile of snakes and seize them by the hand-fuls until all have been picked up. They then run in the four directions, north, south, east and west, off the mesa and down the steep trails onto the plain below, where the snakes are liberated at specified shrines, as messengers to the gods.

The Hopi Snake dance is not snake worship. It is a prayer for rain and the fulfill-ment of adequate crops. The snakes are used as messengers to the underworld gods of rain. Each part of the ceremony carries with it some symbolism toward the bringing of rain. Snakes are symbolic of the rain gods, and are messengers to the rain gods to whom they are allowed to visit in their underground habitat. Rain, and lightning, which can deliver a death-dealing stroke, and the snake, which is also able to deliver a death-dealing stroke, are all entwined in the mythical beliefs.

Rattlesnake Myths:

One of the evidences of the impact made by rattlesnakes on the colonists was the frequency with which geographical and landscape features were named after them. Many rural towns have a Rattlesnake Creek, Rattlesnake Ridge, Rattlesnake Ledge, Rattlesnake Lakes, Meadows, and Mountains.

Most myths and legends that apply solely to rattlesnakes pertain to the rattle. Many of these myths are associated with the rattles used as cures or eradication of disease. Carrying a string of rattles will prevent or cure rheumatism. It will prevent smallpox, and keep a person from having fits. If worn around the neck it is a general disease preventative. One of the most widespread uses of rattles is in the prevention and cure of headaches, by wearing a rattle string in the hair or in a hatband. Rattles were used by Indians to make childbirth easier. Rattles will soothe and pacify teething children. They may be worn as a necklace, placed in a bag, which is hung around the neck, or the child may chew on them. This is an interesting analog to the modern child's affinity to rattles!

The rattles may serve as amulets or good-luck charms. If you receive rattles from someone, you will come to no harm while that person is near. If you kill a rattler, keep the rattles for good luck. If you catch a rattler and rub the rattles on you eyes, you will always see a rattler before it sees you. If you wear the rattle from a dead snake, it will keep other rattlesnakes away. It can also be worn as a charm against rattlesnake bite. Rattles are often put in fiddles to improve the tone, keep out dampness, and give the owner good luck.

There are many myths concerning the relationship of rattlesnakes to weather. If a rattler is draped on its back over a log, it will rain in three days. If rattler tracks are directed to high ground, rain will be abundant. If rattlers are unusually vicious, rain will follow. Turning a live or dead rattler on its back will bring rain.

Myth: Rattlesnakes will always rattle before striking.

Reality: Sometimes they will. Sometimes they don't. It depends upon the conditions surrounding the encounter. Rattlers usually warn before striking. If it is annoyed by an approaching enemy, it will throw itself into its menacing S-shaped coil and sound its rattle. However, if an attack on the snake comes suddenly, the rattler may retaliate with an instant strike, and there will be no interval of rattling. The rattlesnake, like the copperhead, prefers to escape detection by depending on its concealing coloration and its quiet, unmoving posture, to advertising its presence by rattling its tail.

Myth: Rattlesnakes are the pure, concentrated essence of evil. It is their continuous and sole desire to wreak vengeance on all living creatures, especially man.

Reality: Unless injured, attacked, or hunted and forced to turn and fight, rattlesnakes are relatively timid, quiet, peaceful, inoffensive animals that prefer to hide unnoticed, or to escape into some secluded refuge. Unfortunately, their food-gathering apparatus, their fangs and venom, make them dangerous creatures, but they are not naturally.vicious. They represent peaceful power, a gentle giant that seeks only to live and let live. Of all the myths, the one that has most deeply affected human impressions and attitudes toward rattlesnakes is the myth that pictures them as malignant, vindictive and crafty snakes with a special hatred of mankind. A rattlesnake is only a primitive creature with basic survival perceptions and reactions. It cannot vindictively think. Man gives it its thoughts! It seeks only to destroy harmful rodents, and to defend itself from injury by intruders of superior size, such as man. It could not have evolved a special fear of man, since the first human being any rattlesnake ever encounters is usually the last!

CHAPTER FIVE:
CLASSIFICATION OF SNAKES:

Taxonomy is the science of classifying and naming animals and plants. The history of classifying animals is as old as man himself. One of the first modern taxonomists was Aristotle (384-322 BC), who classified animals into groups according to their actions, habits, and where they lived. The real father of taxonomy is considered to be Carolus Linnaeus, a Swedish naturalist, who in the mid-1700s, consistently used a two-name system of naming plants and animals in his work. This system of scientific naming became known as binomial nomenclature. It consisted of a combination of two italicized names. The words were derived from Latin or Greek. Simply translated this means that a two-part name is given to each organism, which is unique for that organism. These assigned names are called generic and specific names, known as the traditional scientific names. Scientific names are usually descriptive, referring to the size, form, color, habits, or other characteristics of the organism. They are sometimes derived from the names of people or places. An example of this is found in the scientific name for the Northern Brown Snake found in New England. Its scientific name is *Storeria dekayi dekayi*. Both names are derived from proper names; *Storeria* comes from David Humphreys Storer, and *dekayi* comes from James Ellsworth DeKay. Since then, the science of taxonomy has changed dramatically.

Today, instead or relying only on structural (morphological) characteristics to compare species, more sophisticated tools are used. These involve biochemistry (a study of the chemistry of life processes), histology (microscopic study of tissue), cytology (structural and functional study of individual cells) and genetic DNA studies.

In general, the animal kingdom is divided into large phyla, which are divided into smaller classes, which in turn are broken down into smaller orders, then into families. The families are subdivided into increasingly precise groupings of genera, which are further defined to species, which are sometimes subdivided into subspecies.

Snakes are grouped in the phylum Chordata. Chordates are a very large grouping of animals having gill slits, tubular nerve cord along their back, and a notochord at some stage of their development. A notochord is an elongated, rod-shaped cellular structure, which forms the primitive supportive structure that later in development is surrounded and replaced by the vertebral column. This highest level of animal classification is subdivided into a subphylum called Vertebrata. These are the vertebrates, which have a backbone consisting of individual segments, or vertebrae. Together with crocodilians, turtles, lizards, and tuataras (primitive lizard-like reptiles of New Zealand with a well-developed third eye), they are included in the class Reptilia (See Fig 5.1). Snakes are then sorted with lizards in the order Squamata. They are then placed in their own suborder, Serpentes. The Serpents are divided into 15 families, whose names end in *-idae*. Two of these families occur in New England; Colubridae and Viperidae. The families are further divided into subfamilies, whose names end in *-inae*, of which 3 are represented by New England snakes; Colubrinae, Natricinae, and Crotalinae. The subfamilies are divided into genera. Twelve different genera are represented in Connecticut.

Changes in scientific names are constantly evolving. Names that applied in the 1970's may no longer be valid today in 2004. Just recently, the genus of the Eastern

57

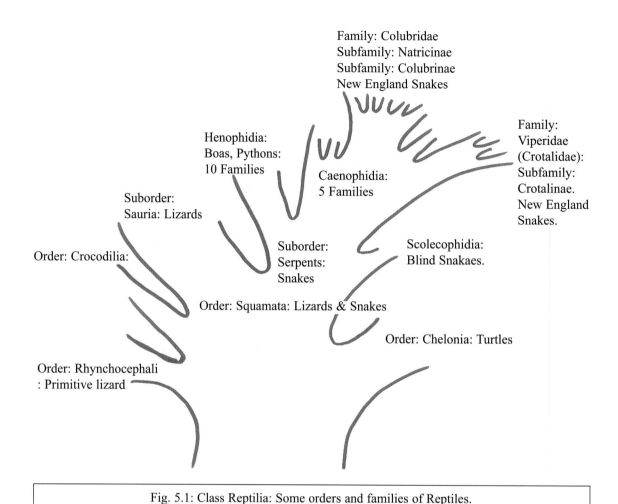

Family: Colubridae
Subfamily: Natricinae
Subfamily: Colubrinae
New England Snakes

Henophidia:
Boas, Pythons:
10 Families

Family:
Viperidae
(Crotalidae):
Subfamily:
Crotalinae.
New England
Snakes.

Caenophidia:
5 Families

Suborder:
Sauria: Lizards

Order: Crocodilia:

Suborder:
Serpents:
Snakes

Scolecophidia:
Blind Snakaes.

Order: Squamata: Lizards & Snakes

Order: Chelonia: Turtles

Order: Rhynchocephali
: Primitive lizard

Fig. 5.1: Class Reptilia: Some orders and families of Reptiles.

Smooth Green Snake of New England was changed from *Opheodrys* to *Liochlorophis*. This particular snake has undergone nine generic name changes since 1827.

One of the problems is that there is no general agreement among herpetologists on the definition of a genus. Webster defines genus as a major category in the classification system of plants and animals, which ranks above a species and below a family. It can include one species or many similar species, subdivided into subspecies. The Latinized or Greek genus name is capitalized and italicized, and precedes the species name which is italicized but not capitalized. Greene, 1997, defines genera as groups of similar, presumably related species. Ernst and Zug, 1996 define genus as originally denoting a group of organisms that looked alike; now it, in combination with higher classification categories, denotes an evolutionary relationship. Because it represents a distinct group of species, the generic name can be used without the specific name, to refer to all the species of that group. The species name is never used alone, without the generic name. A species is a naturally existing population of similar organisms that usually interbreed only among themselves. They are given a unique Latinized or Greek binomial name to distinguish them from all other creatures. Three-part names are reserved for subspecies. If there are three parts to the name (a trinomial), then there are one or more additional related subspecies. Each related subspecies bears the same first two names. For example, *Diadophis punctatus edwardsi,* the scientific name for Connecticut's Northern Ringneck Snake, *Diadophis punctatus regalis* (Mississippi Ringneck Snake), and *Diadophis punctatus punctatus* (Southern Ringneck Snake) are all subspecies of the same species. The repetition of *punctatus* in the name for the Southern Ringneck Snake shows that it was the first member of the group to receive a scientific description. These species have a wide geographic distribution, being found in many areas of the country. They are said to exhibit geographic differentiation, with strikingly different appearances. Because of this geographical difference in appearance, the snakes are represented as distinct geographical races within a species. These races are designated as subspecies. There is frequent disagreement among taxonomists about whether a particular population of snakes is represented by a subspecies or is more correctly classified as a species.

The uncertainties and complexities of snake evolution make it a fascinating area of study. Many biologists are accepting this challenging study with wonderful new tools, which can analyze protein structures and genetic DNA, to identify more closely, how snakes are related.

Common names play an important role in communication among the scientific and ordinary people, and are predominately used in this book, after the initial introduction of each snake, at which time the scientific name is used. In the main body of this book, the species and subspecies accounts are grouped by family. Each of the groups is preceded by a brief description of the family.

Checklist of New England Snakes: The snakes are listed by family, and subfamily. They are in alphabetical order according to their scientific names.

Family: Colubridae:
Subfamily: Colubrinae: (colubrine snakes)

Eastern Worm Snake
 Carphophis amoenus amoenus
Northern Black Racer
 Coluber constrictor constrictor
Northern Ringneck Snake
 Diadophis punctatus edwardsi
Black Rat Snake
 Elaphe obsoleta obsoleta
Eastern Hognose Snake
 Heterodon platirhinos
Eastern Milk Snake
 Lampropeltis triangulum triangulum
Eastern Smooth Green Snake
 Liochlorophis vernalis vernalis
Subfamily: Natricinae: (water snakes)

Northern Water Snake
 Nerodia sipedon sipedon
Northern Brown Snake
 Storeria dekayi dekayi

Northern Red-bellied Snake
        Storeria occipitomaculata occipitomaculata
Eastern Ribbon Snake
        Thamnophis sauritus sauritus
Northern Ribbon Snake
        Thamnophis sauritus septentrionalis
Eastern Garter Snake
        Thamnophis sirtalis sirtalis
Maritime Garter Snake
        Thamnophis sirtalis pallidus
Family: Viperidae
Subfamily: Crotalinae (pitvipers)
Northern Copperhead
        Agistrodon contortrix mokeson
Timber Rattlesnake
        Crotalus horrridus

Special Topic:
List of New England Snakes in 1904:
The following list represents the snakes of Connecticut and New England, as listed in *Fauna of New England,* by Samuel Henshaw, in March, 1904. It is intriguing to note how much the Common names and scientific names have changed in the past 100 years! The Keeled Green Snake, or Rough Green Snake, has not been reported in the state since 1943. The record of the Rough Green Snake *(Opheodrys aestivus)* was from Lamson (1935), who reported a specimen from Waterbury, and a specimen from West Haven (1943) from the W.F. Prince Collection, now stored at the University of Massachusetts (Degraaf, Rudis, 1983). The list is presented in alphabetical order according to the Scientific names:

Carphophiops amoenus, now *Carphophis amoenus amoenus,* changed, from species to subspecies. Past common names were Ground Snake, Little Red Snake, Worm Snake, now the Eastern Worm Snake.

Diadophis punctatus, now *Diadophis puntatus edwardsi,* changed from species to subspecies. Past common name was Ring-necked Snake, now the Northern Ringneck Snake.

Heterodon platirhinos, remains the same with subtle spelling change of species, *platyrhinos.* Past common names were Hog-nosed Snake; Flat-head; Blowing Adder, now the Eastern Hognose Snake.

Liopeltis vernalis, now *Liochlorophis vernalis vernalis,* species names is the same, but the genus name his changed. Past common names were Green Snake, Grass Snake, now called the Eastern Smooth Green Snake.

Cyclophis aestivus, now *Opheodrys aestivus,* species name is the same, but genus name has changed. Past common name was Keeled Green Snake, now the Rough Green Snake, and not considered endogenous to Connecticut.

Zamenis constrictor, now *Coluber constrictor constrictor,* changed from species to subspecies, and genus name changed. Past common names were Black Snake, Black Chaser, now called Northern Black Racer.

Coluber obsoletus, now *Elaphe obsoleta obsoleta,* changed from species to subspecies and genus name has changed. Past common name was Pilot Black Snake, now called Black Rat Snake.

Osceola doliata triangula, now *Lampropeltis triangulum triangulum,* subspecies name is similar, but species and genus name both changed. Common names were Milk Snake, House Snake, Chicken Snake, Chequered Adder, now called the Eastern Milk Snake.

Ophibolus getulus getulus, now *Lampropeltis getula getula,* which is the Eastern Kingsnake, possibly mistaken for the immature Black Rat Snake. The Eastern Kingsnakes closest range is Southern New Jersey. Past common name was Chain Snake, which suggests the pattern of the immature Black Rat Snake.

Natrix fasciata sipedon, now *Nerodia sipedon sipedon,* subspecies is the same, species and genus has changed. Past common names were Water Adder, and Water Snake, now called the Northern Water Snake.

Natrix leberis, suggests a yellow-bellied water snake. The Yellowbelly Water Snakes range in North central Georgia, not found in Connecticut. Possible confusion with dark phase of the Northern Water Snake, but bellies, though sometimes yellowish, usually is boldly patterned. Past common name was Yellow-bellied Snake.

Storeria dekayi, now *Storeria dekayi dekayi,* changed from species to subspecies. Past common name was Dekay's Snake, now the Northern Brown Snake.

Storeria occipitomaculata, now *Storeria occipitomaculata occipitomaculata,* changed from species to supspecies. Past common name was Spotted-necked Snake, now the Northern Red-Bellied Snake.

Eutaenia saurita, now *Thamnophis sauritus sauritus,* changed from species to subspecies, and genus name has changed. Past common name was Swift Garter Snake, Ribbon Snake, now the Eastern Ribbon Snake.

Eutaenia sirtalis sirtalis, now *Thamnophis sirtalis sirtalis,* subspecies has remained the same, genus has changed. Past common name was Striped Snake, Garter Snake, and now called Eastern Garter Snake.

Ancistrodon contortrix, now *Agkistrodon contortrix mokeson,* species has changed to subspecies, genus is the same with subtle spelling change. Past common names were Copperhead, Viper, Deaf Adder, now called the Northern Copperhead.

Crotalus horridus, has remained the same. Past common name was Banded Rattlesnake, now called Timber Rattlesnake.

CHAPTER SIX
KEY TO SPECIES OF New England SNAKES
      The quickest, most efficient way to use this book is to look at the following color photographs. The photos show the most common color phase of each adult and young New England snake.   Once the snake has been tentatively identified from the introductory photo, go to the Table of Contents and look up the chapter for that snake. The keys following the photos can help reach a final determination.

Adult Timber Rattlesnake

Young Timber Rattlesnake

Adult Northern Copperhead

Young Northern Copperhead

Adult Eastern Hognose Snake

Young Eastern Hognose Snake

Adult New England Species

Adult Northern Water Snake

Young New England Species

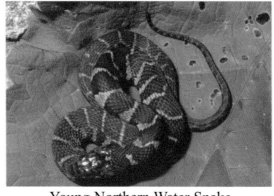

Young Northern Water Snake

Adult Eastern Milk Snake

Young Eastern Milk Snake

Adult Black Rat Snake

Young Black Rat Snake

Adult Northern Black Racer

Young Northern Black Racer

63

Adult New England Species   Young New England Species

Adult Eastern Ribbon Snake

Young Eastern Ribbon Snake

Adult Eastern Garter Snake

Young Eastern Garter Snake

Adult Northern Brown Snake

Young Northern Brown Snake

Adult Northern Red-Bellied Snake

Young Northern Red-Bellied Snake

Adult New England Species

Young New England Species

Adult Northern Ringneck Snake

Young Northern Ringneck Snake

Adult Eastern Worm Snake

Young Eastern Worm Snake

Adult Eastern Smooth Green Snake

Young Eastern Smooth Green Snake

The key that follows is a numbered list of opposite pairs of comparison characteristics. The characteristics appear as a series of couplets, allowing for a choice of descriptions for the snake that needs to be identified. An example of how to choose between the couplets is as follows. Read (1a),"a facial pit between eye and nostril," and (1b) "no facial pit between eye and nostril." Make a choice of which characteristic the snake in question possesses. If the snake in question has a facial pit, refer to (2a) "scaly rattle at tip of tail, top of head covered with small scales, dorsal pattern of body a series of dark chevron-shaped blotches, venomous."

The name of the snake in question is listed as the Timber Rattlesnake. All the names for the various scales and other characteristics are depicted by line drawings in Figs. 6-1, 6-2 and Appendix I. All technical terms are defined in a glossary at the end of the book.

KEY TO CONNECTICUT SNAKES

1a A facial pit between eye and nostril (Fig.6.2d) on each side of head; most subcaudal scales not divided (Fig. 6.1c); pupil vertical (Fig. 6.2d).............................**2**

    1b No facial pit between eye and nostril (Fig 6.2g)...................................**3**

    2a Scaly rattle at tip of tail; top of head covered with small scales (Fig. 6.2c); dorsal pattern of body a series of dark chevron-shaped blotches; venomous; *young,* gray ground color; dark gray to black blotches; prebutton to button on tail ....**Timber Rattlesnake (Crotalus horridus)**

    2b No scaly rattle at tip of tail; top of head covered with 9 enlarged plates (Fig.6.2b); head copper to reddish brown; body pattern of chestnut-brown hour-glass-shaped blotches on beige to pinkish-gray ground color; loreal scale present; venomous; *young,* gray changing to beige; pattern dark gray-brown changing to brown with age; tip of tail <u>yellow</u>...................**Northern Copperhead (Agkistrodon contortrix mokeson)**

    3a Some or all dorsal scales keeled (Fig. 6.1a)...**4**

    3b All scales smooth (Fig. 6.1b)...**12**

    4a Anal plate divided (Fig. 6.1e)..**5**

    4b Anal plate entire (Fig 6.1d)...**11**

    5a Rostral scale not upturned or keeled...**6**

    5b Rostral scale upturned and keeled (Fig. 6.2e); general coloration extremely variable; yellow, brown, gray, olive, orange may predominate; usually spotted, but plain black and olive green are found; belly mottled, gray or greenish on yellowish, white or light gray; *young* have gray ground color with distinct black spots ....**Eastern Hognose Snake (Heterodon platyrhinos)**

    6a Loreal scale present (Fig. 6.2f)...**7**

    6b Loreal scale absent (Fig 6.2g)..**10**

    7a Lateral scales smooth; central scales weakly keeled; 2 postocular scales(Fig. 6.2a); 25-30 scale rows (Fig. 6.1b)..**8**

    7b All scales heavily keeled (Fig 6.1a); 2-3 postoculars (Fig. 6.2a); fewer than 25 scale rows (Fig. 6.1b)..**9**

    8 Head and dorsal color shiny black, often with traces of spotted pattern when distended; belly whitish, clouded with gray with checkerboarding toward neck; *young,* strongly patterned dorsally on body and tail; pale gray ground color with dark brown to black blotches; by 36" most of pattern has disappeared; belly checkerboarded fading to uniform clouded gray, except toward head as snake grows ....**Black Rat Snake (Elaphe obsoleta obsoleta)**

    9 Scale rows 21-25 (Fig. 6.1b); about 30 red, dark brown, or black dorsal bands or blotches; light markings between dark lateral blotches; ground color varies from pale gray to dark brown; some adults plain dark brown or black; belly with red or brownish centered half-moon markings; *young,* strongly patterned; black on a ground color of pale gray or light brown......**Northern Water Snake (Nerodia sipedon sipedon)**

10a Scale rows 15 (Fig. 6.1b); usually 6 supralabials (Fig. 6,2a); dorsum brown to reddish chestnut brown; 4 narrow vaguely defined dark dorsal lines and/or light middorsal stripe; some specimens gray to blue-black; 3 light nape spots at neck; black pigment on head; light spot on 5th upper labial bordered below by black; belly bright red; **young,** dark gray-brown; belly pink; 3 pale spots fuse to form incomplete collar ....**Northern Red-bellied Snake (Storeria occipitomaculata occipitomaculata)**

10b. Scale rows 17 (Fig. 6.1b); usually 7 supralabials (Fig. 6.2a); ground color varies from light brown, beige to reddish brown; 2 parallel rows of blackish spots border light middorsal stripe about 4 scales wide; belly white, yellowish or pinkish; belly scales marked with small black dots at end of each ventral scale: **young,** dark gray-brown to dark gray; yellowish collar..............**Northern Brown Snake (Storeria dekayi dekayi)**

11a Normally 3 yellowish stripes; lateral stripes on rows 2 and 3 only (Fig. 6.2I); scale rows less than 27 (Fig. 6.1b); 2 prefrontals (Fig. 6.2a); ground color black, dark brown, greenish or olive; usually double row of alternating black spots between stripes; belly greenish or yellowish with 2 rows of indistinct black spots hidden by overlapping ventral scales.......................**Eastern Garter Snake (Thamnophis sirtalis sirtalis)**

11b 3 bright yellow stripes set off against dark brown to velvety black body; lateral stripes on rows 3 and 4 (Fig 6.2h); 7 white unmarked supralabials (Fig. 6.2a); pre-orbital scale white; tail length about 1/3 total length of snake; medium to light brown stripe along 2 lower-most lateral scale rows and outer edge of belly; belly plain yellowish to greenish......................…..**Eastern Ribbon Snake (Thamnophis sauritus sauritus)**

12a Anal plate divided (Fig. 6.1e)..**13**

12b Anal plate entire; usually 3 rows brown or reddish brown blotches, bordered in black alternating along body; middorsal blotches large, sometimes resemble bands; ground color gray to tan; belly checkerboarded with black on white; small head; no visible neck; *young,* blotches are red, leading to name "red adder" ....**Eastern Milk Snake (Lampropeltis triangulum triangulum)**

13a Orange or golden yellow ring just behind head; body black, slate gray or bluish gray; belly orange or yellow with few black spots in center; small head; no visible neck.......................**Northern Ringneck Snake (Diadophis punctatus edwardsi)**

13b No neck ring.. **14**

14a Uniform dorsal coloration; no spots, blotches or stripes; preocular scale present...**15**

14b Uniform dordal coloration; scales opalescent; preocular scale absent; dorsal color brown to reddish brown; 2 prefrontal and 2 internasal scales; belly and adjacent 1-2 rows of dorsal scales pink; pointed scale on tip of tail; *young,* light pinkish gray; belly pink..................................**Eastern Worm Snake (Carphophis amoenus amoenus)**

15a Dorsal color satiny plain black; belly dark gray to black; some white on chin and throat; *young,* strongly patterned with middorsal row of dark brown, or reddish brown blotches on gray or bluish gray ground color; tail unmarked; by 30" pattern usually disappeared...............**Northern Black Racer (Coluber constrictor constrictor)**

15b Dorsal color bright green; belly white or pale yellow; young, olive to bluish green.....................**Eastern Smooth Green Snake (Liochlorophis vernalis vernalis)**

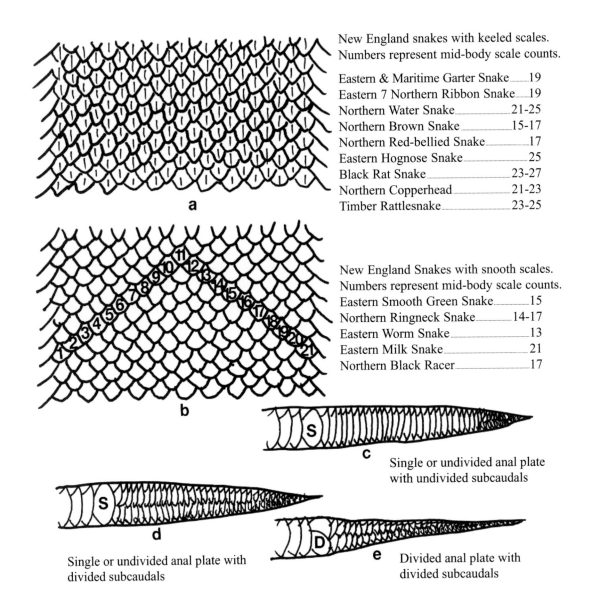

New England snakes with keeled scales. Numbers represent mid-body scale counts.

Eastern & Maritime Garter Snake	19
Eastern 7 Northern Ribbon Snake	19
Northern Water Snake	21-25
Northern Brown Snake	15-17
Northern Red-bellied Snake	17
Eastern Hognose Snake	25
Black Rat Snake	23-27
Northern Copperhead	21-23
Timber Rattlesnake	23-25

New England Snakes with snooth scales. Numbers represent mid-body scale counts.

Eastern Smooth Green Snake	15
Northern Ringneck Snake	14-17
Eastern Worm Snake	13
Eastern Milk Snake	21
Northern Black Racer	17

Single or undivided anal plate with undivided subcaudals

Single or undivided anal plate with divided subcaudals

Divided anal plate with divided subcaudals

Fig. 6.1: Keeled and smooth scale illustrations with mid-body scale counts for 14 species of New England Snakes. (c) New England snakes with a single or undivided anal plate and undivided subcaudals scales are the 2 venomous species, the Timber Rattlesnake and the Northern Copperhead. (d) New England snakes with a single or undivided anal plate and divided subcaudals scales are the Eastern and Maritime Garter Snake, Eastern and Northern Ribbon Snake, and the Eastern Mike. (e) New England snakes with a divided anal plate and divided subcaudal scales are the Northern Water Snake, Northern Brown Snake, Northern RedBellied Snake, Northern Ringneck Snake, Eastern Worm Snake, Eastern Hognose Snake, Black Rat Snake, Eastern Smooth Green Snake and the Northern Black Racer.

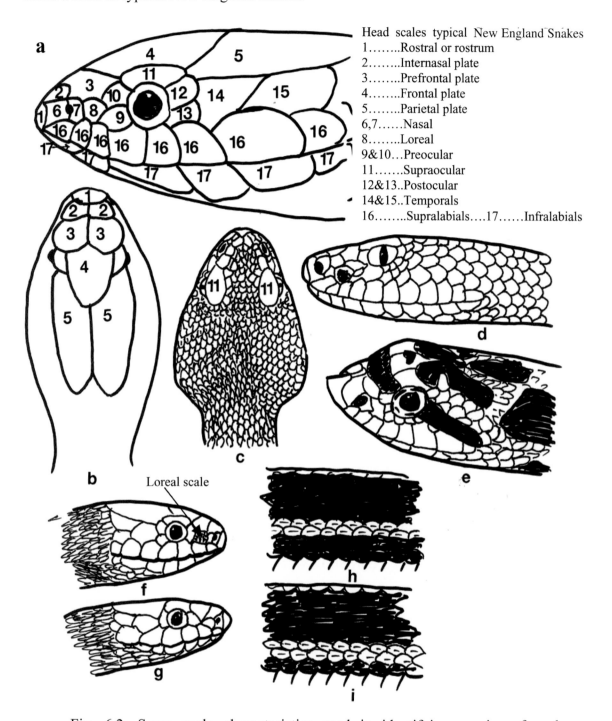

Head scales typical New England Snakes
1........Rostral or rostrum
2........Internasal plate
3........Prefrontal plate
4........Frontal plate
5........Parietal plate
6,7......Nasal
8........Loreal
9&10...Preocular
11.......Supraocular
12&13..Postocular
14&15..Temporals
16........Supralabials....17......Infralabials

Loreal scale

Fig. 6.2: Some scale characteristics used in identifying species of snakes. (a) Represents head scales, side or lateral view, of typical snake. (b) Illustrates top view of enlarged head plates. (c) Illustrates top view of Timber Rattlesnake head with small scales as opposed to the enlarged head plates of all other New England snakes. (d) Illustrates hear-sensing pit of Northern Copperhead and Timber Rattlesnake. (e) Illustrates upturned enlarged rostrum of Eastern Hognose Snake. (f) Loreal scale present. (g) Loreal scale absent. (h) Illustrates position of stripe on rows 3&4 of the Eastern and Northern Ribbon Snake. (i) Illustrates position of stripe on rows 2&3 of the Eastern and Maritime Garter Snake.

CHAPTER SEVEN
COLUBRIDS: The Typical Snakes (Colubridae)

Of all snake families, this is the largest and most varied. To this enormous family belong approximately 75% of all genera and 78% of the species of snakes of the entire world. It contains more than 280 genera and about 1,600 species. Its members dominate on all the continents except Australia, where relatives of the cobras and coral snakes (Elapidae family) are most numerous. In eastern and central North America, Colubrids make up about 85% of the genera and 84% of the species. It is also the most difficult to understand. It includes snakes that do not seem to fit into this family, but are included in it as a matter of convenience. The Colubridae is sometimes called a "trash-can group," because it contains many unrelated subgroups that are thrown together because biologists cannot decide where else to classify them. Colubrids represent the most structurally diverse group of snakes. They have only a left carotid artery. There are no teeth (edentulous) on the premaxilaries (two dermal bones on the roof of the mouth, joining on the midline, forming the border of the nostrils). Few internal or external characteristics can be used consistently to define all members of the family, or those of its subfamilies. Certain species from different groups look very similar but are only distantly related. As time progresses, and more rigorous analytical methods are employed, a highly modified classification of groups of snakes into lineage will undoubtedly occur.

Colubrids have adapted to virtually all-imaginable habitats. They occur in temperate forests and tropical jungles. The may be arboreal (tree dwellers), terrestrial (land dwellers), or aquatic (water dwellers). Colubrids are considered to be highly evolved, or advanced snakes, as evidenced by the total absence of any vestigial hind limb anatomy. Only one lung, the right lung, is functional, and usually elongated. The left lung is either vestigial (remnant organ that had been more fully developed in an earlier stage of development), or absent completely. A tracheal lung can be present or absent. A tracheal lung is a respiratory surface that arises from the trachea (windpipe), between the pharynx (throat area) and the true right lung. In some, it consists of only a highly vascularized surface on the back part of the windpipe, but in others, it is expanded into a baglike, elastic structure.

The feeding habits of Colubrids are equally diversified. Depending on the species involved, they feed on mammals, birds, and reptiles, including other snakes, amphibians, fish and insects. Some are highly specialized such as snail eaters, egg eaters, and frog eaters. Prey may be killed by constriction or swallowed alive.

Some Colubrids are unique by possessing enlarged, rear maxillary teeth, often but not always grooved. A venom-producing, modified salivary gland, the Duvernoy's glands is present. The venom injected by this inefficient apparatus is normally lethal only to the prey that these rear-fanged (opisthoglyphous) snakes feed upon. However, some of the larger species such as the African Boomslang *(Dispholidus)* have caused human fatalities.

In this large, diverse family, species range from small fragile snakes less than 12 inches (30.5 cm) long to some that are greater than 11 feet (3.35 m) in length. All colubrids have large ventral scales. Some have smooth dorsal scales. Others are covered with strongly keeled dorsal scales. Most have a rounded snout. A small number have an unusual modified rostral scale, such as the Eastern Hognose Snake of New England. All of the New England Colubrids have round eye pupils.

The names and divisions of the subfamilies of the family Colubridae are still in dispute among herpetologists. The number of recognized subfamilies ranges from 4 to 7. Of the Colubrids in North America, three subfamilies are recognized in Connecticut. The subfamily Colubrinae contains the Northern Black Racer *(Coluber constrictor constrictor)*, the Black Rat Snake *(Elaphe obsoleta obsoleta)*, the Eastern Milk Snake *(Lampropeltis triangulum triangulum)* and the Eastern Smooth Green Snake *(Liochlorophis vernalis vernalis)*.

The subfamily Natricinae contains the Northern Water Snake *(Nerodia sipedon sipedon)*, the Northern Brown snake *(Storeria dekayi dekayi)*, the Northern Red-Bellied Snake *(Storeria occipitomaculata occipitomaculata)*, the Eastern Ribbon Snake *(Thamnophis sauritus sauritus)* and the Eastern Garter Snake *(Thamnophis sirtalis sirtalis)*, the Northern Ribbon Snake *(Thamnophis sauritus septentrionalis)* the Eastern Garter Snake *(Thamnophis sirtalis sirtalis)* and the Maritime Garter Snake *(Thamnophis sirtalis pallidus)*.

The subfamily Xenodontinae includes the Eastern Worm Snake *(Carphophis amoenus amoenus)*, the Northern Ringneck Snake *(Diadophis punctatus edwardsi)* and the Eastern Hognose Snake *(Heterodon platirhinos)*.

In general, members of the subfamily Colubrinae of Connecticut, or Colubrines, vary greatly in body form, ecology (the study of how living organisms relate to their environment), and behavior. They range from the small green snake to the large black rat snake. Body forms may be slender as in the green snake and racer or muscular as the black rat snake. They occur in mountains and fields. They can be terrestrial or semiarboreal. Different species may be generalists, eating a variety of prey, or specialists, eating mostly one type of food, such as the green snake and its preference for spiders. Colubrines are mostly egg-layers (oviparous), and may lay from 3-40 eggs depending upon the species.

The members of the subfamily Natricinae of New England, or Natricines, can vary in size from the small red-bellied snake to the large water snake. Most of the Natricines are considered water snakes, although they may feed and hide in the water, they regularly exit the water for basking and reproduction. Some are terrestrial, living in moist habitats from swamp to forest. The aquatic species prey on fish and amphibians. Others prefer earthworms, slugs, snails and insects. The New England Natricines, and other American Natricines are live -bearers of young (viviparous).

The American Xenodontinae, or Xenodontines, are also highly diverse groups of snakes. Most are small to moderate-sized snakes. In Connecticut, they range from the small shiny worm snake to the stout rugged hognose snake. They occur in all habitats. Some species burrow, while others are terrestrial. The majority of the species are generalists, eating a variety of preys. The hognose is a specialist, preferring toads to all other forms of prey. Xenodontines are predominantly egg-layers. Clutch size is directly related to body size, the larger the snake, the larger number of eggs in a clutch.

CHAPTER EIGHT

EASTERN GARTER SNAKE *Thamnophis sirtalis sirtalis*

*This chapter is dedicated to **Wyatt Lee Frantz** who went through transition from his physical life to his pure spiritual life on May 30, 2003, he was seven years old and left us doing what he loved, motorbiking. Wyatt was born to be a man before most, and touched thousands of hearts and lives, young and old, with his zest for adventure, excitement and kindness. He will continue to bless us with his spirit and charitable contributions for eternity. This cover photo is Wyatt's pet snake.*

Fig. 8.1: Typical Eastern Garter Snake with prominent dorsal stripe, fading from yellow, to white to tan, against dark gunmetal blue black ground color. Photographed in 1983.

Description: The Eastern Garter Snake, *Thamnophis sirtalis sirtalis,* is a medium sized, moderately stout snake. Adults average between 18 and 26 inches, with a record of 48 **3/4** inches. The background, or ground coloration and striping are extremely variable in this species. Three stripes, a medial or dorsal stripe and 2 lateral stripes are the distinguishing characteristic of this snake. The color of the stripes may vary from cream-colored, to yellow, to a soft golden beige, or pale greenish yellow. The dorsal stripes may be white, bone, buff colored, or absent completely. When the dorsal stripe is present, it starts at the seam between the parietal head shields (Fig.6.2-b) at the top of the head, and goes to the tip of the tail. It is usually a brighter yellow at the head. The yellow fades to pale yellow to white, to a tawny brown color towards the tail. This stripe usually appears, more strongly defined than the lateral stripes, because it is bordered on each side of the body with the dark ground color (Fig. 8.1). The lateral stripes in this snake are bright yellow, creating a dramatic tailored look against the dark ground color. The lateral

Fig. 8.2: Lateral line on scale row 2 and 3, and ventral scale spots.

stripes are always present, and are confined to the 2nd and 3rd scale rows (Figs. 6.2-i, and

Fig. 8.3: Eastern Garter Snake from Old Lyme CT, captured in 2001, by 10-year old field associate Evan Kirk, displaying prominent spotted pattern, and ventral scale spots. Two small yellow parietal spots common in most garter snakes appear on the top of the head.

8.2). There may be a double diagonal row of black spots between the lateral and dorsal stripes. In many Connecticut garter snakes, the dark spots between the stripes dominate the pattern (Fig. 8.3). Most individuals have 2 small yellow or white spots on top of their heads. These two parietal spots on the parietal shields of the head are not present on all individuals, but are prominent on the dark head of the animal in this photo. The aura radiating from this beautiful animal suggests a golden autumn sunset. The stunning snake in the photo was captured by a young, 10-year old field assistant Evan Kirk, in June 2001. Evan lives in Old Lyme Connecticut, and with his friend Chris, spend most of their waking hours after school, and during summer break, hunting and studying snakes. They are conscientious science students and budding herpetologists. Evan has contributed three species of snakes featured in this book. His enthusiasm spreads to his peers and a respect and knowledge of snakes continues to grow because of his involvement.

The ground color on the Eastern Garter Snake ranges from black, bluish-black, dark walnut, chocolate-brown, greenish brown, to olive green. The belly is usually a luminescent pale bluish-green. Some variation in ventral coloration to a cream or yellowish hue is also common. There are black spots on each side of the individual belly scutes. The spots meet at the margin formed with the first row of body scales, as seen in Fig. 8.2 and 8.3. This first row of lateral body scales vary from tan to chestnut brown. The yellow stripes of the sides fuse into this tan band, giving the snake the appearance of having another lateral stripe continuing to the belly. This brown border covers the first

74

Fig. 8.4: Eastern Garter Snake from Southington, CT., displaying brown color on tips of ventral scales and first scale row. Also shows the lateral line well outlined on scale rows 2 and 3. Notice also th e dull appearance created by the keeled scales. The dorsal stripe is faded.

row of scales and the edges of the abdominal plates as seen in Fig. 8.4. The snake in this photo also displays a faded to near-absent dorsal stripe. The body scales are keeled (Fig. 8.6), and usually occur in 19 rows in the neck area and at mid-body, and 17 near the vent (Fig. 6.1-a). The keeled scales create a rough textured feel when handled, and gives the snakes a dull, lack-luster appearance. The anal plate is single, or undivided. The ventral scales average 158, and show no variation between the male and the female. A few Eastern Garter Snakes are found with no stripes and a black over-all coloration (melanistic). An example of this phase is represented in Fig. 8.5. Notice the prominent black spots and white lips. There appears to be a complete absence of yellow pigment.

Fig. 8.5: Melanistic Eastern Garter Snake, 1983.

Sexual Dimorphism: The existence of marked morphological differences (sexual dimorphism) between males and females is noticeable in garter snakes. The females are longer and heavier than the males. The females snout to vent length is about 17 % longer than the males. The average male weighs only about 55% as much as the female. The

Fig. 8.6: Close up photo of dorsal head plates and lateral head scales of Eastern Garter Snake. The keeled scales show very distinctly in this photo. This sunflower beauty was found by Ernie Krulikowski in 1983.

male tail is about 25% as long as his total length, averaging 76 divided subcaudals. The female has a shorter tail than the male, only about 19% as long as her total length, and averages only 67 divided subcaudals. The males noticeably longer rapidly tapering tail has an obvious bulge (Fig. 6.1,e) at the base where the simple himipenis is stored. It is unbranched, has 5 large spines at the base and numerous very small recurved spines in slanting rows on the shaft. Males longer than 19 inches usually have swollen keels on the scales near the vent, which are called knobs. These knobs appear to serve some hedonic, or sexual stimulation function. Shorter males usually have only weakly developed, or completely absent knobs. The females have a shorter more stout tail (Fig. 6.1-d), and lack knobs.

Head Scales: The head of the garter snake is olive-brown, dark brown or black. To help identify the scales discussed in this section, refer to Fig. 6.2(a-b). Fig. 8.6 shows a close-up photo of the head scales of the Eastern Garter Snake. There is a single elongate scale (preocular) in front of the large walnut-brown eye. The preocular scale is in contact below with the 3rd upper lip (supralabial) scale, in front with the loreal scale, and above with the supraocular scale, and prefrontal plate. Notice the golden halo surrounding the round pupil. The eye is in contact with the 3rd and 4th supralabial scales. The loreal scale is in front of the preocular scale, and is in contact below with the 2nd supralabial, above, with the prefrontal plate. The nostril is between the 2 nasal scales. The nasal scales are in contact below, with the 1st supralabial scale, and above with the internasal plate. There are 3 small postocular scales behind the eye. The large temporal

76

scale is in contact below, with the 5th and 6th supralabials, with the 2 lower postocular scales and above with the parietal plate. Above the eye is the supraocular scale, resembling an eyebrow, which is in contact with the frontal and parietal plates on top of the head. There are 7 supralabials, and 10 lower lip scales (infralabials). Most Eastern Garter Snakes have dark lip bars (sutures) on the supralabials. This is an important distinguishing feature when making comparison identifications with the Eastern Ribbon Snake, which has no dark sutures on the upper lip. The lower lip has no dark sutures.

Range: The Eastern Garter Snake ranges from the southern tip of Hudson Bay southeast through western Quebec, New Hampshire, and Massachusetts to Rhode Island. The range extends south to Florida, and southwest to eastern Texas. From eastern Texas, its range extends north through Arkansas, central Missouri, eastern Iowa, central Minnesota, to western Ontario. The Eastern Garter Snake is New England's most widespread and ubiquitous (appears everywhere), serpent. It is found from sea level to the highest elevation of the state, and from urban areas to wilderness. This species is presently secure within Connecticut.

Habitat: The home ranges include forest edges, especially along stone walls, which separate the forested areas from the open fields. The moist habitat areas visited by garter snakes include swamps, along riverbanks, streams, drainage ditches, ponds, quarries, lakes and bogs. They like grassy and shrubby fields, and abandoned farmlands. Trash dumps, decaying old barns and outbuildings are favorite sites. Old poultry farms with discarded sheet-metal incubation trays provide warm, moist hiding places. Garter snakes will be found in city parks, cemeteries and suburban yards and gardens. The snakes will take refuge beneath logs, boards, pieces of old linoleum, flat stones, and any debris that catches the warmth of the sun and keeps them safe from predators.

Behavior: The Eastern Garter Snake is more cold tolerant than many other species of snakes. It's annual cycle of activity ranges from as early as mid March into November. Individuals are often active on warm days between February and March, during the spring thaw (Fig. 8.7). They retreat into their hibernaculum when the temperature drops. Winter, fall, and spring activity is mostly during the day (diurnal). In the spring, some twilight (crepuscular) and nighttime (nocturnal) activity does occur at the time of frog and toad breeding. In the summer, most activity is either during the morning, early evening, or at night. The home range for garter snakes can be as large as 2 acres. However, if abundant food and a suitable hibernaculum are present, a large home range is not necessary, for most of the long-range activity periods involve moving from feeding grounds to the hibernaculum.

Hibernation sites include rock crevices, gravel banks, dams, stone causeways, and old wells. Almost any site will do, as long as it allows the snakes body temperature to remain slightly above freezing, and is moist enough to prevent dehydration. Holes in decaying tree stumps, and old foundations are favorite sites. Woodchuck burrows, mole and vole burrows, muskrat and crayfish burrows are also excellent hibernacula. The hibernation site is largely determined by the maintenance diet of the snake. If the main prey is fish, frogs and other amphibians, the hibernaculum will be near a water site. If the main diet encompasses insects, worms, baby rodents and nestling ground birds, the sites will be near the shared habitats of this prey. Garter snakes over-winter together. They may share their hibernaculum with other species. Pope, 1937, recorded 76 Northern

Fig. 8.7: Garter Snakes found under an old sheet-metal incubation pan, next to their hibernaculum in an old decaying concrete foundation, on a warm March day in 1984.

Brown Snakes, with 10 Eastern Garter Snakes in old rat burrows on Long Island. Among other snakes that share hibernacula with the garter snake, are the Northern Red-Bellied Snake, Northern Ringneck Snake and the Eastern Smooth Green Snake. These snakes are often found sharing anthills as hibernation sites. The hibernating snakes survival is aided by the breakdown (catabolism) of glycogen, which is stored in their liver. The high level of glucose derived from the stored glycogen, acts as antifreeze as well as supplying winter energy.

Studies have shown that the garter snake will voluntarily find temperatures between a low of 48 F, and a maximum of 95 F. The preferred selected temperatures are between 68 and 95 F. After feeding, a warmer minimum temperature of 75 F. is chosen. While undergoing the shed cycle (ecdysis), temperatures of between 61 and 79 F are preferred.

Reproduction: Female Eastern Garter Snakes become sexually mature during their second year, at a total length of about 21 inches. Males mature during their second year at shorter lengths than the female, of about 19 inches. Mating usually occurs after emergence from hibernation. After a mild winter, this can occur as early as mid March, Some researchers have documented fall mating also, but it is not as common as spring courtship. There is evidence dating back to 1882, when Smith recorded garter snakes mating in September and October. The sperm from the fall mating remain viable over the winter, with fertilization of the ovum, taking place in the spring. A period of cold exposure followed by a rapid rise in body temperature is important for the activation of spring mating behavior in male garter snakes. During the mating period, the females

Fig. 8.8: Partial view of Eastern Garter Snakes in a "mating ball." It is not uncommon to find several males pursuing a single female (1983).

release pheromones (sexually stimulating chemicals), from their skin, which help the males find and identify them. These pheromones are specific for each species. Some male garter snakes also release a pheromone that attracts other males. This is apparently a mating strategy of the male snake to try to confuse rival males by mimicking a female. While rival males are attending to the mock male, he is able to spend his time courting and mating with the real female. In mating trial-research by mason and Crews (1985), the "she-males" mated with females more often than the normal males did. This demonstrated a reproductive ability, but also a possible selective advantage to males with this female-like pheromone.

There is a definite courtship ritual between the male and female garter snakes. The general pattern is similar for most snakes. The courtship beginning phase is called *tactile-chase* by Gillingham, 2001, or touch and chase. It is one of the simpler methods of courtship among snakes. After locating a receptive female, the male slides forward, rubbing his chin against her back. He continually rubs his chin on her head, back and sides. There is a lot of tongue-flicking behavior in the male, as he repeatedly attempts to align his body next to the female's. Tongue flicking is necessary for recognizing the correct species of snake. Sometimes the female will flee from the male, and he will have to chase after her, and try again. Often many males will pursue the same female. All this courtship and mating activity can be an amazing site to behold. It is often referred to as a *mating ball,* where many males vie for the attention of one female. Some of this communal activity is demonstrated in Fig. 8.8. The second phase *(tactile-alignment)* of courtship involves a lot of tail quivering, and searching for the proper positioning of the

79

Fig. 8.9: Gravid (pregnant) female Eastern Garter Snake found in 2001 in Old Lyme, CT by field associate John Stearns, a young student of herpetology.

male and female vents. The female must open, or gape her vent to receive the male sexual organ (hemipenis). This is called cloacal gaping. The final phase *(intromission and coitus)* involves the actual mating (copulation) as seen in Fig. 1.8. Although the photo shows another species mating, the procedure is the same. At the end of this phase, the male forms a plug (copulatory plug), which blocks the oviduct opening in the female for a few days. It prevents the rival males from immediately mating with that female. Females may store sperm during winter hibernation. The sperm remain alive for about a year. Research has shown that the stored sperm are discharged from the females storage site in the oviduct within six hours after spring mating. New sperm takes about 24 hours after mating to reach the same place in the oviduct.

The Eastern garter snake is viviparous. The embryos develop fully functional placentas with the mother. There is nutritional, respiratory, and excretory exchange with the mothers circulatory system. The gestation period between mating and birth is about 4 months. Birth occurs in late July to early August. The female has spent the summer basking in the sun, to provide a warm incubation temperature for the developing babies. There is a great advantage to giving live birth, especially in colder climates. The gravid (pregnant), female is able to move to warm areas, bringing her developing young to ideal incubation temperatures. This allows for less stressful embryonic development, and a greater number of viable young. The litter will vary from 2 to 31 neonates, or newborns. The average litter is 23 offspring. Breckenridge (1944) recorded as many as 85 neonates. Notice the beautifully marked female in Fig. 8.9. She appeared to be a well-developed gravid female, robust, swollen with new life. She had a favorite sunning rock, and was

Fig. 8.10: Juvenile Eastern Garter Snake, photo taken in 1983. Markings are vivid agter its recent shed.

located by a young field assistant, John Stearns. John is an excellent young student of natural history, who is totally captivated by snakes and their incredible mysteries of survival. He can always be found around the lakes' shoreline, streams and bogs of Old Lyme Connecticut, alone, or with a couple friends, searching for slithering serpents. It has been wonderful helping him learn about the creatures that he loves so much.

The newborns are 5-9 inches at birth. They are patterned like the adults as seen in Fig 8.11. They must immediately fend for themselves, feeding largely upon earthworms, insects, slugs tadpoles, small frogs, and minnows. Young garter snakes grow rapidly after birth and during the following spring (Fig. 8.10). If prey is abundant, the juvenile can grow as much as 1.5 inches a month during its first year. Growth rate decreases as the snake gets older.

Fig. 8.11: Newborn (neonate) Eastern Garter Snake, one of a litter of 15, August 1984.

Feeding: Adult garter snakes prey upon wood frogs, green frogs, tree frogs, spring peepers, salamanders, small fish, earthworms, soft bodied insects and night crawlers. The prey is seized in the mouth and swallowed alive. There is some evidence that the saliva of the garter snake has mildly venomous qualities. The rear teeth are slightly enlarged. Garter snakes have Duvernoy's glands, which are advanced salivary

Fig. 8.12: Some garter snakes forage around and in lakes, ponds, bogs and streams. Often when fishing or chasing tadpoles and frogs, they become food for aquatic predators.

glands that produce proteins, which are considered to be mildly venomous. The secretions from the glands surround the larger rear teeth, and enter the prey when the teeth are embedded into the flesh of its prey. There have been a few reactions to garter snake bites that have resulted in some bleeding, swelling and bruising. However, no systemic symptoms developed. Some people get a burning rash at the bite site. The enzymes might help to immobilize active prey such as frogs, toads fish and small mice. These prey are usually chewed upon before the swallowing is begun. The secretions also serve to begin digestion of the prey.

Predators and Defense: Eastern Garter Snakes are preyed upon by red-tailed hawks, owls, great blue herons, American bitterns, turkeys, crows, robins, blue jays, free-roaming chickens, pheasants, and some fish eating ducks. Mink, weasels, skunks, opossum, raccoons, shrew, domestic and feral cats kill garter snakes. Bullfrogs, large fish, and crayfish will attack garter snakes that are foraging in the water. Box turtles, wood turtles, the Eastern Milk Snake, and the Northern Black Racer prey upon garter snakes. Humans are the biggest threat to the Eastern Garter Snake. Habitat destruction, automobile slaughter, and use of pesticides kill hundreds of snakes every year.

The temperament of the garter snake is as diversified as the rest of its natural history. When threatened or approached, the garter snake will inflate and flatten its body to appear twice its size (Fig.8.13). It readily strikes when advanced upon. If captured it will bite, hanging onto the offending hand, and chewing. At the same time it is biting, it sprays musk, and smears a foul smelling mixture of potent cloacal waste and musk on its

Fig. 8.13: The garter snake in this photo is displaying a strong defensive flattened posture. He has a stub tail caused by breaking of a section of his tail to escape a predator. His aggressive stance may be more dramatic because of the narrow escape he had that caused the loss of the tip of his tail.

attacker. The smell is pungent, and takes hours of scrubbing to remove its noxious smell.

Henry S. Fitch, 2003, studied tail loss as a defensive strategy of the garter snake. If garter snakes are held by the tail, they rotate their body with a whirling motion that quickly gains momentum and snaps off the tail. When a tail breaks, the broken end is very active, performing a series of sideways contractions which may be so rapid that is it seen as a blur, causing it to skip and hop about on the surface of the ground. The lively movements of the detached tail may distract the attention of a predator, permitting the snake to escape. Snakes do not regenerate their broken tails. The large number of snakes with part of the tail missing suggests the success of the strategy. By sacrificing part of the tail, garter snakes save their lives. In the study, females (Fig. 8.4) had higher frequencies of broken tails than males (Fig. 8.13). Adults had a higher number of broken tails than juveniles.

Common names: Some common names for the Eastern Garter Snake are: garden snake, common garter snake, spotted garter snake, striped grass snake and the three-striped adder. The scientific name, *Thamnophis sirtalis sirtalis* is a combination of Greek and New Latin, meaning the "bush snake that looks like a garter strap." The genus name *Thamnophis* is derived from the Greek *thamnos*, which means, "bush," and *ophio* meaning, "snake." The species name *sirtalis* is New Latin meaning "like a garter," in reference to the resemblance of the pattern of this snake to a striped garter strap.

Similar species: Snakes that may be confused with the Eastern Garter Snake are the Eastern Ribbon Snake and the Northern Brown Snake. The ribbon snake has the lateral stripes on the 3rd and 4th scale rows, whereas the garter snake has the stripe on the

Fig. 8.14: Adult Eastern Garter Snake.

Fig. 8.15: Adult Eastern Ribbon Snake.

Fig. 8.16: Juvenile Eastern Garter Snake.

Fig. 8.17: Adult Northern Brown Snake

2nd and 3rd scale rows. The ribbon snake has a very long tail, about 1/3 the length of its body. It has no dark upper lip marks, and the stripes are always bright yellow against a velvety black ground color. The brown snake has the spots and dorsal stripe, but the stripe is usually difficult to see. The spots are brown, and the ground color is brown. It might be confused with a juvenile garter snake. Photos of these comparisons appear above in Figs. 8.13-8.16.

Garter snakes make good companions for a summer pet pal. When first capturing them, it would be wise to wear a pair of cotton gloves. Garters will usually bite and musk when first handled. See chapter on Captive Care at the end of the book to set up a temporary housing arrangement. It is recommended to keep your snake only for the spring and summer season. Feed it earthworms and small fish. In September, it is recommended to release it at the same place you captured it earlier in the season. The snake needs to return to its home range, and continue living a life of foraging and making new life.

Garter Snakes contributed for photographs were donated by field associates Paul Nager, John Stearns, Ernie Krulikowski, Evan Kirk, and Wyatt Frantz.

CHAPTER NINE

EASTERN RIBBON SNAKE *Thamnophis sauritus sauritus*

This chapter is dedicated to Evan Kirk, who was 10 years old at the time of his many contributions to the collection of specimens needed to complete this 20-year photographic study of New England Snakes. Evan spends hours in the wilderness with his Dad hiking and studying. The magnificent mother featured in Fig. 9.8 was one of many snakes donated by him for this study. He is a passionate student of the natural wonders and enthusiastically shares his love with friends and teachers.

Fig. 9.1: Eastern Ribbon Snake with 3 brilliant yellow stripes against a velvet dark-walnut ground color.

Description: The Eastern Ribbon Snake, *Thamnophis sauritus sauritus* is a medium-sized, streamlined species of the garter snake family. The ribbon snake is one of the most slender of all the snakes in New England. The adults average 18-26 inches in length. One of the distinguishing characteristics of the ribbon snake is its long gradually tapering tail. The tail is about one-third the entire length of its body. An average 26 inch snake has a tail about 9 inches long. The diameter of a snake that size is only about 3/8 of an inch, indicating a very slender snake. The record size is 40 inches. The ribbon snake is easy to recognize, with its three yellow stripes, ranging in color from light sulfur to deep lemon yellow. These highly visible yellow stripes stand out prominently against a rich dark brown or black ground color (Fig.9.1). The two spots on top of the head, near the seam of the 2 parietal plates (Fig. 6.2-a) are smaller and more faint than the spots on the Eastern Garter Snake (Fig.8.3). Most ribbon snakes do not have these parietal spots. It would be interesting to determine the significance of

Fig. 9.2: Female Eastern Ribbon Snake showing faint parietal spots on top of her head just above the beginning of the dorsal stripe. Notice the long tails of some of her offspring.

these spots, why are they present on some ribbon snakes and not on others. The scales are

Fig. 9.3: Photo illustrating keeled scales with prominent ridges, and the position of the lateral yellow stripe clearly shown on scale rows 3 and 4. Notice the light brown coloration on the upturned belly or ventral scales in the right hand corner of the photo.

strongly keeled, with a raised longitudinal ridge running down the middle of each individual scale, like the keel on the bottom of a boat (Fig. 9.3). The rough scales impart a velvety appearance to this graceful serpent. There are 19 scales per row around the neck and midbody (Fig. 6.1-b), and 17 at the vent. The belly is creamy yellow, with a hint of pale iridescent bluish-green. A distinct chestnut brown band separates each lateral side stripe from the belly. The color blends from the first row of scales, onto the side or lateral surface of the belly scales (ventral scutes). The ventral scutes turn upward, so that they actually look like the first row of lateral scales (Figs 9.3 and 9.4). This cinnamon stripe is called a ventrolateral stripe. The upper half of the ventrolateral stripe is bordered with black. The anal plate is single.

The middorsal stripe begins at the junction with the paired parietal plates on top of the head (Fig. 9.2), and runs the length of the body to the tip of the tail. This dorsal, or back stripe is a usually a paler

Fig. 9.4: Close-up showing ventrolateral stripe of light chestnut brown covering the upturned edges of the ventral belly scales and bleeding onto the first half of the first row of scales.

yellow than the lateral stripes. Towards the tail, it usually fades to a buff or fawn color.

Fig. 9.5: Close-up of Eastern Ribbon Snake, found by field associate Al Corey in Old Lyme, CT, August 1984, illustrating origin of the dorsal, lateral and ventrolateral stripes. The head scales and head plates are also well defined.

The color of the dorsal stripe involves the row of scales above the backbone, called the central vertebral row, and half of each row on each side of the vertebral row. This would make the dorsal stripe equal to a width of 2 scale rows. The lateral stripes, are brilliant, sharply defined, lemon yellows. They involve the 3rd and 4th scale rows above the ventral scutes. The upper edge of the fourth row and the lower edge of the third row are black. The lateral stripes extend from the white chin (Fig. 9.5), to the tip of the tail. The chin and lower throat are pure white. The Eastern Ribbon Snake displays white, line-like spots on some scales, and on the skin between the scales, when the body is distended (Fig. 9.1).

Sexual dimorphism: There is no outstanding visible physical difference between male and female ribbon snakes. The females tend to be slightly heavier, but the general length, body dimensions and tail lengths are indistinguishable between the sexes. The males average 161 ventral scutes, while the females average 156. Males have about 117 subcaudals and the females average 113 (Fig. 6.1-d).

Head Scales: The top of the head on a ribbon snake varies in color from a dark walnut to a soft reddish brown. To help identify the scales discussed in this section, refer to Fig. 6.2 (a-b). The dark color extends along the side of the head to the eye. There are 3 small postocular scales behind the eye. The upper postocular is in contact with the parietal plate. The mid-postocular is contacting the single temporal scale, and the lower postocular contacts the 5th upper lip scale (supralabial), with the white color from the supralabial scale coloring its lower edge. The single elongate preocular in front of the eye contacts the supraocular above, and the 3rd supralabial below. It is marked with a snow-white upright streak, parallel to the eye (Fig. 9.5). This white mark, directly in front of

Fig. 9.6: Camouflaged Eastern Ribbon Snake from Salem CT., May 1989. Notice stunning streamlined effect of stripping among the leaf litter, and the distinctive white bar in front of the eye.

the large, beautiful, brown eye creates a stunning identification feature, which is easily recognized in the field (Fig. 9.6). The small loreal scale is located between the preocular scale and the nasal scale (Fig. 6.2-f). It is bordered by the prefrontal plate above, by the nasal scale in front and by the second supralabial below. The large nostril is located in the center of a single divided nasal scale, bordered by the internasal plate above, the rostrum in front and the 1st supralabial below. There are 7 white supralabials, and 10 white lower lip, or infralabials, scales. There are no black bars on the labial scales, as are found in the Eastern Garter Snake. The large golden brown eye is in contact below with the third and fourth supralabials, and above with the supraocular. The iris is chestnut brown with a golden halo around the pupil. The stripes and soft brown hues are especially effective camouflage when the snake is moving through thick leaf litter (Fig. 9.6). Notice that even from a distance the white preocular eyespot is visible.

Range: The Eastern Ribbon Snake ranges from east of the Mississippi River to southern Maine and southern Canada, southward to Florida and the Gulf Coast. A gap in the range exists from eastern Tennessee and western North Carolina northward, through eastern Kentucky and into southern parts of Indiana, Ohio and portions of Pennsylvania.

Eastern Ribbon Snakes are found statewide, but their distribution is very spotty. They are undergoing a ***long-term decline in Connecticut***. This may correlate with a reduction of their preferred habitat, over the last fifty to seventy-five years. This is a result of drainage of wet meadows, and damming of marshy areas to make ponds and reservoirs. In many parts of the state, red maple swamps have replaced the open wet-meadows habitat. The recolonization of beaver, and their associated dam building, may help restore

Fig. 9.7: Young 10-day old Eastern Ribbon Snake, Old Lyme CT, August 2002. This extremely grace-ful fluid serpent glides over the waters surface, without a hint of rippling. The stripes enhance the cam-ouflage effect against the horizontal water reeds.

these open wetlands, thus enhancing suitable habitat for the ribbon snake (Klemens, 2000: 68-69). This principle of synergy, the working together of life forces, is the basic principle of Natures Circle of Life. Man has a way of disrupting the harmonious rhythm of this natural cycle.

The Eastern Ribbon Snakes are listed as ***Special Concern*** under the Connecticut Endangered Species Act. Special concern status provides for no legal protection, however the collection and possession of this species is regulated by the Connecticut Department of Environmental Protection. Under the Connecticut Code, Section 26-55-3-F, possession is limited to a single individual. As wooded swamps and other shallow wet-lands are converted into ponds; bullfrogs, snapping turtles, and painted turtles increase in number, taking over habitats that once supported wood frogs, spotted turtles, and ribbon snakes (Klemens, 2000:14-15). The ribbon snake is an indicator of marsh and wetland habitat health. It feeds mainly on aquatic organisms, thus becoming affected by the accumulation of pesticides and other pollutants that are consumed while feeding on contaminated fish and amphibians. This graceful serpent is a wonder to watch as it glides across the surface of the water, hardly creating a ripple. The stripes are a very efficient camouflage as the snake moves through the water, with reeds and vegetation growing horizontally along its edge (Fig. 9.7). Though visible, the snake's continuous line disguis-es its movements. Its camouflage, speed, and slender streamlined shape cause the snake to rapidly become invisible.

Fig. 9.8: Elegant 36 inch female Eastern Ribbon Snake with 22 neonates delivered on August 15, 2002 in Old Lyme Connecticut. Field associate Evan Kirk.

Habitat: The ribbon snake can be found in a variety of habitats in close proximity to permanent or semipermanent bodies of water, where frogs and other aquatic prey are abundant. They prefer wet meadows, and fallow (uncultivated) fields crossed by meandering streams. The many power lines that crisscross Connecticut provide long tracts of this kind of habitat. The snakes will be found in swampy areas, around bogs, marshes, and weedy lake shorelines. They will be found on the banks and among the vegetation bordering these bodies of water. Ribbon snakes are found near flowing water such as brooks, streams, rivers, swamps and marshes, as well as standing water such as bogs, wet meadows, and naturally occurring ponds. They are often found in the brush and shrubs surrounding the bodies of water.

Behavior: The main period of activity for ribbon snakes generally runs from late February or early March through late October or early November. Hibernation takes place between October and March in a variety of locations. The sites include muskrat bank burrows and lodges, ant mounds, crayfish burrows and vole tunnels. The body temperature of hibernating ribbon snakes averages 42 F (5.6 C). The temperatures preferred by ribbon snakes ranges from about 55 F to 93 F. (12.6-34.0 C) (Ernst and Barbour, 1989). The male activity peaks in March and April when mating takes place as the animals emerge from hibernation. The female activity period peaks in August at birthing time. The home range may average 3 acres. They may be found basking on logs, muskrat lodges, and warm leaf litter (Fig. 9.6). They escape rapidly into dense cover or open water when disturbed or threatened. This species is semi-arboreal and can often be

Fig. 9.9: Newborn Eastern Ribbon Snake. 8.5 inches. Photographed August 1984 in Old Lyme CT. Field associate Billy Ross.

found sunning in the lower branches of bushes. It prefers areas with brushy vegetation at the water's edge for concealment. If captured, ribbon snakes tend to thrash around and secrete musk and feces, but they seldom bite. Because of their nervous, high-strung temperament, and delicate, slender physical physique, they are easily injured during capture. They make poor captives. It is recommended to respectfully observe these beautiful animals in their native habitat, leaving them and their home undisturbed.

Reproduction: Male and female ribbon snakes become sexually mature during their third spring, at lengths of about 23 inches. Mating occurs in late March and April in Connecticut. Ribbon snakes are viviparous, giving birth to live young. The young are usually born in late July or August. The average litter size ranges from 8-13. Some litters have up to 26 newborns. Neonates, or newborns, average eight inches (Fig. 9.9).

The beautiful female in Fig. 9.8 was rescued by field associate Evan Kirk, an enthusiastic 10-year old student of herpetology. Evan retrieved the snake from a dangerous area of heavy vehicular traffic. It is rewarding to have young students as trained field assistants, able to make life saving conservation decisions about animals subjected to extirpation (annihilation of the species by human actions). The robust 36 inch female appeared to be gravid (pregnant), and was set up in a birthing aquarium. She basked every day, and consumed 3 feeder fish twice a week for a month before giving birth. About a week before she delivered, she stopped feeding. The newborns, neonates, averaged 8 inches. It was so rewarding to come home from work and see a nest full of 22 spaghetti snakelings! After their first shed, which occurred within 24 hours of their birth, they grew an average of 3/4 of an inch. Each neonate ate 3, 1/2 inch feeder fish the day

Fig. 9.10: Notice the large eye, nostril and tongue of Eastern Ribbon Snake. The tongues red base and black tip are characteristic of ribbon and garter snakes. Both vision and olfaction, using the tongue and nostrils, are used to detect prey.

after birth. Feeding was carefully monitored, because one fish was often grabbed by two snakes. Snakes have the habit of continuing to swallow past the prey and onto the other snake, which is connected to the opposite end of a shared piece of food. The mother and youngsters continued to eat and rested well for a week. They were released to an historic ribbon snake habitat in Old Lyme CT, on August 22, 2002. The young averaged 9 inches at the time of their release (Fig. 9.7). Growth rate decreases as the snakes mature.

Feeding: Ribbon snakes feed primarily upon amphibians, including gray tree frogs, spring peepers, green frogs, wood frogs, spotted salamanders, redback salamanders, and marbled salamanders. Ribbon snakes will also prey upon minnows. Small ribbon snakes feed on small frogs and toads and their tadpoles. Full-grown ribbon snakes are able to swallow medium sized frogs. Unlike their cousin the Eastern Garter Snake, ribbon snakes do not like to eat earthworms.

Most feeding is done in the morning or early evening, being predominately daytime, diurnal feeders. The snakes actively prowl and forage to find prey. They may become night hunters (nocturnal), during the frog and toad-breeding season. Once found, the ribbon snake seizes the prey in its mouth, and swallows it alive. Prey is detected by the sense of smell, involving the tongue, large nostrils, and vision (Fig. 9.10).

Predators: Eastern Ribbon Snakes are preyed upon by wading birds such as the great blue heron, and American bittern. Small predatory mammals such as the mink, weasel, skunk, opossum, raccoon and shrew also eat this snake. Bullfrogs, large fish and crayfish will attack ribbon snakes. Turtles, including the snapping turtle and wood turtle

Fig. 9.11: Adult Eastern Ribbon Snake, displaying camouflage. March 1984.

Fig.9.12: Adult Eastern Garter Snake, heavier, with shorter tail than Eastern Ribbon Snake.

Fig. 9.13: Newborn Eastern Ribbon Snake, notice large head and thin body.

Fig. 9.14: Newborn Eastern Garter Snake, dark spots compare to solid color of ribbon snake.

prey upon ribbon snakes, as well as other snakes, such as the Eastern Milk Snake and the Northern Black Racer.

Humans are the greatest threat to the Eastern Ribbon Snake. Illegal collecting, vehicular slaughter, careless and indiscriminant use of pesticides and destruction of habitat kill hundreds of ribbon snakes every year. Because ribbon snakes feed largely upon amphibians, they are subject to increased exposure to pesticide poisoning, called biomagnification. The effects of pesticide poisoning are magnified in the food chain. The amphibians are exposed to pesticides by direct application, and by ingesting insects that have been exposed to pesticides. The insects eat plants that have been sprayed with herbicides, and are subjected to direct poisoning from pellets of pesticides, and aerial insecticide application. The ribbon snakes eat the amphibians that have eaten the insects that have eaten poisoned plants. Being at the top of this food chain, the ribbon snakes therefore receive a magnified dose of the pesticides, resulting in a magnification of the poisoning effects.

When disturbed, the ribbon snake rapidly flees. If near water, it will not hesitate to dive in and swim rapidly away. They are fast moving snakes, and, as with the Eastern Garter Snake, will often break off the tips of their tails in an effort to escape a predator (Fig. 8.13). Because these snakes are rapidly declining in population, and the fact that their collection is regulated by state regulations, they should not to be maintained as pets.

Common names: Some common names for the ribbon snake are, the slender garter snake, striped water snake, and the striped racer. The genus *Thamnophis* is derived from the Greek *thamnos.* meaning "bush" or "shrub," and *ophio* meaning "snake" or "serpent." The species name *sauritus* stems from the Greek *sauros* meaning "lizard," in reference to the long lizard-like length of the tail.

Similar species: The Eastern Ribbon Snake is often confused with the Eastern Garter Snake. The ribbon snake is much more slender than the garter snake and has a very long tail. The yellow stripes are more prominent and the ground color is solid, with no dark spots. Comparison photos between adult and juvenile Eastern Ribbon Snakes and Eastern Garter Snakes appear in Figs. 9.11 through 9.14 on the page 94.

CHAPTER TEN

NORTHERN BROWN SNAKE *(Storeria dekayi dekayi)*

This chapter is dedicated to the memory of Anna and Casimer Krulikowski, devoted parents and owners of a small farm in Southington Connecticut, which was the home for many happy herps. The most numerous were the Northern Brown Snakes, affectionately referred to as the "LBJs," little brown jobs. They were everywhere, under all discarded debris. The farm was full of worms and night crawlers, some of their favorite foods. This is a tribute to wonderful country living, which may be physically gone, but alive in love and spirit eternally.

Fig. 10.1: Northern Brown Snake, Southington CT, August 1985. Earth-brown ground color, no prominent dorsal stripe, and dark dorsal spots present one common color phase. Field associate Ernie Krulikowski.

Description: The Northern Brown Snake, (*Storeria dekayi dekayi*), is a small, moderately stout snake with large eyes. The average size is between 7 and 10 inches, with an historic record of 20.75 inches. The brown snake rarely exceeds 15 inches. There can be quite a variation in the brown hues of dorsal ground color. It may range from a grayish brown, to light yellowish brown, reddish brown, chestnut, or dark brown. Two color variations are seen in Fig 10.1 and Fig 10.2. The dorsum or back of the brown snake has two parallel rows of distinct paired dark spots, longitudinally marking the body. The light band seen in Fig. 10.2, is not as marked in all brown snakes, it is usually an indistinct paler band that extends down the middle of the snakes back (Fig. 10.1). The bands outer edges are generally lined with a row of evenly placed dark spots. Sometimes the black spots are intermittently connected by a thin black line. Brown snakes that have recently eaten large meals, or females heavy with young, often appear to be liberally speckled with small horizontal flecks of light and dark specks (Fig. 10.1). These specks of color are usually concealed between the dorsal scales, only becoming visible when the snakes skin is stretched. A dark blotch is on each side of the neck directly behind the head. The scales are keeled (Fig. 10.6), with a ridgelike process on each individual scale, giving the snake a rough feel when handled.

Fig. 10.2: Fawn-soft brown ground color, prominent light-colored dorsal band outlined with black spots.

Fig. 10.3: Close-up of head scales and markings of Northern Brown Snake, June 1983. Notice dark blotch behind head, and dark bar running from the temporal scale to the suture between the 6th and 7th upper lip (supralabial) scales. Small black dots are faintly visible on the belly scales.

There are 17 rows of scales at midbody (Fig. 6.1-b), with the same number at the neck and vent. The anal plate is divided (Fig. 6.1-e). The venter or belly is pinkish to buff colored from about mid body to the tail. The chin and neck are usually white. The belly is unmarked, except for a row of black spots along the edges of the ventral scales or scutes, where the lateral scales meet.

Sexual dimorphism: There is no outstanding physical difference between male and female brown snakes. The females tend to be slightly heavier, but the general length and body dimensions are indistinguishable between the sexes, except when the females are pregnant (gravid), at which time they are noticeably larger in circumference than the males. The males tail is slightly longer than the females tail, averaging 24% of its total body length as opposed to the females, which averages 20% of her total body length.

Head scales: The head of the brown snake is small and usually darker than the body of the snake. The eyes are large, with a golden brown iris and a large round pupil (Fig. 10.3). To help identify the scales discussed in this section, refer to Fig. 6.2 (a-b). The single large preocular scale is in contact with the eye, bordered above by the supraocular eyebrow scale, in front by the prefrontal plate and posterior nasal scale, and below by the 2nd and 3rd supralabial lips scales. The two small postoculars scales are located behind the eye, and bordered above by the supraocular eyebrow scale, on the sides by the large temporal scale, and below by the 4th and 5th supralabial lip scales. There is no loreal scale (Fig. 6.2-g). Several other small brown snakes resemble the brown snake, so checking scale characteristics, such as the presence of the loreal scale is

Fig. 10.4: Northern Brown Snake found under debris on old farmlands, in city parks and disturbed human habitats. Its coloring and markings make camouflage in weeds and dead grasses ideal.

is often necessary. The nostril is located between two nasal scales. There is a dark mark on the temporal scale on the side of the head running down between the 6th and 7th upper supralabial lip scale (Fig. 10.3). Most of the upper and lower lipscales have dark spots on them.

Range: The Northern Brown Snake ranges from southern Maine through New England to North Carolina, and westward from southern Quebec, through New York, Pennsylvania and West Virginia. The Northern Brown Snake is common in Connecticut. They are most abundant in the more developed portions of the state. They are found even in vacant lots in some of Connecticut's largest cities. The brown snake is presently secure within Connecticut (Klemens 2000: 67).

Habitat: The Northern Brown Snake can be found in nearly all ground habitats. The trees associated with the forest edges are white pine, sugar maples, black cherry and red cedar. They can be found around cultivated fields, vacant lots, tall grass fields and around old farm buildings (Fig. 10.4). Before the onset of pollution and the massive use of pesticides, this gentle little brown snake could almost be called the 'city snake' because of its abundance in parks, cemeteries, and under trash in empty lots. Habitats away from cities include bogs, swamps, streams and lake edges. It shows a preference for damp shaded places that offer ground cover and enough surface litter where hiding places, snails, slugs and earthworms abound. Klemens (1993) says that the Northern Brown Snake of Connecticut and southern New England favors disturbed human habitation sites over undisturbed habitats. During his studies over a period of 17 years, approximately

Fig. 10.5: Northern Brown Snake displaying flattened body in threatening posture after being disturbed beneath its hiding place of black tar paper. Notice the beautiful array of mosaic colors of white, black and bluish gray, only visible when the body is distended.

93% of the specimens that he collected came from the following modified natural areas: 31% rural-agricultural, country farmlands, 13 % suburban residential districts on or near the outskirts of cities, 18 % urban, city dwelling, and 31 % in radically disturbed habitats. Although still a common snake, it is so adept at hiding that few people encounter it, and when found it is usually mistaken for a young garter snake. Favorite hiding places are discarded pieces of plywood, old linoleum, sheet metal and tarpaper.

Behavior: Brown snakes become active soon after the ground begins to thaw in late March or April. They are cold-tolerant species, and remain active until late October or November. When the temperature drops they retreat to some shelter beneath the frost line and hibernate. The temperature of the den sites generally stays around 35-40 degrees F. Hibernation sites include animal burrows such as abandoned mole, vole and wood chuck burrows, deep rock crevices, old foundations, anthills, decaying logs, rotting tree stumps, and compost heaps that maintain a warm temperature by heat generated from organic decomposition. Nobel and Clausen, 1936, wrote about discovering over 350 specimens of the Northern Brown Snake in two hibernation sites near Flushing, New York. Northern Brown Snakes often share communal dens with Eastern Garter Snakes. In 1932, Clausen found 76 brown snakes, 10 garter snakes, and 1 water snake in an old rat burrow. The depth of the hibernaculum ranged from 12-36 inches. Brown snakes have also been found inside old rotten stumps about 39 inches deep and foundations of old buildings (Pope 1937:115). The communal gathering benefits the snakes by reducing

Fig. 10.6: Threatening attack posture assumed by Northern Brown snake when cornered. Notice the keeled scales separated by the blue-gray skin.

their body water loss during the long period of winter dormancy. Brown snakes are more active at night (nocturnal) than during the day. They spend the days hidden in a carpet of leaf litter or concealed beneath surface objects. The most commonly used shelters in their wild habitats are logs, rocks, brush piles and loose tree bark. Within the large metropolitan area, where they are often abundant, they typically hide beneath mulch piles, cardboard, shingles, boards, roofing paper and other types of discarded building materials. Suburban yards littered with such rubbish seem to attract this little brown snake like a magnet. It can also be found in thick mats of grass growing along the foundation of houses (Fig. 10.4). The home range of the Northern Brown snake is small, usually involving only a few hundred feet.

This friendly little snake rarely bites, even when provoked. When discovered under surface debris, it remains still for an instant when first exposed, then it tries to escape. When further approached, and unable to flee, it may flatten its body in a threatening gesture, causing the body scales to separate (Fig. 10.5). Accompanying the flattened distended body gesture is a striking threatening posture (Fig. 10.6). Only rarely will the disturbed snake strike. If picked up it will spray musk from its scent glands in its tail and spread feces from its cloacal opening.

Although still abundant, the Northern Brown Snake, over the past 20 years, seems to have been on a slow decline. Where formerly 10-12 snakes could be found in one day on an old family poultry farm in Southington CT, the same site in 2000 produced no snakes. Old farms with discarded debris are being sold off and new neat homes with no

Fig. 10.7: Mother brown snake with babies. Young are born alive, and resemble ringneck snakes, with collars around their necks.

trash piles to hide under seriously affect the microhabitats of this small snake. The brown snake is almost fossorial in its hiding habits, and without debris to hide under, it disappears.

Reproduction: The Northern Brown Snake is viviparous. There has been an ongoing discussion about whether brown snakes are ovoviviparous or viviparous. Ovoviviparous reproduction is a form of live birth in which the female retains the eggs within her body until they hatch. The developing egg contains a yolk sac, which stores nutrients. The snakes delivered in this way still have the attached yolk sac. Viviparous reproduction occurs when there is nourishment to the developing embryo directly from the mothers circulation. Recent research at Trinity College, in Hartford Connecticut, has established that placental membranes, which function in gas exchange as well as in the transfer of water and nutrients from the mothers circulation, are present in the brown snake, establishing the fact that they are truly viviparous (Blackburn, Johnson, Petzold 2002).

Mating occurs from late March through May. Females bear 3-31 young. The female in Fig. 10.7, gave birth to 26 young in August 1985. Each birth took about 1 minute to complete. The mother would raise her tail, contract her body, and push the baby, coiled inside its fetal membrane, from her body every 2-3 minutes. After the young are born, they take about 2 minutes to puncture the birthing sac and slither to their mother. They remained close to their mother until they were released with their mother in her home range. Harding (1997) also made note of this close contact with the parent. The young snakes are small; about 3.5 inches long on the average, and are dark brown or

Fig. 10.8: Close-up of young Northern Brown Snakes after first shed. Notice white collar around neck.

dark slate gray in color. A distinguishing characteristic of the young is a light grayish white colored ring found around the neck (Fig. 10.8). At this age, they are sometimes confused with ringneck snakes. The gestation period, time between mating and birthing, averages 110 days. Females usually reproduce every year. The snakes are sexually mature when they reach a total length of about 7 inches, which, at a growth rate of about 2 inches a season puts them in the spring of their second full year.

Feeding: The brown snake loves earthworms, slugs and snails. Other items on the snakes menu include sowbugs, spiders, small frogs and amphibian eggs. Brown snakes have 15 teeth on each maxillary bone. The teeth closest to the snout are longer than the back teeth. Douglas A. Rossman, in 1990 did some research into reports that snails were listed in the diet of brown snakes. He and P. A. Meyer performed some feeding experiments using brown and red-bellied snakes, both of the genus *Storeria*. The following feeding behavior was noted. The first phase was called the assault phase in which the brown snake seized the snail by the exposed soft body part. There was no aggressive strike, just an opening of the mouth, and firm grabbing hold on the fleshy snail body. The snail was then shoved forward along the ground until the shell became lodged against some firm object. Snails were only chosen if most of the soft body was exposed. With its prey firmly pressed against a rock, the snake twisted its head and forebody in a half to three-quarter rotation and held it there, while continuing to maintain its grip on the soft morsel. After about 10 minutes the snail became fatigued and could not resist the tension any longer. It relaxed the large muscle that held it to its shell. It was then easily pulled free from the protective casing. The snake was rewarded for its patience with a

Fig. 10.9: Northern Brown Snake enjoying its favorite food, warm wiggly worm delight.

superb delicacy of fresh snail. The question of why have not more snails been found in the stomachs of dissected wild-caught specimens of brown snakes was discussed. One explanation might be that some of the food items that were identified as slugs, were actually snails. Earthworms are also a favorite food as seen in Fig. 10.9. The worm is actively trailed and seized by the snake. It gradually works the body in its mouth, getting to the closest end. Once the end of the worm is reached, it is quickly swallowed. The use of pesticides to control grubs and slugs will adversely affect the population of the brown snake.

Predators: The predators of the brown snake include other snakes, such as the Eastern Milk Snake and Northern Black Racer. Birds that prey upon the brown snake include the American Crow, turkeys, domestic chickens, red-shouldered hawks and robins. Mammals that attack brown snakes include domestic and feral cats, raccoons, opossums skunks, and weasels. Large toads and bullfrogs will also prey on the young snakes. Shrews forage in similar subterranean areas and have been know to attack brown snakes (Linzey, 1981).

Common names: The Northern Brown Snake is often called DeKay's Snake. It is also called the ground snake, brown grass snake, house snake, spotted adder, and little brown snake. The scientific name is derived from proper names of people. The genus name *Storeria,* honors an American physician and naturalist David Humphreys Storer, March 26-1804 to 1891. The species name *dekayi,* honors James Ellsworth DeKay, a New York naturalist who first described this pretty little brown snake. The snake does well for short periods of captivity, eating earthworms readily. As long as there is a hide-box, or clean debris to hide under, plenty of water and love, its company may be enjoyed for a season, with release in September so natural life cycles may resume.

Similar species: Snakes that can be confused with the young Northern Brown Snake (Fig.10.10) are the young Northern Ringneck Snake (Fig. 10.11) and the young Northern Red-Bellied Snake. (Fig. 10.12).

Fig. 10.10: Young Northern Brown Snake with light colored neck collar and rough keeled scales.

Fig. 10.11: Young Northern Ringneck Snake with bright yellow neck ring and smooth shiny black scales,

Fig. 10.12: Young Northern Red-Bellied Snake with light cream-colored neck collar, pink belly, and rough keeled scales.

Fig. 10.13: Young Eastern Garter Snake resembles light-phase Northern Brown Snake (Fig. 10.4)

Fig. 10.14: Dark-Phased Northern Brown Snake similar to Northern Red-Bellied in Fig. 10.15.

Fig. 10.15: Adult Northern Red-Bellied Snake in opaque-phase.

The adult dark-phased Northern Brown Snake in (Fig 10.14) can be confused with the Northern Red-Bellied Snake when it is in its opaque, preshed phase as seen in (Fig. 10.15).and the young Eastern Garter Snake seen in (Fig. 10.13).

CHAPTER ELEVEN

NORTHERN RED-BELLIED SNAKE   (*Storeria occipitomaculata occipitomaculata*)

This chapter is dedicated to Christopher Guiles. Chris was 10-years old when this photo was taken in July 1987, seventeen years ago. An enthusiastic young herpetologist and naturalist in Ashford CT, he led me to the most treasured photos in my long 20-year research-photographic-study of New England Snakes. I will forever be grateful to him for the excitement, innocence and passion for life that he shared with me in our quest for the ruby gem of the forest.

Fig. 11.1: Northern Red-Bellied Snake, July 1987, Ashford CT, found by field associate Christopher Guiles.

Description: The Northern Red-Bellied Snake, *Storeria occipitomaculata occipitomaculata,* is a beautifully delicate, small woodland snake. Adults average 8-10 inches in total length and about 1/4 inch in diameter. The record length is 16 inches. The usual color variations are brown or gray above. A pale longitudinal dorsal stripe, running the length of the body, is present on some individuals, and absent in others. Red-bellied snakes can be olive-brown, tan-brown, russet-brown, bronze, chestnut-brown, gray-brown, steel gray above, or even black.

Fig. 11.2: Final days of ecdysis of Northern Red-Bellied Snake, 2 days before actual shedding. Notice the pink belly.

The more common color variations in Connecticut are chestnut brown and slate gray. The animals photographed from Windham County Connecticut, in 1987, were a soft medium brown above with no visible dorsal stripe (Fig. 11.1). The bellies varied from pink to scarlet red. One snake was kept for study, and returned to the site a week later. It appeared to be in the final stages of the preshed cycle. The eyes were not cloudy, but the colors were dull, with a dusky dark haze, and the belly was pink (Fig. 11.2). The snake was misted twice a day to keep its skin moist. The 10-inch male did shed in two days. The final stage of shed, or ecdysis, with the scarlet red belly almost blinding in its radiance is illustrated in Fig.

Fig. 11.3: Beautiful bright scarlet red belly of its namesake, the Northern Red-Bellied Snake immediately after shedding, August 1987.

11.3. An incredibly stunning Northern Red-Bellied Snake emerged as a golden brown, knight in shining armor. It was like the transformation of a caterpillar chrysalis into a beautiful, golden monarch. The ventral scutes are bright red, edged with a blue-black border, formed from dark bluish spider-like flecking on the lateral edges of the belly scales. There are three light yellow or bone white spots behind the head, at the nape of the neck. One of the neck spots can be seen in Fig. 11.4. It is formed by six light cream-colored scales that are mottled with reddish brown flecks.

The plates or shields are also well outlined in Fig. 11.4, showing the elongate paired parietal shields that outline the anterior or top half of the dorsal spot. The frontal shields are between the eyes and supraoclular scales, or eyebrows. The paired prefrontal shields are in front of the single frontal shield, and the two internasal shields touch the nasal scales, and are in front of the rostral scale, or rostrum. To aid in identifying these head plates refer to Fig. 6.2 (a-b). Each scale in the first row of scales next to the belly is marked with a yellow

Fig. 11.4: Close-up of dorsal view of red-bellied snakes head, showing large head plates and the light colored circle at the nape of its neck.

Fig. 11.5: Stunning pecan-colored Northern Red-Bellied Snake illustrating blue-gray ventrolateral stripe along the belly, and the golden yellow spots along the side and back of the snake. This helps to distinguish this species from the Northern Brown Snake. The white line behind the eye is also characteristic.

horizontal spot, creating a thin lateral line just above the margin of the belly. The light lateral line runs parallel with the blue-gray ventrolateral stripe on the ventral scales (Fig. 11.5), creating an artistic identification characteristic, to differentiate it from its close relative, the brown snake. The three rows of vertebral scales are outlined by another thin line of highlighted golden spots (Fig 11.5). These spots run the length of the body, and outline a dorsal stripe that is sometimes, but not always, a shade lighter than the golden pecan on the sides of the snake. The scales are heavily keeled, with prominent ridging (Fig. 11.10). There are 15 row of scales at midbody, and the anal plate is divided (Fig. 6.1: b&e). Another color phase found in Connecticut has a dark gray ground color. A representative specimen was photographed by researcher Robert W. Fritsch II. It has a dark slate-gray ground color with a narrow light colored dorsal stripe, which begins at the light spot behind the head, and extends the length of the body. The venter or belly is deep blood red (Klemens, 2000: 68).

Sexual dimorphism: The females are generally longer and heavier than the males. The tails of the males are longer than the females, being about 25% of their body length, whereas the females tail is about 22 % of her total body length. Both sexes average about the same number of 125 ventral scales. The males average 47 subcaudals, and the females average 42 subcaudals.

Head scales: The head is small, and darker than the body. There is very little indentation at the neck, the neck and head having about the same diameter. A white spot

Fig. 11.6: Illustration of facial scales and gorgeous pastel mosaic of color representing the Northern Red-Bellied Snake in its entire splendor. Notice the white line behind the eye on the 5th supralabial scale.

is found behind the eye. It is located on the 5th upper labial or lip scale, contacting the lower postocular scale, and is a visible field characteristic (Fig. 11.5). The single large temporal scale is in contact with the 2 postocular scales. The 5th upper supralabial lip scale with the white line, and the 6th enlarged upper lip scales, both contact the temporal scale, which is bordered above by the large parietal plate. The two preocular scales can be seen contacting the front of the large golden brown eye, but no loreal scale is present between the eye and the 2 nasal scales (Fig. 6.2f). The nostril is located between the 2 large nasal scales. The snout is white with light flecking of blue and reddish brown specks. The white scales forming the lateral spot are visible with faint evidence of pecan brown flecking. The spider-like blue-black webbing can be seen marking the gray-blue ventrolateral line on the upturned edges of the belly scales. These above mentioned facial scales and the splendid display of pastel colors are illustrated in Fig. 11.6. To aid in identifying the scales described in this section, refer to Fig. 6.2, a&b.

Range: The Northern Red-Bellied Snake ranges from Nova Scotia, west to the southeastern tip of Saskatchewan, and south through eastern South Dakota. The range then extends from eastern Iowa, the eastern fringes of Kansas, Oklahoma, and Texas, to the Gulf of Mexico. Summarizing the range; the species is widely distributed in North America, in a line extending east from Manitoba, Canada, to eastern Texas, and from Nova Scotia south to northern Florida.

The Red-Bellied Snakes range in Connecticut includes the following counties: Litchfield, Hartford, and Windham (DeGraaf and Rudis 1983: 60). There is no special

Fig. 11.7: Northern Red-Bellied Snake in moist woodland habitat, displaying some defensive posture with twisting body contortions and showing of its brillant red belly.

state status designated for the Northern Red-Bellied Snake. The snakes secretive, almost fossorial, underground burrowing lifestyle made it difficult to assess its abundance. Until recently, most authorities in the nongame areas believed the animal to have a spotty population density, and the sites were kept confidential. Craig, 1979 had created five categories, to designate the status of reptiles and amphibians in Connecticut. Under Craig's 'mode of occurrence' designation, the Northern Red-Bellied Snake was listed as **RL** (rare and local). This refers to individuals or small populations, which occur in one or a few highly restricted localities. Under the 'degree of threat,'designation, Craig listed the Red-Bellied Snake as **V** (vulnerable). This refers to reptiles and amphibians that, although not currently in danger of extinction, are nonetheless sufficiently rare to warrant concern (DeGraaf and Rudis 1983: 9). These special snakes were unofficially listed for future consideration. However, recent fieldwork has greatly increased the number of known sites for this species in Connecticut (Klemens, 2000:68). It appears to be widely distributed in upland regions. Almost all documented populations are from the northern counties, but some animals have been documented from southeastern Connecticut, near the Rhode Island state line. The Red-Belly Snake is presently secure within Connecticut.

Habitat: Northern Red-Bellied Snakes prefer woodlands of pine, oak, hickory, and hemlock groves. They are frequently found in upland wooded ridges. This forest dweller can be found in moist woods (Fig. 11.7), well-drained rocky hilltops, and near bogs that border high, stony, wooded areas. Sometimes they are found in quite arid conditions, of sand and gravel. Because the red-bellies are know to hibernate in anthills,

Fig. 11.8: Red-bellied snakes spend most daytime hours hiding and burrowing for slugs, their favorite food.

the travels to sandier areas may be in search of such mounds. They are rarely found in debris around old barns and abandoned buildings, which are regular haunts for their cousin, the brown snake.

Behavior: These secretive, shy snakes like hiding under stones, leaf litter, logs, boards, discarded debris, and inside large decaying logs and stumps. Red-bellied snakes are active during early morning and afternoon hours, being crepuscular in spring and fall. During the summer months, they become active at twilight and nighttime, avoiding the heat. This burrowing, hiding (Fig. 11.8) nocturnal behavior makes it very difficult to locate them. They tend to be solitary, except when they congregate with other snakes at hibernation sites. Anthills, unused rodent burrows, soil containing crevices and passageways, such as root systems of old trees and stumps, and foundations of deserted buildings are common hibernation sites. These sites are often shared with brown snakes, garter snakes, and green snakes.

One of the most startling snake stories is a true one published by Stuart Criddle of Treesbank, Manitoba, in an article entitled, "Snakes from an anthill". On September 25, 1934, two smooth green snakes were found dead on an anthill located on the farm of the author. The anthill was about 6 inches high, with a 3-foot diameter, and was occupied by black ants, probably of the genus *Formica*. It had an abandoned appearance. After the hill had been carefully examined, 6 Red-Bellied Snakes were found. The next day, four more were dug out. The spot was revisited again on October 6. Careful digging with a spade revealed lower galleries of the anthill that were almost alive with snakes. In 40 minutes of digging, 75 snakes were removed. On October 10, the hill was completely dug

Fig. 11.9: Baby Northern Red-Bellied Snake, August 1987. Notice the cream-yellow spot, leading into a light dorsal stripe. There are 2 parietal spots on top of the head. This baby assumed the defensive rollover posture typical of red-bellied snakes. To get an idea of its size, it is coiled up on a white oak leaf.

out. The diameter of the anthill increased with depth, taking on an inverted funnel appearance. The soil was sandy. Water was found at 4 feet 9 inches. No snakes were found below the water level, but some had the lower parts of their bodies submerged in it. A total of 257 snakes were removed from this single anthill. Eight were young *Thamnophis radix*, Plains Garter Snakes, 101 were *Storeria occipitomaculata,* Northern Red-Bellied Snakes, and 148 were *Opheodrys vernalis*, Smooth Green Snakes (Wright and Wright, 1957: 561-562). Red-Bellied snakes form mass migrations to and from their hibernation sights in spring, usually April, and September to October. There have been records of many snakes being killed on roads during this migration time. Some private landowners that know about a hibernation trail, will go out on patrol during the expected migration times, and guard the roadways until the snakes have safely crossed.

Reproduction: Mating most often takes place after emerging from hibernation in April. Late summer to fall mating has also been reported. Mating that occurs in the fall results in spermatozoa remaining alive in the females oviducts over the winter. An oviduct is the duct in female snakes, which connects the ovary, where the eggs are produced, to the cloaca, where birthing takes place. The cloaca is the common chamber in snakes, into which the urinary, digestive and reproductive systems discharge their contents. The cloaca opens to the exterior through a vent, referred, to as the anal opening. The male deposits his sperm seed into the cloaca of his mate. This fall mating guarantees spring fertilization. The females are viviparous, giving live birth in late summer or early autumn, usually from the first week of August, into the middle of

Fig. 11.10: Northern Red-Bellied Snake consuming its favorite slug meal. Notice the curling up of the upper lip scales, showing a characteristic lip curl so often described in their defensive behavior, October 1988. The golden harvest pecan color is stunning in the autumn light, and the keeled scales are dramatic.

September. The young snakes are nourished during development by placental organs present in the mother. The average litter is between 8 and 12 neonates, or newborns. The brood size can be as large as 21 young snakes.

The young snakes are dark brown, with a light dorsal stripe, and three yellowish spots on their necks (Fig. 11.9), which may fuse, to form a collar that looks like a ring from above. This ring causes confusion in identification between young brown snakes and young ringneck snakes. The background that the baby is on is a white oak leaf. Newborn Red-Bellied Snakes are between $2^{1}/_{4}$ and 3 inches in length. The smallest neonate on record is from an observation made by Ruthven, in 1906, which recorded a neonate only 45 mm, or about 1.75 inches long (Wright and Wright, 1957). This led Ditmars to make the following often quoted statement: "The young are so diminutive that a large earthworm appears quite gigantic in comparison. One of these youngsters could coil comfortably upon a dime and leave a margin around it"(Ditmars, 1936: 178).

Defensive Behavior: The defense tactics of the Red-Bellied Snake include a partial rollover, displaying its colored undersides (Fig.11.7). This appears to be an inborn trait, as seen by the posture of the young snake in Fig. 11.9. This kind of exhibition has recently been interpreted to be part of an ancestral defensive response to threatening situations. It resembles the turning over and playing dead of the Eastern Hognose Snake. Jordan, in 1970, had found red-bellies stiffening and playing dead when attacked, displaying the vermilion bright red belly (Vogt 1981:160). Presenting the bright red belly

115

Fig. 11.11: Northern Red-Bellied Snake at home in low shrubs and berry bushes foraging for slugs and spiders in predawn hours. The low-angle morning rays enhance the snakes brilliant beauty.

may be enough to startle a predator, and allow time for a quick escape. The snake also flattens its body and curls its upper 'lips' in a form of warning (Fig. 11.10). When handled or attacked, the Red-Bellied Snake will emit a foul smelling combination of musk from its scent glands, and fecal waste, and rub it all over the attacker. Its regular defense is to make a rapid retreat under a rock, log, or leaf litter.

Feeding: The Northern Red-Bellied Snakes favorite food is slugs. In Fig. 11.10, a simply magnificent animal is enjoying his favorite meal. Notice how the 'lips' are turned upward. This adaptation is very useful, not only for the sneer tactic of scaring off predators, but for maneuvering into snail shells and gaining access to the scrumptious meal inside. They also eat soft-bodied insects, earthworms, sowbugs, pill bugs, tiny frogs and snails. Red-bellied snakes are abundant in Nova Scotia, where they are a big help controlling the slugs and snails that thrive in the blueberry fields. Red-Bellied Snakes are great predators of slugs, which cause a lot of damage to the blueberry fruit. They are comfortable foraging in berry patches and low shrubs during predawn hours (Fig.11.11).

Predators: Some birds that are predators of the red-bellied snakes are the American Crow, hawks, chickens and turkeys. The Eastern Milk Snake has been reported to eat these small snakes. Raccoons, opossum, domestic and feral cats, are known predators of the red-bellied snake. Skunks and shrews have been known to dig them up in the leaf litter and make a meal of these snakes.

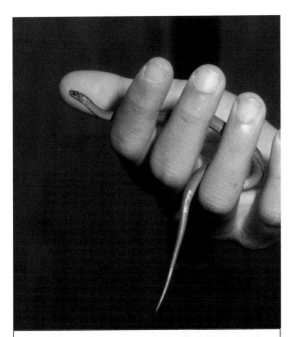

The Red-Bellied Snakes are shy, and gentle creatures that never bite. When handled too much, they may musk and release cloacal waste onto the offending hand, but that's as aggressive as they get. If they were more common, they might make an interesting captive, but keeping them is against the best interest of the snake. These small snakes are susceptible to pesticide poisoning because of their insectivorous diet. Fragmentation of their habitat and vehicular snake slaughter has reduced their numbers considerably.

Common names: This species is also known as the little brown snake, red belly snake, red-bellied_brown snake and the spot-necked snake. In the 1930s, Pope, and Ditmars, referred to the Red-Bellied Snake as Storer's Snake. Until 1999, the snake was called the Northern Redbelly Snake. In 1999, the common name for this snake was listed as Red-Bellied rather than Redbelly (Crother 1999).

Fig. 11.12: A Northern Red-Bellied Snake in the hand is a treasure beyond belief. The gentle hand belongs to 10-year old Chris Guiles, August 1987, a budding naturalist, herpetologist and field associate. Thank you Chris, 17 years later our dream has materialized.

The scientific genus name *Storeria*, honors an American physician and naturalist David Humphreys Storer. The species name *occipitomaculata* is derived from the Latin, *occipit* meaning the back of the head, and *macula,* meaning spot, referring to the three light nape spots at the back of the head.

Similar Species: The Northern Brown Snake is the same genus as the red-bellied snake, and similar in physical appearance (See page 105). The Northern Ringneck could be confused with the gray to black colored red-bellied snakes. The young of the Northern Brown Snake, Northern Ringneck Snake and young Northern Red-Bellied Snake (See page 106) are very similar. The Eastern Worm Snake and Northern Red-Bellied Snake look similar at certain stages of their shed cycles, and from a distance they could be confused, with the pink bellies and pointed tails (See page 139).

At the time that the photos of the Northern Red-Bellied Snakes were taken, in August of 1987, it was thought by most experts in the field, that these snakes were very rare in Connecticut. The few sites that were known were kept secret, to save the population. The photo in Fig. 11.12 was an answer to an impossible dream. Young Christopher Guiles was the dream-maker. After several years of legwork and research trying to locate Red-Bellied Snakes for photographs and study, this young man was the beacon to that dream. While lecturing at UCONN, in the summer of 1987, mention was made about the elusive red-belly, and the inability to locate any for the Snakes in Connecticut study. A young man in the auditorium jumped up and said he had them in his backyard! Two days later a field trip was planned to visit Chris. We took a hike, on a 90-degree day in August, not really expecting to find snakes. Within 30 minutes, Chris

Fig. 11.13: Delicate ruby of Ashford, Connecticut, found by Chris Guiles.

had captured two adult red-bellies, and before the tour was finished, he had come up with a spectacular find, a 3 inch baby snake. This trip was beyond miraculous. Those magic moments with Chris will be treasured as the ruby gems he so professionally produced. A sensitive, enthusiastic lover of all things great and small, Chris was an excellent student, and budding naturalist. The only more elusive snake in the state was the Timber Rattlesnake, beautiful, demure, and dangerous. Times spent with them were especially charmed, sharing the honor of close up photography in the wild. However, the work with Chris, and the dainty, gentle rubies of Ashford, will never be forgotten. Thank you Chris, seventeen years later, your treasure is finally published. The colors of this splendid serpent may only be compared to a spawning Brook Trout on a golden bed of sand, after a warm summer rain in the glow of a Labrador sunset surrounded by a radiant rainbow.

NORTHERN RINGNECK SNAKE   *Diadophis punctatus edwardsi*

This chapter is dedicated to Sandra and Jim Tripp of Old Lyme CT whose love of nature, and enthusiasm for education and healing, have led to an exciting Mill Pond Restoration Project named The Tributary Mill Conservancy. The Center is a dream come true for Sandy and Jim, and their sons Morey and Greg. Conservation and love of life is our theme. Preserving respect for all forms of life, through education and passion for peaceful coexistence is our dream.

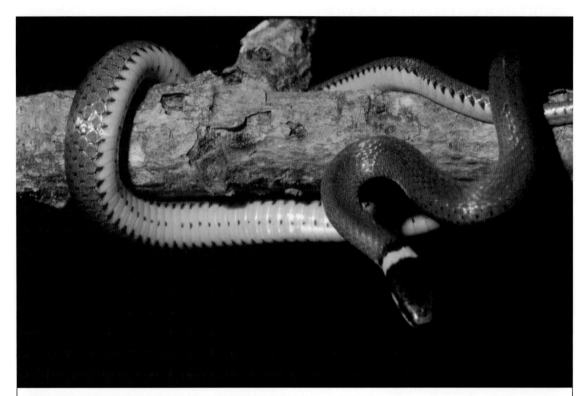

Fig. 12.1: Beautiful representative of the Northern Ringneck Snake. The apricot-yellow belly of this subspecies usually has no black spots on its belly. Some however, such as the elegant blue-gray slate colored animal illustrated here, have tiny black dots, intermittently scattered in a partial row down the center of the belly. This splendid Ringneck was found by 10-year old field associate Evan Kirk, June 2001 in Old Lyme CT. Notice the yellow neck collar, smooth scales and black spots bordering both sides of the belly scales.

Description: The Northern Ringneck Snake, *Diadophis punctatus edwardsi,* is one of 12 subspecies of *Diadophis punctatus*. It is a small, slender, dark colored snake, with a golden collar around its neck. The adults average between 10 and 15 inches. The record length is 27$^{11/16}$ inches. This dark, moderately slender woodland snake has a body diameter of between 1/4 and 3/8 of an inch. The dorsal ground color varies from slate gray (Fig 12.2), to black (Fig. 12.3). The scales are smooth with single apical pits (Fig. 12.1),

Fig. 12.2: Slate smoky gray color phase Northern Ringneck, June 1983.

Fig. 12.3: Black color phase Northern Ringneck, May 1983.

120

Fig. 12.4: Gun-metal gray, Northern Ringneck Snake illustrating the pebbled effect created by the apical pits or depressions on eaach smooth scale. Notice the collar behind the head on this satin serpent changes from yellow to a creamy white as it joins with the white chin and neck. The uniform tubular shape and tapered tail are well documented.

or depressions, which give the snake an iridescent, pebbly satin luster (Fig. 12.4).

The scales row count of 15 at the neck, midbody, and tail, gives the snake a uniform tubular shape (Fig. 12.4). The anal plate is divided (Fig. 6.1-e). The head joins the body with only a small visible neck. The ring, or collar around the neck is 2 to 4 scales rows deep, and may vary from pale lemon yellow to tangerine orange. It is outlined by the dark head and by a black line behind the collar where the body joins the neck. The snout is nearly truncate, having a square, flat, broad shape, when viewed from above. The head is distinctly flattened above, and the widest portion is at the area of the angle of the jaw. There are usually 17-18 maxillary teeth on each side of the mouth. The last two teeth are slightly larger than the front ones, and are separated from the rest of the teeth by a very short interspace called a diastema. The mandibular teeth on the lower jaw average 20, the palatine teeth on the upper palate average 10, and there are 20 ptery-

Fig. 12.5: Northern Ringneck with apricot-yellow belly with no mid-verntral spots. Defensive feigning death roll illustrated above is often mentioned in literature, but rarely seen in this subspecies. This elegant female was donated by Sandra and Jim Tripp, July 2003, Old Lyme CT.

Fig. 12.6: Female Northern Ringneck Snake with stub tail, indicating a close encounter with a predator. She is in a preferred habitat area of moist moss in a forested area between a quaking bog and rock ledges in Old Lyme CT, June 1988.

goid teeth (Fig. 2.2). There is a slight taper behind the ring, forming a small neck indentation. The body maintains a uniform width to the vent. The tail tapers to a horny tip (Fig. 12.4). The entire ventral, or belly surface, from the white chin to the tip of the tail is either yellow or orange (Fig. 12.5). The ends of each ventral scale or scute are tipped with black (Fig. 12.1). This creates the appearance of a black longitudinal line between the belly and lateral scales running the length of the body. It marks the margin where the belly scales meet the shimmering smooth lateral scales. There are also some midventral black dots in the same photo, which occur on the center of most of the ventral scales from the chin to about 1/3 the length of the body. The dots then become scattered in a random pattern, with no dots on the last half of the body.

Sexual Dimorphism: The tail in ringneck snakes tapers gradually in males, and more suddenly in females. The tail of the male averages 23% of his total length, while the females tail averages 20% of her entire length. Mature males possess small but definite anal ridges (Blanchard, 1942: 106). Males reach maturity at about 8 inches. Females are sexually mature at about 10 inches and possess no anal ridges. Males and females are similar in size, with the gravid females being heavier during their pregnancy.

Head scales: Location and identification of all scale characteristics can be understood by studying Fig. 12.6. The head is noticeably flattened and glossy black, with tan flecking. The top of the head is darker than the body. The black of the head extends down to the upper border of the rostrum and upper supralabial lip scales. The eye is small, with a dark brown iris, and difficult to distinguish on the black background of the

122

Fig. 12.7: Close-up of head scales of Northern Ringneck Snake. Notice the small eye, large nostril and yellow-orange ring at the base of the head, bordered on both sides by black scales. The ring is about 2 sale rows deep. Notice how the black head color outlines the upper supralabial lip scales.

head. To help identify the scales discussed in this section, refer to Fig. 6.2 (a-b). There are 2 postocular scales behind the eye, and 2 small preocular scales in front of the eye. The upper preocular is in contact with the supraocular eyebrow scale above, and the prefrontal plate. The lower preocular is in contact with the loreal scale and the 4th supralabial lip scale. The upper orbit of the eye is marked by the eyebrow or supraocular scale, and the lower margin is bordered by the 4th and 5th upper labial scales. The internasal head shields and rostrum are tan, which give the rounded, broad snout a lighter color than the top of the head. The tan color may continue through the upper portion of the eye. The rostrum has a black line through the middle of the scale, which runs from the nostril and single nasal scale, through the loreal scale, to the eye, along the top margin of the upper labials, or lip scales. The nostril is large, and seems to fill the entire area of the nasal scale. The dark line outlining the 8 white, or cream colored upper labials, and neck, along with the apricot-yellow ring, provide a dramatic identification characteristic. The brilliant yellow collar or ring is 2 to 3 scales rows deep. The dark apricot yellow of the collar changes to the same cream-color as the neck and lip scales (Fig. 12.7). The black from the head extends onto a few dorsal and lateral scales, posterior to the ring. This makes the yellow ring stand out even more dramatically. The ventral part of the ring marks the beginning of the belly, which changes from white, or cream to yellow or orange. Identification, number and placement of head and facial scales are important in distinguishing different species and subspecies.

Range: The Northern Ringneck Snakes range is from Nova Scotia to northeastern

Fig. 12.8: Male Northern Ringneck Snake in upland habitat, rocky area above quaking bog. Habitat is shared with Northern Copperhead, Black Rat, Northern Black Racer, Eastern Ribbon and Eastern Worm Snakes.

Minnesota; south through the uplands to northern Georgia and northeast Alabama; north in the Mississippi Valley to the southeastern tip of Illinois. It is absent from large areas in Wisconsin, Indiana and Ohio.

In Connecticut, the ringneck snake is found from sea level, to Connecticut's highest elevations on the Taconic Uplift, in the northwestern corner of Litchfield County. The ringneck snake is presently secure in Connecticut (Klemens, 2000: 61).

Habitat: The ringneck snake is reported from a variety of habitats in Connecticut, ranging from pitch pine barrens to hemlock ravines. It is most frequently encountered under flat stones and logs, or beneath the loose bark of decaying stumps. The preferred habitats are cool forested areas. In southeastern Connecticut, the forested areas contain oak, hemlock and mountain laurel. They are particularly drawn to cutover timbered areas with abundant ground cover, and rocky wooded hillsides (Fig.12.8), near bogs, swamps, and streams, with mossy areas (Fig 12.6). They are found under the loose rotten bark of fallen trees, especially hemlocks, in old logs channeled by insects or decay, under boards or piles of boards that have lain undisturbed for years, and in piles of hemlock bark. With the massive death and decay of Connecticut's Hemlock groves in the past 10 years, the ringneck habitat has expanded. Ditmars (1907:335) refers to finding ringneck snakes under the bark of trees infested by ants. He also found them in anthills.

Behavior: Ringnecks are active from April to October. They are nocturnal and secretive. The Northern Ringneck is a sociable animal, found in aggregations of two or more companions. In favorite areas, such as a rock or board that has become an active hangout, it is common to find several ringneck snakes underneath the same hideaway, for a period of several years. With all the decaying hemlock trees in the southeastern corner of the state, several ringnecks are often found together in the tunnels made by ants, in these rotting logs. The logs provide warmth, moisture, concealment and food.

Hibernation sites include mammal burrows such as those of the woodchuck, rat, vole and chipmunk. Hibernating ringnecks have been found along the foundations of old stone structures with lots of crevices, as well as inside the dirt-floored basements of these buildings. Other reported hibernacaula are old wells, stone walls, brush piles, rotting logs and stumps, sawdust piles, gravel banks, and in south-facing pockets and crevices in rocky slopes. Winter temperatures in hibernation sites have been determined to be between 32 and 50 F (Fitch 1975).

The Northern Ringneck Snakes do not always like being handled. They may musk and defecate, and on rare occasions attempt to bite, but on the average, although nervous, they settle down rapidly in ones hand, and patiently await their release. The snake will often completely collapse in the hand, and cease all movement, feigning death (Fig. 12.5). Being of such slender and delicate constitution, it is not recommended to keep these snakes as pets. They are usually poor feeders in captivity, although ant eggs, and red backed salamanders have been eagerly consumed by some captives.

Reproduction: Male and female ringnecks reach sexual maturity during their third spring in colder climates. Males have active sperm throughout the year, allowing for mating at any time during their seasonal activity period. Female ovulation occurs in June. The greatest numbers of active sperm were found in the female ringnecks tested in May. June and September (Fitch, 1975).

Courtship and mating is a very rare site to witness in these secretive shy individuals. Under laboratory conditions they are inhibited by capture and handling, and almost no observations of sexual behavior has been recorded. However, Fitch 1975: 27, described a courtship observed in open woodland, on September 24, 1959 at 4 PM. The female involved was in the process of shedding her skin. The attending male reacted to the scent emanating from her moist, newly exposed skin with animated courtship movements. The snakes moved out of sight beneath leaf litter. The leaves were gently brushed aside, exposing the pair. Another male had joined the female, and both males were pressed against her. The snakes again moved out of sight. Mating was observed at 5 PM, when they were relocated in damp soil beneath a heavy decaying plank. The female was nervous and active, continually flicking her tongue and shifting her position often, sometimes dragging the passive male after her. During the observation, the snakes often coiled together with the male often pressing his snout against the female's side. The snakes disappeared from sight and they could not be relocated.

The Northern Ringneck is oviparous, or an egg-layer. Average clutches of three eggs are deposited in a nesting site late in June to early July, but 2 to 4 are common. Most natural nests have been found in rotted logs with a shell of solid wood on the outside. The eggs are usually found in a cluster in the soft part of the decaying wood, just underneath the shell, on the sunny side of the log (Blanchard, 1942). The decaying log provides warmth and moisture for incubation. Other natural sites include nests under flat rocks, tarpaper, shingles, leaf litter, bark and sawdust piles, and decaying stumps. Preferred nests may be used by several females at the same time. Blanchard has reported

Fig. 12.9: Female Northern Ringneck Snake with eggs laid on July 2, 2003 in Old Lyme. Jim and Sandra Tripp generously donated this female for photographs.

nests containing from 7-48 eggs in one nest that could be sorted into small groups of eggs that were similar in shape and proportions. Communal nesting sites with up to 55 eggs have been found in one decaying log cavity (Vogt 1981:127). A report from Nova Scotia documented 117 eggs found in a communal nest in Halifax County under a boulder.

The eggs ranged in size from 0.82 inches to 1.40 inches in length, and between 0.25 and 0.33 inch in width. The eggs contain large embryos when laid, and hatch in less than half the time required for the development of the eggs of most snakes. The eggs are elongate, and very thin, with a parchment-like texture. They are cream-colored with sulfur-yellow ends (Fig. 12.10). After being laid, they gradually swell, and show irregularities in shape. By the time of hatching, they've increased on an average of 14 % (Blanchard, 1942:111). Incubation time varies with temperature, and may last from 40-60 days between laying and hatching. It takes about five minutes from the first appearance of the egg in the vent to be completely extruded and deposited in the nest. The average time between eggs being laid is about 38 minutes. The

Fig. 12.10: Elongate white eggs from Northern Ringneck Snake, with yellow tips, July 2, 2002.

hatchlings take an average of 20 hours to completely emerge from their eggs. An egg

Fig. 12.11: Freshly shed young Northern Ringneck Snake, September 2003, with stunning iridescent satin-black color and brilliant yellow neck ring. Hatchlings average 3.75 inches. This young snake was rescued from a spiders web.

tooth is present, which is used in cutting the shell, and is shed a day or two after hatching (Blanchard 1942: 111-112). The hatchlings are delicate satin-black threads of shimmering new life. The neck ring is pale apricot-yellow, and the belly is a translucent pinkish yellow. Hatchlings average between 3 and 4.5 inches. Their first shed usually occurs within a week from hatching (Fig. 12.11).

Feeding: The favorite food of the Northern Ringneck Snake is the slender red-backed salamander. Other prey of the ringneck snake are earthworms, slugs, grubs, salamander and ant eggs, sowbugs, beetles, small frogs, and ants. Ditmars recorded ringneck snakes eating green snakes and red-bellied snakes (1936: 277). Hatchlings and young snakes devour termite and ant eggs. The captured prey is swallowed alive. With larger quarry, partial or weak constriction is used to subdue the animal.

Predators: This small gentle snake has many natural predators, including snake-eating serpents such as the Northern Copperhead, Northern Black Racer, and Eastern Milk Snake. Bullfrogs also have been reported to devour ringneck snakes. Birds that prey upon these snakes include the American Crow, blue jays, robins, hawks, owls, and turkeys. Mammals such as the opossums, domestic and feral cats, and shrews prey upon ringneck snakes. A small snake such as the ringneck snake, is the occasional prey of spiders, Ernst and Zug, 1996 and authors field observations. Raccoons and skunks will raid the nesting sites, devouring the eggs. One of the few times that the snakes are seen in the open is when the family cat brings one into the living room. The snakes are also seen on warm tar roads in the fall. Otherwise, they are very reclusive and unseen unless

Fig. 12.12: Typical defensive posture of the Northern Ringneck Snake is the head-hiding behavior illustrated in this photo. "I'm hiding my head, so you cannot see me!"

the rock under which they hide is lifted.

Defensive behavior: A common defensive behavior of the Northern Ringeck Snake is to hide its head underneath its body (Fig. 12.12). A less common behavior of the Northern Ringneck Snake is to play possum, roll over and show its brilliant belly colors. Of the dozens of ringnecks studied over the past 25 years, only the female in Fig. 12.5 exhibited this behavior.

The stunning animal presented in the cover photo and in Fig. 12.l, with the tangerine orange belly was presented for photographs in June, 2001, by 10-year old naturalist and field assistant, Evan Kirk, of Old Lyme, Connecticut. Evan is encouraged by his parents, Wayne and Tish, in his study of herpetology. Evan also contributed an Eastern Garter Snake and elegant female Eastern Ribbon Snake for photographs. Evans best friend, Christian Tompkins, accompanies him on most of his reptile adventures and shares his love for the wonders and mysteries of the natural world. The other specimens photographed for this chapter were found by field associates Steve Berube and my son Ernie Krulikowski, between 1983 and 1988.

Common names: The Northern Ringneck Snake is also known as the eastern ringneck snake, collared snake, and yellow-bellied snake. The scientific name for the genus *Diadophis,* comes from the Greek *diadem,* for crown or turban, and *ophi* for snake (Borror 1960), in reference to the golden ring around the snakes neck. The species name *punctatus* is Latin for dotted, probably in reference to the black dots on the ringnecks belly scales. The subspecies name, *edwardsi* relates to a proper name, and honors George Edwards, an English naturalist, April 3, 1694-July 23, 1773. He was the author

128

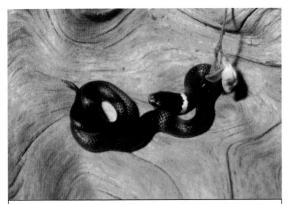

Fig. 12.13: Young Northern Ringneck Snake with smooth scales with light pinkish yellow belly and bright yellow collar.

Fig. 1214: Young Northern Red-Bellied Snake with keeled scales, pink to salmon belly and light cream-colored collar.

Fig. 12.15: Young Northern Brown Snakes with keeled scales, grayish white belly and white to buff colored collar.

of many books on Natural History, one of which contained an index of Lennaean names prepared by Linnaeus (the father of taxonomy) himself. The adult Northern Ringneck snake looks like no other Connecticut snake. **Similar species:** However, the young Northern Brown Snake (Fig. 12.15) and the young Northern Red-Bellied Snake (Fig. 12.14) resemble the young Northern Ringneck Snake (Fig. 12.13). The brown snake and red-bellied snake both have keeled scales, and the collars around their necks are pale in color.

CHAPTER THIRTEEN
EASTERN WORN SNAKE *(Carphophis amoenus amoenus)*

This chapter is dedicated to Phil Trowbridge, a handsome and award winning stone mason from Old Lyme CT. Phil's work takes him to snake habitats constantly, and he honors their right to life, saves them from death and destruction, and when their homes are destroyed by reconstruction of human habitat, he relocates the otherwise doomed animals. Phil has donated many snakes for photographs over the past 5 years, and the Eastern Worm Snake featured above is one of them. Conservation and respect for life are his code of honor.

Fig. 13.1: Eastern Worm Snake, June 1987 Old Lyme CT. Stunning contrast between salmon-pink belly and purple-chestnut back color distinguish this snake. At fast glance in the field, it is often mistaken for a large earthworm or night crawler.

Description: The Eastern Worm Snake, *Carphophis amoenus amoenus,* is a small, round-bodied unpatterned snake (Fig. 13.1). It looks so much like an earthworm, or nightcrawler, that it is often mistaken for one, until it is picked up. The dorsal or upper surface is a dark chestnut brown, to purplish-black. During periods of shedding, ecdysis, the dark dorsal tone, fades to a smoky gray (See Fig. 13.2). The ventral, or belly surface is pink to reddish-pink, almost salmon colored (See Fig. 13.3). The pink belly color extends upward onto the first row, and half of the second row of lateral scales. There is a line of demarcation between the second and third row of dorsal scales. This is where the dark chestnut brown meets the contrasting pink belly color The snakes head is small and the same width as the neck. It is difficult to distinguish from the rest of the body. The head is slightly flattened, and terminates in a bluntly rounded snout. The eyes are small. Its short tail ends in a sharp intimidating spine (Fig. 13.4). The adults range from 7¹ᐟ² to 11 inches. The

Fig. 13.2: Opaque worm snake, notice gray back and pale pink belly. Excellent example of the divided subcaudal scales (See Fig. 6.1-e)

131

Fig. 13.3: Pink belly of Eastern Worm Snake. The head burrowing twisting behavior is characteristic of this snake.

record length is 13¼ inches (Conant and Collins, 1998: 333-334). The body scales occur in 13 rows at the neck, midbody and anal area, giving it the tubular cylindrical shape so characteristic of this snake. Scale numbers are specific for each species of snake, and do not change with the growth of the snake. The number and arrangement of scales is the same at hatching and in adulthood. The anal plate is divided. The opalescent, iridescent smooth scales shimmer with a play of colors like that of the opal (Fig. 13.1). **Sexual dimorphism:** Female Eastern Worm Snakes are heavier than the males, and have more ventral or belly scales than males, averaging 130 scales. The males average 122. The males tail is longer than the female, averaging 18% of its total body length, with an average of 35 subcaudal scales. The females tail is about 13% of her total length and she averages 27 subcaudals. Adult males have ridges on the body scales behind the area next to the anal plate (Ernst, and Barbor, 1989:15).

Fig. 13.4: Notice sharp spine-like scale at the tip of the tail. When this snake is captured, it will press this sharp tip into the palm of its captor, often causing the person to release the snake. It may also be used in burrowing activities.

Head scales: The head of the Eastern Worm Snake is small and darker brown

Fig. 13.5: Close up of lateral head scales and dorsal head plates of Eastern Worm Snake. The head scale placement is important in subspecies identification.

than the body. The elongated paired parietal head shields on the top of the head, look like armor plates. The frontal head shield spreads between the supraocular, or eyebrow defining scales. The prefrontals form part of the front orbit of the eye. The large loreal scale completes the front orbit of the eye. There are no preocular scales in front of the eye. A large single nasal scale, with a very small, almost invisible nostril in the middle of the scale, is located in front of the loreal scale. The internasal head shields and rostral scale or rostrum forms the blunt, slightly pointed snout. There is 1 postocular scale behind the eye, and 2 temporal scales behind the postocular scale. The eye is small and beady in appearance. There are 5 supralabials, defining the upper lip area, and 6 sublabials, (infralabials) or lower lip scales. All the described scales are important in the identification of species and subspecies, and can be seen in Fig. 13.5.

Range: The Eastern Worm Snakes range extends from south-central Massachusetts, to south-western Rhode Island, through Connecticut, south through South Carolina, and northern Georgia, west into southern Ohio, eastern Kentucky, eastern Tennessee, and north-central Alabama.

The Eastern worm snake is a southern species, with southern New England and New York State being its northern most range. It is most widely distributed in the lowlands of Connecticut, but some individuals have been recorded from elevations up to 900 feet. The principle threat to this species is suburban development, which has been spreading across the low-lying portions of the state. This suburban sprawl has resulted in the loss of large areas of favorable habitat. Worm snakes are rare in Massachusetts, Rhode Island, and southeastern New York. They are considered a species of

Fig. 13.6: Moist moss habitat, with characteristic burrowing posture displayed by Eastern Worm Snake in Old Lyme CT, 1983.

conservation concern (Klemens, 2000: 59).

Habitat: The Eastern Worm Snake favors tracts of forested land with a natural leaf litter cover, and mossy areas, which maintain an adequate moisture level (Fig. 13.6). The humus layer, a brown or black substance resulting from the partial decay of leaves and other vegetative matter is the favorite hunting ground for the worm snake. The areas need to be damp, and must contain well-drained organically rich soils, littered with rocks and logs under which the snakes take cover. The woodlands favored by these small delicate snakes have stands of white and northern red oak, hickory, swamp and sugar maples, and peripheral cedar groves. Mountain Laurel is also prevalent. The forest canopy provides a leafy umbrella to help conserve the soils moisture. The soil type is a mixture of clay and loam, with at least 25% moisture content.

Behavior: The worm snake is usually found under logs and stones, which rest directly on the soil, not imbedded in the ground. Under these stones, the worm snake enlarges the channels made by earthworms. Every spring, for over three years, a worm snake was found under the same rock at a bog in Old Lyme, Connecticut in the 1980's (Fig. 13.7). Worm snakes may also be dug up from loose soil while working a garden, or forest debris. These snakes are also often unearthed by the farmers plow. It is a true burrower, and is seldom seen on the surface. This type of underground life-style is termed fossorial. It has several physical characteristics that make burrowing into the soil easier. These include a narrow head, a cylindrical body, small eyes, smooth scales and a short tail. They may also be found under loose bark of fallen and decaying tree trunks. Sites in garden areas and farmlands have diminished due possibly to the extensive

Fig. 13.7: Beautiful Eastern Worm Snake found for over a period of 3 years under the same rock at a bog in Old Lyme CT. between 1985-1988.

use of diazinon. It is a strong insecticide, a nerve poison, and. is applied by homeowners and agricultural workers to control grub infestation. Diazinon is applied to flower gardens, lawns. and haying fields. Unfortunately, it has caused long lasting reductions in earthworm populations, (Potter, 1990). Diazinon is no longer being manufactured (2004), and once the stock on store shelves is sold, the product will no longer be available,

During dry warm summers, the snakes retreat deep into the soil. Earthworms are the major food source for the worm snake, and it is thought that the snakes follow the worms deep into the soil in dry weather.

The home range of the worm snake is surprisingly small. Specimens have been found in the same area year after year (Fig. 13.7). A study by Barbour in 1969 with radio-isotope tagged Eastern Worm Snakes showed a home range of between 75 and 1594 square feet (23 and 486 square meters), with an average of 835 square feet (253 square meters). This translates into less than one half of a basketball court, a very small range for a very small snake! The longest movement in a 24-hour period was 148 feet (45 meters). Most active periods were less than 12 hours long, and periods of no movement ranged from a few minutes to over 14 days.

The worm snakes emerge from hibernation on warm days in March, or April. They hibernate in rotting logs, especially pine stumps, rodent burrows, and woodchuck burrows. They are also capable of burrowing below the frost line, often following the worms down deeply into the ground. On cool spring nights or cold days, they retreat into the ground until rising temperatures warm the earth enough for activity. They are diurnal, daytime hunters, in the spring an fall, and become nocturnal during the summer months.

Fig. 13.8: Female Eastern Worm Snake from Clinton CT with five eggs deposited on June 5, 1989. The eggs hatched on August 25. The eggs averaged 1 inch long by 1/4 inch in diameter.

Worm snakes are exceptionally cold tolerant, choosing temperatures averaging 73 degrees F. Body heat and skin moisture loss are probably the most important factors in habitat selection and activity pattern for the worm snake.

Reproduction: Male worm snakes are sexually mature at an average snout to vent length of 6.6 inches (170mm), which translates to an average total length of about 7.5 inches. Most males have developed ridges on the dorsal body scales near the vent by the time their snout to vent length averages 6.2 inches (159mm) (Ernst and Barbour, 1989), which is about 7 inches in total length. Females reach maturity at an average total length of 8 inches.

There appear to be two mating periods for the Eastern Worm Snake. One period is between April and May, the second mating occurs between September and October (Behler and King 1979:591). The fall mating results in the storage of viable sperm by the female until the following spring. Because of their secretive burrowing life style, mating and courtship behavior of the worm snake has not been recorded.

The gravid females will deposit from 1-8 eggs, about 45 days after mating (Ernst and Zug, 1996: 52). The average clutch is 5 eggs. The eggs are laid inside rotting logs or stumps, under flat rocks, inside old sawdust piles and compost piles or in small underground burrows, which the female digs in soft moist soil. The eggs are white, and elongate, with thin, leathery shells. The average size is 1 inch long and a quarter of an inch in diameter (Fig. 13.8). Incubation is about 7 weeks. Eggs hatch between mid-August and early September. The hatchlings range in size from 3 to 4 inches (Conant 1998: 334). The female in Fig. 13.8 from Clinton Connecticut deposited 5 small eggs on

Fig. 13.9: Two of 5 young Eastern Worm Snakes that hatched on August 25, 1989. They were about 3 inches long after hatching. When first emerging from their shells, they were a dull gray, (Fig. 13.10), but after their first shed, which happened about 7 hours later, they transformed into these stunning shimmering gunmetal gray bullets with brilliant reddish-pink bellies. Notice the empty shell next to one of the beauties on the left.

June 5, 1989 in a nest she made in the incubation aquarium. On August 25, the eggs hatched (Fig 13.9). The 3-inch, opaque, hatchling in Fig. 13.10 is one hour old. The

Fig. 13.10: Newborn Eastern Worm Snake with dull translucent body and soft pink belly. After shedding, the young are more sharply two-toned with dramatic gunmetal gray backs and reddish-pink bellies (Fig. 13.9).

actual emergence from the shells was not observed, for it happened underground, but the newborns all worked their way to the surface within a 5-hour period. The 7-hour old, freshly shed, shiny gunmetal-gray hatchlings, with an abandoned eggshell, are seen in Fig. 13.9. The young were fed small worms before being released.

Feeding: The adult worm snakes are almost exclusively earthworm consumers. Other reported prey include grubs, soft-bodied insects, slugs, small hatchling snakes such as the ringneck, and small salamanders. The small head and mouth would limit their food to soft-bodied, narrow-shaped prey.

Predators: Besides man, the worm snakes main predators are other larger snakes, such as the Eastern Milk Snake, the Northern Black Racer, and the Northern

137

Fig. 13.11: Evidence of predation of the worm snake is evident in this photo of a large female with one eye missing, and several scars on her body. This snake was found on the ground near a robins nest in August 1985. She was 11 inches long.

Copperhead. Domestic and feral cats, shrews, and the opossum are reported predators. Toads have been reported to eat worm snakes. Birds, such as owls, crows, blue jays and robins have been know to attack the worm snake. The robin is often confused by this serpentine imitation of its favorite food, the earthworm (Fig. 13.11). The nesting sites full of eggs are easy prey for skunks and raccoons. Humans remain the most destructive element in this snakes survival. Habitat destruction (See page 133) and indiscriminate use of pesticides are slowly eliminating this gentle creature. Ernst (1962) reported the death of a worm snake, which had eaten chlordane-poisoned insects (Ernst and Barbour, 1989). Another destructive chemical is diazinon (See page 134). Unfortunately, the pesticide also poisons and kills earthworms. Not only are the worm snakes harmed from consuming poisoned earthworms, but they are also starved or forced to move into less favorable habitats in search of food, for their earthworm supply has been annihilated.

Defensive Behavior: The worm snake is a harmless reptile, which neither strikes or bites when handled. If it is uncomfortable in a captors hand, it will smear a noxious, messy combination of musk from its scent glands and waste from its cloacal vent all over the hand holding it, or other predator attacking it. During the struggle, it strongly presses its sharply tipped tail (Fig13.4) into one part of a person's hand, while its head is busily probing in another spot. The posture exhibited in Fig. 13.3 exemplifies this attitude of burrowing into a resistant surface. When found a worm snake usually tries to escape by crawling under a rock or other surface debris. If no hiding place is available, it will twist and turn its head, rotating it from side to side, up and down, in a rolling motion, until it has made a hole large enough to disappear into (Fig. 13.6).

Fig. 13.12: Adult Eastern Worm Snake with shiny smooth iridescent scales, short pointed tail, pink belly, and reddish, purple-brown back.

Fig. 13.13: Adult Northern Red-Bellied Snake in opaque, preshed phase with keeled scales, long pointed tail, pale pink belly and brown back.

Common names: The Eastern Worm Snake is also known as the ground snake, blind snake, and twig snake (Wright and Wright, 1957: 105). The scientific genus name *Carphophis* is derived from the Greek *carph* meaning twig, and *ophio,* meaning snake. The species name, *amoenus* is Latin for lovely, charming or pleasing. This descriptive word came from Say's (1825) description of the worm snake as a being very pretty and a perfectly harmless serpent.

Similar species: The only snake that the Eastern Worm Snake could be confused with in New England would be the Northern Red-Bellied Snake. The red-bellied snake has keeled scales, and more chestnut-brown back, and brilliant red belly. When the red-bellied snake is in its opaque stage before shedding, it resembles the worm snake the most (Fig.13.13). Comparison photos appear in Fig. 13.12, the Eastern Worm Snake and Fig. 13.13, the opaque phase of the Northern Red-Bellied Snake.

CHAPTER FOURTEEN

EASTERN SMOOTH GREEN SNAKE   *Liochlorophis (Opheodrys) vernalis vernalis*

This chapter is dedicated to Everett Lee of Lyme Connecticut. Everett has been the inspiration for many students of herpetology in Southeastern Connecticut. He took young enthusiasts on "snake hikes", taught them the ethics of habitat preservation, and instilled a respect for and understanding of the often-misunderstood serpents that he knew so well. His help in locating specimens (this beautiful emerald included) for photographic purposes was invaluable. This 20-year study would never have been complete without his influence, inspiration, and calm patient presence. Thank you Everett Lee.

Fig. 14.1: Beautiful 22 inch female Eastern Smooth Green Snake from Essex CT, September 1986. Notice iridescent emerald green scales, so smooth they shimmer. Found by field associate Everett Lee of Lyme CT.

Description: The Eastern Smooth Green Snake, *Liochlorophis vernalis vernalis (Opheodrys vernalis vernalis),* is a small, streamlined bright green snake with a long tapering tail. The adult varies in length from 12-20 inches. The record length is 26 inches. (Conant and Collins, 1998: 347). The beautiful emerald green female in Fig. 14.1 measured in at 22 inches. She was found in Essex, Connecticut. A good friend and field associate, Everett R. Lee, found this snake in August 1986. The Eastern Smooth Green Snake is a moderately small snake with a uniformly bright green back. The belly of this brilliant green snake is usually a soft yellow. The head is slightly wider than the neck. The scales of the Eastern Smooth Green Snake are smooth; hence, the name smooth green snake. The scales are in rows of 15 at midbody, and the anal plate is divided (Fig.6.1:b&e).

Fig. 14.2: Close up of smooth scales of Eastern Smooth Green Snake, thus its namesake *smooth*. Notice how the yellow-green ventral belly scales blend into the side scales. There is a hint of yellow tinting bordering each body scale, giving a sunshine glow to this beautiful snake.

Sexual dimorphism: There is very little difference between the male and female smooth green snake. The tail of the male is longer, averaging 85 subcaudal scales, and more tapered than the female.

141

Fig. 14.3: Close up of Eastern Smooth Green Snake showing head scales and dramatically beautiful emerald green color. Notice the color change to yellow on the upper lip scales, and the prominent nostril at the tip of the long snout. The eye is large and golden, accentuating this snakes beauty.

The females tail only averages 72 subcaudal scales, and her tail is more bluntly tapered. Females average more belly or ventral scales than the males, averaging 138 or less, while males average less than 130. The females tend to be heavier than the males.

Head scales: The head of the smooth green snake is elongate, tapers only slightly into a short neck, and is deep emerald green. The prominent large golden eye is a distinguishing characteristic (Fig 14.3). There is a distinct line of demarcation on the upper lip scales (supralabials) from green to yellow. The nostril of the Eastern Smooth Green Snake is located in the center of a single nasal scale as seen in Fig. 14.3. The internasal and prefrontal head shields above the nostril are rounded to contact the nasal and loreal scales to form the long snout. Posterior to, or behind the nasal scale, is the loreal scale. Positioned immediately after the loreal scale are two preocular scales, in front of the eye. The upper preocular is larger than the tiny lower preocular scale. See Fig 6.2: a, e, f to help with identification of these scales. The supraocular scale is above the eye and defines the eyebrow. There are 2 postocular scales behind the eye followed by the large temporals. The green snake has 7 supralabial scales, which define the upper lip area. The 5th supralabial is triangular-shaped, with the apex in contact with the lower postocular scale. The large 6th supralabial is in contact with the temporal scale. The change in color from green to yellow, fading to a cream tone, can be seen in Fig. 14.3. The 8 lower labials, that define the lower lip, are white. The neck is white, changing gradually to a pale yellow. The more mature snakes seem to have more yellow bellies, with the younger snakes having a whiter belly color (Fig.14.7). The angle of the jaw lifts, giving the impression of a smile (Fig. 14.3), which emphasizes the gentle natural beauty of this ele-

Fig. 14.4: Notice dramatic iridescent greens and yellows on this elegant Eastern Smooth Green Snake.

gant animal. Notice how dominant the eye appears. The iris surrounding the round pupil presents an outstanding golden yellow halo, which is outlined in black.

An interesting color change occurs following the death of a smooth green snake. The postmortem snake turns blue. A discussion of pigment containing cells might help explain this phenomenon. All colors except blue arise from color cells called chromatophores, which are embedded in the deepest layer, or dermis of the skin. There are four main types of chromatophores. Melanophores contain melanin, a dark pigment, which can produce shades of black, browns, depending on the thickness, or density of melanin present, and the amount of, and position of, the melanophores in the skin. Melanin, is the dominant pigment in snakes. Xanthophores contain carotenoids, and pteridines, which are pigments that produce shades of yellow or orange. Erythorphores also contain carotenoids and pteridines, which produce shades of red and orange. Iridophores contain purines, which are colorless, crystalline compounds, which have reflective properties, and are often iridescent. Some shiny smooth-scaled snakes such as the Eastern Smooth Green Snake appear iridescent, due to the play of light on the scales outer surfaces, and on the buried iridophores (See Fig. 14.4). Blue color is a result of a scattering of light from the scales surface and subsurface. The various chromatophores are stacked in layers in the skin. The different arrangements of these color cells produce the range of colors seen in snakes. Green snakes appear green because the blue of scattered light combines visually with the yellow of the xanthophores, thus producing a green color. The yellow pigment, which is a fat-based compound, breaks down when the snake dies, and the skin slowly changes from green to blue (Ernst and Zug, 1996: 34). Preserved specimens are also blue (Vogt 1981: 132).

143

Fig. 14.5: Juvenile Eastern Smooth Green Snake demonstrating climbing ability and excellent camouflage. Notice the brown-gray hue of the young snake, compared to the deep emerald green of the adult, in Fig. 14.4.

Range: The range of the Eastern Smooth Green Snake extends from Nova Scotia, westward to southern Ontario, into central Minnesota to southern Wisconsin, Michigan, to northeastern Ohio, to the Appalachians of Virginia and West Virginia, north throughout New England (DeGraaf and Rudis 1983: 69). There has been some discussion between herpetologists about the species and subspecies definition of the smooth green snake. Most authorities continue to describe the Eastern and Western Smooth Green Snakes as separate subspecies, but some authorities consider them as different races, but not subject to the subspecies categories (Conant and Collins, 1998: 9, 10, 347). This text defines the Eastern Smooth Snake as a separate subspecies with a separate range, while Peterson's Field Guide by Conant and Collins, 1998, combines the ranges of the Eastern and Western Smooth Green Snakes into one large area.

The New England Natural Heritage Program of the Nature Conservancy has listed reptiles and amphibians according to their relative rarity and endangerment for all the New England States. The Eastern Smooth Green Snake, has been ranked R, rare, on Connecticut's concerned list. Small populations are widespread in the state, but are limited in overall frequency of occurrence in relation to other animals in the same family. The Conservancy has also listed the smooth green snake as T, state threatened. This refers to animals that have been undergoing a long-term decline in the state. The smooth green snake is becoming depleted to the point where it is approaching "endangered" status. Natural or man-induced events may be responsible for this decline. These lists are unofficial, and are meant for future consideration of the species status. No legal status has been provided (DeGraaf and Rudis 1983: 8-10).

144

Smooth green snakes are irregularly distributed in Connecticut. The most recent records are east of the Connecticut River. There are current and historic records from the western portion of the state. Green snakes were once more widespread in Connecticut. Their populations have undergone a slow decline in the past 50 years, due in large part to pesticide spraying. Loss of their preferred habitat, such as open grasslands that are associated with wetland systems, has also contributed to their decline. It is difficult to assess whether smooth green snake populations are stable, or declining. There may be a recent increase in eastern Connecticut (Klemens, 2000: 66).

Habitat: The Eastern Smooth Green Snake lives in a variety of mesic (moderately moist) habitats such as meadows, bog, marsh and stream borders, and adjoining open woodlands. Eastern Smooth Green Snakes are primarily terrestrial. They prefer foraging on the ground, although they are capable climbers. The juvenile in Fig. 14.5, was well camouflaged in the mountain laurel. The green snakes can be found in grassy fields, meadows along streams, around bogs, swamps, and marshes as well as mountain meadows. They are also associated with Christmas tree farms, orchards, and cultivated blueberry and raspberry fields. In Connecticut, they can be found in association with Aspen, Cottonwood and Willow stands.

When growing up in Cheshire Connecticut in the 1950's, little green snakes were always found in a meadow near an aspen grove. The memory of the aspen trees is a vivid one. Whenever a thunderstorm was imminent, the leaves of the aspen would turn up and warn of the approaching storm. The grassy habitat area was next to a beautiful spring-fed brook, full of native brook trout up to 12.5 inches! It was such a beautiful spot with the babbling brook, warm radiant sunshine and gorgeous gentle green snakes to play with. The cold fresh-water springs were so refreshing on a hot summers day. We would often go to wild blueberry patches and pick berries for pies and jam. Delicate little green snakes were often in the blueberry shrubs feasting on the spiders.

Revisiting this paradise 40 years later was heartbreaking. There were no snakes, no salamanders, no crayfish or beautiful brook trout. The stream had no signs of life. The water had a brownish yellow tint, and slimy greenish algae covered the once pristine gravel bottom. The old cart paths through the woods were paved roads and driveways. This was a perfect example of suburban sprawl. To have grown up in the early 1950s, before the pollution of our environment had accelerated, was one of the miracles gracing a life filled with natural wonders. The goal of life is living in agreement with nature, a disappearing philosophy. Photographing these beautiful animals was a way to bring that miracle to future generations.

Behavior: Smooth green snakes are primarily diurnal, active during the day, from mid-April to mid- October. Documenting the blossoming of the dogwood trees with the snakes emergence from hibernation in the spring, has proven to be a reliable guide year after year. When the dogwood blossoms are about one half to three-quarters of an inch across, the snakes that are in deep hibernation chambers usually become visible near their den sites. The foliage is an accurate weather broadcaster, taking into consideration all the variables that also affect the reptiles.

The hibernation sites are quite variable, and depend upon availability The site may be an underground rat, vole, chipmunk or woodchuck burrow. Old trees with deep crevices among the roots; large decaying logs, southern facing rocky slopes with deep

Fig. 14.6: Swaying motion described by Cochran, 1987, as rhythmic lateral head movements.

fissures, and abandoned wells, are recorded hibernation sites (Gregory, 1997). Many references are made to anthills as hibernation sites for green snake. The sites are often shared with brown snakes, red-bellied snakes and garter snakes, see pages 113-114. Smooth green snakes demonstrate an unusual swaying behavior, called rhythmic lateral head movement, described by Cochran, 1987. When Cochran returned 2 captive smooth green snakes to their cage, each swayed its head and neck slowly from side to side, at a rate of 1 cycle per second. It is possible that the gentle swaying (Fig. 14.6) could be simulating a plant moving slowly in the breeze, helping the snake to blend with its surroundings. This behavior was observed and photographed by the author in September 1986 (Fig. 14.6).

Reproduction: Mating occurs in spring and late summer (Behler and King 1979: 640). The female lays from 3-12 eggs in late July or August. It is common to find communal nesting sites where several females share a rotting log, sawdust pile, or small dug out areas under a rock or plank. The eggs are white and cylindrical in shape, measuring a little less than one inch (23mm) long, and about half an -inch (13mm) wide (Vogt 1981: 133).

Incubation time can vary from 14 to 30 days (Ernst and Zug, 1996: 46), and as short as 4 days (Greene, 1997: 128). The young hatch in July to early August. The most interesting thing about breeding habits of the smooth green snake is the short time it takes for the eggs to hatch, particularly in colder climates. Eggs laid in the more northern climates are in an advanced stage of development when deposited. They have experienced longer periods of time incubating in the mother, where temperatures are warmer and more constant than in a nest subject to the colder temperatures. Although they may hatch in

146

Fig. 14.7: Close up showing grayish blue hue of young smooth green snake when viewed from the side, and the whitish belly. Fig. 14.4 illustrates a dorsal view showing the brownish dorsal coloring.

about 10 days, the actual out-of body incubation can be as brief as a 4 days. This may represent an intermediate condition between egg-laying and live-bearing snakes. (Werler and Dixon, 2000).

The hatchlings average 6 inches in length. The young are not the same bright green above and yellow-bellied as the adults, but appear grayish or brownish and more bluish-green when viewed from the side with a whitish belly (Fig. 14.5 and 14.7).

Feeding: Smooth green snakes feed almost completely on spiders, centipedes and moth larvae, crickets and beetles. The insectivorous diet makes this delicate animal very susceptible to insecticide poisoning. The toxins are introduced directly when insecticides are sprayed, or indirectly when contaminated insects are consumed. As early as 1961, Smith commented on the fact that the insectivorous diets of the green snake made it more susceptible to the ravages of pesticide poisoning. In 1972, Minton noted that two green snakes taken from an area sprayed with insecticide, died within two weeks. In 1992, Johnson talked about the need to take special measure to ensure the survival of this delicate animal. Their habitat must be protected and improved where feasible, and the use of pesticides reduced or eliminated in their home range.

The state of Missouri has listed the smooth green snake as extirpated This is a. form of extermination producing total annihilation of an animal by human neglect; destruction of habitat; and poisoning by pesticides and herbicides (Levell 1997). Because the spider is a favorite food (Fig. 14.8) the animal is subject to what is called biomagnification. The insects that the spider eats live off plants that have been sprayed with herbicides. They are also subjected to direct poisoning from pellitized and aerial

Fig. 14.8: Close-up illustration of smooth green snake eating its favorite food, a spider. Biomagnification of insecticide poisoning affects this insectivorous predator.

insecticide application. The spider eats these contaminated animals and gets a higher dose of the poisons, because of the toxic build up in the insects it consumes. The toxins are stored and magnified in the spider, which in turn is eaten by the green snake.

Defensive behavior: Eastern Smooth Green Snakes are very docile and nonassertive. Very rarely, they will feign an open-mouthed attack, but do not bite (Fig. 14.9). When approached, the snake will back off and retreat. When encountered in a field, they will dart off for a short distance and either freezes, or rises up and gently sways with the vegetation. When handled, the snake settles down quickly after a brief hyperactive period, and entwines around the fingers of the handler, docile and gentle. The snake does not bite, and rarely musks, which is the discharge of a foul smelling substance from glands in the cloaca, sometimes called the anal glands. Although a green snake is gentle and easy to handle it does not make a good pet.. The delicate snake refuses to eat in captivity and soon the fragile snake dies.

Fig. 14.9: Smooth green snake, 1986, feigning open mouth gaping behavior, but the snake will not follow this behavior by striking or biting.

Predators: One of the biggest predators, of the green snake is the household cat, and its wild feral partner. These domestic cats gone wild cause a lot of devastation in the snakes

Fig. 14.10: Captivating large, hauntingly beautiful eyes of the delicate green snake. Preservation of this gentle creature is a top priority of conservationists.

natural range. Crows and Blue Jays, are very aggressive, loud predators. Raccoons, skunks and opossums have been known to raid incubation sites devouring the entire nest.of eggs. Bullfrogs also eat these small snakes. Robins have been seen attacking small green snakes, pecking them until they are limp and easy to swallow. Poultry farms used to dot the landscape of Connecticut. The chickens on the open ranges enjoyed chasing and pecking at the little green snakes. Man and his excessive use of pesticides and insecticides, along with habitat destruction are the greatest predators of this gentle doe-eyed emerald of the forest (Fig. 14.10).

Common names: The Eastern Smooth Green Snake is also called the American smooth green snake, grass snake and spring snake (Wright, Wright, 1957:555). A long history of the taxonomy of the Eastern Smooth Green Snake, has been well documented by Vogt, 1981. The species name *vernalis* is Latin for springtime. This could be a reference to the time of year the snake is most often found, or a reference to its spring-like green color (Mitchell 1994). The genus name *Liochlorophis* is from the Greek *lio*, meaning smooth, and *chlor* meaning green. The latest name change came about in 1997, with a new genus name *Liochlorophis* (Collins 1997: 40). The species name has remained constant, but the genus name has changed 9 times since 1827

Similar species: No other snake in Connecticut or adjoining New England states can be confused with the Eastern Smooth Green Snake. The Rough Green Snake, which has keeled scales, is not found north of southern New Jersey.

CHAPTER FIFTEEN

NORTHERN BLACK RACER   *Coluber constrictor constrictor*

This chapter is dedicated to Gary Hall of Lyme Connecticut. In the 1980's when Gary was a young naturalist and herpetology student, he contributed many snakes towards the photographs in this book. The typical partial albino juvenile in this chapter was one of his most unusual contributions.

Fig. 15.1: 52 inch male Northern Black Racer, photographed in Old Lyme CT in May 1986. The slender streamlined serpent has an iridescent shimmer to its smooth scaled black body. The apical pits, faintly evident depressions in the scales, are evident on some of the scales. This magnificent animal was presented for photographs by field associate Steve Berube of Old Lyme CT.

Description: The Northern Black Racer, *Coluber constrictor constrictor,* is a satiny black, slender, swift snake with a long tail. Adults range from 36 to 60 inches in length, the record length being 73 inches. It is strikingly beautiful and graceful, with glossy smooth, textured scales. The smooth dorsal scales have apical pits (Fig. 15.7), which are depressions faintly evident on the posterior end of the scales, seen as lightened areas on the tips of the scales in Fig. 15.2. The smooth scales give a satiny blue-black, gun-barrel luster to the snake (Fig 15.1). When the sun hits it at a certain angle, a stunning, iridescence is seen. The mature adults are all black with the exception of a buff, tan-yellow snout. The buff to yellowish color bleeds onto the infralabials (lower lips), and chin shields in the more mature, older individuals. The degree of yellowing on supralabials (upper lips) varies with individual snakes. The belly is a lustrous slate or bluish-gray, with no markings (Fig 15.2). The scale rows are 17 at midbody and 15 at the posterior end of the snake. The anal plate is divided.

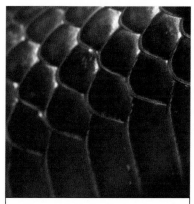

Fig. 15.2: Smooth scales of Northern Black Racer with hint of the apical pits as lightened spots at the tips of the scales which are bordered with a fringe of gold. The dark belly scales blend into the side scales.

Sexual dimorphism: The males and females are very similar in the field, with the females having a heavier

151

Fig. 15.3: Close-up portrait illustrating head scales and color of snout and lip scales. Notice ridged eyebrow scale (supraocular) suggesting the no-nonsense, quick-tempered behavior exhibited by these streamlined, nervous reptiles. The head has a flattened elongated appearance, with large eyes and nostrils.

build, and shorter tail. Males are longer than the females, averaging 180 ventral scales and 99 subcaudals. The females average 168 ventral scales and 84 subcaudals. The males have tails that average 25% of their total length, while the females tail averages 22% of her total body length.

Fig. 15.4: Chin (gular) scales and whitish snout and lips blending into black belly of racer.

Head Scales: The racers head is black with a buff colored snout. The snout includes the rostral, internasal, and nasal scales. The light coloring also blends onto the frontal head shield. The upper labial scales have a narrow margin of white, fading to gray (Fig. 15.3). The chin shields spread at the tips, with 3 rows of gulars between the tips and the ventral scales. Gulars are scales below the jaw between the lower lip scales, chin scales, and ventral or belly scales. Notice that in this mature animal there is considerable yellowish coloration on the lips and snout (Fig. 15.4). The head is only slightly distinct from the neck. See Fig. 6.2, a & b for help in identifying the scales mentioned in the following descriptions. The 2 nasal scales are surrounded by the internasal above, and the 1st supralabial (upper lip) below. The nostril is located between the two nasal scales. The loreal scale is present between the frontal shield and the nasal scales. The frontal shield is concave on the sides: anteriorly it is wider than the supraocular, and meets the loreal and the 2nd nasal scale. There are also two preocular scales present. The lower preocular is very small and is wedged between

Fig. 15.5: Sleek 4-foot racer with raised head hunting posture in typical habitat of leaf littered forest floor. The racer requires large tracts of mixed old fields and woodlands. Photographed in May 1988 in East Haddam, Connecticut.

the 2nd and 3rd supralabials. The eye is above the 3rd and 4th supralabials. There are 7 supralabials and 9 infralabials (lower lip scales). There are 2 postocular scales. The supraocular scale forms a thick looking ridge over the eye, which resembles a scowl, or frown (Fig. 15.3). This enhances the notorious fierce reputation incurred by this beautiful animal. The eye is large and the iris is brown, with a light amber halo surrounding the round black pupil. The sleek beautiful mature black racer featured on these pages was captured by Steve Berube; friend, dedicated herpetologist and field associate. Steve's assistants were Al Corey, and Billy Ross (1986).

The Northern Black Racer is known for exceptional eyesight. Dr. Gordon L. Walls, in 1942, described a yellow lens in the snakes eye. The yellow optics markedly increases visual acuity. He concluded from his studies that the swiftest snakes pursuing the swiftest prey have the deepest yellow lenses. Generalizing from his observations he concluded that diurnal snakes have yellow lenses, the color being deepest in species that are swift and sharp-sighted. The lenses of sluggish and secretive snakes are pale, and the nocturnal snakes, have perfectly colorless lenses (Ditmars, 1936:185-186).

Range: The range of the Northern Black Racer extends from southern Maine to southwestern Ohio to central Alabama, to South Carolina, and throughout the eastern United States. The northern black racer is widely distributed in Connecticut, except in the state's northwestern corner. They are a declining species within the state, having disappeared from many areas due to habitat change, fragmentation, and loss. The racer has an extensive home range, and if this area is reduced because of urban development,

153

Fig. 15.6: Young Northern Black Racer in typical habitat of stonewalls, threading through deciduous and evergreen forests. Notice the dorsal row of reddish brown saddles, which stand out against a light gray background color. Toward the rear of the body the markings become gradually less distinct until they disappear entirely, before reaching the end of the tail. The aggressive strike position and vibrating tail are characteristic of the racer, young and old.

the populations decline or disappear. The northern black racer does not have a special status designation in Connecticut at this time (Klemens, 2000).

Habitat: The Northern Black Racer may be encountered in most any terrestrial situation. They may be found in brushy country; undergrowth near streams; thickets of alder and mountain laurel; edges of woods, swamps, and marshes; margins of thick woods covered with leaf litter (Fig. 15.5), either deciduous or pine (Fig. 15.6); open fields; clearings, meadows and grassy fields; road borders; around farms and stone walls, and rock ledges. Bogs, ponds and swamps are frequented in the spring when the frogs and toads are mating and abundant. These species are very partial to the edges of meadows and fields that are fringed along their borders with brush and stone walls. In such places, they find an abundance of birds, small field mice, and deerfoot mice that make their nests in the undergrowth and stone walls.

Behavior: The racer is an alert, nervous, quick-tempered, active, and locally abundant serpent. It is quick to flee when approached, and darts off to disappear as if by magic. Because of this speed, it is often referred to as the *satin streak, terrestrial rocket,* and *black meteor* (Ditmars, 1933). This species is a diurnal day-time hunter and enjoys basking in the branches of bushes such as mountain laurel. When hunting it characteristically travels with its head raised above the ground (Fig 15.5), looking for small rodents, frogs, bird nests, and small snakes. When approached the racers first

Fig. 15.7: The racers pugnacious, nervous, quick-tempered personality is well illustrated in this photo. The apical pits in the smooth dorsal scales are also visible. A provoked individual will strike repeatedly, its head and forebody slightly raised off the ground, and its tail frequently whirring, sounding like the buzz of a rattlesnake, in the leaves of the forest floor.

reaction is to flee at top speed, quite often upward into bushes. If cornered it will fight bravely and savagely, striking strongly (Fig. 15.7), almost jumping off the ground for half the length of its body. It will vibrate its tail in dried leaves, producing a buzzing sound very reminiscent of the sound made by the rattlesnake. This is a very disconcerting, adrenaline-rushing experience, especially when it is heard in a den site area shared by the Timber Rattlesnake. If caught it will bite repeatedly, or grab on with a bite and jerk its head to one side, ripping the skin, causing quite a nasty abrasion. While biting and thrashing to get away, it will also release foul smelling musk and feces, and smear it all over its attacker. Because of this unusually aggressive behavior, which is a self defense mechanism, human persecution of this animal is high. The racer has been known to approach people who happen upon them during mating season. Stories abound about people being chased by these black lightning snakes, but they are merely defending their breeding grounds. Humans react in a similar manner if so disturbed!

Over most of its extensive range, averaging 25 acres, it is active from late March to late October. The racer is often active at warmer air temperatures than other snakes, often being encountered prowling and hunting in fields on hot, 90 F summer days, when other snakes are resting in cool shelters. The preferred temperature range is between 72 F and 86 F (Ernst and Barbour, 1989:58). Racers enjoy basking. They are often seen stretched out on low branches of Mountain Laurel, or on lichen-covered stones and logs on warm spring days.

Fig. 15.8: Top view of young Northern Black Racer illustrating extensive pattern and light colored mottled head. The young racers do not look anything like their satin black parents. Notice how the pattern gradually disappears towards the tail. Because of this patterning, and the habit of vibrating its tail rapidly, producing a buzzing sound, these young snakes are often mistaken for rattlesnakes, and instantly killed by frightened humans.

Reproduction: Mating occurs in April and May after emergence from hibernation. The Northern Black Racers often congregate at den sites with other snakes such as the Timber Rattlesnake, Northern Copperhead, and Black Rat Snakes. These sites tend to be historic sites that have been in use since recorded history, and revisited every year. They are in deep rock crevices on southeast facing slopes or trap rock ridges. Racers will also use abandoned woodchuck burrows and red fox dens. The racers are among the earliest snakes to emerge from these sites. Occasionally they will use deep caves and rotting stumps that give passage below the frost line. Upon emergence, the snakes linger for a few weeks around the openings to the den sites, until danger of deep frost dissipates. The males seek out and find pheromone scent trails left by the mature females. When a receptive female is encountered, the male attempts to lie alongside her, and crawl over and under her. The male has been observed to bite the females neck just prior to mating.

Eggs are deposited 4-6 weeks after mating between June and July. The clutches range in size from 7 to 40, with an average of 16 eggs. The eggs are about $1^{3/4}$ inches long and 3/4 inch in diameter. Ditmars recorded eggs laid on July 20, that were 2 inches long and 7/8 inch in diameter. By August 15, the eggs had increased in size and diameter. They had a globular rather than symmetrical look. The eggs hatched on September 5th. Eggs are white and granular, looking as though they were sprinkled with salt granules (Ditmars, 1936: 195). Dirt readily clings to the eggs giving them a dirty-white look

Fig. 15.9: Young Northern Black Racer in defensive posture, ready to strike. Notice the stunning half-moon markings on its silvery-white belly. Adults have steel gray to black belly scales, with no pattern. Most of the juvenile pattern has disappeared by the time a racer reaches 3 feet in length.

shortly after being deposited in the nest sites. The nests are sometimes communal and are formed 2-3 inches deep in loose soil, piles of sawdust, hollow logs, decaying wood or stumps, under flat rocks, discarded sheet metal, and in aged manure piles or compost piles. Incubation averages 51 days. Hatchlings emerge from late July to early September, and average 9 inches in length. The young Northern Black Racers are radically different in color and pattern from the adults (Fig. 15.8). The young racer in this photo was rescued from a work site in southeastern Connecticut, by stone masons Paul Maturo and Larry Burke. Rather than having a solid unmarked body, young racers are boldly patterned with a middorsal row of dark gray, brown or reddish-brown blotches or saddles, on a ground color of gray or bluish gray. The dorsal brown or reddish brown blotches are outlined in black. The flanks are marked with dark irregularly shaped spots. The belly is white with half-moon shaped black spots (Fig. 15.9), dotting its length from chin to vent. The head is light colored and irregularly spotted with black and varying amounts of gray. The eyes appear very large on the young snakes. As the snake grows, the ground color becomes darker, but patterning is still noticeable. The pattern has become less distinct by the second year, and is completely gone by the time the snake is 36 inches long. The young racers eat crickets, grasshoppers and young frogs and toads. **Predators** include larger snakes and crows. Their boldly spotted color pattern affords excellent camouflage.

Some interesting folklore concerning the young black racer began in the late 1960's. The following story began to circulate throughout the eastern United States about black snakes mating with copperheads and rattlesnakes. Black-colored snakes, either the northern black racer, or the black rat snakes were said to mate with copperheads and rattlesnakes. The fable continued to state that the patterned young snakes that were produced not only resembled their venomous parents in markings, but were also venomous themselves. The fact that the black snakes commonly hibernate in the same historic den sites as the Northern Copperhead, and the Timber Rattlesnake, and are often seen together, made this assumption even more believable. There is absolutely no truth in this recently invent-

Fig. 15.10: Atypical juvenile Northern Black Racer, photographed in 1986, showing no dark patterning so typical of young racers, as seen in Fig. 15.8. All scale counts matched, the youngster simply lacked the genes needed to create the dark saddles so common in other young racers. This could be considered a partial albino, lacking the dense layer of black pigmentation common in other black racers.

ed myth. It is impossible for snakes of such different heredity to breed. The breeding of copperheads and rattlesnakes with black snakes is as impossible as breeding a dog and a cat, producing *dogats*, and *catogs* (Ernst and Zug, 1996:81-82)! Occasionally a snake will be found that does not fit the usual description of other snakes of the same species. One such

Fig. 15.11: Pugnacious young atypical black racer captured in Old Lyme Connecticut in September, 1986 by a young field assistant Gary Hall. Notice similar look of his adult counterpart in Fig.15.7.

individual was found by a young field assistant, Gary Hall on a warm September afternoon in 1986 along the railroad tracks near his parents home in Old Lyme Connecticut. The snake in Fig.15.10, shows a juvenile Northern Black Racer, lacking the usual dark saddle-markings common to young racers. A discussion of the cells in snakes skins that gives them their distinctive markings and color variations can be reviewed on page 143. These color cells contain melanin, a dark pigment, which produces blacks, and dark shades of browns, depending on the thickness of the melanin layer, and upon the abundance and position of the color cells in the dermis, or second layer of skin. Melanin is the dominant pigment in snakes. When this

158

Fig. 15.12: Northern Black Racer caught in plastic deer netting, the latest human predation on this snake.

dark pigment is spread throughout the color cells in a snakes skin, the animal appears dark. If the melanin is concentrated in small spots within the color cells, the animal appears light colored. The placement of the melanin pigment is genetically determined. If the gene that controls this placement mutates, or undergoes a sudden variation in this inheritable characteristic, then an atypical or mutant individual will be produced. (Ernst and Zug, 1996). This mutation is distinguished from a variation that results from generations of gradual change.

Feeding: The Northern Black Racer is what is called an opportunistic feeder, eating anything that is available. Prey eaten include small snails, spiders, grasshoppers, crickets, cicadas, beetles, caterpillars and moths, frogs, salamanders, small turtles, other snakes, nestling birds and eggs, moles, voles, shrews, mice, rats, chipmunks, squirrels and will even feed upon its own young. There are also reports of racers swallowing their own shed skins (Ernst and Barbour, 1989: 61)

The racer hunts by stealth and speed. It moves through brush and tall grass, with its head held several inches above the ground (Fig. 15.5). It flushes its prey from hiding. As soon as the prey moves, the racer dashes forward in a burst of speed to overtake its prey. After the prey is found, it is seized in the racers mouth, and if small is eaten alive. Larger prey may be pressed to the ground with the snakes body, while it chews on the preys head to subdue and kill it. Many of the insects and rodents that the racers eat are destructive elements to farmers, so this snake should be regarded as beneficial to the farmer and not indiscriminately slaughtered.

Predators: Many young racers are eaten by other snakes such as the copperhead, black rat snake, milk snake and rattlesnake. Red-shouldered, red-tailed and sparrow hawks

Fig. 15.13: Close-up study of damage done to racer caught in plastic deer netting.

prey upon the racer. Other birds that attack them are owls, crows and blue jays. Opossums, raccoons and skunks devour their eggs. Humans are by far the most destructive predators to racers. Widespread habitat destruction, indiscriminant use of pesticides and vehicular slaughter has drastically reduced the numbers of Northern Black Racers. Because of their defensive, aggressive temperament, they are often brutally slaughtered by people frightened by their behavior.

One of the latest destructive elements introduced into the home ranges of the racer and black rat snake is plastic deer netting (Figs 15.12 and 15.13). Many homeowners install this netting around their gardens and ornamental shrubs. The snakes, foraging in the area after mice, voles, moles and insects, become entangled in this plastic death trap. The suns warmth softens the plastic, so as the snake writhes and twists to get out of the mesh, it expands just enough to completely imprison the snake in its grip. The thin mesh cuts into the snakes skin (Fig. 15.13), creating an inescapable trap. The innocent snake is attacked by crows and other birds, is baked by the hot sun, is unable to move to cooler shelter, or to find shelter for the night, is unable to get water, and death becomes a blessing for this tortured animal. The snake in the photos was rescued by Marsha Kohutovic of Old Lyme, who was drawn to the area where the snake was found, by the sound of screaming crows. Marsha respects and loves all forms of fauna, be it feathered, furry or covered with scales! She exhibited courage and caring by rescuing the injured black racer, and has joined in the campaign to inform people about the dangers of plastic netting.

Large black rat snakes have also been brought to the author by concerned neighbors to be saved from the talons of this plastic death. The mesh is surgically removed. During the procedure, none of the victims ever attempted to bite or thrash about while they were being rescued from the plastic prison. They seemed to sense that they were being helped. Fortunately, all the snakes rescued to date have survived. After a short rehabilitation time with food and water, they were healthy enough to be released to their home ranges.

Racers are high-strung nervous animals, and make poor captives. They will usually bite and thrash around when handled, usually defecating and spraying musk all over the handler. They usually refuse to eat in captivity, fall victim to parasites and infections, and are best left alone and observed from afar in their home ranges.

Common names: The Northern Black Racer is also know as the eastern racer, black snake and horse racer. The scientific name *Coluber constrictor* is derived from Latin. *Coluber* means a serpent or harmless snake, and *constrictor*, means squeezer. The name implies that the snake is a constrictor, but it does not constrict its prey.

Similar species: Adult snakes that could be confused with the Northern Black Racer are the Black Rat Snake, the black phase of the Northern Water Snake, and the black

Fig. 15.14: Adult Northern Black Racer, with smooth scales, satin black back and belly, with white lips and chin.

Fig. 15.15: Adult Black Rat Snake with keeled scales, white checkered belly, faint white pattern on body, and dark sutures on white lips.

Fig. 15.16: Adult black phased Northern Water Snake, keeled scales, reddish-white patterned belly and black sutures on light colored lips.

Fig. 15.17: Adult black phased Eastern Hognose Snake with keeled scales, cream-colored belly and lips, white chin, broad head and upturned snout.

Fig. 15.18: Young Northern Black Racer with dark saddle-pattern on gray ground color.

Fig. 15.19: Young Black Rat Snake with dark blotched-pattern on gray background.

phase of the Eastern Hognose Snake. These three snakes have keeled scales, and are stockier in build. They all display aggressive behavior when first encountered. The water snake is found near bodies of water, rarely in open fields and grasslands, and the hognose snake, though similar in color has a distinctive wide neck, and upturned snout.

161

Fig. 15.20: Young Timber Rattlesnake with dark blotched-pattern on gray ground color and pre-button on tail.

Fig. 15.21: Young Eastern Hognose Snake with light and dark blotches on gray ground color and broad head with upturned snout.

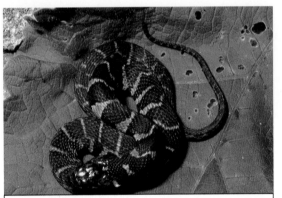

Fig. 15.22: Young Northern Water Snake with dark bands on gray ground color, and black broad head.

Young snakes that are confused with the *young* Northern Black Racer are the young Black Rat Snake (Fig.15.19), the young Timber Rattlesnake (Fig. 15.20), the young Eastern Hognose Snake (Fig. 15.21) and the young Northern Water Snake (Fig. 15.22).

CHAPTER SIXTEEN

BLACK RAT SNAKE *Elaphe obsoleta obsoleta*

This chapter is dedicated to William (Billy) Ross and Alfred (Al) Corey, 2 young naturalists and herpetologists in the early 1980's who were extremely energetic snake hunting enthusiasts, and contributed dozens of snakes for photographs in this book.

Fig. 16.1: Juvenile Black Rat Snake September 1987 from Old Lyme Connecticut. Notice shiny black lightly keeled, pitted scales with a scattering of faint white patterning. Lip area and neck snow-white.

Description: The Black Rat Snake, *Elaphe obsoleta obsoleta* is a graceful, strong constrictor that conveys a feeling of ease and power as it moves. Its adult length varies from 42 inches to 72 inches. A specimen captured near Forestine, Sullivan County, New York, measured eight feet four inches long (Ditmars 1935: 20). The average adult is 48 inches long. The Black Rat Snake is the longest snake in Connecticut, and one of the largest snakes in North America. The mature snake is polished, iridescent black ebony, and becomes more melanistic (black) with age (Fig. 16.8). Some adolescent snakes have a faint gold or rusty colored pattern on their back (Fig. 16.1). The large adult snakes retain specks of white pigment on some of the scale edges of their body. These speckled areas of white are scattered along the length of their bodies. When the body is distended, white shin between the black scales will also give a speckled appearance to the snake.

At midbody, 23 rows of dorsal scales encircle the snakes body (Fig. 6.1-b). The ratio is 25-23-17 (Ernst and Zug, 1996), with a count of 25 at the neck and 17 near the vent. The dorsal or back scales are pitted, weakly keeled and polished (Fig. 16.1). The lateral or side scales gradually become less and less keeled, looking smooth and shiny toward the belly. This gives the body a smooth and glossy appearance. The anal plate is divided.

The snakes general body build has a suggestion of power, strength and weight. Its trunk, when visualized in cross-section is shaped like a loaf of bread. In other snakes, it is more circular. The abdomen is flattened, forming almost 90-degree right angles with the sides of the body. This shape is referred to as being angulate-bellied (Wright and Wright 1957). The specially angulated belly scales have enabled the snake to become an

164

Fig. 16.2: Black Rat Snake in typical rearing-strike posture. Notice the white chin and throat and checkerboard pattern of belly.

excellent climber.

The head, which is shinny black on top, is white on the lip scales, across the lower jaw, chin and throat (Fig.16.1). The lip scales contain dark bars where each supralabial (upper lip scale) and infralabial (lower lip scale) meets (Fig. 16.2). The rat snakes head is wide at the base of the neck, tapering to a bluntly squared off snout. When observed from above, and underneath, the head has a definite triangular shape (Fig. 16.3), which is accented by the narrow neck. This defies the age-old myth that only venomous snakes have a triangular-shaped head. It is widest behind the eyes near the corner of the mouth, giving it a distinct oblong appearance.

Fig. 16.3: Belly of mature male Black Rat Snake showing the change from white chin and neck, to spotting on cream-colored scales, to a checkerboard pattern, which gradually changes to a solid gunmetal blue-black color.

The belly changes dramatically from the white chin and throat, to a pale cream, color, which modifies to a pinkish vanilla with random spots of slate gray. The spotting gradually intensifies, into squarish dark blotches that form a checkerboard pattern. This checkerboard pattern is held over from the juvenile pattern. The last three-quarters of the belly, including the

165

Fig. 16.4: Close up of juvenile Black Rat Snake showing head scales. The adult head is so shiny black, that refractive light rays make it impossible to distinguish the separate scales. Notice the large beautiful copper-colored eye, with pupil outlined in white.

tail, loose the checkerboard pattern and become a solid shiny gunmetal blue-black (Fig. 16.3). The anal plate is divided. The top of the head is a glossy polished black. The eye is large and the iris of the adult is a purple-black color. The round black pupil is outlined with a thin white line.

Head scales: The photo in Fig. 16.4 is the head of a juvenile black rat snake. It was chosen to show the facial scales. The black head of the adult is too refractive and shiny to give a good example of the arrangement of the facial scales, which are so important in species identification. The iris of the eye is extremely remarkable with the threads of copper and black and a white halo around the pupil. The eye is large and dominant. Vision is important in this semi-arboreal snake as it hunts for birds. The 8 supralabials (upper lip scales) next to the eye are dusted with gray flecks of silver. The dark lines between each of the upper and lower lip scales are called sutures.

These dark sutures help distinguish the black rat snake from the black racer, which has no black sutures on its lower lip scales, and only a few faint ones on the upper lip. Below the silver flecking, the supralabials are white, as are the 11 infralabials (lower lip scales). There is one large preocular scale in front of the eye. The loreal scale is present between the nostril and preocular scale. The large nostril is positioned between the nasal scales. The large eye is above the 4th and 5th supralabials. The 2 postocular scales border the posterior orbit of the eye. The second postocular scale meets the margin of the 5th and 6th upper labials. The rostrum, internasals and prefrontals form the blunt square snout.

Fig. 16.5: Black Rat Snake in typical terrestrial habitat. Compare this with Fig. 15.5 of the Northern Black Racer. These photos show the similarities between the two species, especially in similar habitats. The differences are seen in the glossy finish of the rat snake as opposed to the smooth satin racer. The rat snake also has snow-white lips, with black sutures between each scale, a white chin, and throat, leading to a white checkerboard belly, which does not turn dark until halfway down the body. The racer has a buff colored snout, and whitish lower lips, which blend slightly upward onto the upper lips scales. The chin is whitish, but the throat turns dark gunmetal gray immediately, with the entire belly being black. The racer will usually take off rapidly when it is encountered in the field, while the black rat tends to freeze, and stand its ground.

Sexual Dimorphism: There is no color or pattern difference between the male and female black rat snakes. The only sexual dimorphism displayed is that the male has a longer tail than the female. The male rat snake averages 232 ventral scales, while the female averaging 239. The tail of the male averages 86 subcaudal scales, and is about 17% as long as his total body length. The females tail averages 77 subcaudal scales and her tail is about 16% as long as her total body length. The females are generally heavier than the male rat snakes.

Range: The range of the Black Rat Snake extends from southern Vermont through southern New England; across New York, and the southeastern tip of Ontario; west through southwestern Wisconsin, central Iowa, and southeastern Nebraska; south to Georgia, eastern Alabama, and Arkansas.

The center of abundance for the Black Rat Snake in Connecticut encompasses the southeastern hills and coastal regions of the state, from New Haven eastward to the Rhode Island border. They are irregularly distributed in the coastal areas and southwestern hills up to southern Litchfield County. In the Central Connecticut Lowland, they are found along the trap rock ridge formations northward into central Massachusetts

Fig. 16.6: Black Rat Snakes are semi-arboreal, spending a lot of time in trees and bushes, either basking, hunting for nestling birds and bird eggs, or taking shelter in tree holes as much as 50 feet above the ground. This Black Rat Snake was photographed in May 1986 languishing in the spring sun on black birch boughs.

(Klemens 2000: 62).

The status of the Black Rat Snake in Connecticut was listed in 1983 as "**S**". S refers to a condition describing apparently secure populations, although a "watch" status may apply. This ranking was established by the New England Natural Heritage Programs of the Nature Conservancy. Amphibians and reptiles of New England were rated according to their endangerment and rarity. Species are listed according to their vulnerability to extirpation (DeGraaf and Rudis 1983: 7-9).

State regulations: In 1985, state regulations, in Section 26-666-14-B of the Connecticut Code, were set up to limit the collection of the Black Rat Snake in Connecticut. The open season is declared as, a single adult animal, obtainable only during the period between May 1 and August 31. This regulation was established as "preventative medicine." The populations of the rat snake have diminished in many areas of Connecticut in recent years. Collection of Black Rat Snakes by people interested in their pet-trade appeal put a lot of pressure on the native population. Because the Black Rat Snake does not breed until its fourth season, the population is greatly affected by the removal of juveniles. This is the reason that the regulation restricts the collection to adults only. Eggs are strictly protected against collection. Compliance with this regulation will ensure healthy maintenance of the present population of Black Rat Snakes. This is a much better management position than being faced with the recovery of an endangered or threatened species (SCOPE 1985).

Habitat: The rat snake is primarily a forest animal, which occupies many other

types of habitats, ranging from rocky hillsides with pockets of leaf litter (Fig. 16.5) and mountain ledges, to deep forest edges that border overgrown fields of tall grasses and wild flowers. Barbed wire fences and stone walls separate the woods from the fields and farmlands. The snake is often attracted to human habitations. Poultry ranchers consider them one of their greatest enemies and kill the rat snake on sight. They prey upon young chicks, eggs and many rodents, which are abundant in the range shelters. The rat snake also finds shelter in the rafters and upper-story wood flooring of barns and chicken coops. They often enter abandoned, or little used buildings; barns, and silos; attics, basements, and wall spaces looking for rodents. The Black Rat Snake is semi-arboreal, spending a great deal of time in trees. They can often be observed resting and basking with their long body draped loosely across a leafy branch (Fig. 16.6). It will often establish residence in arboreal retreats 20 to 50 feet above the ground, and will revisit the same favorite tree every year. Its muscular trunk and the sharp right

Fig. 16.7: Young Black Rat Snake climbing a vertical tree trunk. Adults climb just as successfully, be it a barn, tree or chimney. The blotched pattern of the young affords a great camouflage.

angle created by the union of each body flank with the belly, greatly increases the snake's ability to climb trees, cliffs, and walls. As the snake inches upward along a tree trunk (Fig. 16.7), the angular, outward projecting belly scales press firmly against the irregularities in the bark. Like cleats, the belly scales provide sufficient traction to hold the snakes body securely against the trunk. The young snakes cryptic camouflage coloration makes it difficult to see against the bark. Large adults climb trees and buildings just as easily as the young.

Summer ranges occur on the north and east sides of bluffs and rocky forested areas. This is not a common haunt for snakes, because it is quite cool, so the rat snakes are often overlooked. It also provides less competition for habitat, as the black racers range on the warmer southern side. The rat snake is a diurnal (daytime) forager that typically stays close to protective cover as it prowls for prey.

Some radio telemetry studies were conducted in Vermilion Country, Illinois to assess the habitats preferred by black rat snakes and two other species of snakes that appeared to share the same habitats. The snakes in the study were anesthetized with isoflurane gas, and a small radio transmitter was inserted into the body cavity. The antenna was inserted immediately under the skin. The snakes movements were recorded and plotted on maps. The research was set up to determine how species of similar size,

Fig. 16.8: Black Rat Snake in typical strike stance when cornered or threatened. The adult snakes will rarely bite when first captured in the wild, but the young and adolescent rat snakes are quite aggressive, and will bite and musk when first handled, but become more forgiving as they grow into gentle giants.

who share similar diets, are able to coexist in a shared summer range. The study involved black rat snakes, fox snakes and blue racers. The data revealed that almost 50 % of the black rat snakes were found high up in trees, and that another 15% were located in shrubs less than 10 feet above the ground. The remaining 35% were found on the forest floor or in underground shelters. The fox snakes were all found on or below the ground, and the racers showed only about 5% above ground in shrubs. The research provided a fascinating view into how snakes can share the same space, and share similar diets, yet due to the different areas of the habitat used, such as trees, terrestrial and underground activity space, each snake thrived in what would otherwise appear to be a crowded space. The racers indicated a tendency to be more active at higher temperatures than the fox snakes and rat snakes. The difference in habitat use and temperature sensitivity explains how similar animals may coexist in shared habitats. Understanding the serpents secretive natural history will lead to productive management decisions (Heske and Keller, 2000).

Behavior: The Black Rat Snake has been observed participating in combat dances. Stickel et al, 1980 described such combat behavior in 1951 and 1952 in Maryland. He recorded two episodes, a year apart, and involving one of the same snakes in both years. One snake had about 40% of its body twisted spirally around the latter part of the other snake. It kept its head elevated and kept forcing the other snake to the ground, while the other snake kept trying to throw off the coils. They drew their forward parts away from each other and turned their head inward, facing one another, forming an

Fig 16.9: 2 Black Rat Snakes emerging from hibernation site in late April 1988. Northern Black Racers and Northern Copperheads were photographed leaving the same den opening.

open-heart shape. There was a constant contest to keep their heads above the opponents. The more aggressive snake was observed biting the other across its back. Gillingham (1980), has studied and analyzed combat behavior in Black Rat Snakes and described the behavior patterns observed in the following 7 categories: touch mount, dorsal pin, hover, push-bridge, avoidance, head raising, and no response (Ernst and Barbour, 1989:81).

Defensive Behavior: The natural defense of the Black Rat Snake is to remain motionless when first encountered in the field. A completely still snake is likely to be over looked, especially among sticks, leaves and rocks. The snake may also avoid pursuit by escaping upward into trees. When cornered or annoyed, the rat snake forms a coil, raises itself off the ground, vibrates its tail, and sometimes strikes (Fig 16.2 and Fig 16.8). Generally it prefers to maintain its peaceful pleasant temperament, and remains motionless.

Reproduction: The Black Rat Snake usually mates shortly after emerging from hibernation. The hibernation sites are often shared with Timber Rattlesnakes, Northern Black Racers, and Northern Copperheads. The racers emerge first, and then the rat snakes, followed by the copperheads (Fig. 16.9). These historic sites are usually on the southeastern-facing exposure of rock ledges, trap rock, or talus slopes, often overlooking a bog, reservoir, or lake. Other hibernation sites include old wells, deep caves, stone quarries, old abandoned buildings, and attics and basements of occupied old homes.

Mating and courtship usually takes place close to the den site, in late April to early May. As the excited male moves his chin along his mates back, undulations ripple forward along his flanks, and the tip of his tail vibrates. The female responds with

Fig. 16.10: Baby Black Rat Snake emerging from egg. The tip of the nose and eye can be seen below the body roll. It took over 12 hours for this hatchling to free itself from the egg on July 30, 1985.

twitching along her body. If more than one male is in the arena, a vigorous combat ritual ensues, page 170. The rivals become entwined, trying to press the opponents head to the ground, not hesitating to bite each other. The dominant male mates with the female.

Fig. 16.11: Clutch of 10 eggs deposited in June 1986, in a decaying tree stump.

After mating, the snakes leave the den area, and start their journey to the summer range. Gestation, the time between mating and depositing the eggs, averages 44 days. The clutches averaging 10-14 eggs are usually deposited in June (Fig. 16.11). Some successful sites are reused annually. The nesting sites are sometimes communal, and are found in rotting stumps, decaying vegetation, garden mulch piles, compost piles (Fig. 16.12), and old sawdust piles. Some individual females will deposit eggs under a favorite flat rock, in a sunny location that absorbs the rays and acts as an incubator. Sites are also found in leaf litter, manure piles and under boards or tarpaper in old farmyards. Incubation time averages 60 days, depending upon the ambient (surrounding) temperature. The warmer the incubation site is, the faster the eggs will develop.

An interesting event was reported by Pope, concerning the incubation of a

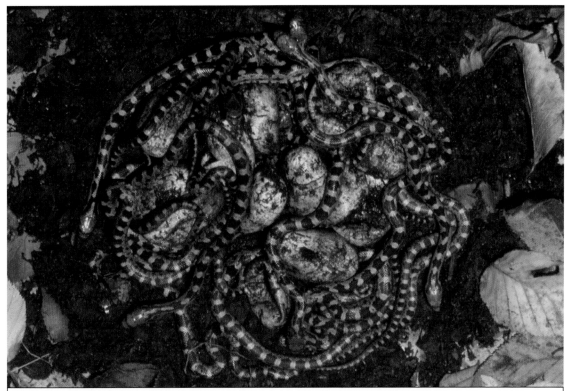

Fig. 16.12: Communal nesting site in compost pile from Haddam Connecticut in late September 2003. The nest was found by John Morrell and his children John Wyatte and Maranda.

communal egg site. Dr. Oliver P. Medsger observed some unusual behavior of two black rat snakes, in Pennsylvania. For a period of 3 weeks, he watched two black rat snakes at an old lumber mill. Their movements around an old sawdust pile made Dr. Medsger curious enough to take up an observation post. The snakes would spend hours basking in the sun on top of the sawdust pile. They would then bury themselves out of sight, into the sawdust. After the third week of observation, Dr. Medsger dug into the pile of sawdust and found a black rat snake coiled around 44 eggs. He concluded that the snakes were carrying heat that they had absorbed from basking in the sun, down to the eggs, and the coiling created a higher incubation temperature (Pope 1937: 71).

The white eggs are a flexible leathery texture, about $1^{3/4}$ inches long by three-quarters of an inch in diameter (Fig. 16.11). The hatchlings range from 11 inches to 16 inches. The hatchlings shown in Fig. 16.12 averaged 14 inches in length. The hatchling featured in Fig. 16.10, after making 2 longitudinal slits in the egg, took over 12 hours to emerge. Every time its head started to poke out, it did a 180, and refused to leave its safe home. By morning, it was found hatched and happy. It must have been camera shy.

The young Black Rat Snake is remarkably different from the adult snake. It has a pattern of about 40 black patches or saddles along the length of its body. Notice in Fig. 16.13, how the blotches continue to the tip of the tail, looking more like stripes than random blotches. Many visits to check out rattlesnake calls have culminated with the resident describing the buzzing rattlesnake sound, and the fact that they did see a rattle. When the young rat snake vibrates that striped tail in the leaves it does look like a rattle. A trained field observer knows that a rattlesnake of that size would not have a rattle, but

Fig. 16.13: Young Black Rat Snake in tight coil. Notice the dark blotches on the tail. When threatened, these young snakes vibrate their tails, producing a buzzing sound very similar to the rattlesnake. The dark blotches, when vibrating, form a blurred image, resembling a rattle.

just a button, which does not rattle, the young rattlesnake would be shorter and stockier in build. The usual residential caller has no such knowledge, at least not at the time of the call. After visiting with them, and discussing the two snakes in question, education and relief go hand in hand.

The ground color of the young Black Rat Snake is a light dove gray (Fig. 16.12 and 16.13). There is a black, Y-shaped pattern at the base of the neck, which resembles the Y-shape on the Eastern Milk Snake. The young rat snake is often confused with the milk snake. A black bar extends from the back of the eye, to the 8th upper labial scale, also similar to the milk snake. The top of the head is a light tan color, with areas of mottled gray. The parietal shields, at the back of the head, are a darker gray than the rest of the head. A dark line runs from the right eye, across the "forehead", or prefrontal shields, connecting to the left eye, representing another similarity with the milk snakes markings (Fig. 16.14). The iris of the large prominent eye is pinkish white. It becomes

Fig. 16.14: Eastern Milk Snakes markings are similar to the young Black Rat Snake, but the colors are dramatically different, as well as the shape of the head.

174

Fig. 16.15: Black Rat Snake constricting its prey.

laced with silver and gold flecks as the youth matures. The light line surrounding the pupil changes from gold to white with maturity.

Darkening of the dorsum, or back, occurs rapidly as the animal grows, and the melanophores (black pigment cells) expand. In its fourth spring, at sexual maturity, the pattern has all but disappeared (Fig. 16.1). The young adult in Fig. 16.1 was found by Tyler Malcarne. The snake was rescued from Tyler's flooded home basement. The snake was undernourished, and after a period of rehabilitation it was photographed and released.

Feeding: A Black Rat Snakes diet includes rats, mice, chipmunks, red and gray squirrels, voles, shrews, bats, flying squirrels, nestling birds and eggs. Some Black Rat Snakes will take up seasonal residence in a Bank Swallow colony for a guaranteed bundant food supply. They will often enter barns and raid barn swallow and phoebe nests of young birds or their eggs. Large prey is subdued by powerful constriction (Fig. 16.15). The rodent is grasped by the head after an incredibly rapid strike. It is held by the conical-shaped teeth that curve inward toward the back of the mouth. A few coils are rapidly thrown around the animal, and steadily increasing pressure is exerted until the prey no long struggles, can no longer breathe, and suffocates. Several adaptations enable the rat snake to eat animals much larger than it would seem its mouth could hold. The snakes mouth extends well behind the eyes, and its jaws are adapted to handle large prey. The lower jaw consists of two halves, connected by a flexible ligament. The halves can move independently in any direction. As the snake swallows, it manipulates it jaws to actually walk over the prey. The upper and lower jaw are not fused as in mammals, so there is almost no limit to how wide the mouth can be opened.

Black Rat Snakes are very aggressive hunters. They occasionally enter poultry houses and eat the eggs and fledglings, but their economic importance outweighs the occasional raid upon chicken houses. They are highly effective rodent catchers, and consume many destructive mice and rats on farms each year. They are also very efficient vole hunters. Voles attack the hair roots of many shrubs, killing the plants. The elimination of these voles promotes healthy gardens and landscaping efforts.

Predators: Adult Black Rat Snakes have few enemies. Their impressive size and strength make them gentle giants in their realm. Red-tailed Hawks are often seen with a rat snake hanging from their talons. The juveniles are preyed upon by the Eastern Milk Snake and the Northern Copperhead. Domestic and feral (wild) cats attack young rat snakes, as well as crows and owls. Opossums, raccoons and skunks devour their eggs. Man is their greatest enemy, killing hundreds every year with automobiles, habitat fragmentation and destruction and indiscriminately slaughtering them on sight. Because of its search for mice and rats, it is often found inside buildings. This proximity to human habitation exposes it to great danger.

Ditmars recounts a story about a farmer that killed every black snake he'd seen around his grain fields and storage facilities. The snakes were drawn to the fields and silos because rats and mice were feasting on the grain. With the appearance of numerous snakes in the area, the farmer was determined to eradicate the "plague" of evil serpents. He fumed about the damage done to his grain, but continued to slaughter every snake he saw. When Ray Ditmars tried to educate the man about the value of having the harmless, nonvenomous snakes on his farm, he was greeted with a sarcastic belligerent attitude. An agreement was reached between the two men. All the murdered snakes would be brought to the herpetologist for dissection. The stomach contents would be examined, and the results recorded. Nearly every snake contained either a full-grown rat, several smaller rats, or an entire brood of young rodents. Even with this evidence the farmers stubborn reply was to the effect that a snake is a snake, and as such, fit only to be hammered to death with a club. "The only good snake is a dead snake" (Ditmars 1933;172-175). Unfortunately, this attitude is still prevalent today, seventy years later.

Humans have inadvertently invented a new death trap for the innocent Black Rat Snake and Northern Black Racer. It is the extensive use of plastic deer netting around gardens and decorative plants. White tail deer have become an increasing menace to gardeners, and landowners, becoming an epidemic proportion in recent years. Small lots of less than 1\4 of an acre are under siege by 3-5 deer every morning in predawn hours. In an effort to save their gardens, flowers and shrubs, homeowners have been applying yards of plastic deer netting to keep the deer from destroying their plantings. See pages 159-160 for pictures and discussion of this latest threat to these beneficial snakes.

Common names: The Black Rat Snake is also known as the pilot snake. It got that name from the mistaken idea that it leads copperheads and rattlesnakes away from danger and leads them safely to their communal den sites. It is also called the black chicken snake, because it will raid chicken coops and hen houses, eating chicks and chicken eggs (see page 169). Other names for the Black Rat Snake are; black tree snake, and mountain blacksnake (Wright and Wright, 1957). The scientific name *Elaphe obsoleta obsoleta* is from Latin derivatives. *Elap* is Latin for serpent, and *obsole* is Latin for worn out (Borror,1960). This is probably in reference to the loss of the juvenile patterning in the adult Black Rat Snake

Fig. 16.16: Young Black Rat Snake.

Fig. 16.17: Young Eastern Milk Snake.

Fig. 16.18: Young Timber Rattlesnake.

Fig. 16.19: Young Northern Black Racer

Fig. 16.20: Young Eastern Hognose Snake.

Fig. 16.21: Young Northern Water Snake.

Similar Species: The young Black Rat Snake (Fig. 16.16) is often mistaken for the Timber Rattlesnake (Fig. 16.18). It resembles the Eastern Milk Snake (Fig. 16.17) more than any other snake. The young Eastern Hognose Snake (Fig. 16.20) and the young Northern Black Racer (Fig. 16.19) are also confused with the young Black Rat Snake, as well as the young Northern Water Snake (Fig. 16.21).

The adult Black Rat Snake is often confused with the Northern Black Racer. see Fig. 15.5 and Fig. 16.5 for this comparison.

The Black Rat Snake plays a very important role in controlling destructive rodents. Educating the public about the snakes natural history and economic impact is very important in preventing indiscriminate slaughter of this powerfully beautiful black beauty.

177

CHAPTER SEVENTEEN

EASTERN MILK SNAKE　　*Lampropeltis triangulum triangulum*

This chapter is dedicated to Tyler Malcarne, a young naturalist, encouraged by his Mom and Dad, Dale and Steve, to follow his love for all creeping, crawling, and buggy creatures. His enthusiasm and sense of discovery at the mysteries of reptilian life encourage his friends, Ethan Makuck and Kyle Krulikowski to share in his adventures of discovery.

Fig. 17.1: Mature female Eastern Milk Snake photographed in May, 1984 in Southington Connecticut found by field associate Ernie Krulikowski. Notice the pearl-finish created by the two apical pits (depressions) on the smooth scales.

Description: The Eastern Milk Snake, *Lampropeltis triangulum triangulum*, is a slender, cylindrically shaped snake, with a small head. The head and neck are the same diameter. The average adult is 36 inches long, with a record length of 52 inches. Two distinct color phases have been found in Connecticut. The brown color phase is seen in Fig. 17.1. This snake has brown to chestnut-brown saddles along its dorsal surface. The saddles are approximately 8 scales wide and 10 to 12 scales deep. The saddles extend down the sides, to about the fifth row of scales above the abdominal plates. The first of the dorsal blotches covers the head and a portion of the neck. It is elongated and encloses a patch of pale fawn ground color. The point of the light pattern is directed toward the body. This is often referred to as a Y- shaped patch of ground color, on the back of the head (Fig. 17.2). There is an alternating row of similar but smaller blotches on the side of the snake. A row of still smaller dark spots is located lower down the side near the

Fig. 17.2: Close-up showing the pale fawn colored Y-shaped marking on the head and neck, which is surrounded by the first black-bordered, brown body saddle.

belly. All the saddles and blotches are outlined in black. A narrow band extends from

179

Fig. 17.3: Red-phase Eastern Milk Snake found August 2001 from Chester Connecticut by Steve and Tyler Malcarne while removing an old deck. Notice how the deep reddish-brown saddles seem to form bands of color.

behind the eye to the angle of the mouth. The ground color on the back has a buff or fawn tint, and the ground color on the sides, is grayish flecked with tan. The flecking can be seen on each scale in the close-up in Fig. 17.2. The scales are smooth, with 2 apical pits or depressions, which give the snake a satin pearl finish with a shiny luster. The neck and middbody scale row count is 21 rows, with 19 rows near the vent (Ditmars 1936: 239). The anal plate is single.

The snake in Fig. 17.3, is a red phase of the Eastern Milk Snake found by Steve and Tyler Malcarne, while removing an old deck in Chester Connecticut. The saddles are deep reddish brown, and encompass the dorsal and lateral portions of the snake. The red phase snake in Fig. 17.4 was found by Phil Trowbridge while doing masonry work in Lyme Connecitcut in April 1989. The saddles on this snake extend down the sides to the third row of scales, above the abdominal or ventral scales, giving the snake a stripped or banded look. Notice the white U-shaped

Fig. 17.4: Red phase Eastern Milk Snake with banded look. Notice the U-shaped white mark at the neck, characteristic of the milk snake.

mark on the head and neck area, so characteristic of the Eastern Milk Snake. The belly is

Fig. 17.5: Close-up of head scales of Eastern Milk Snake. Notice the dark diagonal stripe from the beautiful rusty-red eye to the angle of the jaw, also present in the young Black Rat Snake (Fig.16.13). The upper and lower lip scales have dark lines called sutures between each scale, as in the Black Rat Snake.

alternately checkered with black rectangular spots (See photo on cover page 178). The red saddles and blotches are all outlined in black as they are on the brown phase. A red bar, outlined in black runs between the eyes, crossing over the 2 large prefrontal scales on top of the head (Fig. 17.4). There is also a narrow red band, outlined in black, that extends from behind the eye to the angle of the jaw at the 7th upper labial lip scale as seen in Fig. 17.5.

The iris surrounding the large round pupil is rusty red. The eye is located above the 3rd and 4th upper labials. There is 1 preocular scale in front of the eye, and 2 postocular scales immediately behind the eye. The nostril is located between 2 nasal scales, or 1 divided nasal scale. The loreal scale is present between the preocular scale and the nasal scales. The prefrontal head shields taper down and around the blunt, square snout to meet with the small loreal scale. The labials are white, with tiny flecks of black and brown in older individuals. There are prominent black markings, called sutures, between the 7 individual upper lip (supralabial) scales. These sutures are outlined with a thin halo of nectarine red. The 9 lower lip (infralabials) scales are white with thin black sutures between the scales. See Fig. 17.5 for the scales discussed in this paragraph and Fig 6.2: (a-b) for specific scale locations. The throat and chin are white. There are about 13 maxillary teeth, with the two deepest ones larger than the front teeth (Ernst and Barbour, 1989: 94).

Sexual Dimorphism: There is not a marked sexual dimorphism, or physical difference between the male and female Eastern Milk Snake. The females tend to have a heavier build than the males. The body and tail lengths are about equal in both sexes, but

Fig. 17.6: Eastern Milk Snakes are found in a variety of habitats, including pine forests. This 43 inch individual was photographed in September 1974 in Cheshire Connecticut.

the male tail will taper more rapidly to a more slender tip than the female, who has a more blunt tail.

Range: Eastern Milk Snakes range from southern Maine, Quebec and Ontario, west to southeast Minnesota and northeastern Iowa, and southern Wisconsin, south to North Carolina, Tennessee and Kentucky. The milk snake is abundant in all counties of Connecticut, and no special status has been designated, though many are killed each year because they are confused with the venomous Northern Copperhead (Klemens 2000: 64).

Habitat: The Eastern Milk Snake appears to have no well-defined habitat preference. It can be found in a variety of habitats from pine forests (Fig.17.6) to oak, hickory, birch and cherry woodlands full of leaf litter (Fig. 17.7). They are terrestrial snakes, rarely found in trees. They can be found in meadows, farmlands, rocky hill-

Fig. 17.7: Eastern Milk Snake camouflaged in leaf litter on forest floor near den site in Old Lyme Connecticut, April 1989. Notice red tongue, most snakes have black tongues.

sides and slopes, edges of bogs, swamps, rivers and streams. They can be found in suburban yards, rural farm buildings, and along powerline right of ways. They flourish in

Fig. 17.8: Eastern Milk Snakes are almost as pugnacious as the Northern Black Racer (Fig. 15.7 and Fig. 15.9). When approached or threatened it will form a strong S-striking poise. If it bites the offending hand, it sometimes hangs on and chews, creating mild abrasions.

human altered landscapes, especially where a mix of fields, pastures, woodlands, and housing occurs. They are found from sea level to the Taconic Uplift in Connecticut, which are the state's highest peaks (Klemens, 2000: 64).

Behavior: Milk snakes are often found when dismantling old buildings, decks and stone walls. Wherever mice are found, the milk snake may also be found. Foraging milk snakes are rarely found during the day. Individuals are invariably found under flat stones, the bark of rotting logs or stumps, boards, pieces of discarded sheet metal, tarpaper, stone walls, and any debris that provides cover (Fig.17.9). Basking in the sun is not a common behavior for milk snakes. They obtain body heat by having

Fig. 17.9: Eastern Milk Snake found under old boards at an old foundation. The snake is in preshed opaque mode, to shed in about 5 days

contact with the underside of the sun-warmed objects under which they take cover.

Their cryptic color affords fantastic camouflage in almost any landscape (Fig. 17.7). Notice the snakes red tongue. Most nonvenomous snakes have black tongues. When encountered in the field, or sighting prey, they will form a coil, and strike quite viciously (Fig. 17.8), vibrating their tail, making a buzzing sound, especially in the

183

Fig. 17.10: Mating pair of Eastern Milk Snakes, early May 1984 in Cheshire Connecticut.

leaves, that resembles a rattlesnakes buzz. This is a very common trait, which unfortunately causes people to think that they are rattlesnakes, and it gets them killed. It can serve either as an attraction to the mouse that it is stalking, or act as a deterrent to a predator in the area.

Milk snakes become active in mid April. They often hibernate around foundations of houses, other buildings, and old wells. The rodent burrows, especially deep rat burrows found along foundations make excellent sites. Abandoned woodchuck burrows, also common in pastures and farmland fields, make a fine hibernaculum. The woodland milk snakes hibernate in rock crevices similar to Northern Copperhead den sites.

Reproduction: Milk snakes breed in late April to early May after emerging from hibernation. The courting pair in Fig. 17.10, was found by field associate Ernie Krulikowski in early May 1984 in Cheshire, Connecticut. They were found near an old farm under the power lines right of way. The habitat is hilly, with stone walls and rock piles separated by swamps in the valleys. When a mate is found, the male tries to crawl alongside the female. He will occasionally wrap coils around her body. He then crawls over and under the female waiting for a receptive

Fig. 17.11: Eastern Milk Snake eggs, June 2, 1986

moment. When the female is receptive, she lifts her tail off the ground. In the final stages

184

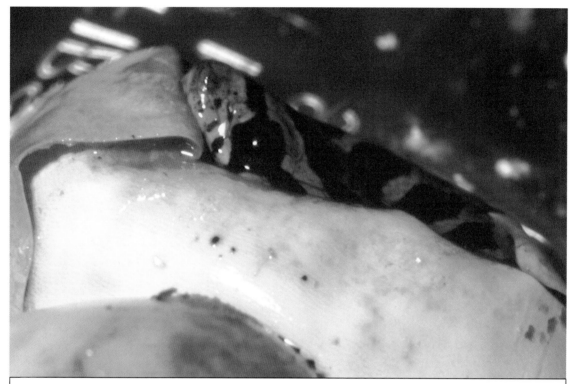

Fig. 17.12: Hatchling Eastern Milk Snake July 28, 1986. The egg tooth used to slice the leathery egg can be seen on the tip of the snakes snout, disappearing shortly after birth. It took 6-12 hours to hatch.

of mating, the male may grasp the head or neck of the female (Tyning 1991: 327).

Eastern Milk Snakes are oviparous, laying clutches of 6-18 eggs. The eggs are long white, and cylindrically oval. They are leathery, and have a smooth texture resembling the surface of a toadstool (Ditmars 1936: 241). The average size of the eggs is $1^{1/3}$ inches long, by **1/2** inch in diameter. Female milk snakes will often gather at communal nesting sites in decaying logs, in loose soil under incubation planks, pieces of plywood or discarded sheetmetal. The sites are in places that get the warm afternoon sunshine, but have enough humidity to avoid dehydration. Most eggs are deposited between June and July, depending upon the climate. Warm spring temperatures lead to earlier mating and earlier egg laying. The eggs in Fig.17.11 were found on June 2, 1986. The nine eggs were kept in the damp wood pulp from a decaying hemlock log in which they were found. The incubation temperature was maintained at about 80 degrees during the day and 70 degrees at night. The average incubation time is about 60 days. The hatchlings began emerging on July 28 (Fig. 17.12), 56 days after the eggs were found. The hatchling in Fig. 17.13

Fig. 17.13: Hatchling with yolk sac, which was absorbed in about 48 hours.

was unable to extract itself from the shell. The shell was surgically removed, and the egg

185

Fig. 17.14: Young Eastern Milk Snake, September 1986. The snake was about 10.5 inches long with bright rusty red saddles, giving it the popular name "red adder." It was found by Linda Stark of Old Lyme Connecticut in a site shared by the Northern Copperhead.

yolk was absorbed within about 48 hours. Notice the unusual mark on the top of the hatchlings head. Some say it resembles the sign of the devil, an interesting analogy, considering the snakes reputation. The young snakes were healthy and robust, and were released to a milk snake range of about 15 acres, on a farm in Southington, Connecticut.

The hatchling milk snakes are about 8.5 inches long but grow rapidly. After the first shed, the young snake adds about three quarters of an inch to its length, and that is usually within an hour of birth. The young milk snakes have the same patterning as the adults, but the saddles and blotches are dark rusty red (Fig.17.14). This is where the vernacular, or nickname, "red adder" stems from.

Feeding: The young snakes head and mouth are so small, and the body so narrow, that it must eat slender prey such as other hatchling snakes that share their habitat. These hatchlings include ringneck snakes, and brown snakes. They also eat young frogs and salamanders. Adults are nocturnal, hunting at night for small rodents. They are known for their constricting powers. They will grasp their prey by the head and rapidly wrap coils around the rodent. Each time the animal exhales, the snake squeezes a little harder until the animal suffocates. Smaller prey is usually swallowed alive. The head and mouth of the milk snake never gets very large, not allowing it to consume large rodents. It specializes in young mice, rats, voles and chipmunks. Shrews, frogs and nestling ground birds are also consumed. The forest dwelling Eastern Milk Snakes are found in the same habitats as the Black Rat, Northern Black Racer, Northern Ringneck and Northern Copperhead. This is especially true in the fall, when the young snakes appear and provide easy meals for the milk snake. This might also indicate similar hibernation sites.

Fig. 17.15: Adult Eastern Milk Snake.

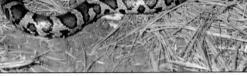

Fig. 17.16: Juvenile Northern Copperhead

Fig. 17.17: Juvenile Eastern Milk Snake.

Fig. 17.18: Young Black Rat Snake.

Fig. 17.19: Juvenile Northern Water Snake.

Fig. 17.20: Young Northern Black Racer.

Common names: Another name for the Eastern Milk Snake is house snake, but 'barn snake' would be more descriptive, because it would reflect how often farm buildings are entered in search of rats and mice (Conant and Collins 1998: 371). It is also called the checkered adder, the common milk snake, the highland adder, and the cow-sucker (Wright and Wright 1957: 366). The name cow-sucker and milk snake stems from an Old World story about a snake that would come into the house and suck milk from nursing mothers. This is similar to the tale that says this species sucks the milk from cows, and causes them to go dry. The snakes are in the dairy barn in search of rodents, not to milk the cows.

The highland adder name comes from its superficial resemblance to the copperhead. The scientific name *Lampropeltis* is derived from two Greek words meaning shiny shield. *Lamp* is Greek for shine and *pelt* is Greek for shield (Borror1960:51,71). The specific name, *triangulum* is Latin for "having 3 angles", or triangle, which is in reference to the shape of the first saddle on the head and neck.

Similar Species: Snakes that are often confused with the Eastern Milk Snake are the Northern Copperhead (Fig. 17.16), which has an unmarked head, distinct neck, weakly keeled scales, elliptical pupils, a pit between the nostril and eye, and a single row of dorsal crossbands. The juvenile Black Rat (Fig. 17.18) is the most likely snake to be mistaken for the milk snake. It even has the Y mark at the base of its neck. The scales are only weakly keeled, and the saddles are similar to the milk snake, but dark brown to black in color. The rat snake also has a large head, with a thin neck. The juvenile Northern Water Snake (Fig. 17.19) has keeled scales, saddles that run all the way to the reddish patterned belly, and a divided anal plate. The juvenile Northern Black Racer (Fig. 17.20) has reddish blotches that are outlined in black, but the background color is very dark gray, and the blotches cover only two thirds of its body.

Predators: Ernst and Barbour report possible cannibalism in the Eastern Milk Snake. They also list the bullfrog and brown thrasher as predators. Predatory mammals such as the raccoon, coyote, fox, skink and opossums, along with hawks, and owls probably take milk snakes as prey. Many die on the highways and through the destruction of their habitat (Ernst and Barbour, 1989).

CHAPTER EIGHTEEN

EASTERN HOGNOSE SNAKE *Heterodon platirhinos {platyrhinos}*

This chapter is dedicated to Carl Kotzan, a teacher and stimulator of young minds. His enthusiastic teaching techniques involved his students in many field activities, which instilled in them a passion for nature and respect for the mysterious world of reptiles. Carl contributed the beautiful olive-green Eastern Hognose Snake in this cover photograph.

Fig. 18.1: Orange phase of Eastern Hognose Snake in September 1985 from Old Lyme Connecticut. Notice beautiful tangerine-orange background color, inflated body and spread head and neck, characteristic of this gentle "bluff-artist" snake.

Description: The Eastern Hognose Snake, *Heterodon platirhinos {platyrhinos}* affectionately referred to as the Spreading Adder (Fig. 18.1) is one of the most interesting snakes, not only in Connecticut, but in North America. These moderately sized snakes, are, in proportion to their length, one of the thickest bodied snakes in the Northeastern United States. A 3-foot specimen is about $1^{1/2}$ inches in diameter (Ditmars, 1939: 35). The average adult ranges in size from 20-33 inches, with a record length of $45^{1/2}$ inches (Conant, and Collins, 1998: 327). The Eastern Hognose is the largest of the three species of Hognose snakes, which include the Western and Southern species.

Colors and markings are extremely variable in the hognose snakes. The variations in ground body colors are orange, yellow-brown, pinkish beige, and gray. Solid colored snakes with no patterns can be found in olive green and black. Seven color variations, including the young hognose, have been photographed in the past 20 years, from 1983, to 2003, in central and southeastern Connecticut. The most common variation encountered in the many animals found was the orange phase (Fig. 18.1). The jet black, melanistic phase was the most rare (Fig. 18.2), followed by the gray, (Fig. 18.3), olive-green (Fig. 18.4), pinkish beige (Figs. 18.5), yellow-brown (18.6), and the unique gray, white and black phase of the young Eastern Hognose Snake (Fig. 18.7). The gray patterned young hognose snakes were rare, as single finds, but abundant as hatchlings. The adult gray phase has a pattern, but the blotches are light colored, outlined in black. The more common patterned snakes have dark brown to black irregular blotches. These blotches may appear as crossbands along the middorsal line. Smaller blotches appear along the lateral

190

or sides of the snake, and alternating spots are present along the belly margin. The boldly patterned back and sharp-edged, three-sided scale on the tip of the upturned snout are distinguishing characteristics of the hognose snake. The head is wide and distinct. When threatened, the head and neck are excessively flattened, producing a rather frightening, sinister, yet strikingly stunning appearance (Fig. 18.1).

Fig. 18.2: Dark-phase Eastern Hognose.

Fig. 18.3: Gray phase of Eastern Hognose

Fig. 18.4: Olive-green Eastern Hognose

Fig. 18.5: Pinkish beige Eastern Hognose

Fig. 18.6: Yellow-brown Eastern Hognose.

Fig. 18.7: Gray young Eastern Hognose.

The venter, or belly color is a combination of vanilla-cream, tawny tan, and slate to gunmetal gray. The chin is immaculate snow-white. At the first ventral scale or scute, the color changes to a cream color with rusty-red spots. Fig. 18.8 shows an outstandingly

Fig. 18.8: Eastern Hognose showing upturned snout, which gives it the namesake hognose snake. Notice snow-white lower lip, chin shields, and small chin (gular) scales. The throat scales are peach tinted and speckled with orange and black dots.

gorgeous animal! The belly scutes become progressively flecked with gray. The flecking gradually becomes a darker mottling, which blends into a more solid blue-gray bar on each scute. The last half of the belly to the vent is usually solid steel or gunmetal gray. The tail is peach colored with spotty rusty orange and gray spots (Fig. 18.13). The scales are keeled and pitted, giving the snake a pearl finish. The scales are in rows of 23 or 25 at midbody, and the anal plate is divided (Fig.6.1:a,b,e).

Sexual dimorphism: Sexual dimorphism, the physical differences between male and female individuals, is expressed in body length, and tail length in the hognose snake. The males have proportionally longer tails than females. They have a fewer number of ventrals than the female, averaging 126, with the female averaging 140, and more subcaudal scales, averaging 45, with the female having about 43. The males tail is about 19% as long as his total body length, with the females tail being about 14% of her total body length. Females are on the average, heavier than male hognose snakes (Mitchell, 1994).

Head Scales: The photo in Fig. 18.9, is a close up of a young eastern hognose. It is chosen to show the head scales. The color in the adults masks the fine divisions between the individual facial scales and head plates (Fig.6.2: a&b). The dark phase (Fig. 1.18), represents the black head that is very common on the black, olive and dark gray phases. A dark band crosses the top of the head between the eyes. It starts at the front of the eye, across the wide supraocular (eyebrow), and the prefrontals, to the opposite supraocular. This band is missing in the dark phase snakes. There is another band that extends from the 2nd subocular ring scale at the eye, to the angle of the mouth at the 8th upper labial.

Fig. 18.9: Close up of young Eastern Hognose Snake illustrating head and facial scales. The scales are easier to see in the light colored youngsters face compared to the dark colors of the adult snakes which mask the individual scales. Note the black mask from the corner of the mouth to the eye, and across the forehead. The upturned snout points to the azygous scale, present only in the hognose snake in Connecticut. The ring of ocular scales around the eye is also easy to see.

Parallel to this band is a broken band starting on the top of the head at the parietal shields, spreading to the beginning of the neck where it expands to form a large black patch (Fig. 18.10. This is also present on all color phases, though difficult to see on the truly black melanistic phase, unless the neck is expanded. A single azygous plate separates the internasal plates on the top of the head, just at the tip of the upturned rostrum (nose) scale. The large nostril, which looks surprising like a pit, is located between 2 nasal scales. The iris of the eye varies from a buff color to soft olive, with dark brown to black mottling. The eye is surounded from one end of the supraocular (eyebrow) scale to the other by a complete ring of small ocular scales. The frontal and 2 parietal shields are shorter than in most snakes. The upper and lower labials are pale to deep lemon yellow on the solid colored snakes. The upper labials are cream colored with specks of orange on the patterned snakes, and the lower lip scales (infralabials) are white. The distinctive upturned-ridged rostrum scale,

Fig. 18.10: Black V-shaped mark present on many patterned Eastern Hognose Snakes is especially dramatic on this tangerine beauty.

193

Fig. 18.11: Stunning gray Eastern Hognose in sandy habitat in Old Lyme Connecticut, July 1989.

resembling the upturned snout of a hog, is the outstanding feature and namesake of the hognose snake (Fig. 18.8).

Range: The Eastern Hognose Snake ranges from: Cape Cod, to extreme southern New Hampshire and central Massachusetts; west to central Ohio, east central Indiana, and southern Ontario; west to central Minnesota, to southeastern South Dakota; south to central Texas and southern Florida (Conant and Collins. 1998: 328). The center of distribution of the Eastern Hognose Snake in Connecticut is in the central portion of the eastern and western hills. This area represents extensive glacial sand and gravel deposits. Recent sightings have declined in the central Connecticut lowlands and coastal zones, possibly due to the intense development in this area of the state. The hognose appears to have a lower population level compared to other snakes in the state. Reports of declining populations along the entire northern limit of their range, from New England westward to Michigan, have been documented. The Eastern Hognose is a *"Special Concern"* species in Connecticut. Under the Connecticut Code (Sec. 26-55-3-E), possession is limited to a single specimen (Klemens, 2000: 63). *"Species of Special Concern"* means: any native plant species, or any native nonharvested wildlife species, documented by scientific research and inventory, to have a naturally restricted range or habitat in the state; to be at a low population level; to be in such high demand by man that its unregulated taking would be detrimental to the conservation of its population, or has been extirpated from the state.

Habitat: This species distinctly likes sandy habitats (Fig.18.11). It prefers dry areas, rather than wet or marshy ground. It is found along swamp, bog and marsh edges, while hunting for frogs and toads, especially during the amphibians spring mating season. It prefers open or thinly wooded tracts of land rather than dense dark woodlands. The

Fig. 18.12: Eastern Hognose in threatening posture after being encountered in the field. It first tries to escape, but being slow and cumbersome due to its stout and burrowing nature, its retreat is followed by a defensive strike position, with head and forebody spread in a cobra stance, raised above the ground. The entire body expands and contracts as the snake inhales and exhales, producing a loud hiss with each breath.

hognose is often found in meadows, grassy areas next to woods, plowed fields along riverbanks, beaches, and railroad tracks. Many of the animals captured by Gary Hall, an ardent field associate and lover of the hognose snake were found along the railroad tracks in Old Lyme, Connecticut leading to the Connecticut River.

Behavior: The Eastern Hognose Snake has one of the most complex defensive reactions of any snake. When the snake is first encountered, its reaction is to retreat. If its retreat is blocked and it feels in danger, the alarming antics of this threatened hognose snake are among the most complex defensive displays of any reptile repertoires. An attitude of uncompromising hostility, more ominous than Clint Eastwoods sneer, "go ahead, make my day", is at once assumed. An incredible bluffing behavior begins that makes the snake appear larger and more aggressive than it really is. The snake backs into an exaggerated coil, and inhales air to enlarge its already heavily built body. Its head and neck are elevated, and expanded. The anterior ribs are elongated and are spread in a manner that makes the neck as wide as that of a cobra (Fig. 18.12). The hognose snake thus flattens and widens its head until it assumes a formidable, triangular outline. The flattening of the neck distends the scale rows and makes the patterning and colors especially vivid (Fig. 18.1). Air is expelled from the inflated body by rapidly constricting the body wall. This forces the air out through the glottis, an opening on the floor of the mouth that leads to the trachea, or windpipe. The sounds created come in short, violent hisses, as the head is thrust forward in quick false strikes with a closed mouth. If the threat

Fig. 18.13: Final stages of playing dead in wreathing thralls of exotic defense behavior of Eastern Hognose Snake.

persists, the snakes body assumes its normal shape, begins to coil, and seems to go into convulsions, twisting and writhing violently. The head is twisted to one side, and the body kinks. The mouth gapes helplessly open, oozing blood from engorged membranes (autohemorrhage), as seen in Fig. 18.14. The tongue hangs out, and the snake rolls over on its back playing dead (letisimulation or thanatosis) (Ernst and Zug, 1996:58-59). The snake actually has its body's midsection inside its mouth in what appears to be a self inflicted bit, during a final convulsion before becoming totally limp. The flaw to this behavior is that if the snake is turned over, this supposedly dead snake will immediately roll back over again. When left alone for a while, the snake cautiously raises it head, looks around, and if the threat is gone, slithers off to safety. When the snake lets out the loud hisses of breath, mythology has it that it is releasing venomous breath.

Fig. 18.14: Open mouth, tongue hanging out, blood vessels engorged and oozing blood display last stage of death act of the hognose. Notice the two rows of teeth, the palatine and maxillary (Fig. 2.2) on the roof of the mouth and near the upper lip scales. The enlarged rear teeth can be seen, as well as the diastema, or space between them and the smaller front teeth.

An account related by Minton, 1980, recounts a story that took place in 1793, in an area around Lake Erie: "Of the venomous serpents, which infest these waters, the hissing

Fig. 18.15: Eastern Hognose Snake eyeing up his next meal. Hognose snake love toads, but frogs are a close second on their menu list.

snake is the most remarkable. When you approach it, the snake becomes flat, appears of brighter colors, and opens its mouth hissing. At the same time, it blows from its mouth with great force, a subtle wind. If drawn in by the breath of the unwary traveler, it will infallibly bring a decline, which in a few months must prove mortal. No remedy has yet been found to counteract its baneful influence" (Minton and Minton, 1980: 61-62).

Along with the twisting convulsions, and open mouth, the snake discharges fecal material from its cloaca, along with a foul-smelling fluid from its musk glands at the base of its tail (Fig.2.27). If it has recently eaten, it will regurgitate its last meal.

The mouth of the hognose snake has 4 rows of upper teeth (Fig. 2.2), two rows of palatine teeth on the roof of the mouth, and one on each maxillary, or upper jaw bone. Two of these rows can be seen in Fig. 18.14. The front teeth are smaller than the enlarged sword-like teeth on the rear of the upper jaws, which are separated from the front teeth by a gap known as a diastema. The teeth serve to catch, hold and engulf its food.

The hognose snake loves toads as its favorite prey (Fig. 2.9). The hognose has a physiological resistance to the powerful digestive toxins produced by the skin glands on a toad. The toxins are so poisonous that few animals can eat large toads without suffering severe illness or death. Toads puff up their bodies in defense when captured. The enlarged rear teeth were once mistakenly assumed to penetrate the toad's body wall and puncture its lungs, deflating the toad. Experiments and behavioral observations indicate that the teeth are too short to deflate the toad. Instead, the teeth serve to channel venom from the Duvernoy's gland, into the bite, which relaxes the toad. The toad deflates, and is easily swallowed (Ernst and Zug, 1996: 7,8,29).

Duvernoy's gland: Two types of ophidian (serpentine) oral glands are known to

197

produce venom. These are the Duvernoy's glands found in most colubrid snakes, and the venom glands of vipers, elapids (front fixed fanged snakes), and sea snakes. The gland is composed of branched tubules rather than simple groupings of cells, and is situated immediately under the skin, above and near the angle of the jaw. It is derived from the same tissue as tooth enamel. The Duvernoy's gland opens by a duct at the base of the posterior, enlarged teeth. The secretions from the glands flow down the enlarged, rear teeth and into the prey, by the chewing motions of the snake. The secretions are introduced slowly into the victim, by indirect pressure from the nearby jaw-closing muscles (Green.1997: 78-95). The secretions of Duvernoy's glands are colorless, whereas true venom glands secretions are typically some shade of yellow. These clear secretions immobilize the victim and help the snakes digest the prey.

Bites from hognose snake: There have been reports of negative reactions to bites from hognose snakes. In 1960 the late Arthur N. Braggs, a herpetologist, best known for his studies on spadefoot toads, reported pain and swelling of his hand lasting several days after he had been bitten by a western hognose snake. In 1973, a sixteen-year-old boy had similar symptoms after being bitten by an eastern hognose snake. Hognose snakes are considered exceptionally docile and harmless. Bragg therefore believed the bite was a feeding, rather than a defensive response, since he had been handling frogs just before he was bitten. The smell of food would also activate the digestive glands (Minton and Minton, 1980: 60-63).

Feeding: An Eastern Hognose was maintained for a few years as a companion (*Hoggie*) and study animal. It was often difficult to capture enough toads and frogs to maintain its hearty appetite. Many studies have been done on enticing a snake to consume food other than their favorite, by rubbing the substitute food with their favorite food, to put the scent of the desired food on the less desirable prey. An alternative method was used to get *Hoggie* to eat mice (Fig. 1.2).

In the spring, 1985, some American toads were captured as food for the hognose snake. The toads were frozen for future feeding. One thawed toad was mixed with water and a puree was made. Then a frozen mouse was thawed in warm water, soaked in the puree, and then offered to the hognose. Snakes do not usually take food while in shed mode (Fig. 1.2), but *Hoggie* did not hesitate. He could not see the food, only smell it, and he immediately consumed the mouse. The snake was fed *puree of toad-mouse,* when toads were not available. This procedure supports Bragg's theory, that he was bitten because he had the scent of toad on his hands. It is now common knowledge that, if the scent of food is on the hands of the keeper, the keeper will be bitten.

Other prey taken by the hognose snake includes frogs, salamanders, and red-spotted newts. The newts have a toxic skin secretion, which, as with the toads, does not adversely affect the hognose snake. Other reported prey includes hatchling turtles, nestling ground birds, and young mammals such as mice and chipmunks. Insects are often found in the snakes stomach remains, but researchers believe that most of these insects were originally in the stomachs of the amphibians that the snake consumed, thus being secondarily ingested with the amphibians.

Eastern hog nose snakes are diurnal daytime hunters. Their sense of smell (Fig. 1.18) is very important in locating prey above and below ground (See p. 6-8). The hognose snake is completely terrestrial, never found in trees. They are occasionally seen

Fig. 18.16: Olive-green female Eastern Hognose Snake with gray patterned youngster, Old Lyme, Connecticut, 1986.

swimming, with their bodies flattened and their heads are held a few inches above the water line, presenting a frightening appearance, especially when at eye level with them. They are often killed by frightened swimmers.

They are accomplished burrowers, digging into soft soil to find concealed toads, and to create underground tunnels for shelter, egg laying, and hibernation. The hognose snakes wedge-shaped snout acts as a plow that pushes its way through the sand, forcing the loosened soil to either side. Its short thick body and keeled scales help to anchor it more firmly in the tunnel, permitting stronger head thrusts for the plowing process.

Two kinds of tunnels are created. One is a shallow tunnel, only a few inches below the surface, used for temporary shelter. The other burrows are deeper and more permanent, to which the snake often returns. Platt described one such tunnel as dropping downward sharply for the first 3 inches, then continuing diagonally for another 4.5 inches, finally ending in a small chamber that held the snake. Other chambers have been found 8 inches deep and 3 feet long (Werler and Dixon, 2000: 142).

Predators: Predators include the red-tailed hawk, and owls. The young are preyed upon by other snakes such as the Eastern Milk Snake, Black Rat Snake, Northern Copperhead and Northern Black Racer. The eggs are harvested by skunks, raccoons and opossums.

Humans are the worst enemy of the Eastern Hognose Snake. Many are killed because they appear so ferocious, and are mistaken for venomous snakes. They are also sub-jected to magnified pesticide poisoning, as a result of being at the top of a food chain that contains insect-eating amphibians. The insects are exposed to herbicides and insecticides, and pass this poisoning onto the hognose when the insects are consumed by the snakes.

Fig. 18.17: Juvenile Eastern Hognose Snake, found by Mike Naumowitz, Lyme Connecticut, September 2001, with color change that seems to be tending toward the adult orange phased adult.

Reproduction: The hognose snakes are usually active from April to early October. They are cold tolerant, and able to crawl slowly, spread their necks and hiss at a body temperature of only 42F. Their preferred activity temperature ranges between 72 F and 93 F (Platt, l969).

Females are mature when they are 22 months old and about 24 inches in total length. Males mature at the same age, but are shorter in length, averaging 22 inches in total length. The females grow more rapidly than the males. The main breeding period for the hognose snake is the time shortly after leaving hibernation, between mid-April and through the month of May. The male finds a receptive female by following her scent trail. They may travel as far as 5.8 miles during the breeding season (Platt, 1969). If fall breeding occurs, the sperm remain alive through hibernation, until the following spring when the female ovulates. Shortly after hibernation, and after the successful search for a mate, the male courts the female and mating occurs. The females usually produce young every other year. The eggs are laid in June to early July, in nests about 5 inches deep constructed by burrowing into loose loam or sandy soil. Some nests are excavated under flat rocks.

Clutches vary from 4-61 eggs, depending upon the size of the female. The average clutch for the Eastern Hognose Snake is 22 (Greene, 1997:117-139). The eggs are cream-colored, elliptical, shaped more round than long, and have a thin parchment texture. Some females have been observed coiled around their eggs.

Most hatchlings emerge between August and September, after an incubation time averaging 57 days. Platt (1969) observed hatchlings emerging from a clutch of 12 eggs. The average time between the appearance of the first slit in the egg to the hatchling

Fig. 18.18: Adult orange phase Eastern Hognose.

Fig. 18. 19: Adult Northern Copperhead.

Fig. 18.20: Red phase Northern Water Snake.

emerging from the egg was 27.5 hours! It took 55.5 hours for the entire clutch to finish hatching. The hatchlings average length is 7.6 inches. The young snakes are patterned like the adults snakes, but their color are entirely gray, with different shades and intensities. As they grow, the gray gradually changes to the background color of the adult stage. The juvenile in Fig. 18.17 is probably changing to an orange adult.

Similar species: The adult orange phase hognose snake (Fig. 18.18) is sometimes confused with the Northern Copperhead (Fig. 18.19), and the red-phase Northern Water Snake (Fig. 18.20). The black phase hognose (Fig. 18.2) resembles the dark phase of the adult Northern Water Snake. The young hognose snake resembles the immature Black Rat Snake and Northern Copperhead (Fig. 18.21). The immature Northern Water Snake (Fig. 18.22) and Timber Rattlesnake (Fig. 18.23) are also mistaken for the young hognose.

Common names: The hognose snake is also known as the spreading adder, hissing sand snake, blowing viper, and puff adder. The scientific name *Heterodon* is Greek, for different tooth. The Greek *hetero* means different and *odon* means tooth. This is in reference to the different sized enlarged rear teeth in this genus. The specific name, *platirhinos* is from the Greek *plati*, which means broad or flat, and *rhino*, meaning a nose (Borror 1960). This is in reference to the enlarged rostrum or snout that characterizes the hognose snake.

A name change back to a preexisting spelling has been introduced by Platt, 1985. He found that the oldest available name for the Eastern Hognose Snake was proposed by Latreille in 1801, which was spelled *platirhinos*, not *platyrhinos*. He has suggested that the proper scientific name for this snake should be *platirhinos*. Most publications printed after 1985 have accepted this spelling. A notable example is Conant, 1975, in his Peterson Field Guide to Reptiles and Amphibians of Eastern/Central North America, the spelling was *platyrhinos*. In Conant and Collins, 1998-revised edition, the spelling is changed to *playirhinos*. A notable exception to accepting the change appears in Ernst and Barbour,

201

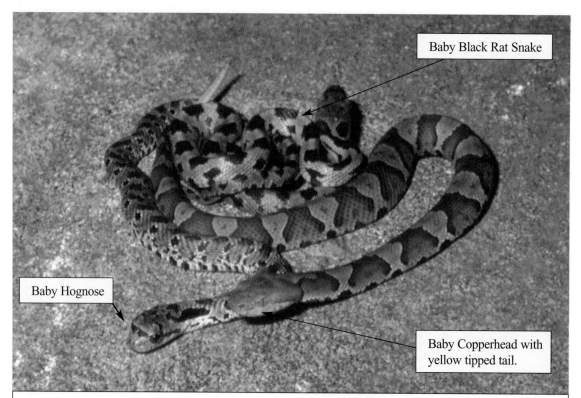

Fig. 18.21: Photograph of three young look-a-like snakes; the Eastern Hognose, Northern Copperhead and Black Rat Snake.

Fig. 18.22: Baby Northern Water Snakes.

Fig. 18.23: Baby Timber Rattlesnake with prebutton.

1889: 38, where it is stated: "We believe that to adopt this spelling now would cause confusion, and feel that the name *platyrhinos* should be retained because of its common use for many years.

202

CHAPTER NINETEEN

NORTHERN WATER SNAKE   *Nerodia sipedon sipedon*

This chapter is dedicated to my son Ernie Krulikowski who has been the inspiration to create this book for the past 20 years. He loves all snakes, but the Northern Water Snake was his favorite, for it was the most difficult to tame, and had the same wild independent nature that possesses my son. The snakes would strike, bite, chew and musk, but Ernie thrived on the challenge, loved the fight, and reveled in the capture and release of this worthy opponent and survivor of a child's curiosity and thrill of the hunt.

Fig. 19.1: Stunning red phase female Northern Water Snake found by Allan and Helen Aroh of Old Lyme Connecticut, September 1987. The red phase is common in southeastern Connecticut, and often mistaken for the Northern Copperhead.

Description: The Northern Water Snake, *Nerodia sipedon sipedon*, is extremely variable in color. It is a large heavy-bodied nonpoisonous snake. Its average adult length varies from 24 inches to 40 inches, the record being 55$^{1/8}$ inches (Conant and Collins 1998: 293). The scales are heavily keeled and doubly pitted, with a very prominent ridge running down the middle of each individual scale (see Fig. 19.2), and occur in 21 rows at midbody. This can give a lackluster appearance to a dark snake, (Fig. 19.3) especially when dry and dusty. The common water snake has been described as a dingy, dull, lusterless, brown, rough-scaled serpent, that has a flat head, a thick body, and looks very ugly (Ditmars 1933: 164). The photos on this page contradict this "ugly" presentation. The water snakes in these photos represent a minority, as far as beauty is concerned. Notice the delicious apple red, and the sculptured white, peach and black speckling on each scale, along with the white and black mottled belly scales (Fig. 19.6), of carrot orange, flecked with black. This is truly an artists rendition of a midsummer nights sunset. The snakes texture is rough to the touch. The anal plate is divided. There are so many patterns and

Fig. 19.2: Illustration of strong keel in scales of Northern Watersnake. Dramatic colors evident in this beautiful specimen.

204

Fig. 19.3: Dark phase Northern Water Snake. This gravid (pregnant) female had 40 babies September 12, 1987. Her appearance emphasizes the immense bulk of these snakes, and dull sheen created by the heavily keeled scales. Water snakes are often seen basking on rocks in the spring and fall.

color variations in individual water snakes; it is impossible to describe them all. Generally they have a gray, buff, or tan ground color. The pattern starts out at the neck as a banding, which gradually changes to 30 or more, brown, dark brown or red-brown saddles along the length of its body (Fig. 19.4). There are alternating blotches, usually rectangular shaped, along the sides. The ones closest to the belly have a tendency to have a reddish color. Many of the water snakes in southern Connecticut have a red lateral coloration. The sides of the snake have wide reddish-brown bands. On the first third of the body, the bands are wider at the belly than on the back of the snake, forming a triangular gray pattern ((Fig. 19.4). Along the remainder of the body, the lighter ground color changes to narrower lateral bands about 2 scale-rows in width. The bands and saddles are outlined in black. The pattern generally becomes less noticeable as the water snake grows larger (Bowens,2003), and often results in a uniformly dark snake (Fig. 19.3). Sometimes, when a dark snake is seen in the water, a pattern will often be revealed in

Fig. 19.4: Typical dusky water snake demonstrating changing pattern from neck area to mid body.

what seemed to be a black colored snake. The tail is sometimes ringed in the same color as the dorsal markings, but it is generally black.

Fig. 19.5: Belly of gravid female Northern Water Snake displaying rich red colors with mottled dark pattern on off white ground color.

The belly colors are as varied as the dorsal colors of water snakes. The chin is white, with well-developed chin shields. They are separated by one row of gulars, which are the scales below the jaw between the lower labials, chin shields and ventral scutes (scales). The colored pattern begins immediately, on the second ventral scute. The crescent shapes become larger (Fig. 19.7), and as seen in Fig. 19.6, change from orange to red. This is also visible in Fig. 19.5, which shows a very beautiful and extremely gravid female. There is a tint of creamy-yellow down the center, mid ventral line of the belly, with gray

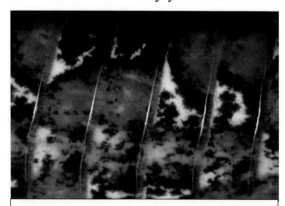

Fig. 19.6: Dramatic red patterned belly of Northern Water Snake.

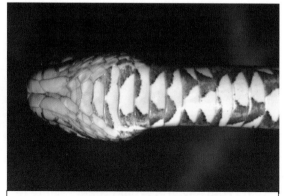

Fig. 19.7: Chin, throat and neck scales visible on *nonvenomous* triangular shaped head

to black flecking. A random pattern is formed, with black crescents interspersed between the red half-moons. The overall effect has a forest fire intensity with blackened charcoal

Fig. 19.8: Close up of head of mature Northern Water Snake demonstrating head scales. Notice the swollen enlarged look of the upper lip scales, and the dark suture lines between each lip scale

against a snow-white ground color. Some other Northern Water Snakes have bellies that are almost uniformly speckled with gray, except for an orange-yellow or pinkish midventral stripe.

Head scales: The dark head of the northern water snake is large, rounded, chunky and distinct from the neck. The prominent eye is located above the 4th and 5th upper labial, or lip scales. There are 3 small postocular scales. The 3rd postocular scale is triangular in shape, and angles down around the eye to contact the 5th and 6th upper labials. The eye is centered between the 4th and 5th upper labial. The round pupil is surrounded by a light yellow halo that spreads into a pale olive-tan colored iris. The eyes often look yellow. There is a large single preocular scale, in front of the eye. The prefrontal head shield rounds down to meet the loreal scale, and the upper half of the single preocular scale. The nostril is small and is located on the upper half of a single divided nasal scale. The nasal scale is above the 1st and 2nd upper labials, and contacts the internasal head shields, and the rostal scale, to form the snout. There are 10 lower labials (infralabials), each with dark sutures where they meet. The temporal and upper 8

Fig. 19.9: Swollen upper lips, triangular shaped head and generally menacing look of water snake.

labials (supralabials) are swollen, making them wider than the top of the snout. These swollen supralabials are visible in the dorsal view in Fig. 19.9, and give the head an even fuller stout, triangular appearance, one more reason that they are mistaken for being venomous. This snake looks menacingly sinister with the yellow eye, swollen lips, wide triangular shaped head, thin neck and polished black head. It sends an unmistakable *do not tread on me* message.

Because of its heavy body, chunky, triangular-shaped head, aggressive behavior when cornered, and constant association with water, this snake is almost invariably confused with the venomous Eastern Cottonmouth (*Agkistrodon piscovorus piscovorus*), or water moccasin. However, the venomous water moccasin lives no farther north than southeastern Virginia. This confusion is particularly true in the north, even though no true water moccasins occur. From a distance in the field it is not easy to distinguish the two snakes. If you are visiting the southern states, from southern Virginia to Florida and the Gulf Coast, it is an excellent idea to avoid all water snakes.

There are four remarkable features distinguishing the Eastern Cottonmouth from the Northern Water Snake. These features are extremely helpful when assuring a New England resident that the snake that has just been killed, because it was a dangerous water moccasin, is in fact a harmless water snake. (1) The plates under the tail, subcaudals, are in a double row on the water snake, and in a single row in the cottonmouth. (2) There is no pit between the eye and nostril on the harmless water snake. A prominent pit is present between the eye and nostril on the cottonmouth. (3) The pupil of the water snake is round. The pupil of the cottonmouth is elliptical as a cats eye. (4) The upper teeth of the water snake are small and uniform. The water moccasin or cottonmouth has a pair of large folding fangs in the front part of the upper jaw. ***THERE ARE NO VENOMOUS WATER MOCCASINS IN NEW ENGLAND.*** The northern most range of the Eastern Cottonmouth, or *true* water moccasin is southeastern Virginia.

Sexual dimorphism: The sexually mature male Northern Water Snakes, have knobbed keels in the anal region called supra-anal keels (Shine, 2001). Among adults, the female normally has a more massive heavier body (Fig. 19.1), than the males. The females have larger and broader heads than the males, and a longer total body length. The males and females have similar ventral scale counts, averaging 140. The females tail is shorter, equaling about 23% as long as her total length and more rapidly tapered. The adult male is usually smaller, more slender and has a longer uniformly tapered tail, equal to about 26% as long as his total length (Fig. 19.10).

Range: The range of the Northern Water Snake extends from southern Ontario, extreme southern Quebec, and southern coastal Maine, south to northern South Carolina, Georgia and Alabama, and west to Nebraska, Kansas, eastern Colorado and northeastern Oklahoma (Ernst, Barbour, 1989).

The water snakes are widespread in southern New England, flourishing in and near human-altered bodies of water, including reservoirs and farm ponds. They have been recorded from sites as high as 15,000 feet, but this is not a common finding. The Northern Water Snake is presently secure in Connecticut, although many are killed each year in the mistaken belief that they are venomous (Klemens, 2000).

Habitat: Northern Water Snakes live in or near most permanent bodies or water, including rivers, lakes, ponds, bogs, marshes, swamps, reservoirs and drainage ditches.

Fig. 19.10: Mature male Northern Water Snake basking at favorite spring and fall hangout in low bushes and shrubs overhanging bodies of water.

They prefer fairly open, sunny locations with plenty of cover and basking sites. Low overhanging shrubbery such as blueberry and mountain laurel bushes are favorite sunning spots in the spring and fall (Fig 19.10). Some other favorite basking sites are clumps of cattails, swamp bunch grass, beaver and muskrat lodges, exposed root systems on riverbanks and lake shores, logs, piles of rocks (Fig. 19.3), and driftwood. They are often found around waterside structures such as wooden docks, patios, boathouses, pier bridge supports, earthen or rock dams and causeways, spillways, culverts, and old quarries. The water snake adapts well to moderate human interaction. City and urban parks with ponds, and heavily used fishing spots may have healthy populations of Northern Water Snakes. They are uncommon in deeply forested woodland swamps and ponds. The Northern Water Snake prefers quiet slow-moving water to fast moving streams and rivers. They prefer the edges of ponds and lakes rather than the open deep water, where they are usually only seen when retreating from a threatening situation.

Behavior: The water snakes are wary and will slip off their basking perches at any sign of danger. Some may swim with their heads above the water to the other side of the bank, or circle in the deeper water until the threat has disappeared. If the threat persists, they will dive to the bottom and anchor themselves to a log, branches, or vegetation. Most will surface again after five to ten minutes. Breathing in snakes is a 2-stage process, consisting of a brief ventilation cycle, and a longer pause cycle. Constriction of the trunk forces the air out of the lung, (1) exhalation, and expansion of the trunk creates a semi-vacuum, which draws air into the lung, (2) inhalation, at which time breathing stops. This breathing pause, or apnea, can last from a few seconds to several minutes in a resting and undisturbed snake. In diving snakes, the period of apnea is prolonged. Physiological

Fig. 19.11: Postpartum female with her 36 babies delivered on September 15, 1987, after retrieval from Allan and Helen Aroh's property on September 12.

studies on water snakes indicate that submergence can last from 5-25 minutes while foraging (Ernst, Zug, 1996). Ferguson and Thornton (1984) found that a water snake could remain underwater for over 65 minutes with no signs of stress. During this time the snake's heart rate fell to 9% (5 beats/min) of its resting heart rate (Ernst, Barbour, 1989).

Northern Water Snakes are active from April to October. They forage during daylight hours (diurnal), in the spring and fall, but adopt nocturnal habits in the summer. Their hibernation sites include crevices of rocky ledges found close to bogs, lakes, and reservoirs, and in root systems on riverbanks and shorelines adjacent to summer water habitats. Other possible hibernation sites are foundations of old country bridges, and dams where masonry is of dry construction with deep crevices, earthen dams, and abandoned wells. Muskrat burrows and dens, along with water rat and crayfish burrows are possible den sites, as well as beaver lodges.

The water snake tends to be a sedentary animal, with a small home range. The same snake will be found year after year at its favorite pond. As long as the food is plentiful, there is no need to range long distances.

Reproduction: The Northern Water Snake emerges from hibernation in Late March or early April. After the temperatures have stabilized, and threats of freezing temperatures have subsided, spring mating occurs, usually in early May. Males and females reach sexual maturity at 2 years. The 2 year old females, averaging 28 inches, are longer than the males of the same age, who average only 20 inches.

Mating may take place on land, in the water, and on branches overhanging the water. Courtship and mating take place during the daylight hours and may last 2 hours. A single female may be courted by several males. Greene, 1997, recounts such a courtship.

Fig. 19.12: Newborn (neonate) Northern Water Snake forcing it head through the embryonic membrane in which it was born. Notice that the tongue is flicking immediately upon breathing fresh air.

A female northern water snake and two courting males were seen lying beside a stream. A third male flicked his tongue rapidly while swimming near by, as it gained access to the shore and joined them. One male mated with the female, while the other two continued rubbing the female with their chins. Eventually the writhing mass rolled into the water. After returning to shore, two more snakes swiftly joined the group. The female reentered the stream and remained motionless for a few minutes, after which the mating male unwrapped his tail disconnected from the female, and rejoined the others, while she proceeded to swim away.

The Northern Water Snake is viviparous, bearing live young, which have had nourishment by placental organs in the mother (Fig.19.12). Aldridge and Bufalino, 2003

Fig. 19.13: Neonate in birth sac with blood vessels that sustained its life inside its mother.

state that water snakes appear to be predominantly lecithotrophic, which means that the developing babies obtain most of their embryonic nourishment from a yolk sac placenta (Fig. 19.13) inside the mother. They also discovered that pregnant water snakes consume food all during their pregnancy, or gestation period, and do not go into a fasting or anorexic state, as do some snakes, such as the Timber Rattlesnake. There is a strong correlation between the size of the female and the size and number of babies.

211

Fig. 19.14: Newborn water snakes averaging 8.5 inches after first shed. Notice dark black pattern on gray ground color. The white belly with dark half-moon spots is also evident. As the snakes grow, the patterns change. Some older snakes become totally dark in color (Fig.19.3).

Northern Water Snakes produce enormous litters of up to 100 neonates, newborns (Greene 1997). The gestation period between mating and birth of the young is about 58 days. The young are born between late August and September. The average litters range from 15 to 40 (Fig. 19.11) neonates.

An opportunity arose to obtain several gravid female water snakes in September 1987. Allan and Helen Aroh of Old Lyme needed to have several snakes removed from their property. Because they were described as reddish snakes, with a pattern on them (Fig. 19.1), the fear that they were copperheads was quite real, especially since an active copperhead den site was in the area. The snakes had been seen under a tarp, which was covering a stone wall that was under construction. When arriving on the scene at 8:00 p.m., September 13 1987, the tarp was removed, and 6 very large snakes fell out. The snakes were all pregnant Northern Water Snakes, which were removed from the site, with sighs of relief from the Aroh's. Two females were kept for study. The others were released to a safe habitat. One pregnant (gravid) female began delivering at 6:30 a.m. on September 15. The last birth, number 36, was at 9:48 am. The average birth took 3 minutes. A rest period occurred after every 4th birth, of between 12 and 20 minutes, before another set of babies were expelled. The first few snakes given birth to, remained in their sacs for up to 15 minutes before thrusting and pushing their way through the membrane. The last neonates born, pushed their way out of their sacs immediately. After puncturing the membrane, the neonate rested for about a minute, then proceeded to work its way out of the sac, crawling out of an attached membranous material, with its tongue flicking (Fig. 19.12). The emergence took an average of 3 minutes, and looked like the neonate was actu-

212

Fig. 19.15: Juvenile one year old Northern Water Snake, 15 inches long. Notice how the blotches are wider, forming bands with less gray ground color showing. Reddish brown tones are developing near the belly.

ally shedding its first skin, as it left the tight membrane behind. Seven to ten minutes later a second shedding, ecdysis, occurred. This shed took 2-4 minutes. The average length of the newborns, after shedding the membrane, was 7.5 inches. After the second shed, the average length was 8.5 inches. The baby snakes had grown an average of one inch in the first 15 minutes of their life! The young snakes have shiny black heads, and a pattern of black saddles along the length of their bodies. This pattern appears on a gray ground color, which shows as bars and triangles on the sides of the snake (Fig. 19.14). As the snakes grow their patterns change. The saddles become more like bands and different tones of brown begin to develop on their flanks (Fig. 19.15).

Feeding: Northern water snakes eat mostly cold-blooded prey. Small fish make up the largest part of their diet, followed by frogs, tadpoles, aquatic salamanders and larvae, hatchling turtles, and crayfish. Young water snakes will eat insects, earthworms, and young frogs. Adults will actively forage for prey underwater, by probing into clumps of vegetation or under rocks. They have been observed herding schools of minnows into a reef or onto the shoreline and charge at them with their mouth wide open. They will also hunt with a deliberate slow stalk for larger fish and frogs. One of the least mentioned preys of the Northern Water Snake is the eel. Many local residents in Old Lyme Connecticut have witnessed water snakes swallowing eels. Jim Tripp and his family, who are starting a Nature Center on Mill Pond have a large resident population of water snakes, and have observed them eating eels many times.

Predators: Natural enemies of the Northern Water Snake include large predatory fish such as bass and pickerel, bullfrogs, snapping turtles, larger water snakes, hawks, herons, and other wading birds, raccoons, skunks, and mink. Humans are the most serious enemies of these snakes.

Defensive behavior: When threatened the snake will first try for a rapid retreat, usually into the water. From a basking branch, it will just dive into the water and make a rapid retreat. If cornered or seized, it may flatten its head and body and strike out repeatedly at the attacker. While not venomous, its many rows of curved teeth, in a large head, with massive jaw muscles, can inflict a nasty bite.

The bite from a water snake can be compared to a bite from a pickerel fish, verses a bite from a brook trout. The snakes saliva has an anticoagulant that causes thinning of the blood, so that the broken skin will bleed rather profusely. My son, Ernie Krulikowski, can attest to the fact that the bite of a Northern Water Snake is indeed painful and bloody. Ernie was the field associate for all the water snakes collected for the study and photography of this chapter. The 36-inch beauty in the cover photo was one of the largest and more aggressive snakes. Ernie jokes that the red color was his residual blood. The snake was captured in August 1983. Ernie was 12 year old at the time. He is now 33 and still an ardent amateur herpetologist.

In addition to biting and thrashing about, the captured snake will release a surprising amount of noxious smelling musk and fecal material. If sufficiently stressed it will also regurgitate its latest meal, which is also a smelly affair. The water snake is completely harmless if not molested.

These snakes are thought to have an adverse impact on sport fishing. In the 1930's, Boy Scouts received bronze "Junior Conservationist" medals for killing Northern Water Snakes, believing they were protecting trout.

In 1973 a 15 cent bounty was put on water snakes that were threatening a goldfish hatchery in Camden County, Missouri. In that year, 6328 water snakes were killed. 4958 of these were turned in for the bounty, equaling a paid-out of $743.70. It was estimated that 6,328 snakes would have consumed over 19,083 pounds (8,656 kg) of goldfish at about $4.53/pound ($10.00/kg) commercial value. This calculates out to $86,560 worth of fish that would have been consumed in 1973 by the 6,328 snakes that were killed! This amount of indiscriminate killing is not condoned. It may be necessary to trap the snakes and release them elsewhere. (Ernst, Barbour, 1989).

In defense of the Northern Water Snake, it tends to eat smaller, slower-moving or injured fish, which are easier prey than fast moving trout. They may actually have a positive impact on fishing by feeding on the fish stunted by overpopulation, and by eating dead or diseased fish.

Similar species: Adult snakes that may be confused with the Northern Water Snake are as follows: the black phase of the adult Northern Water Snake (Fig. 15.16) resembles the Black Rat Snake (Fig. 15.15); the Black Racer (Fig. 15.14), and the black phase of the Eastern Hognose Snake (Fig. 15.17), see page 161. The red phase of the adult Northern Water Snake (Fig. 18.20) resembles the red phase of the Northern Copperhead (Fig. 18.19), and the rusty orange phase of the Eastern Hognose Snake (Fig. 18.18) see page 201. The immature water snake (Fig. 19.14) resembles the immature Northern Black Racer (Fig. 15.18), Black Rat (Fig. 15.19) and Eastern Hognose Snake (Fig. 15.21) see pages 161-162.

Common names: The Northern Water Snake has many other names such as;

banded water snake, black water snake, common water snake, and water adder (Wright and Wright 1957: 511). The scientific name, *Nerodia sipedon sipedon*, is Greek. *Nero* is Greek for wet or liquid, and *sipedon* meaning siren (Ernst, Barbour 1989), one which snares and entangles. Translated it means a wet serpent whose bite causes decay and death, in apparent reference to the large teeth and nasty bite of this snake (Mitchell, 1994).

CHAPTER TWENTY
VIPERS: FAMILY VIPERIDAE
PIT VIPERS: SUBFAMILY CROTALINAE

All dangerously venomous snakes except the Coral Snakes belong to this group of snakes called Vipers. They are called solenoglyphous snakes (see pages 27-28), which have evolved a highly advanced and specialized dental apparatus for the injection of venom. Their hollow fangs are not fixed in place, but are attached to a short, modified bone, called the maxillary bone (pages 25-26). This maxillary bone is capable of rotating through an arc of about 90 degrees.

Erecting the fangs is not an automatic reaction; it is controlled by the snake. During the strike, the mouth is widely opened (Fig. 3.3 and 3.5). The fangs are erected, and a rapid stab, rather than a bite, injects the venom. The fangs can be erected simultaneously, at the same time, or erected one at a time, or not at all. Each fang has a supply of embryonic or replacement fangs behind it. When a replacement fang reaches full size, the functioning fang becomes loosened at its base, as the new fang moves into place, slowly pushing the old fang out (Fig. 3.2). During this process, a snake may have 3 or even 4 fangs instead of two. When the new fang is securely in place, the old one is usually lost in the body of the next prey animal that is bitten. This fang replacement process continues for the life of the snake.

The Viperids, or Viperidae are the most advanced family of living snakes. This family is further divided into three subfamilies, but only one, the Crotalinae, occurs in the Americas. One subfamily is made up of primitive snakes in the Azemiopinae family, which has only one living representative, the Fea's Viper (*Azemiops feae*) of Asia. The second is the family of true vipers, Viperinae, of the Old World, which are found throughout Europe, Africa, and Asia. They range from a 12 inch *Vipera ursinii* which preys upon small grasshoppers, to the huge African Gaboon Viper (*Bitis gabonica*) (Fig. 20.1), with a length of about 7 feet and a circumference of over 18 inches, which can consume a small antelope! The third

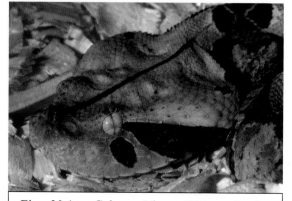

Fig. 20.1: Gaboon Viper (***Bitis gabonica gabonica***), Africa's largest viper, a member of the subfamily Viperinae of the Old World has fangs that can be more than 2 inches long!

family, is the advanced pit vipers of Asia and North and South America, the family of Crotalinae, of which New England has two representative members, the Northern Copperhead, and the Timber Rattlesnake.

The Crotalids, or snakes of the family Crotalinae, are called *pit vipers*. The most important external feature that immediately identifies a pit viper is the presence of a pair of thermorecptive infrared-sensing facial pits (see pages 5-6) on either side of the head, between the nostril and the eye (Fig. 1.16). The pit is a sensory organ, which allows the snake to locate warm-blooded prey even in total darkness. It also allows the snake to gauge its distance, and to actually visualize its size and shape. Any snake with such a pit is venomous.

Fig. 20.2: Northern Copperhead, *Agkistrodon contortrix mokeson*, one of two of New England's venomous snakes, a member of the Crotalinae subfamily of pit vipers, which is a subfamily of the family Viperidae, the hollow-fanged vipers.

Fig. 20.3: Timber Rattlesnake, *Crotalus horridus,* the second of the two New England venomous snakes, also a member of the Crotalinae subfamily of pit vipers, which is a subfamily of the family Viperidae, the hollow-fanged vipers.

In North America, the rattlesnakes, *Crotalus,* copperheads and cottonmouths, *Agkistrodon,* represent the family of Crotalinae (Crotalids). In Connecticut, only the Northern Copperhead, *Agkistrodon contortrix mokeson,* (Fig. 20.2) and Timber Rattlesnake, *Crotalus horridus (Fig. 20.3)* are representatives of the pit viper family.

These two species are stout-bodied, with the scales under their tails (subcaudals), in only one row (Fig. 6.1c); not divided (Fig. 6.1d) as in the nonvenomous snakes in New England. Their heads are much wider than their necks, forming a triangular shape; and the pupils of their eyes are vertically elliptical cat's eyes. In New England, all snakes with elliptical pupils and a pit are venomous, and it goes without saying that any snake with a rattle on its tail is venomous.

Snakes in the genus *Agkistrodon* are the venomous "moccasins" (Conant, Collins, 1998). The copperheads are called "highland moccasins" and the cottonmouths are called "water moccasins." ***There are no water moccasins in New England***; their closest northern range is southeastern Virginia! The Northern Copperhead (Chapter 21) is the only member of this genus in Connecticut. The large head scales or plates on top of the head are similar to the harmless colubrids (Fig. 6.2b).

The only New England snake in the genus *Crotalus,* the rattlesnakes, is the Timber Rattlesnake (Chapter 22). The rattle is its defining characteristic (page 22). It is a unique structure consisting of a row of flattened dry horny segments that interlock in such a way as to produce a buzzing sound when it is shaken vigorously. A new segment is added each time the snake sheds its skin, which is usually 2 to 4 times a year. Another identifying feature is the difference in the head scales on top of the Timber Rattlesnakes head. Instead of being large plates as in all the other 15 New England snakes (Fig. 6.2b), the top of the Timber Rattlesnakes head is covered with small scales (Fig. 6.2c).

Pit vipers seem to be the most highly evolved snakes. They are well organized for capturing, killing and consuming large warm-blooded prey. Their venom is a distinctively complex substance of many types of proteins, which act primarily on a victims blood tissue (hemotoxic), but also has some effect on the nervous system (neurotoxic). Extreme caution should be exercised around these serpents, for even an apparent dead venomous snake can inflict a serious wound by reflex action. Most pit vipers are night hunters during the warm months, and bear live young.

CHAPTER TWENTY ONE

NORTHERN COPPERHEAD *Agkistrodon contortrix mokasen*

This chapter is dedicated to Steve Berube, who as a child, and now a man, has a mystical peaceful power which allows the spirits of all natures creatures to flow through him with no waves of fear. Steve removed my paranoid fear (false evidence appearing real) of snakes, and in its place supplied me with the power to photograph Spirits Serpents in the pure light of enlightenment, showing their beauty, grace, power and regal right to live. Without Steve this book would never had been created.

Fig. 21.1: Beautiful pecan-brown Northern Copperhead recently out of hibernation, May 1984 in Old Lyme Connecticut in typical woodland habitat near its rock ledge winter home.

Description: The Northern Copperhead, *Agkistrodon contortrix mokasen,* is one of the two venomous snakes in New England. It is a richly colored, heavy-bodied snake. The average adult length is between 24 and 36 inches with a record length of 53 inches (Conant and Collins 1998). It has vivid and characteristic rich chestnut, or pecan brown cross-bands, which are narrow on the back and wider on the sides. When looked at from above the crossbands resemble an hourglass shape. From the sides, the majority of the bands appear as blunt Y's, with the stems directed upward. Notice the distinct ground

Fig. 21.2: Red color phased Northern Copperhead.

Fig. 21.3: Beige colored Northern Copperhead.

color phases in the photos on this page, of pecan brown (Fig. 21.1), red-brown (Fig. 21.2) and light beige, found in the southeastern population. The cross-bands are out-lined in a

Fig. 21.4: Yellow colored Northern Copperhead from central Connecticut is one of many studied by Chuck Smith during radio-telemetry studies. Notice the characteristic pits visible even at a field distance of several feet.

dark brown border that is about 2 scale rows deep. The color of the cross-band is a lighter brown, than the border, but darker than the ground color. A dark spot, the same color as the outlined border is in the center of the Y- shaped lateral portion of the band, and is about 2 scale rows wide. The pattern on the red phase in Fig. 21.2, is the same as the beige animal but with different color enhancements. The chestnut saddles are outlined in

Fig. 21.5: Spotted pink belly of this gorgeous female, is characteristic of the Northern Copperhead.

black walnut borders with a dark spot in the middle of each Y-shaped section. The ground color is pinkish lavender with middorsal dark spots in the center of the ground color interspace. The scales are finely stippled with dots of color. There is a row of prominent black spots on the first row of scales, below the saddles and interspaces of ground color, which extends onto the pink checkered belly, as dark half moons (Fig. 21.5). The stunning animal in Fig. 21.4 displays another color phase characteristic of animals in central Connecticut. The ground color is soft yellow-pecan with small middorsal black spots. The chestnut saddles are outlined in dark russet brown, with central spots of deep russet. The animal is alert, but in a loose relaxed coil. The copperheads distinguishing

Fig. 21.6: Stunning artistically sculptured and colored head of Northern Copperhead. Notice the elliptical pupil, and pit between the eye and nostril. The white speckled lip scales are also an identifying characteristic.

features are its vertical elliptical cat's eye pupil, copper colored head and deep pit between its eye and nostril (Fig. 21.7). The neck tapers noticeably, making the head appear very broad, distinct, and triangular-shaped. The scales are weakly keeled, and in middorsal scale rows of 23, and the anal plate is undivided (Fig. 6.1c).

Sexual dimorphism: In adult copperheads, the sexual differential in length is much greater than it is in the newborn, and it increases with advancing age. Males grow faster than females, especially in the fourth years. The largest males are greater by 1/4 than the largest females (Fitch, 1960). The tails of the males, on the average, were slightly longer than the females of the same size, but in both sexes, the relative tail length progressively decreases as the snake size increases. It is difficult to distinguish the male from the female in the field. They appear very similar, except if the female is pregnant, she will be noticeably heavier than the nongravid females, and males.

Head scales: The head is triangular-shaped, flat, and a shade of copper, hence the popular name, copperhead. The facial scales can be identified in Fig. 21.6. The upper lip area to the nostril forms a mask that is a shade lighter than the top of the head. Some animals have a grayish-beige mask, with orange flecking as seen in Fig. 21.6, while others wear a copper mask (Fig. 1.16) .A white line outlined with dark chestnut separates the two tones. It begins behind the eye and extends to the angle of the mouth. Each nostril is between a prenasal and a postnasal scale, which is in contact with the internasals above, and the first upper lip scale (supralabial) below. The loreal pit is located at a level with the lower edge of the eye, between the eye and the nostril. The pit is bordered above by an oval, supraloreal, scale, and is bordered below by a small, rectangular infraloreal

Fig. 21.7: Close up of heat-sensing pit of Northern Copperhead. The freckled chin and lip scales are also well illustrated, as well as the elliptical pupil.

scale (Fig. 21.7). The pit is bordered in the front by the second supralabial lip scale, and in back by the lower preocular scale, in front of the eye. The upper preocular is approximately twice as large as the lower. It contacts the eyebrow, or supraocular scale, which has a ridge overhanging the eye that gives the impression of a Clint Eastwood frown: "go ahead, make my day". There are 2 subocular scales under the eye, which are bordered by the 3rd and 4th supralabials. There are 3 small postoculars, behind the eye. Above the last four upper labials are several rows of temporal scales. The first is small and contacts the 4th and 5th supralabials. Temporals of the upper rows become progressively smaller, and blend into the small scales on top of the head. Below the upper lip scales, there are 10 infralabials (Fig. 21.7), or lower lip scales. The upper half of these scales are the same orange flecked, light color as the upper labials. A dark russet red line marks the border to the lower half of the scales, which are dark brown or chestnut colored. This line marks the lower edge of the facial mask.

There is a rounded triangular mental scale, on the chin, which is located below the rostral plate, or snout. The first pair of infralabials borders the mental plate, and contact the pair of elongate genials, which are the chin shields. There are approximately six rows of gulars, which are the scales between the chin shields, and the anterior, or forward ventral scales (Fig. 21.7).

Eyes perceive light in the visible spectrum, that is, in the light frequencies visible to the human eye. Some snakes also "see" in the infrared spectrum, which are invisible rays just beyond the red of the visible spectrum, and have a penetrating heating effect. They use heat receptors called pit organs to form these images. Heat radiates or reflects

Fig. 21.8: Illustration of hinged fangs of Northern Copperhead. Notice the fangs are surrounded by a membranous sheath, which helps direct the venom from the duct to the hollow fang. The replacement fangs can be seen behind the functional fangs, as they slowly move forward to eventually replace the older worn fangs (See page 25).

from all objects as infrared rays, and the frequency and intensity change with the temperature and size of the object. Infrared vision detects a temperature difference between an object and its surroundings. This difference produces a heat spot on a uniform-temperature background. Infrared vision is ideal for hunting warm-blooded, endothermic, prey, such as birds and mammals.

The infrared receptors lie in the pit organs. Each paired receptor organ consists of a double chamber, which is divided by a membrane. The pit organ is positioned against a cavity in the maxillary bone, which is part of the upper jaw. The pit membrane is a double sheet of epidermis, with tiny blood vessels, and free nerve endings from the trigeminal, or fifth cranial nerve. The trigeminal nerve, among other sensations, is sensitive to sensations of heat. A small pore in front of the eye connects the inner pit chamber with the outer air. The outer chamber forms the visible pit on the snake's face. The pit organs are oriented forward. The left and right field of infrared vision overlaps, and provides precise directional information for aiming a strike. Recent work shows that in the snake's brain, the image projected by the pits largely overlaps the visual image, so the snake actually sees an infrared image of the warm object. The pits appear to be used chiefly in directing the strike. Snakes that have had their other sense organs blocked can still strike accurately. The linking of the heat-sensing organs with the highly developed fangs and powerful venom gives the pit vipers the most sophisticated weapons system known among snakes (Ernst and Zug, 1996).

Fig. 21.9: Open mouth Northern Copperhead showing how the fangs can be rotated forward as the mouth opens nearly 180 degrees.

The copperheads' fangs (Fig. 21.8) are modified teeth. A fang is simply a tooth that is modified to inject venom into prey. The fangs work together with other structures to form a complete venom-delivery apparatus, which functions like a hypodermic syringe and needle (See pages 25-28).

The hinged fangs of the copperhead allow the snake to strike, envenomate, inject the venom, and withdraw, without injury from the struggling prey. The hinged fang is positioned at the front of the mouth, on a short maxillary bone, that can rotate forward, and backward. When not in use, the fang folds backward and upward against the roof of the mouth, where it lies enclosed in the sheath. During a strike, the maxilla bones rotate forward, erecting the fangs, and the mouth opens nearly 180 degrees (Fig 21.9). As the snake strikes, the jaws close, propelling the fangs, and injecting the venom into the prey. The right and left fangs can be rotated independently. The copperhead often works its fangs back into their resting sheaths, one at a time after swallowing its prey (Fig. 2.8).
Newborn copperheads are fully operational. They have fangs and are able to inject venom when they bite (Fig. 21.10). Throughout their lives, all snakes shed and replace their teeth and fangs. A series of replacement fangs are arranged in a graduated series, the largest next to the functional fang. As the functional fang wears down, it is replaced by the next fang. The reserve-fang series then shifts forward, so a replacement fang is always available to replace an old or damaged functional fang, as seen in Fig.21.8.During the replacement phase, the copperhead may briefly have two fangs on each side of the head. The normal cycle of replacement for each fang is slightly more than a month. The replacement period takes approximately a week .The length of the copperhead fang is less

Fig. 21.10: Newborn copperhead is equipped with venom and fangs, and can inflict a dangerous bite. Notice the dull gray ground color of the baby, with muddy brown saddles. Its eyes are opaque after escaping the placental membrane, and will clear up when accomplishes its first shed after about an hour.

than half the length of a typical rattlesnake fang (Fitch, 1960: 111, 269). Each fang seldom measures more than 5/16 inch.

An average of five cases of copperhead bites is reported each year in Connecticut. According to information gathered by Karant in 1980, only a single human death was discovered in the review of 2,000 cases of copperhead bite. Amaral, 1927, reported a human death from a copperhead bite involving a 14-year-old bitten on a finger. P. Wilson, 1908, reported 5 deaths from copperhead poisoning.

Sherman Minton, a herpetologist and physician treated over 50 copperhead bite cases in his career. The generalized symptoms that Minton observed include local pain and swelling, nausea, vomiting, sweating, and thirst. The victim usually experienced enlargement and tenderness of local lymph nodes, and the presence of blood, or serum-filled blisters was not uncommon. In only one case involving a young girl were symptoms of shock observed. Minton treated tissue necrosis (decay), but not severe enough to warrant skin grafting. Upon being bitten, the victim may feel a burning, intense pain at the site of the bite, followed by bluish discoloration and rapid swelling, with blood and fluid oozing from the puncture sites. In any case of a venomous snakebite, the victim should be taken to a hospital immediately. Most copperhead bites, as a result of the short fangs, are subcutaneous bites, and usually are not treated with antivenin unless indications of severe poisoning develop. For discussion of snakebite and treatment, please see pages 28-43. Pages 41-43 detail a personal account of a severe copperhead bite to a Lyme Connecticut resident, Bob Mariani in 1976. All venomous snakebites should be reported to the Poison Information Center in Farmington, Connecticut (Petersen and Fritsch II, 1986:36-39).

Fig. 21.11: Copperheads seek shelter from the hot summer sun, often in cool rock crevices. A hiker could reach into such a rock-hold while climbing, and accidentally get bitten by the startled snake.

In a chart of toxicity on a selected number of 81 venomous snakes, the copperhead is listed as number 81. The species are listed approximately in order from most to least toxic. The toxicity is measured in terms of the dose of venom it would take to kill 50 percent of the test mice that were injected with the dose of venom (Ernst & Zug: 120-124). The lethal dose is recorded as the LD $_{50}$. The total amount of venom contained in both venom glands of an average adult copperhead is between 40 and 70 mg. of dry weight (Minton and Minton , 1969). The minimum lethal dose required to kill an adult human is estimated to be 100 or more milligrams.

Because of the quiet nonassertive temperament of the copperhead in its natural habitat, snakebites are rare in the wild. The victim has to accidentally step on or touch the copperhead while hiking or climbing in the snakes summer range (Fig. 21.11). Copperheads will seek cover from hot summer temperatures, and if homes are built in their ranges, the snakes will enter garages, sheds and workshops if the doors are left open. The victim of this kind of encounter usually reaches into a box of tools, a drawer, or box of rags, etc, and is bitten by the startled snake. Cover is also sought in woodpiles, stone walls, and loose piles of debris. The most common bites occur from people handling the snakes, not the snakes being aggressive towards the people.

The other critical senses for the copperhead are vision and smell. The vertical or elliptical cat's eye pupil (Fig. 21.6), which is one of the remarkable physical features of the copperhead is able to open wider than a round pupil, thus allowing more light to enter the eye. This is an important feature for a snake that hunts at night. Fig. 21.12, shows how the elliptical pupil will fully dilate, or open up in the dark, during a night on the prowl. In addition to the night vision and heat-sensing pit, odor is also important in locating prey.

226

Fig. 21.12: Photograph illustrating night vision of Northern Copperhead, showing how the vertical elliptical pupil will dilate in the dark for more effective vision at night.

See pages 6-8 for discussion on the importance of the tongue and Jacobson;s organs in the snakes elaborate sense of smell.

Range: The Northern Copperhead's range extends from Massachusetts and Connecticut southward on the piedmont and highlands to Georgia, Alabama, and northeastern Mississippi, and westward through southern Pennsylvania and the Ohio Valley to Illinois.

The copperhead is one of two venomous snake species found in New England. It occurs in the coastal zone, as well as in the southwestern and southeastern hills. In the Central Connecticut Lowland, it is primarily associated with the trap rock ridge system on the west side of the Connecticut River. The copperhead is absent from large portions of Litchfield, Tolland and Windham counties. Populations have declined rapidly in Fairfield County, where they are now rare. The encroachment of development to their den sites in the Central Connecticut Lowland has resulted in increased mortality at these sites. Copperheads are considered a species of conservation concern in both Massachusetts and New York (Klemens, 2000: 71-72).

Habitat: The hibernation habitat of the southeastern populations, is glacial granite and quartz outcroppings which abound with mountain laurel, oak, birch, beech and hemlock stands. The sites are always associated with permanent bodies of water, such as bogs, lakes, streams dotted with old millponds, and reservoirs. There is a definite preference for ground that is shaded by a leaf canopy and blanketed with leaf litter from deciduous trees. The home range is approximately 24.5 acres for males, and 8.5 acres for females.

Fig. 21.13: Pair of Northern Copperheads enjoying last basking rays of a late autumn sunset on granite ledges in Old Lyme Connecticut, before they must retreat to their ancient historic winter den.

The home range includes historic den sites on southern to southeastern facing rock ledges or traprock outcroppings, depending upon the location of the population. Studies done by many researchers, including radiotelemetry research by C. F. Smith of the Department of Ecology and Evolutionary Biology at the University of Connecticut, have greatly enhanced the understanding of home range activity of the Northern Copperhead (See Appendix I, Radiotelemetry Research) in Connecticut.

After leaving the hibernation sites, the male and nongravid females migrate to their summer ranges. These areas include areas bordering stone walls; old abandoned saw mills and the accompanying log and sawdust piles, as well as old quarry sites. They have been found in hollowed-out decaying timbers of old bridges over drainage ditches, and in rock crevices filled with leaf litter. Later in the summer when the temperature rises, they become nocturnal, travelling and foraging at night. Daylight hours are spent sequestered under logs, deep inside hollow tree stumps, under flat rocks, or forest debris, at stone and earthen dams, and in bunch grass along swamp edges (Smith, personal communication 2002). They become diurnal again in the fall when the nights get too cool for activity. On the last days of autumn, the snakes spend the warm afternoons basking in the golden glow of the afternoon sun on ledges near their den (Fig. 21.13), enjoying the last days of their active season.

The hibernacula are in deep crevices in trap rock, or granite outcroppings, along hilltops with an eastern or southern exposure (Fig. 21.14). Copperheads usually share their dens with other snakes. Black rat snakes have been photographed leaving the same den sites (See Fig. 16.9). Black racers have also been observed at the same sites in the spring. The black racers are usually first to emerge, followed by the black rat snakes. The

Fig. 21.14: Copperhead emerging from winter hibernation at granite outcropping in Old Lyme Connecticut, April 1988.

copperheads are the last to emerge. The same historic den is used every year.

Reproduction: Mating may occur any time in the snakes' season of activity, especially when the snakes are concentrated along the hibernation ledges in spring and fall. There is some tendency for concentrated breeding activity a few weeks after the spring emergence, during the latter half of May, when the females are in heat. At this time, the receptive female gives off an odor (pheromone) from her body during ovulation. The scent emanating from her skin leaves an odor trail, which the males follow. Once the male-female encounter has occurred, the females scent further arouses the male when he is exposed to the skin on her back. Courtship and mating has rarely been observed in the wild, probably because it normally occurs at night or under cover.

Schuett and Gillingham, 1988, did extensive laboratory studies on copperhead courtship. They found that courtship was always initiated and performed by males. The male begins courtship by touching the female with his snout. His head and neck are raised and placed on the back of the female. The female is usually resting coiled or outstretched when the male makes contact (Fig. 21.15). The male rubs his chin along the female's back with side-to-side movements of his head and neck while he presses his chin into the females body. The male will sometimes display a head-jerking behavior, while he advances toward the female's head. When he gets to the female's neck-head region, he stops moving forward but continues to rub his chin on her head and neck. Tongue flicking' is about 1-2 flicks/second during the entire courtship behavior. The male's tail quivers next to the female's tail, as his tail is pushed beneath the female, forming a loop, as tail and cloacal caressing follows. If the female is receptive, mating occurs. The pair is

Fig. 21.15: Pair of Northern Copperheads in beginning stages of courtship, 1983, Old Lyme Connecticut, pair was located by Everett Lee.

usually stationary during the mating, but sometimes the female will advance shortly after mating has begun and just before the end of coitus (mating). If the female moves, the male crawls backward during her advancement. She will sometimes move her tail in a wave like motion during mating, which averages over 6 hours, 366 minutes (Schuett and Gillingham, 1988: 374-380). Mating that takes place in the fall, results in storage of sperm in the female until the following spring.

Combat dance: Male combat behavior, or the combat dance, can be considered a form of social aggression. Competition definitely occurs for access to food and mates. Larger males won the staged combat (agonistic) trials in laboratory tests conducted by Schuett and Gillingham, in 1989. It was also observed that if an individual that won a contest with an opponent, was reintroduced to that same opponent, the previous winner would win again. This suggests that dominant-subordinate relationships develop in male copperheads. Larger males were always able to defend their mates, and able to interrupt and dethrone smaller males from their attempts at courtship. However, once mating was in progress, no introduced males were able to interrupt the mating.

In observed combat rituals, the male copperheads make contact, and within seconds, both individuals begin to rise off the ground and display rapid tongue-flicking behavior. When the animals have about one-third to one-half of their bodies raised, or elevated, off the ground, both individuals begin a rhythmic swaying motion. Often their heads, necks, and trunks are parallel to one another as they sway, and the heads are always bent at a sharp angle at the neck. The swaying postures observed were front-to-front, side-to-side, and front-to-back. Eventually, one individual starts an offensive-hook, by leaning over and arching his head or neck over the back of his opponent and pushing downward.

Fig. 21.16: Illustration of Northern Copperhead combat dance in spring habitat of oak leaf litter and rocky terrain.

As this occurs, one animal makes a strong effort at forcing the other to the ground, therefore "topping" its opponent. Often the other snake responds by doing the same thing, and the necks and trunks become entwined (Fig. 21.16). Both snakes immediately return to the vertical display. After 8 to 145 minutes of this vigorous activity, one snake shows a spontaneous rapid retreat. The dominant male often follows in pursuit of the loser, or sub-

231

Fig. 21.17: Gravid (pregnant) female copperhead at favorite basking rock near den site. Several expectant mothers spend the spring, summer and fall in areas called rookeries, which have minimal forest canopy, and abundant warming rocks where they await the birth of their young.

ordinate male. This ends the combat bout. This combat and establishment of dominance, demonstrates competition for access to females and is thus an important factor in sexual selection (Gloyd and Conant, 1990).

After mating, gravid or pregnant females tend to stay near the hilltop ledges, close to the den sites, and spend a lot of time basking (Fig. 21.17). This raises their body temperature to enhance the development of the embryonic snakes. Basking rocks are used annually and sometimes by more than one female. The gathering basking areas of pregnant females are often referred to as rookeries. Many females will be completely hidden under large flat rocks. The basking rocks are exposed to sunshine from morning until late afternoon.

Copperheads are viviparous, giving live birth. Most births occur between mid-August and mid September. The number of young per litter increases with the size of the female. A gravid female, 22 inches long, which had been rescued from a residence in June 1984 in Old Lyme Connecticut, gave birth to 4 young on September 11, 1984. In July 1985 a 26-inch pregnant female was saved from a work site, and gave birth to 6 young on September 25. The birthing had been anxiously awaited, feeling like an expectant parent, with camera equipment loaded and waiting. What else happened on September 25, 1985!

Hurricane *Gloria* happened. Penny (Fig. 21.18), the expectant mother, was giving birth, as preparations for a very strong hurricane were underway. Plywood was being nailed to cover the picture windows, facing the waterfront, where the direct impact was expected. Drinking water was being drawn, and everything that could be battened down

232

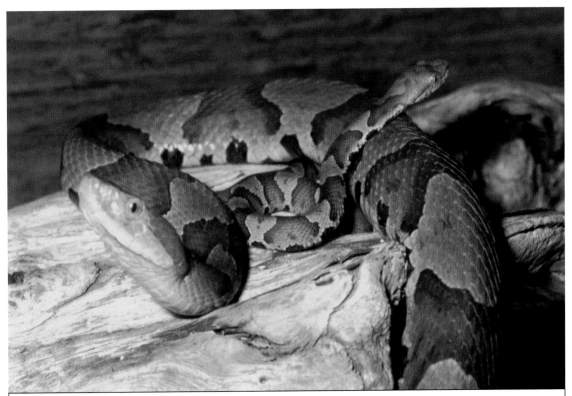

Fig. 21.18: Mother copperhead with one of six young born during hurricane Gloria on September 25, 1985.

had to be secured. Well, photographs just had to be taken. An opportunity like this does not come along every day. Penny did not appear greatly distressed by the parturition, or birthing process. She would move her lower body from side to side occasionally, and waves of muscular contractions could be seen, but she remained quiet and composed. There were 3 neonates already born by 7 a.m. The fourth fetus appeared at her cloacal opening, or vent at 7:30. It was encased in a strong fetal membrane. (Fig. 21.19) The contractions slowly rippled along the lower portion of her body. The beautiful package

Fig. 21.19: Neonate copperhead birthing. Notice sturdy placental membrane through which the baby must force its way out to avoid suffocation.

was advancing slowly through her birthing canal. The head could be seen as Penny slowly pushed the bundle of life from her body. The young snake was folded in a tight bundle, with its head in the middle, and its dark eyes very visible through the membrane. The other three neonates were already moving around, exploring their surroundings. They were very gray and dull in general coloration, with blackish crossbands. Their markings resembled the adults, but gray was the dominant color. As seen in Fig. 21.20, about 15 minutes after extrusion, or birthing, the newborn had pushed its head through the membrane and was actively forcing the folds of its body against the restraining birth blanket. It took the neonate in the photo about 10 minutes to

Fig. 21.20: Newborn copperhead, 15 minutes after birthing, forcing it head through the tough birth sac. Notice the dull gray ground color and dark cross bands.

millimeter its way out of the membranous birth sac. The process resembled the first ecdysis, as the placenta with its blood supply and life-sustaining properties, is gradually shed. The young copperhead measured about 8.5 inches. Its pupils were elliptical, but more open than the adults, and clouded over with a gray film. The tail was light colored, but the deep yellow sulfur color was not visible. The young snakes were immediately social, and as each one crawled away from its birth sac, it joined its siblings in a healthy pile of young copperheads. Penny rested for 25 minutes before her body started the waves

Fig. 21.21: Six one-day-old copperheads camouflaged in leaf litter, except for the alluring yellow tails.

of contractions again. The last two babies were seen as obvious enlargements at the vent area (Fig. 21.10). It took only 7 minutes to push the fifth baby out, and its head ruptured the membrane as it was birthed. With only a rest period of 10 minutes, the last baby was born. It also forced its head and neck out of the sac as expulsion occurred. A slight variation in color was evident between the recently born, and the later births, the youngest were grayer, and the older individuals were taking on a brownish hue. After shedding occurs, which happened during the neonates first night, the newly shed young now have a more iridescent brownish hue and a bright sulfur-yellow tail

Fig. 21.22: Recently shed day old baby Northern Copperhead with brilliant iridescent brown hues and stunningly sulfur-yellow tail which may be used to entice amphibians to approach in hopes of obtaining an easy meal, but instead is ambushed by the young cunning copperhead. Notice the gray head of the newborn is now the characteristic copper color of the adult.

(Fig. 21.22). When among dried leaf litter, the colors of the 6 young snakes blend so perfectly with their surroundings that it is almost impossible to discover them, with the exception of the bright yellow tail (Fig. 21.21). An unsuspecting young wood frog, hopping along in search of food, could be attracted to the lure of the yellow tail, which may look like a twitching yellow grub, maggot, or worm. The young snake lying in ambush, entices the frog to within striking distance, and has its first meal. The yellow tail disappears as the young snake matures. In its second full year, the only remnants of the yellow tail, is a very pale lime-yellow, with the white rings from infancy, as seen in Fig. 21.23.

Fig. 21.23: Juvenile 2-year old copperhead with stripped white tail, the only remnants of its brilliant yellow infants tail.

Feeding: Among the foods favored by copperheads are the following: voles, cicadas, white-footed mice, short-tailed shrews, ring-necked snakes, large caterpillars of the silk moths such as luna, cecropia, polyphemus, oak worm, io moth, imperial moth and regal moth, field mice, young wood rats, nestling ground birds, baby rabbits, worm snakes, garter snakes, young

235

Fig. 21.24: Beautiful 43 inch red-phase copperhead found by Mark Kus in Lyme Connecticut. This animal represents well the common name "red snake". This magnificent animal is displaying the slow retreat so characteristic of the docile tempered snake.

black racers, frogs and salamanders. The small snakes, especially the ring-necked snake, proved to be important in the food of young copperheads. Frogs and toads are abundant in the ranges of the copperhead, especially after warm summer rains, when the amphibians and the copperheads are both active. Large prey is bitten and released, to be tracked after the venom has taken effect. Small prey such as frogs, salamanders, cicada and birds, are kept in the mouth until dead. Studying the scats or feces of the snakes is an excellent way to determine prey that has been consumed. However, amphibians are completely digested by the snakes, and no remains, except possibly some of the insects eaten by the amphibian before it was eaten by the copperhead, show up in the scats.

Cicadas, a favorite food when available, are mainly sought when recently transformed into adults or still in the soft defenseless nymph stage as they emerge from their underground habitat. They prove to be easy prey for the easy-going copperhead. Although the copperhead is ordinarily a terrestrial being, it can often be found in low bushes or shrubs feasting on cicadas in late summer evenings. It was reported by Conant in 1951 about a Northern Copperhead dying after eating a 17-year cicada. The cicada apparently was not dead when the copperhead swallowed it, and the cicada successfully burrowed its way through the snake's neck, killing it!

Defensive Behavior: The copperheads strongest line of defense is its concealing pattern (Figs.2.22, 21.4 and 21.21). In the words of Ernst and Barbour, 1989; "In our opinion, copperheads are better lovers than fighters".A copperhead tends to lie quietly, coiled motionless on leaf litter with its cryptic pattern matching the varied brown hues of the forest floor. If it must move to avoid danger, it does so very slowly (Fig. 21.24), and

236

Fig. 21.25: Fully aroused copperhead that feels threatened, displaying flicking tongue, intense spring-loaded S-coil strike position and vibrating tail.

heads directly to the nearest shelter. The copperhead is not an aggressive animal, but if the threat continues, and the snake is not near a shelter, it will change from a resting coil to strike position with one sudden rotation of its head, as it turns to face the danger, and prepare to strike. If caught out in the open and approached openly by an aggressor, the copperhead will make lunging movements towards the enemy. Vibrating of its tail is a response to severe alarm or disturbance. It is characteristic of copperheads that are cornered. A copperhead that vibrates its tail is thoroughly aroused and ready to strike. The snake in Fig. 21.25 illustrates an animal in just such an aroused state. The tail is a blur of vibrating tension; the S-coil is exaggerated, and as taunt as a spring-loaded trap. The fore-body is raised off the ground, ready for a lunge-strike. This is a dramatically beautiful animal. A copperhead that is being restrained and struggling emits jets of musk in a fine spray from the cloacal or tail glands. The musk is usually only discharged when the snake is threatened or being handled.

Predators: Adult copperheads do not have very many predators. Among their natural enemies are the Eastern Milk Snake, opossums, coyotes, feral and domestic cats and red-tailed hawks. First-year young are more vulnerable to predators. Moles will come up under young copperheads that have nestled under flat rocks, attack them from underneath, and drag them into their tunnel to eat them (Fitch 1960). Opossums, cats, and snake eating snakes, or ophiophagous snakes, such as the eastern milk snake, have been known to eat young copperheads.

Man is by far the copperheads greatest enemy. Over most of the copperhead's range, habitat destruction, and the automobile have severely reduced populations. The F.O.R.D.(found on road dead) illustration in Fig. 21.26 is an unfortunate way to locate a

237

Fig. 21.26: Evidence of vehicular snake-slaughter, one of the greatest man-made predators of the Northern Copperhead. Many copperheads are killed on roads in the summer months, for they forage at night, and are easy prey for the automobile. The warm roads provide pleasant hunting, often supplying an easy diet of injured rodents.

copperheads range! For many years, some counties placed bounties on copperheads, and people were paid varying amounts of money up to $3.00, for turning in a dead copperhead in the 1950's.

Common names: The copperhead is known by many vernacular or common names. The most common ones are, chunk head, high land moccasin, red adder, red snake, and red viper (Wright and Wright, 1957). The genus name *Agkistrodon* means hooked tooth. The species name *contortrix* means twister, and the subspecies name *mokeson* translates to moccasin (Ernst and Barbour, 1989).

Similar Species: The adult copperhead (Figs. 21.27 and 21.29) is often confused with various harmless snakes, especially the Eastern Milk Snake (21.28), the Eastern Hognose Snake (Figs., 21.30) and the red phased Northern Water Snake (Fig. 21.31).

The young copperhead (Fig. 21.32) is often confused with the harmless Northern Black Racer (Fig. 21.33), and young Black Rat Snake (Fig.21.34). These young harmless snakes are found in similar habitats as the copperheads, often sharing the same den sites.

All of these harmless snakes lack a facial pit, have rounded pupils, not the vertical elliptical pupil of the copperhead in daylight, and usually have patterns on their heads, not plain copper-colored head as the copperhead has. The young rat snakes and racers are more slender in body build, but because they tend to be defensive when approached by a large human predator their aggressive behavior often causes people to consider them dangerous. The rapid vibration of their tails in the leaves is especially frightening, and they will strike repeatedly when threatened.

Fig. 21.27: Tan colored Northern Copperhead.

Fig. 21.28: Adult Eastern Milk Snake.

Fig. 21.29: Red-brown Northern Copperhead.

Fig. 21.30: Orange Eastern Hognose Snake.

Fig. 21.31: Red phase Northern Water Snake.

Fig. 21.32: Young Northern Copperhead.

Fig. 21.33: Young Northern Black Racer.

Fig. 21.34: Young Black Rat Snake.

The majority of the Northern Copperheads in this chapter were found by Steve Berube, Everett Lee, Al Corey, and C.F. Smith who also contributed abundant field data.

CHAPTER TWENTY TWO

TIMBER RATTLESNAKE *Crotalus horridus*

This chapter is dedicated to a fine friend and fellow lover and protector of the Timber Rattlesnake in Connecticut, Al Bagley. Al has been educating children around the state on the natural history of our native king of the wilderness for years, and I owe him an immeasurable debt of gratitude for sharing a day in this beautiful animals kingdom. The photos in this chapter are a result of that day in Gods country, a silent place of peace, power and respect. A day that will live with my readers and me forever. Thank you Mr. Bagley, from the bottom of my heart.

Fig 22.1: Magnificent king of his entire domain. The massively beautiful Timber Rattlesnake was photographed at its den site on October 1986 in a secluded area on the Mesonic Mountain Range in Connecticut. He represents the yellow phase. He presented a calm peaceful demur as he posed for the photo, seeming to understand that no threat was present. It was an incredible experience to lie on the forest floor with this symbol of power and freedom, and share his view.

Description: The Timber Rattlesnake, *Cortalus horridus* is one of the two venomous snakes in New England, and is one of the most beautiful of all the North American rattlesnakes. This heavy, stout-bodied, snake ranges in length from 10-inch newborns to 60-inch mature adults. The average length of Connecticut Timber Rattlesnakes is about 39 inches. The record length of 74 $^{1/2}$ inches is held by a snake captured near Sheffield, Massachusetts in 1931 by Raymond L. Ditmars of the New York Zoological Society. In 1969, a 5-foot animal was reported from Litchfield County, but a 6-foot specimen would be unlikely to be found in Connecticut.

Adult Timber Rattlesnakes show extreme color and pattern polymorphism, with variations on two distinct color phases, and different crossbands and chevrons. The light phase animals have at least three distinct variations in color. The outstanding individual in Fig. 22.1 is dramatically patterned with dark black walnut bands and chevrons on a ground color of fawn-yellow. The dark saddles and chevrons are outlined in light yellow-white scales. The head is dark straw yellow.

The young snake in Fig. 22.2, is in its second summer, located by Everett Lee, and photographed in June 1984, in Portland Connecticut. The large spots on the first third of its body, that gradually expand into wider and wider bands, which cover the remainder of the rattlers body are outlined in white. The head is more mustard colored than tawny-yellow as in the animal above. The background color is grayish olive-brown. The dark

Fig. 22.2: Young Timber Rattlesnake found by Everett Lee June 1984. The olive yellow and tan ground color with dark chevrons blends in with the surrounding forest leaf litter, providing awesome camouflage. This animal still retains the first button and three additional rattles, indicating it is probably in its second season, having shed 4 times since birth.

bands join with the lateral spots on the side of the animal to form chevron shaped bands. A rusty brown dorsal stripe, about 3 scales wide, runs the length of the body. The tail on both snakes is dark velvet black. The young animal has recently shed, as evidenced by its bright color, and blue coloration of the newest distal rattle segment at the base of its tail.

A variation in the light phase coloration is portrayed in Fig. 22.3, of an older animal, located by Al Bagley, and photographed in September 1986 in central Connecticut. Notice the rattle has 8 segments, including the original segment from its first shed. The background color is light mustard. The large blotches behind the head, that grade into saddles and then bands are olive-brown, outlined in black, spotted intermittedly with a white border. The head is light olive-mustard yellow. There is an indistinct dorsal stripe, of a light rusty mustard color.

The dark phase of the Timber Rattlesnake is illustrated in Fig. 22.4. The ground color is gray-black near the head and neck, and becomes darker towards the tail. Some dark phased snakes have a walnut-brown ground color with bands outlined in a thin yellow border. Notice the black head and black blotches that grade into saddles. The saddles become more like bands toward the tail. These dark markings are stunningly outlined in white on this beautiful animal. A prominent mustard yellow dorsal stripe begins at the nap of the neck, and runs the length of the body of this individual. The lower lip or labial area is also white, leading into a white throat and white to cream colored belly. This is a young animal with 6 rattle segments, and was about 2 feet long. Its temperament was not docile and laid back as was the case with the light colored animals. Of the 18

242

Fig. 22.3: This elegant animal represents a variation on the yellow or light phase Timber Rattlesnake. It has an olive-mustard ground color with darker olive chevrons outlined in black. Notice the 9 rattle segments and perfectly tapered string indicating no breakage from its origin at birth.

snakes located, this was the only dark phased individual. The light specimens seem to prefer sites abundant with leaf litter, and are more common than the dark phase individuals in Connecticut.

Black or dark phased rattlesnakes are more common in the mountains of the Virginia, Pennsylvania and New York. In describing the dark-colored animals, Ditmars (1936) words express their stunning presence as follows "…after freshly casing their skins, they have the soft, rich effect of black velvet."

Size: No trait is more easily exaggerated than the size of the Timber Rattlesnake. Most people upon seeing one for the first time estimate its size as between 4 and 5 feet, which, especially in modern times, is an overestimate, probably based on the sheer massive build of these beautiful animals, especially when seen in their natural surroundings. Brown, 1993 has listed the average sizes of adult males as 43.5 inches total length, and adult females averaging 38.5 inches total length. The maximum size in total length may be 8 feet in the south and 6 feet 2 inches in the north. In Browns 13-year study of New York animals, he found the largest male to be 54 inches, and the largest female to be 47 inches in total length. When raised in captivity, growth is enhanced. Brown's 10-year old males, raised from birth reached a length of 56 inches with weights of 5.5 lb. for the black phase captive and 6.7 lb. for the yellow phase animal. It is generally agreed that along with the depletion of the rattlesnake population, the average body size is also decreasing, probably because the larger snakes have been the easiest to kill and capture.

Sexual Dimorphism:.Ditmars, 1936, stated that in the mountainous districts of the northern United States, the greater number of females are sulfur yellow, while the males

243

Fig.22.4: Black or dark phase Timber Rattlesnake photographed in central Connecticut, September 1986. Defining characteristic is the black head and dark gray ground color. The black chevrons are dramatically outlined in white, as is the lower jaw. This individual had a more pugnacious temperament than the yellow variations.

are blackish, though this rule does not always hold true. Klauber, 1956, agreed with Ditmars, and states that the yellowish specimens are nearly always females, whereas the black specimens are generally males. Petersen and Fritsch, 1986 also state that it was once commonly thought that dark individuals were males and light colored animals were females. Seigel and Collins, 2001 (p. 69) state that the male coloration in *Crotalus horridus* is usually yellow, and the female coloration is usually black. Because Klauber (1956) is stated as an authority in the Table 2.2 where this statement was recorded, it is believed that the statement is a typographical error, for the reverse statement is the more prominent theory. An extensive discussion of color in the sexual dimorphism or Timber Rattlesnakes is presented on pages 225 and 668 in Klauber, 1956. Recent studies have led herpetologists to finally agree that *color is unrelated to the sex of the Timber Rattlesnake*

Male Timber Rattlesnakes are larger than females (Brown, 1993). Sex may be determined by the short tail in females, consisting of an average of 20 subcaudal scales and a tail that is about 6 percent as long as the total length of her body. The longer males tail consists of an average of 25 subcaudals, and the length is about 8 percent as long as the total length of his body (Ernst, and Barbour, 1989).

Head scales:.The Timber Rattlesnake is the only snake in the state that does not have the typical nine large head scales or shields on the top of its head. The head scales on the other Connecticut snakes, which are designated as prefrontal head shields, are represented in the Timber Rattlesnake by 2 enlarged scales located between the supraoculars. The supraoculars are the thick eyebrow shields, which are located above the beautiful

Fig. 22.5: Dramatic illustration of head scales of Timber Rattlesnake. This is the only Connecticut and New England snake that has small scales on top of its head, all others have large head plates (See Fig. 6.2, a, b and c). The prominent eyebrow scale above the eye (supraocular) give the impression of a primitive rough and tumble character, when in reality the Timber Rattlesnake is a highly evolved individual.

reticulated iris and elliptical pupil in the photo above. These enlarged scales, called canthals, are in contact with the supraocular eyebrow shield, and the internasals, which are above the nostril. The cluster of small scales between the canthals is called the intercanthals, which occupy the prefrontal area. The numerous small head scales located between the supraocular eyebrows occupy the frontal area of the scull and are called intersupraoculars. The large nostril is located between the prenasal and postnasal scale on the lateral or side of the head, as seen above. The prenasal scale is in contact with the first upper labial or lip scale, and the large scale on the front of the nose, called the rostrum.

Fig. 22.6: Three photographs illustrating color variation of the Timber Rattlesnake as exemplified by the color of the small scales on the top of the heads. From left to right are the olive, black and yellow versions.

The 2 scales behind the postnasal scale are called loreal scales, which are in contact with the large upper preocular scale, and elongated lower preocular scales, located just in front

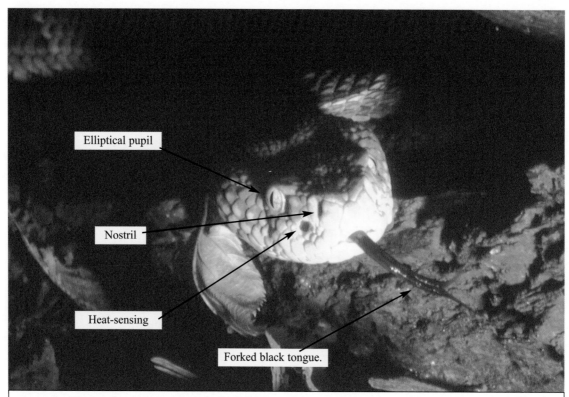

Fig. 22.7: Illustration of the important senses utilized by the Timber Rattlesnake. The tongue, nostril and heat sensing pits all aid in locating, identifying and striking at its prey, all aided by the elliptical pupil.

of the eye. The pit is directly beneath the elongate lower preocular, and the scales which line the pit, called lacunals, are visible just beneath and in front of the pit. The cluster of small scales under the nostril between the upper lip scales, loreals, and lacunals, in front of the pit, are called prefoveals. The small scales behind the lacunals and under the pit are called postfoveals. It is difficult to determine where the last postfoveals scale and the first subocular scale begin. The suboculars line the lower edge of the eye, and the 3 postocualars, seen in the photo above, outline the back or posterior edge of the eye. Notice the beautifully stippled scales, all marked with dots of black, navy blue flecks, and iridescent spots of teal blue. Although a marked feeling of the primitive emanates from this spectacular animal, a sense of power and peace also floods the photo. The arrangement of head scales, how they contact each other, and their numbers are important in classification and identification of rattlesnakes. This study of the different scale characteristics is called squamation. See Appendix III for help in locating the many scales mentioned in this section.

Hunting and Feeding Behavior: The photo in Fig. 22.7 illustrates all the important senses of the Timber Rattlesnake. The Timber Rattlesnake uses several of its senses in its ambush technique for obtaining prey. In its favored feeding areas, it uses its highly developed sense of smell to locate runways made by mice, especially white-footed mice, and voles. Odors in the air are breathed in through the nostrils, in the conventional sense of smell, which sends messages to the brain to identify the particles. To further track the prey, the rattler uses its tongue to sense the trail. The extended glistening black tongue flicks in and out through an opening in the rostrum plate located in the front of the upper

Fig. 22.8: Portrait of captive Timber Rattlesnake, June 1984 illustrating the ability of the elliptical pupil to dilate to a round shape in dim lighting situations. The animal was used in teaching seminars by Al Bagley.

lip, between the nostrils, as seen in Fig. 22.7. The tongue tips wave up and down along a scent trail, with the odor particles sticking to the tips. The odor particles are then deposited on the roof of the mouth, when the tongue is drawn back into the mouth. These particles then enter the fluid-filled Jacobson's organ, which is a special organ, full of sensory cells, close to the larger olfactory chambers used in the conventional sense of smell. The cells send messages to the brain to identity the odors. These combined methods of detecting odors enhances or magnifies the snakes sense of smell, and gives the snake exceptional ability to track its prey.

Reinert Posture: The rattlesnake then follows the scent trail until it finds an ambush site where the rodents path runs along the top of a fallen log. Researcher Howard K. Reinert found that out of 225 randomly sampled logs, 75 percent of them were used as runways by white-footed mice and other small mammals, at least once a day. Ambushes peaked between 9:00 P.M. and 8:00 A.M. The snake then positions itself along the log. It coils on the forest floor, with its chin resting on the side of the log, at right angles to the pathway. This is referred to as the "Reinert Posture", Brennan, 1995. The Timber just rests and waits for the mouse to come along. As the mouse moves closer, the snakes sense of hearing picks up its approach by picking up the vibrations made by the mouse. The sounds are felt by the skin lining the temples of the snakes head. This is where the sensations are passed on to the muscles, and then to the quadrate bone, which is connected loosely to the skull. These tiny vibrations are passed along to the small columella bone, to the inner ear, and its sound-sensitive cells send messages to the brain. The snake is also able to feel vibrations through its lower jaw when it is in contact with any surface. If there is sufficient light, the snake also uses its sense of sight to locate the mouse.

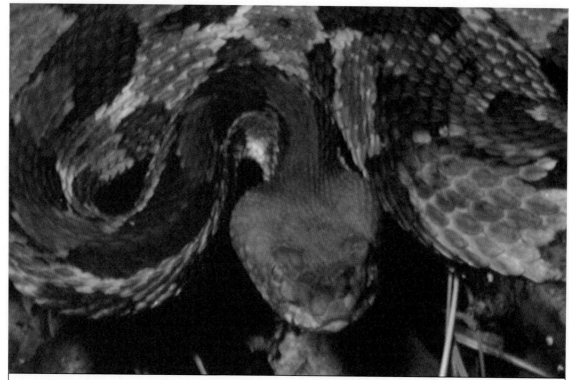

Fig. 22.9: Large venom glands at the base of the head give this snake a very distinctive triangular-shaped head.

Ambush hunters such as the Timber Rattlesnake that live in dense habitat, have eyes that are positioned laterally, or towards the side of the head to produce a wider, broad field of vision. Their eyes are large with vertical elliptical pupils, which are able to gather more light in low intensity lighting, as encountered in the evening, nighttime and dawn. As seen in Fig. 22.8, the pupil can open wider to allow more light to enter the eye. The eye registers light in the visible spectrum, which are the frequencies the human eye is able to see.

The rattlesnake also is able to see in the infrared spectrum, using the heat respectors called pit organs. This pit is very visible in the close up photos (Figs. 22.5, 22.7 and 22.8). It is a cavity about 1/8-inch wide, and about 3/16-inch deep. This external opening is facing forward, and is located between and below the nostril and eye. There is one on each side of the head. At the rear of the cavity is a concave membrane, shaped like a shallow bowl, which has nerves which connect to the snakes brain. These nerves respond to tiny sudden changes in infrared radiation.

A mouse radiates heat from its body, and the frequency and intensity change with the temperature and size of the prey. The rattlesnake is able to detect a temperature change as slight as 0.003 degrees C in only 0.1 seconds and at a distance of about 18 inches in total darkness. The left and right field of vision overlaps and provides precise information to direct an accurate strike. This infrared vision is perfect for hunting warm blooded or endothermic prey such as birds and animals at night. Recent studies suggest that the pit vipers are able to see images generated by the pit organs.

As the mouse passes in front of the snake, the pit organs and eyes aim the strike. Injection of venom is triggered by contact with the mouse's body. The snake releases the mouse from the strike, and returns to its pre-strike position. The strike is more like a stabbing motion with the mouth opening nearly 180 degrees, but the lower jaw does not clamp down. The snake recoils, avoiding injury from the struggling prey, as the mouse continues to hop a short distance before collapsing from the shock of the venomous bite, and is usually dead within one minute. The rattlesnake uses tongue flicking to follow the brief scent trail of the crippled mouse. It then grabs the dead mouse by the snout, and begins to swallow it. This swallowing may take from a few minutes to up to a half-hour depending upon the size of the snake and prey.

The venom is manufactured in modified salivary glands located behind the eyes. The glands and muscles (See Appendix III) that inject the venom give the rattlesnake the extremely enlarged triangular shaped head as seen in Fig. 22.9. The rattlesnake is able to voluntarily control the injection of venom during a strike. It is able to inject venom through one fang, both fangs, or inject no venom at all, resulting in a dry bite. Studies have shown that when a rattler is finally antagonized enough to strike, there is a 30 percent or greater chance that it will not inject venom. The use of venom is related to feeding, not defense. Venom glands must replace the lost venom from each strike-bite, and that takes time. Wasting venom on an animal such as the human is not a natural phenomenon, and only occurs when the snake is harassed, extremely frightened or injured. The venom immobilizes, kills, and begins to digest the prey immediately.

Rattler venom is hemorrhagic, hemolytic, or hemotoxic, which means that it destroys muscle tissue and blood. It also contains agents that induce shock. The Timber Rattlesnake is more dangerous than the Northern Copperhead as far as the amount of venom that can be injected, and the potency of the venom. The standard way to estimate the potency of venom is to test the venom's killing power on mice. This test estimates the strength of venom by injecting calculated amounts of venom into a sample of mice. The dose that it takes to kill 50 percent of the tested mice within 24 hours is recorded. This dosage is called the LD_{50}. LD stands for "lethal dose" and is measured in milligrams of venom per kilograms of mouse weight. The copperhead has an LD_{50} of 10.90, whereas the Timber Rattlesnake has an LD_{50} of 1.64. It takes much less venom from a Timber Rattlesnake to kill a mouse, than it does from a Northern Copperhead. The total amount of venom that a snake is able to inject is also a factor in determining how dangerous a snake is. The amount of available venom from a copperhead is 40-75 mg., compared to 75-210 mg. from a rattlesnake. This amount is given as the dry weight of all the venom that could be milked from an adult snake. Taken the increased strength of the venom, and the increased amount of venom available to be delivered in a bite, the Timber Rattlesnake is potentially more dangerous than the Northern Copperhead. Rattlesnake bites are rare in Connecticut. In the past 50 years, only two people have been bitten by the Timber Rattlesnake, and they were both handling the snakes (See page 24).

Large specimens of the Timber Rattlesnake have curved fangs, which form an arc of from 60 to 70 degrees, and measures about 1/2-inch along this arc. The fangs of larger snakes are thicker, heavier-walled, stronger, and have a more hooked fang, with a greater curve. The hollow, elongated teeth are hinged at the front of the snakes mouth on a short bone that is able to rotate forward and backward. When not in use, the fang folds backward and upward against the roof of the mouth, where it lies enclosed in a membranous sheath. The fangs erect together, but may be rotated independently, and moved back into their resting sheaths one at a time, after swallowing prey. Throughout the life of a snake, the teeth and fangs are shed and replaced regularly. Several replacement fangs are

Fig. 22.10: Illustration of young rattle, which has a definite tapered appearance, and retains the button from the snakes first shed.

arranged in a graduated series, with the largest replacement fang behind and above the functional fang. The fangs are replaced as they wear down or are broken. A rattler may shed several pair during its active season (See pages 25-28).

Climbing Behavior: Rattlers will also ambush prey at the animals burrow entrance, and at nesting sites of ground birds. They have been documented to climb trees and shrubs. Timber Rattlesnakes have been personally seen in Mountain Laurel bushes, and documented by Fritsch, in October 1986, as being found high up in some brush. It is always questionable whether these animals are simply sunning themselves or actively hunting birds. Most herpetologists that have studied these animals for years feel that, especially in the spring and fall, sightings of timbers in bushes are sunning themselves. The ground temperature is colder than the air temperature at those times of the year, so basking in bushes is common. When striking birds, rattlers will clamp down after the strike, holding onto the bird until the venom takes effect. Clark's research on the diet of the Timber Rattlesnake in 2001, revealed that 91 percent of the prey consumed by the northern population of Timber Rattlesnakes were mammals such as shrews, white-footed mice, house mice, chipmunks, wood rats, young squirrels and rabbits. About 7 percent of the diet consisted of birds, and about 1 percent was reptiles. He found that Timber Rattlesnakes exhibit an unusual degree of specialization on warm-blooded prey, even as juveniles. The neonates or newborns with prey in their stomachs, contained small mam-mals. It may be the case that these snakes simply are rodent specialists from birth. It would be interesting to see if juvenile timber rattlesnakes will even eat amphibians in a captive situation, personal communication Clark, 2003.

Rattle: Another feature that is distinctive to the Timber Rattlesnake is the rattle

250

itself, as seen in Fig. 22.10. A question that is often asked is whether rattlesnakes always rattle before they strike. Brennan's comment, 1995, puts this question at rest. "Left unmolested in the wild, the only striking a rattler does is for the purpose of obtaining food. If the snake buzzed every time it intended to strike its prey, it would probably die of starvation in a year or so." Klauber, 1972, states"…those of us who live in areas where rattlesnakes are quite common…almost never hear one unless we ourselves have disturbed it." The rattle is used as a warning, or bluffing device, to frighten animals that might injure the snake, thus avoiding damage to itself. Sounding the rattle is an automatic nervous reaction, to a frightening situation. It is not true however, that the rattlesnake will always sound a warning vibrating sound before every strike. Many conditions will affect whether a snake will sound its rattle or not. Some variables will include: the individual temperament of the snake; the suddenness of the intruding invader; whether the snake was frightened out of sleep; whether the snake is gravid or pregnant; the temperature of the snake and its surroundings; and the closeness of a hiding place. Vibrating the tail when angered or annoyed, is a common snake reaction used by venomous and harmless snakes. Some snakes, such as the Black Rat Snake, Northern Black Racer and Eastern Milk Snake in Connecticut will vibrate their tails among leaves, producing a sound similar the sound of a rattler's rattle.

The rattling sound comes from the rapid vibration of a series of loose-fitting, interlocking, cone-shaped scales on the tip of the snakes tail. The rattle is a series of these loosely linked thickened skin sheaths which are partially telescoped into each other like a column of hats, in such a way that they vibrate against one another from the muscular action of the snakes tail. Vibrating the tail at about 50 cycles per second, causes the edges of these scales to rub against on another. This produces the spine chilling buzzing sound that really does not sound like the usual, rattle vibration. It has often been likened to the sound of the cicada. Quite often the sound will be first heard when a person steps on a flat rock, under which a rattler is resting. The sound is amplified as it reverberates off the rocky enclosure. There is no vocabulary strong enough to describe the chills that run up along your neck, or the tingling sensation of your entire body as your senses all become alert as the rush of adrenaline floods your sympathetic nervous system, until you feel as high as an eagle soaring towards the sun. Large snakes produce louder, lower pitched sounds. The temperature of the snake and its surroundings will also affect the rate of vibration. The speed of vibration increases with higher temperature.

When the baby rattlesnake is born, it has a single rattle segment which is called the prebutton as seen in Fig. 22.11. This prebutton is lost when the newborn sheds its skin for the first time. This first skin molt typically occurs within ten days of birth. The youngster in Fig. 22.11 is close to its first molt. Notice how the eyes are clouded over, and the general appearance of the snake is dull and whitish. The technical term for the process of skin shedding or molting is ecdysis. Ecdysis begins with the death and dissolving of the bottom cells, which cause the outer skin to soften and become dull. The spectacle, or scale covering each eye, becomes milky and opaque which temporarily clouds the snakes vision. During this time, the snake stops feeding and remains hidden. In a few days, the spectacle clears, and within three to five days the snake sheds the old skin sheath in a single piece. Shedding usually beings at the lip scales, as the snake rubs its chin against a rough surface to loosen the skin, and continues rubbing, catching the loose skin on a rock or branch to act as an anchor. The snake crawls out of the old skin, much as peeling off a

Fig. 22.11: Newborn Timber Rattlesnake showing prebutton and opaque eyes, evident of preshed mode, September 1986.

girdle. The shedding cycle usually takes fourteen days. The new skin is more boldly colored and the patterns are more vivid.

The prebutton (Fig. 22.11) is thus replaced by the underlying button, which becomes the first retained rattle segment. The button is the end of the rattle, as seen in the photo above, until such time that it is broken off from injury. The hardened thickened skin or keratin, covering the living hidden tip of the rattlesnake's tail, upon which the rattle is formed, is called the matrix. In Fig. 22.10, the matrix of this recently shed snake appears as the blue basal button that is firmly attached to the tip of the muscular tail. The end of the snake's backbone, or vertebral column, which is connected to the rattle, is called the style, or shaker. The vibratory muscles are attached to the base of the shaker. Six bundles of muscles make up the vibratory mechanism, with three on each side. If the button is intact, counting the number of segments will indicate the number of times the snake has shed its skin, but not necessarily how old the snake is. As the rattler grows, so does the matrix, so that each new segment is slightly larger than the previous one. This is seen in Fig. 22.10, taken in June of 1984, of the rattle of a third-year snake, which has a definite tapered appearance. The more mature animal in Fig. 22.3 has a perfect string of 9 segments, which still has the tapered structure and retains the button. An older snake, seen in Fig. 22.1, with nine segments, carries a uniform rattle in which every segment is the same size. The tapered section has been lost due to weather, wear and breakage. It is uncommon for a Timber Rattlesnake in the wild to carry a rattle with more than a dozen segments.

Reproduction: The massive elegant bulk of the gravid female in Fig. 22.12, is breath-taking in magnitude and spirit. She has at least ten segments to her rattle, with a

Fig. 22.12: The massive girth of this gravid or pregnant female Timber Rattlesnake is awe-inspiring. She was one of over a dozen females photographed in September 1986, and was basking in a sunny ledge area with abundant low-bush blueberry shrubs.

noticeable taper. Connecticut Timber Rattlesnakes do not produce their first litters of young until an average age of eight years, and thereafter produce young either every second or third year, depending upon climate, availability of food, and the health of the female. The gravid or pregnant females congregate in a warm, rocky area with no forest canopy cover, extensive low bush blueberry and mountain laurel, and an abundance of large flat warming, incubation rocks. The photo in Fig. 22.13 shows the immediate area of a rookery with several gravid females, postpartum females and newborns. In the center of the photo, another gravid female can found concealed in the low brush. Notice the emaciated postpartum female in Fig. 22.14. These photos were taken on September 14, 1986 in central Connecticut. Extreme gratitude and appreciation is acknowledged to Al Bagley for his help on this important photographic field trip.

Timber Rattlesnakes are known to mate in both the spring and the fall. Males locate females by tracking the pheromone scent trail left by the receptive females. Mating takes place on the summer foraging range as well as near the den. Males appear unusually active during mating season, not only seeking out females, but many observers have noticed a combat dance preformed by males around the denning areas. Brennan, 1995, recounts an encounter with two four-foot snakes that shot out from beneath a den rock. Their necks were intertwined as they muscled each other each other from side to side. The snakes were separated by Brennan. The snake that did not retreat remained poised for battle. The snake remained tense, holding its upright stance as it was placed back on the den rock. Upon release, it began patrolling the surface of the rock where two females had been basking. The other male returned to the rock, resting its head on the rock, watching

253

Fig. 22.13: Mother Timber Rattlesnake with her newborn. The mothers usually stay with their babies until the young have had their first shed, which is usually 8 to 12 days after birth. If conditions permit, the mother and young then forage for a couple of weeks before the babies follow their mother into the den. Youngsters can survive on stored yolk in their bodies, over the winter if they cannot get a meal first.

the other male. Fall mating results in the female storing the sperm throughout the winter hibernation time, with resulting egg fertilization the following spring. The average is a litter of eight newborns, which average 12.5 inches. The size of the litter is proportional to the size of the female. The young in Fig. 22.13, photographed with its mother was opaque, getting ready to shed for the first time in a few days. The postpartum females are very emaciated and weak after delivery, as seen in the Fig. 22.14 insert. They need at least three years of foraging, to become heavy enough to support another litter of young. The Timber Rattlesnake is a slow-reproducing species in its northern localities, with three to four year reproductive cycles, and late age for the first litters, as late as nine to ten years, Brown, 1991. The young stay with their mother until after their first shedding, at which time they forage for a meal, but it is not critical that they feed before entering hibernation. The young must follow the scent trails of the

Fig. 22.14: Mother Timber Rattlesnake illustrating extreme emaciation after the trial of pregnancy and delivery.

mother to the winter quarters, a den they will use for life.

Fig. 22.15: Two Timber Rattlesnakes at den opening October 1986. Notice 10-segment rattle, with the first few years string of rattles broken off. The remaining segments are all about the same dimensions, with no tapering, indicating an older animal.

This congregation of pregnant female Timber Rattlesnakes is one of the many reasons for the snakes extirpation, or annihilation by humans. During times of bounty hunting, before the protection of the Timber Rattlesnake, hunters would search out these nursery sites, kill the pregnant females, and then cut the baby snakes from their womb, so that the number of snakes turned in for bounty was increased tenfold, by turning in the unborn babies. This is a tragic example of mans inhumanity to life forms other than his own.

Range: The Timber rattlesnake is endemic, or native to North America. The range of *Crotalus horridus,* which includes the snakes commonly known as the Timber Rattlesnake, the Banded Rattlesnake, and the Canebrake Rattlesnake, includes 30 states. It ranges from New Hampshire and Vermont south through the Appalachians to northern Florida and Alabama; from southern Illinois, Indiana, and Ohio south through Kentucky and Tennessee to the Gulf Coast of Mississippi and Louisiana; and from southeastern Minnesota and southwestern Wisconsin south through eastern Iowa, Missouri, Arkansas and eastern Kansas, eastern Oklahoma and eastern Texas.

It seems to be most abundant in the Appalachian Mountains from northeastern Alabama to Pennsylvania. It is also abundant in certain heavily wooded portions of the Coastal Plain from North Carolina to Louisiana (Brown, 1993). The Timber Rattlesnake has been significantly reduced in at least 20 states including Connecticut, Massachusetts, New Hampshire, New Jersey, New York, Pennsylvania and Vermont. It was extirpated from Maine in the 1860s and from Rhode Island in the 1970s. It formerly occurred in southern Ontario, Canada, but has been extirpated there for over 50 years.

Fig. 22.16: Granite escarpment and ledge with accumulated talus, another den site for the Timber Rattlesnake in New England. May 1984.

Range in Connecticut: The rattlesnake's decline in Connecticut since colonial time is well documented. It is presently confined to small areas of northwestern and central Connecticut. Many dens are in state forests, but rattlesnakes are still killed both at the dens and at when they forage on private property during the summer. The Nature Conservancy has been purchasing land adjoining Meshomasic Forest and Berkshire Taconic Landscape as part of its "Last Great Places" campaign to preserve essential ecological gems remaining in southern New England. The Conservancy works with the DEP's Land Acquisition Unit to protect the home of one of the most important populations of Timber Rattlesnakes in New England. The Conservancy has been funding research on the Timber Rattlesnake and the Black Racer, for several years to better understand the movements and needs of these fascinating reptiles. Rattlesnakes require large tracts of unfragmented forest. Individual snakes forage a mile or more from their dens during the summer months.

Status: Heavy collection pressure at well-known den sites threatens the fragile population. The Timber Rattlesnake is fully protected and listed as an "Endangered Species" under CT ESA in Connecticut. It is strictly protected on public lands from persecution and collection. They are considered a high conservation concern throughout the Northeast, Klemens, 2000. A scientific permit system is in place.

According to the TNC/Heritage distribution Ranking System the Timber rattlesnake in the other New Enalgand states is as follows: Maine it is extirpated; Massachusetts, critically Imperiled: Rhode Island Extirpated; Vermont, Critically Imperiled; and New Hampshire, Critically Imperiled.

The state regulation in Massachusetts is fully protected and listed as Endangered under MA End. Spp. Act. Education and scientific permit system is in place. The state of New Hampshire lists the Timber Rattlesnake as fully protected and is listed as Endangered under NH Nongame Spp. Mgmt. Act. Research, conservation and exhibition permit system is in place. Collection and possession permits allowed with cutoff date of Jan. 1, 1996. In Rhode Island, the Timber Rattlesnake is listed as Extirpated. It is fully protected and listed as Protected under General Laws of Rhode Island. The state status in Vermont if fully protected and listed as Endangered under VT ESA. Scientific, propagation, zoological, education, economic hardship and special purposes permit system is in place in northern parts of the species range,

Habitat: Brown, 1993, has classified three distinct habitat types based on the snakes seasonal activity. These include den sites, transient or temporary migratory habitat, and summer range.

Den sites: In the northern colder zones, and mountainous parts of its range, the Timber Rattlesnake is defined by its den (Fig.22.15). The den sites, as previously discussed are usually rocky outcroppings, slopes, or fallen rock that provide underground crevices for protection from predators and extreme weather. In northeastern New England and New York, granite slopes and ledges with rockslides of talus are distinctive features at den sites (Fig.22.16). The dens typically face east, southeast or southwest. Elevations range between 500 and 1300 feet. In the Pine Barrens of southern New Jersey, den elevations are only between 80 and 140 feet, and are located along streams in white cedar swamps and bogs (Zappalorti and Reinert, 1992). In Connecticut and parts of New England, hibernation may last as long a seven months, from October to mid April or early May.

Transient habitat: Transient habitat is an area close to the den through which snakes migrate as they leave and return to their dens. These areas are rock outcroppings

Fig. 22.17: Example of transient habitat. The area has many shelter rocks, low bush blueberries and open canopy. The habitat a few feet above this secluded sunlit area was occupied by many pregnant and postpartum females with their young, September 1986.

with specific shelter rocks that are repeatedly used by individuals. Generally, it is located within 600 feet of the den. It tends to be rocky, but support more open woodland with exposed clearings and shelter rocks. The shelter and basking rocks are used by rattlesnakes migrating away from a den in the spring or toward the den in the autumn (Fig. 22.17). Timber Rattlesnakes are known to use specific shelter rocks year after year.

Transient habitat is also used by pregnant females. The warmer exposed rocky areas favor gestation. During this time of gestation and birthing, they are especially vulnerable. Reinert (1990) found that of all the females turned in during an organized Timber Rattlesnake hunt in Pennsylvania, 84% of them were gravid. The rocks provide warmth and some protection (Brown, 1995).

Summer habitat: Summer habitat of males and non gravid females are primary or secondary forests with 50-75 percent canopy closure overhead. The *gravid females* as mentioned earlier, inhabit more open, very rocky ranges with less canopy tree closure and warmer temperature for incubation. The surface vegetation for gravid females is about 25 percent, involving laurel and blueberry shrubs for concealment, but not significant shade. The *male* rattlesnakes prefer mature timber stands with about 75 percent closed forest canopy, with a supply of fallen logs, few rocks, and dense carpet of surface vegetation. *Non-gravid females* prefer a canopy closure of about 50 percent, with less surface vegetation, and can be found around old stone fencerows, foundations, and rock formation on abandoned farmland. These areas are referred to as rodent hotels for the summer. They will also utilize old stumps, logs and boulders as summer haunts. Piles of fallen timber at abandoned sawmills provide attractive summer dwellings, as well as old car dumpsites within their summer range. The non-gravid females need the abundant food supply and increased radiant warmth to restore their strength for future breeding seasons.

Reinert's extensive radiotelemetry work with the Timber Rattlesnake discovered that the largest part of the population spends most of the season in thick forest, lying motionless as they wait for prey. Howard Reinert's love and devotion to the salvation of the Timber Rattlesnake and other elegant snakes, has lead to increased knowledge about their natural history and microhabitat needs. He is on a deadline mission to save these stunning animals from imminent annihilation. We have a friend, who believes in peace, poise and power, in Pennsylvania (Brennan, 1995) and New England, in saving the Timbers from extinction.

Defensive behavior: The defenses of the Timber Rattlesnake, in addition to producing a spine- tingling buzzing cadence with its rattle, can cause ones neck hackles to stand on end, by emitting an incredibly ominous hiss, Brennan, 1995. It sounds like a combination of a stiff breeze swirling through a pine thicket and a balloon being inflated. Another defense tactic is the "swish," sound produced by a rattler's tail as it hastily disappears into a rock hideaway. When a rattler senses danger, it prefers to lie motionless, relying on its natural camouflage to conceal it. The Timber Rattlesnake is a very docile, strong quiet giant of the forest, and prefers to be left alone. If the threat continues, the snake will try to retreat to the closest hiding place. With no retreat available, it will form into a tight defensive coil, rear up off the ground, (Fig. 22.18), and if the harassment continues, it may feign a strike.

Predators: Timber rattlesnakes have been said to live to over thirty years, but the mortality rates during the first few years of life is high. One snake in a litter of eight may be fortunate to live to be four years old. Many others fall victim to starvation, freezing temperatures, parasites and perdition. Hawks, foxes, skunks, opossums, and coyotes have been well known predators of the rattlesnake. Deer and wild turkeys will also stomp rattlers. It has been suggested by some naturalists that the recent increased population of wild turkey in Connecticut could be influencing the declining rattlesnake population. However,

Fig.22.18: Fully aroused Timber Rattlesnake, with inflated body, hissing, and lifted, buzzing rattle. With raised head, it is suggesting one leave it alone, and step lightly around its turf.

humans have been the greatest predators. Since the earliest settlement of North America, hunting rattlesnakes at their dens became a regular seasonal activity.

Conservation:. In 1929, Babcock stated "It is probably only a matter of time when the timber rattlesnake in New England will share the fate of the passenger pigeon." (Brown, 1995). It was extirpated from Maine in the 1860s and from Rhode Island in the 1970s. As of 1992, Vermont population had been reduced to only two viable colonies. Taylor and Soha stated that the New Hampshire species status was precarious and well on the verge of extirpation in 1992 (Brown, 1995).

The major threats to the long-term survival of the Timber Rattlesnake include habitat degradation and destruction, collection for rattlesnake roundups and commercial skin and pet trades, intentional killing, and highway mortality. Other threats included bounty hunting, which is now illegal in most states, and logging and mining industries. Extensive disturbance to snake microhabitats has occurred in Connecticut and the Northeast, in the form of turning over rocks looking for snakes, thus disturbing dens, basking sites and shelters. Martin, 1992, feels that the population decline in the Northeast is due to hunting, and that depleted populations can recover if gravid females are not collected. He feels that summertime snake hunting is the biggest factor in the extirpation and reduction of the rattlesnake populations. The most well known case of illegal trade was the conviction of snake handler Rudy Komarek for poaching, illegal sale and murder of these beautiful snakes in 1993. Scientists say that Komarek, in collecting from 4,000 to 9,000 snakes illegally, devastated the populations of rattlesnakes in New York, Massachusetts and had a major impact on those of Connecticut and New Jersey. One primary snake collector is reported to account for the species decline in both New Hampshire and Minnesota.

DONT TREAD ON ME

Fig. 22.19: The "Don't Tread on Me" flag is the first Navy Jack flag displayed on the ships of the Continental Navy in 1775. This reproduction of the flag is courtesy of Chris Whitten.

The Timber Rattlesnake was once a prominent and respected predator in the forests of eastern North America. Excerpts from a letter, theoretically written by Benjamin Franklin, in *The Pennsylvania Journal* in 1775, elegantly speaks of the high esteem this snake was held in during our founding days as an independent proud nation. "Her eye exceeds in brilliance, that of any other animal, and she has no eyelids. She may therefore be esteemed an emblem of vigilance. She never begins an attack, or, when once engaged, she will never surrender. She is therefore an emblem of nobility and true courage. She never wounds until she has given her enemy just warning against the danger of treading on her. The poison of her teeth is the necessary means of digesting her food, and at the same time is the certain destruction of her enemies. The rattles are just thirteen, exactly the number of colonies united in America. One of the rattles, singly, is incapable of producing sound; but the ringing of thirteen together is sufficient to alarm the boldest man living. She is beautiful in youth and her beauty increases with age. Her tongue is also blue, and forked as lightning and her home is among the impenetrable rocks."

Less than two centuries later, these elegant, velvety creatures are endangered or already extinct throughout their former range. Native Americans and early colonists did not wipe out entire populations of Timber Rattlesnakes. It was the widespread persecution of them in the late nineteenth and twentieth centuries that removed tens of thousands of them from the continent, just as with the demise of the Passenger Pigeons and the American Bison. This disrespect of life parallels the decline in human quality of life and thought for country life, and the pursuit of happiness. All creatures great and small deserve their place of peaceful coexistence, and right to life.

Fig. 22.20: Eastern Hognose often confused with Timber Rattlesnake. The tight coiled tail, large girth, hissing, and defensive behavior often frightens onlookers, and the harmless hognose becomes a rattler.

As a symbol of power and pride, the U. S. Navy Jack flag is again being displayed by all ships during the War on Terrorism. The photo of this flag and its history are credited to Chris Whitten. The **"Don't Tread on Me"** first Navy Jack flag was displayed in 1775 on the ships of the Continental Navy. The first U. S. Navy Jack is traditionally shown as consisting of 13 horizontal alternating red and white stripes with a superimposed rattlesnake and the motto "Don't Tread on Me" (Fig. 22.19). The rattlesnake had long been a symbol of resistance to British repressive acts in Colonial America. Along with the long diligent work of many people to save the rattlesnake from extinction, comes the renewal of the countries respect and love of freedom as represented by flying the First Navy Jack flag promoting pride, enhancing our country 's morale and dedicating respect for life and the pursuit of freedom.

The Timber Rattlesnake has a demure, docile temperament when unmolested. While photographing these awesome giants of the forest, lying upon the same birthing grounds used for centuries, a feeling of peace and wonder swarms through my soul. To be allowed to share their world and bring its beauty to hundreds of readers, I feel privileged to be a part of their salvation. Knowledge eliminates fear, replacing it with understanding and respect. Lying on my belly with my macro lens inches from these magnificent animals put me in a place of awe felt by few. The warm smell of humus, dried pine needles, blueberries, and fern, with the soft caresses of Septembers breath, I have found my secret place, and share the dedication to save these peaceful, beautiful, and elegant masterpieces of creation.

"The bottom line is that a formerly abundant predator is on the brink of disappearance in states where it once was emblematic of freedom and independence. Now Timber Rattlesnakes remind us that truly pristine landscapes no long exist in the eastern United States, and that only strict protection and carefully planned intervention will maintain many vertebrate populations into the twenty-first century" (Greene, 1997). ***Dedicated to Love and the preservation of free-ranging timbers for our children to respect and admire.***

Common Names: The Timber Rattlesnake has been known as the banded or velvet-tail in the north, and the canebrake rattler in the south. The scientific name *Crotalus* is Greek for rattle, and *horridus* is Latin, for terrible or fearful.

Similar species: The following snakes are sometimes confused with the Timber Rattlesnake. These errors in identification are made in the field, usually because a startled

Fig. 22.21: Dark phase Timber Rattlesnake and the dark phase Eastern Hognose look a lot alike in the field.

Fig. 22.22: Newborn Timber rattlesnake about 10 days old looks like baby Eastern Hognose in field.

Fig. 22.23: The young Black Rat and the young Northern Black Racer are notoriously mistaken for the Timber rattlesnake because they occupy the same habitats, and they have pugnacious temperaments. Being high-strung youngsters, they often strike and vibrate their tails, causing a buzzing sound, especially in dried leaves. Almost every call to a frightened homeowners property leads to the identification of one of these two youngsters.

snake starts vibrating its tail in the leaves, and the immediate response, without even looking, is that a rattlesnake has been found, and the rumors spread like wild fire. The Eastern Hognose snakes in Fig. 22.20 frighten people because they hiss, form tight coils with their tails that resemble a rattle, and often rear off the ground and strike.

Appendix (I): Timber Rattlesnake Head Scale Identification

Head Scales of Timber Rattlesnake: dorlolateral view of Connecticut animal.

A: nostril.

b: prenasal: scale directly in front of the nostril.

c: postnasal: scale directly behind the nostril.

d: rostral: large scale on the front of the nose.

e: internasals: two scales in contact with the *rostral* and nasal scales.

f: canthrals: the border scales on top of the head between the *internasals* and the *supraoculars*.

g: intercanthrals: the small scales on the top of the head between the *canthrals.*

h: supraoculars: the large scale extends above and over the eye, resembling a furrowed eyebrow.

263

i: intersupraoculars: the small scales on top of the head between the supraoculars.

j: upper preocular: the large *ocular* scale in front of the eye.

k: lower preocular: the narrow elongate *ocular* scale below the upper preocular in front of the eye.

l: postocular: the small scales directly behind the eye.

m: subocular: the small scales under the eye, between the *postoculars* and the *lower pre-ocular.*

n: interoculabials: the small scales below the center of the eye between the eye and lip, which include the *suboculars* and *supralabials.*

o: pit: the opening to a heat sensing imaging receptor.

p: lacunal: the cells lining the inside of the *pit,* which are usually visible from the outside, and contact the small *foveal* scales.

q: subfoveals: *foveal* scales (small scales that surround the outside border of the pit), between the *lacunal* (p) and *supralabials* (u).

r: prefoveals: cluster of small scales (*foveal*), which are located within a triangular area between the *lacunals* (p), *loreals* (v), *postnasal* (c), and *supralabials* (u).

s: postfoveals: *foveal* scales between the *subfoveals* (q) and the *suboculars* (m).

t: infralabials: scales that extend along the lower lip, also called lower *labials,* from the *mental* to the *angle of the mouth.*

u: supralabials: scales that extend along the upper lip, also called upper *labials,* from the *rostral* to the *angle of the mouth.*

v: loreals: the scales (two) between the *postnasal* (c) and the *preoculars* (j and k)on the side to the head.

Diagram of Rattle: (Adapted from Klauber, 1972)
(b): *button:* the first permanent rattle.

p): *proximal rattle*: last rattle formed.

(t): *terminal rattle:* previous segments lost.

Diagram of *Fang* of pit viper: (Adapted from Klauber,1972)

(m): *maxillary bone.*

(p): *pedestal* or pedicel which forms the union with the maxillary bone, and is usually left on the bone when the fang is broken off.

(e): *entrance lumen* where venom enters from the venom gland.

(d): *dentine* or enamel covers the venom canal and outer surface of the fangs.

(v): *venom canal* through which the venom flows to the tip.

(o): *discharge orifice* through which the venom flows into prey, etc.

(c): *pulp cavity.*

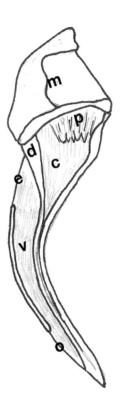

Venom mechanism of pit viper.

(g): *venom gland,* one located on each side of the head, behind and below the eye, just above the angle of the mouth. Several lobes of secretory cells in the gland produce the venom. The secretions strain though small tubes into the lumen, or hollow space of the gland.

(v): *venom duct,* a tube, which carries the venom from the lumen of the venom gland, through the maxillary bone (m), to the base of the fang.

a): *accessory glands* are small masses of glandular tissue surrounding the venom ducts. The glands may serve as valves to control the flow of venom to the fang, and the secretions, though not toxic, may act as a catalyst to activate components in the venom, for the venom taken from the fang is more toxic than venom removed from the lumen of the venom gland.

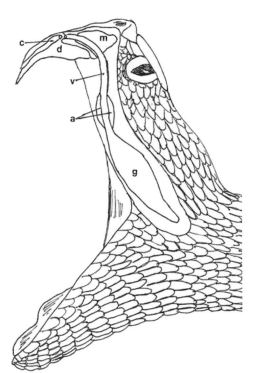

(c): *venom canal* receives venom flow from the sheath of connective tissue that surrounds the base of the fang.

(v): *venom duct,* does not flow directly into the venom canal, but passes through the *maxillary* bone **(m)**, opening next to the fang, in the sheath, where the venom is directed into and through the canal , through the discharge orifice, just above the solid *dentine* **(d)** covered tip and into the prey

Appendix II:
Radiotelemetry Studies on Snakes. The following is a review of Howard K.

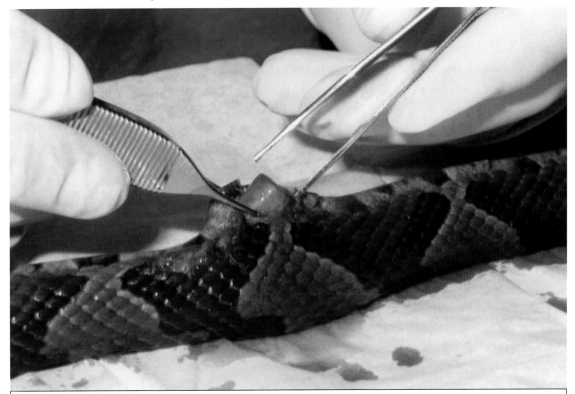

C.F. Smith, Department of Ecology and Evolutionary Biology at the University of Connecticut removing depleted transmitter apparatus to be replaced by unit with new battery, July 2002.

Reinerts work on pioneering surgical implantation in the body cavity of snakes.

Through trial and error and persistent, diligent effort, radiotelemetry, or radio tracking, has evolved into one of the most valuable tools in wildlife biology. With its use, the field researcher is able to consistently locate and relocate free-ranging research animals. There has been no greater achievement for the study of mysterious, colorfully camouflaged animals, into which group the elusive snake fits beautifully.

The first use of radiotelemetry involving snakes was reported by Osgood in 1970. He studied thermoregualtion, which is the study of how animals keep their body temperatures at a constant level by processes of heat production and heat transfer, in the Banded Water Snake, *Nerodia fasciata*, and the Brown Water Snake, *Nerodia taxispilota* in outdoor enclosures. Later, in 1971, Fitch and Shirer reported their results of a radiotelemetric study of free-ranging relationships in some common snakes. Both research studies used ingestion as the method of attachment for the transmitter unit. This method has several shortcomings. Transmitter units that are small enough to pass into the snakes intestinal tract are evacuated in the feces rather rapidly. Larger transmitters that are forced down the snakes esophagus are usually regurgitated. To prevent this, a constriction band was applied around the snakes body (Fitch and Shirer, 1971, and Fitch, 1987). In both cases, the duration of the tracking is limited, and the ingested units interrupt normal feeding and digestion. The normal health and behavior of the unfortunate snake is severely disrupted. Reinert does not recommend the use of a constricting band under any circumstances where normal behavior is desired!

The use of telemetry in the study of the ecology; which is the branch of biology that deals with the relations between living organisms and their environment, and physiology; which is the.branch of biology dealing with the functions and vital processes of living organisms, under field conditions is increasing rapidly. Pitvipers have been well represented in recent telemetric studies from 1973 to the present. Reinert has been intimately involved in the study of the copperhead *Agkistrodon contortrix*, and rattlesnakes of the genus *Crotalus* and *Sistrurus*.

Transmitters containing a crystal controlled oscillator, measuring the values between minimum and maximun frequencies, are the most commonly used for wildlife tracking. They have greater stability than the early transmitters that operated in the AM and FM frequency bands. They also have longer transmission distance and more precise transmission band width. The band width feature allows for the use of several transmitters within the same limited area, with minimal overlap in the signals received. These transmitters usually operate at either CB or VHF frequencies. CB bands are used a lot because of the relatively low cost of the receiving systems, but they are generally very crowded with unwanted signals and the transmitters have short lives. Transmitters that operate with the VHF 150-151 MHz frequency range are preferred for the field study of snakes.

The transmitters are usually powered by a 1.35-volt mercury battery and a whip antenna. The whip antenna allows for the greatest transmission distance. The length of the antenna is determined by the frequency of the transmitter, the transmission distance and the length of the snake. The assembled unit, transmitter, battery and antenna are coated in a 1:1 mixture of beeswax and paraffin. This forms a water-resistant coating, which also prevents tissue irritation. Some snakes (*Crotalus horridus*) have carried these coated transmitters inside their body cavities for as long as nine years with no obvious tissue irritation or transmitter damage.

The receiver is the most important piece of telemetric equipment. Most transmitters produce very weak signals that require sensitive receiving equipment. A hand-held 3-element Yagi tracking antenna is the most suitable for locating snakes.
Headphones are a valuable addition to the tracking unit. They reduce irrelevant external sounds such as planes, motor vehicles and static. A weak signal that is accompanied with considerable static may only be recognizable with the aid of headphones.

The preferred method of implantation is the body, or coelomic cavity. Reinert and Cundall, in 1982, described the simple surgical implantation of long rang transmitters with external whip antennae. Reinert has used this method to successfully implant well over 100 snakes of 8 different species including 4 species of pitvipers (Copperheads, *Agkistrodon contortrix*, Timber Rattlesnake, *Crotalus horridus*, Prairie Rattlesnake, *Crotalus viridis*, and theMassasauga Rattlesnake, *Sistrurus catenatus)*. Infection and death assigned to the transmitter implants have been negligible. Snakes have shown normal growth rate and feeding behavior. Implanted females have produced healthy broods of young snakes.

Snakes should be anesthetized before surgery. Inhalable anesthetics such as halothane or isoflurane are recommended over injectable anesthetics. Reinert introduces the first anesthesia to snakes in a 5-gallon glass aquarium which is fitted with a sliding Plexiglas lid. A small wad of cotton, saturated with anesthetic is placed in the bottom of the aquarium. The snake is placed into the aquarium, and the sliding lid is gradually pushed down toward the floor of the aquarium, the distance depending upon the size of the snake. This forces the snake to remain at the bottom of the aquarium where the anesthetic is strongest.

After the anesthetized snake has been removed from the aquarium, its head is placed into clear plastic tube, which has been fitted with a stopper at one end, followed by a wad of cotton saturated with the inhalable anesthetic, which in turn is followed by a piece of screening. The anesthetized snake can be moved closer to the cotton if more anesthesia is needed, and pulled away, if the need for anesthesia is reduced. This chamber can also be used for the beginning anesthetic dosage.

Transmitters should be placed in the body cavity where they will cause the least interference with body functions and internal organs. For most pitvipers this is approximately three-fourths of the distance from the head to the vent.

The actual field radio tracking is an art that requires extreme patience and practice. Transmission signals are influenced by the location and body position of the snake, by the surrounding surface features and canopy structure, which pertains to the upper leaf layer of the forest. The best signal will usually be obtained from the highest position that allows a clear and broad view. In valleys and canyons, reflected signals may appear stronger than signals coming from the actual direction of the animal. In hilly mountainous terrain, it is best to approach a snake from above its position. This will reduce disturbing the animal, and increase the probability of seeing the snake before it sees you. In most cases, it is necessary to locate snakes a minimum of once every two days, simply to keep from losing individuals that are dispersing.

The use of radiotelemetry in snake research has proven to be far superior to the old traditional random surveys and mark and recapture methods. Many previously accepted *facts* about snake behavior and the habitats that they use have been overturned. Because of the humane, gentle monitoring methods established by Reinert and Cundall, researchers are able to monitor a greater number and variety of individuals for longer periods. This reduces the bias, or systematic error, resulting from the differences between statistical values pertaining to an entire population of snakes, and the random sample drawn from that population.

The limitations of telemetry include the relatively high cost of the equipment and the high cost in terms of time and effort. Frequent location of specimens is required to avoid loss of the snakes. Reinert found that simultaneously monitoring 25 Timber Rattlesnakes, and Copperheads, required nearly constant fieldwork. The information gained from such studies tends to be based upon a large body of data obtained from a small sample size of the real population of snakes under study.

Telemetry also puts restrictions on the physical size of the animals, which are monitored. Transmitters are too large for use in many of the smaller snake species, or in the young individuals of larger species. Smaller transmitters and passive transponders may help to remove this problem in the future. However, the data that is presently being accumulated is strongly biased toward larger snakes.

The frequent handling, surgery, and constant disturbance of the monitored snakes, along with the physical burden of the transmitters themselves may all tend to alter the behavior of the snakes.

With the aid of telemetry, a dedicated researcher can gain insight into the biology of free-ranging snakes that cannot be obtained by any other method. During the past two decades, telemetric studies have contributed greatly to the understanding of the natural history of snakes. Much of what will be learned during the next two decades will also be directly attributable to the use of radiotelemetry. The new generation of researchers can use this technology to monitor a free-roaming snakes temperature, heart rate, blood pressure, neuromuscular activity, digestion, reproduction and much more (Howard K. Reinert, 1992).

Appendix III:

Captive Care: Before any attempt to collect snakes in Connecticut, or any other state, is attempted, you should check with your state authorities, the Fish and Game, Nongame, or Wildlife Departments to find out what species are protected, and what restrictions apply to collection. Although regulations have been presented in each chapter of this book, one must realize that these regulations quickly become outdated, and it is of paramount importance that up-to-date regulations are acquired and abided by. The Department of Environmental Protection will also provide a list of endangered or threatened snakes that are protected by federal regulations.

Rules and restrictions vary from state to state, and in some, you may need a permit to collect any animals. The number and kinds of snakes are sometimes strictly controlled. There are also closed seasons, which must be abided by. Transporting snakes across state lines may also be prohibited. Sometimes a permit is required to keep your captive as a pet in your home. After the above information has been obtained, the following protocol may help in making and transporting your catch.

The best tools for catching snakes are your own two hands. Most harmless snakes can be grabbed by the tail, and gently pulled towards you. Slip your free hand under their belly, and, without restricting them in any strong hold, allow them to glide between your fingers, and up your arm with no restraint. If the snake does not feel threatened, it will not become defensive, and no biting or striking postures are presented. If the snake is approached head-on, it is likely to become defensive, assume a strike position, and possibly inflict a frightening strike, and/or bite.

The standard approach has always been to pin the head of the snake to the ground with some kind of *snake stick*. I have found in the 25 years of search and seizure tactics, that the frontal attack is not only dangerous to the attacker, but also injurious to the snake. With all but venomous snakes, and they should not be molested, captured or in any other way handled; a quick tail grab, and gentle backward tension is the safest, least harmful to captor and captive, method of capture. I recommend wearing a light pair of cotton gloves, just in case the snake wants to bite. The wearing of gloves removes the apprehension of the bite, and thus reduces the negative vibrations that you send towards your friend. If you are not frightened and on guard, then the snake will not be frightened and on the defensive. After years of experience, I personally do not recommend the use of snake sticks. I do not condone the capture of venomous snakes. Research specialists have their own methods of search and seizure, which are not applicable to the everyday snake lover and enthusiast, so their methods are not recommended for hobbyists.

Once the snake is gently captured, it can be put in a collecting bag, or simply admired, studied and immediately released.. If you choose to keep the precious animal for a period of time, I have always found a pillowcase to be an adequate collection bag. The simplest way to confine the snake is to tie an overhand knot in the top of the bag. Care must be taken not to tie the neck of the snake in the knot, be careful to keep the snake from climbing up the bag when the knot is tied.

If you chose to house the snake at home for a short period of observation and friendship, I have found that the best enclosure is a 10 gallon glass aquarium., with a slate bottom. The bottom of the aquarium is to be covered with newspaper (about 4 pages in thickness) cut to fit the sized aquarium that you chose for the snake. Terrariums of moss, earth and other substratum are not recommended, due to the introduction of parasites and fungi. It is also very difficult to clean this kind of substratum, so the snakes feces may contaminate the environment, and cause illness and death in a short period of time. The aquarium should have a tight-fitting lid. The standard top is made out of wire screening. This is adequate, but I have found that when the snake rubs against such a lid, it can cause abrasions on the snout. I recommend a custom fit top made from pegboard, and a snug wooden frame. To secure it I used one or two bricks, depending upon the size and strength of the snake being housed. Hinged tops with locks may also be built if there is any chance that curious smaller children would try to get into the cage. Most snakes such as the garter, brown and black rat (check regulations here, juveniles are not to be taken, and to date only one adult is allowed to be removed from the wild) will tame easily with occasional handling and become good companions.

It is important to provide your snake with a hide box. I have found that one made from paneling or thin plywood is very durable and easy to clean. One can be easily constructed to fit the size snake you have housed. Cardboard boxes may become damp and disintegrate. Plastic butter tubs, with an opening cut on the side at floor level, can be easily cleaned , and make good hiding places.

Install a water dish large enough for the snake to submerge itself completely, but heavy enough so the snake cannot tip it over. Most snakes, including water snakes, do best if their temporary home is kept dry except for the water dish. If the snakes quarters are too damp, it will often develop skin blisters and infections.

Snakes are cold-blooded animals whose temperatures are similar to the temperatures of the cage in which it lives. When they are cold, their body functions slow down and appetites are poor or nonexistent. If they are exposed to too much heat, they can die. Temperatures of between 75 and 85F are best for most snakes. Small round stick on thermometers are available at pet stores that are highly recommended to monitor the temperature inside the aquarium. Never set a cage entirely in the sunshine or in a spot where the sun may strike it later in the day, for your captive will be baked. Morning sunshine is gentle and less intense.

It is highly recommended to release your native snake where you found it no later than September, so it can find its hibernaculum, and over-winter safely. If you keep it during the winter, it will usually refuse to eat, and should be maintained at a temperature in the fifties until spring, but must be supplied with water.

Snakes have specialized feeding habits, and their food is mentioned in the text for each species. Keeping a snake as a pet is an interesting pastime, but it takes time and effort. You will find it practical to keep an animal for only a few days or weeks as you study them and become friends then free them where you caught them. Never turn them loose in a strange environment where it will almost certainly die (Conant/Collins, 1998).

Appendix IV: Range Maps of New England Snakes adopted from Conant/Collins, 1998.

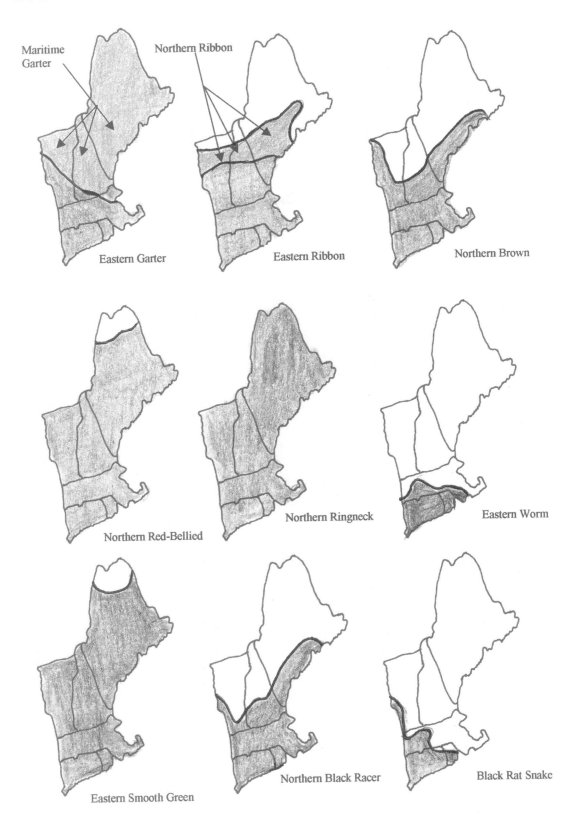

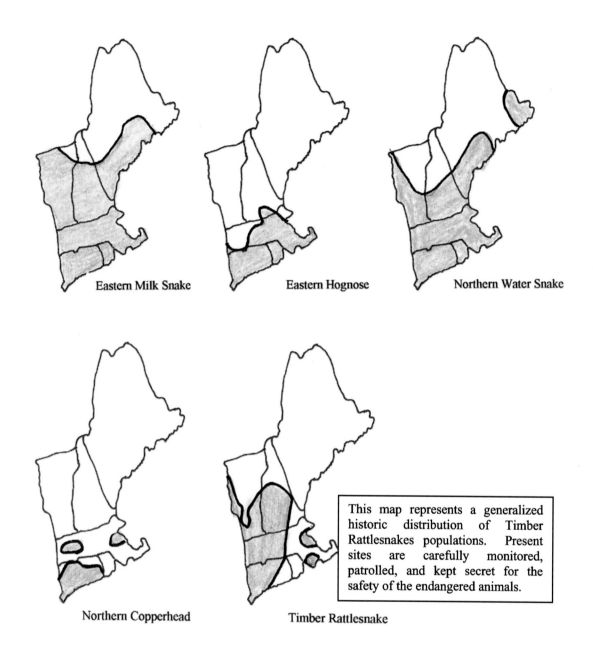

Eastern Milk Snake

Eastern Hognose

Northern Water Snake

Northern Copperhead

Timber Rattlesnake

This map represents a generalized historic distribution of Timber Rattlesnakes populations. Present sites are carefully monitored, patrolled, and kept secret for the safety of the endangered animals.

Subspecies of Snakes in Northern New England that are not present in Southern New England:

Maritime Garter Snake: The Maritime Garter Snake (*Thamnophis sirtalis pallidus*) inhabits the extreme Northeast. It is a subspecies of the Eastern Garter Snake, and is one of the 2 subspecies of snakes that inhabit northern New England, but are not present in Connecticut. Its maximum length is 36 inches. The ground color is cinnamon brown, yellowish olive or olive-gray with alternating rows of black or dark brown spots in a checkerboard pattern. The dorsal stripe can be gray, tan or yellow, and is often lacking, or visible only on the front of the snake and poorly developed. The side stripes are whitish, gray or tan with very little contrast. The belly is whitish near the neck and becomes progressively dusky gray towards the tail. The young resemble the adults and average 6.4 inches in length at birth. Its range extends from Southern Quebec, to the Eastern Shore of

James Bay, east to the Gulf of St. Lawrence and Nova Scotia, and south in New England to extreme northeastern Massachusetts.

Northern Ribbon Snake: The Northern Ribbon Snake (*Thamnophis sauritus septentrionalis*) is a subspecies of the Eastern Ribbon Snake, and is second of 2 subspecies of snakes that inhabit northern New England, but are not present in Connecticut. It is very similar to the Eastern Ribbon Snake, but is smaller and darker. The back is velvety black to dark brown. The yellow middorsal stripe is not always complete, and becomes partly obscured by brown pigment. The tail is shorter than the Eastern Ribbon Snake, being less than 1/3 the total length of its body. It ranges from Maine to Michigan, south to Indiana and northern Ohio with isolated colonies in Nova Scotia and eastern Wisconsin.

Snakes inhabiting the 5 other New England States:

Maine: The following snakes inhabit the state of Maine: The Eastern Milk Snake, Eastern Smooth Green Snake, Northern Black Racer, Northern Water Snake, Northern Brown Snake, Northern Red-Bellied Snake, Maritime Garter Snake and the Northern Ringneck Snake.

Vermont: The following snakes are found in Vermont: The Timber Rattlesnake, Eastern Milk Snake, Black Rat Snake, Eastern Smooth Green Snake, Northern Black Racer, Northern Water Snake, Northern Brown Snake, Northern Red-Bellied Snake, Eastern Garter Snake, Maritime Garter Snake, Eastern Ribbon Snake, Northern Ribbon Snake, and Northern Ringneck Snake.

New Hampshire: The following snakes are found in New Hampshire: The Timber Rattlesnake, Eastern Milk Snake, Eastern Smooth Green Snake, Northern Black Racer, Northern Water Snake, Maritime Garter Snake, isolated population of Eastern Garter Snake, Eastern Ribbon Snake, Northern Ribbon Snake, and Northern Ringneck Snake.

Massachusetts: The following snakes inhabit Massachusetts: The Timber Rattlesnake, Northern Copperhead, Eastern Milk Snake, Black Rat Snake, Eastern Smooth Green Snake, Northern Black Racer, Northern Water Snake, Northern Brown Snake, Northern Red-Bellied Snake, Eastern Garter Snake, Northeastern population of Maritime Garter Snake, Eastern Ribbon Snake, Eastern Hognose Snake, Northern Ringneck Snake, and Eastern Worm Snake.

Rhode Island: The following snakes are found in Rhode Island: the Eastern Milk Snake, Black Rat Snake, Eastern Smooth Green Snake, Northern Black Race, Northern Water Snake, Northern Brown Snake, Northern Red-Bellied Snake, Eastern Garter Snake, Eastern Ribbon Snake, Eastern Hognose Snake, Northern Ringneck Snake and the Eastern Worm Snake. *Rhode Island has no venomous snakes*, the Timber Rattlesnake was extirpated over 30 years ago, and the Northern Copperhead has no historic record in Rhode Island.

Appendix V: Northeast's only Reptile, Amphibian Rescue Rehabilitation Center. Ashleigh's Garden and Rainforest

Allison Sloane has made a dream come true, very similar to my own journey, to

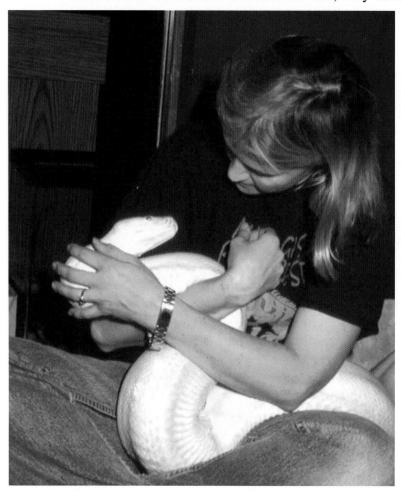

help save the unloved and misunderstood reptiles and amphibians of our world. Allison graduated from Southern Connecticut State University, another circle of life, as often mentioned in this book, the same university that I attended 20 years earlier! Allison always dreamed of operating a safe house for abused and rejected pet herps. Many people purchase reptiles and amphibians on a whim, to have a different type of pet. This new enthusiasm rapidly turns to neglect, and most pets die, usually a long slow suffering death from starvation, dehydration, infection, disease and torture.

It is a sad, eye-opening experience to enter Allison's haven of love. As soon as I met her, there was an instantaneous spiritual unity, and an immediate huge hug ensued. She has a healing soul-quality about her, which just radiates like a lovely rose.

There are over 150 reptiles and amphibians in Allison's care. The accommodations are clean, airy, and warm! The tropical rainforest feeling is very poignant as one enters the protected herp hotel.

The entrance to this marvelous facility is a beautiful floral and gift shop, full of unusual treasures and antiques. The flower arrangements accentuate the feelings of caring and love that just seem to surround everything. Patrons and guests are greeted by Oliver, a magnificently colorful, vociferous Blue-Gold Macaw.

The rainforest section of the facility is in the rear of the building. There is a large snake room filled with now healthy happy herps. Burmese and Ball Pythons are plentiful, and well as boas and cornsnakes. The large snakes are often the most abundant rescue-animals. When purchased by the unwitting new pet owner, the snakes are usually only 2-3 feet long. They rapidly become 6-8 footers, needing more food, care and maintenance. These animals become objects of neglect quickly, and unless someone like Allison hears about them and provides a warm loving home, they usually die. The lovely albino python in the photo was one such abused animal, which was put into rehab and intensive care. Recovery was slow but steady, and now the affection expressed by both Allison and the python is evident in the aura of love radiating from the photo.

There is a large terrarium with turtles, and a lizard room adjacent to it. Large lizards are also subjects of neglect, for the same reasons as the large snake species. They are purchased as small adorable creatures, which eventually become large, and can be dangerous. Monitor lizards grow quickly to a 3-foot length, and when neglected, hungry and thirsty, they become aggressive and dangerous. As soon as Allison puts these abused animals into her care, within a short few weeks, they are docile, well fed, and healing from whatever bodily wounds were inflicted upon them. This healing spirit emanates from all the rooms.

Allison has always loved reptiles and amphibians, and felt a strong need to save the abused animals, and give them a place to recuperate and heal. Her 20-year study of captive care and herp-medicine has made her quite the expert on the art of healing and saving these previously unfortunate animals. The manner of abuse is beyond belief. Snakes and lizards have been burned, stabbed, had their tongues cut out, and been inundated by terrible infections from dirty cages. This abuse is a testimonial to the cruelty so often expressed toward "cold-blooded" animals, and is tragic to witness.

One of Allison's main interests is to educate people about the care and handling of reptiles and amphibians as pets. She has education programs constantly, and does a lot of birthday-party gatherings, where children have fun learning about these wonderful animals, and get the chance to feel, touch, hold and admire a life form so unique and different from theirs. A respect develops. Education smoothes the rough edges of fear, and children learn to treat all creatures with love and tenderness.

Allison has over 20 years of experience nursing injured herps, and do incredible intensive care and surgery on sick reptiles. She works with area veterinarians and herpetologists to provide the best care possible in this one and only, unique rehabilitation center in the New England area. She has an army of over 30 volunteers, many of them students. One such student, Jeffrey Ackley drives many miles from his school, the Franklin Academy, to give his time and love to this wonderful establishment. As Jeff muses, as he holds a bull snake, "The best part of the job is to hold and soothe the troubled animals, and feel them reciprocate the love."

The facility has been open for almost 3 years, and already has over 150 rescued and rehabilitated animals. It is a haven of healing and love. There are rescue facilities for other animals, but not for reptiles and amphibians. Allison's dream was to fill that void, and open a rescue center for abused and neglected herps.   She has fulfilled her dream, and given life to so many abused turtles, lizards and snakes.   She offers hope to the generation of children that she teaches, so that the abuse may stop, and tenderness and understanding may take its place.

The center is funded by contributions, and donations, and by Allisons flower shop, "Ashleigh's Garden and Rainforest of Centerbrook Connecticut, which is named after her daughter, Ashleigh.

GLOSSARY

Abdomen: the lower surface of the body between the neck and the anus.

Adaptation: any structure, behavior, or biological changes that gives an organism a better chance to survive and reproduce in its environment.

Adult: a fully developed and mature animal, physiologically capable of breeding, but not necessarily doing so until social and/or ecological conditions allow.

Aestivate (estivate): to become dormant during the summer or dry season, when food is scarce.

Aestivus: summer.

Aestivation: the reduction of activity by an organism, usually as a response to high temperatures or scarcity of water, draught.

Agkistrodon: hooked tooth.

Aglyphous: possessing teeth with no grooves or a closed canal.

Albino: any animal that is born with no skin pigment.

Ambient temperature: the temperature of the environment surrounding the animal in question.

amoenus: pleasing, charming.

Anal gland: A sac-like structure in the base of the tail of a snake, with an opening through the cloacal wall near the anus, which is present in both sexes, and usually paired. The secretion is a foul smelling, musky substance, which is often excreted with cloacal contents when the snake is handled.

Anal plate: the last ventral scale lying just in front of the anus, vent, or cloacal opening in snakes. It marks the division between the body and the tail. It is single or paired,(entire) or (divided).

Anaphylactic (shock): a severe reaction of allergy or hypersensitivity following injection of a foreign substance. There may be respiratory, circulatory, and neurological symptoms; the condition is often fatal if untreated.

Anavenom: Snake venom which has been treated to destroy its toxic properties, while keeping its ability to stimulate the formation of antibodies. When this detoxified venom is injected into the blood of a living animal such as a horse, these antigens cause antibody formation in the horse, and the development of immunity to the anavenom. The serum from the blood of the animal, called *antivenin*, can then be used in snakebite treatment. Sometimes the use of the horse-based antivenin in humans can cause sever reactions in the blood of humans that are sensitive or allergic the horse serum. Similar words used to express the same meaning are: anatoxin, anavenin, and toxoid.

Angle of the jaw: The angle formed by the bony joining of the lower jaw and the skull.

Angle of mouth: The angle formed by the fleshy tissue surrounding the *angle of the jaw*. This angle is covered by the junction of the upper and lower *labial* or lip scales in snakes. It is also called the rictus of the mouth, or commissure.

Anguiform: Snake-shaped, or snake-like.

Anterior: The front or head end of an animal.

Antibody: A protein produced by the body in response to the introduction of a foreign substance, or *antigen*. The antibody reacts with the antigen to neutralize its harmful effect on the body.

Antigen: A substance, usually a protein, which, when introduced directly into the body through the blood stream, causes the production of an *antibody*, which has the specific ability to neutralize the foreign protein, or antigen.

Antivenin: a serum that is prepared from the blood of an organism, commonly horses, that has been immunized against the venom of a specific snake species through injecting increasing strengths of *anavenom*, venom, or a combination of the two. When this serum is injected into a second organism, such as man, to treat snakebite envenomation, the immunity is transferred to the second organism. Anitvenin for one species can act against venom of a second species. Similar words used to express the same meaning are anti-serum, antivenom, snakebite serum, and snake venom antitoxin.

Anticoagulant: Inhibits the clotting of blood.

Anti-predator behavior: Actions an animal takes to keep predators from eating it.

Anus: The posterior opening of the digestive tract which marks the division between the body and the tail.

Apical scale pits: Depressions, usually two, which are faintly visible on the posterior end of a scale.

Apnea: A pause in breathing.

Aposematism: Characterized by bright or contrasting coloration, which serves to warn off potential predators. Animals that are bright red or yellow are often toxic or distasteful, their colors discourage predators from eating them.

Aquatic: Frequenting water, or living in water. Technically, only animals that have gills for extracting oxygen from water are aquatic, others, such as snakes are semiaquatic.

Arboreal: Inhabiting or frequenting trees and or high bushes.

Auditory mechanism: In snakes, this mechanism is referred to as the vestibulo-quadrate mechanism, which is a bone-conducting system of "hearing" in which the *columella,* or inner ear bone, receives vibrations from the lower jaw and is responsible for sound transmission.

Autotomy: Self-mutilation or self-division. A part of the defensive strategy in some snakes. It refers to the easy fracturing and resulting breakage and loss of the tail as a response to seizure of the tail by an aggressor, in which the tail is broken by the pull of the seizure, not spontaneously (urotomy), as in some lizards.

Azygous: Not being paired, single and placed in the middle line. Often describes a plate on the head of some snakes, which is different from the typical plates.

Azygous plate: Usually elongate scale located on the middle front portion of the head between the internasals, as seen in the Eastern Hognose Snake.

Bask: To rest in the direct rays of the sun, which raises the body temperature of the snake allowing for increased activity, better digestion, and in females, improving incubation of eggs, or embryos in the case of live birth. It is a part of their thermoregulatory behavior, because direct absorption of radiant heat from the sun can raise their temperature above that of their surroundings.

Basal (rattle): Relating to or forming the base.

Belly scutes: The enlarged scales seen on the undersurface of most snakes.

Bifurcated: Forked.

Binominal: A name consisting of two parts, e.g., a genus name and a species name.

Blotch: A large body marking that differs in color from the ground color of a snake. It is usually rounded or squarish and with a border that contrasts with the blotch and ground color. Primary or dorsal blotches are usually confined to the back or dorsal surface, and may extend slightly onto the lateral sides of the body. Secondary or lateral blotches are found on the sides, usually alternating with the primary blotches.

Body length: Measurement from snout to anus, or vent, referred to as *SVL* It may also pertain to the entire length of the snake, from snout to tip of the tail, referred to as the total body length.

Brooding: Physical contact between a mother and her eggs for part or all of the eggs' incubation period.

Button: The terminal segment on the tail of a rattlesnake.

Camouflage: Colors or patterns, which disrupt or confuse bodily outline or shape.

Canthals: Scales on the edge of the crown of the Timber Rattlesnake, and some other rattlesnakes, between the internasals and supraoculars.

Carphophis: Dry twig snake.

Carnivore: A flesh-eating organism or animal.

Cast: Term referring to the shed skin.

Caudal: Any scale or plate on the tail of a reptile.

Cervical: Pertaining to the neck.

Chin shields: Paired, elongate scales on the chin of a snake between the lower labials, or lips.

Chromatophore: Any cell which bears pigment, and thus plays a role in the overall color pattern of the animal. There are four main types: *lipophore; guanophore*; *melanophore: and allophore*.

Cloaca: The common chamber into which the digestive, urinary, and reproductive systems empty, opening to the outside through the anus or vent.

Coil: A series of loops used to refer to the position of a snake commonly referred to *striking coil* and *resting coil*.

Cold-blooded: Often used in describing snakes, it is inappropriate, for many times, the temperature of reptiles may be well above the warm-blooded animals in the same area.

Coluber: serpent, harmless snake

Columella: The bone or bones, and/or cartilage which form the auditory, or hearing, apparatus of the middle ear, with the primary function of sound transmission.

Combat dance: A behavior pattern displayed by two male snakes. When the snakes meet, one challenges, the other accepts. Each lifts the front part of its body off the ground, and the two snakes twine around each other,

rising higher and higher until one gains the advantage and throws the other down to the ground. This action is repeated until one becomes discouraged and moves away. Although suggested to be part of a mating ritual, the real significance of the dance has not been determined. The Northern Copperheads in the illustration display the dance. Color codes: (1) tan; (2) brown-red; (3) pink; (4) black.

Complete rattle: An unbroken rattle string with the button intact.

Concertina locomotion: One of the four basic types of movement in snakes in which the snake anchors its tail and stretches its body full length, and then the head and front part of the body is anchored, and the rest of the body is drawn up into an accordion fold. The progress is like an inchworm, with side or lateral folds rather than vertical, straight up and down folds, also referred to as earthworm movement. The name comes from the accordion-like appearance of the snake as it moves.

contortrix: Twister.

Constrictor: A snake, which kills its prey by wrapping coils of its body tightly around it causing suffocation.

Crepuscular: Active during the hours of twilight and/or dawn.

Crotalus: The generic name of the rattlesnakes. In the noncapitalized usage, it is a mixture of one part rattlesnake venom with nine parts of glycerine, used at one time for the treatment of epilepsy.

Crotalus: Rattle.

Crown shields: Used in reference to the enlarged scales on the top of the head in snakes, including the nine typical normal head plates.

Cryptic: Serving to conceal, having markings, coloration, shapes, or other features that cause an animal to be camouflaged in its natural habitat.

Death feint: The assuming of a position similar to that of a dead individual. The Eastern Hognose Snake goes completely limp, rolls over on its back, with its mouth wide open and the tongue trailing in the dirt, motionless unless turned onto its belly, whereupon it immediately spins back over. Similar words for this behavior include: hypnotic reflex, thanatosis; tonic immobility and ascaphus reflex.

dekayi: A proper name, James Elsworth DeKay.

Deciduous: A shedding, falling off, or falling out, i.e. loosing leaves.

Delayed fertilization: The union of egg and sperm after the sperm have been retained in the oviducts of the female for more than one season after mating.

Diadophis: Divided, through, snake.

Diastema: A space or gap between teeth, which is a true gap, not one caused by the loss of a tooth.

Dichromatism (sexual): A color difference between sexes of the same species.

Dimorphism: Difference in color, form, or structure between members of the same species.

Diosmesis: Refers to double smelling, or the ability to test both the outside odors and the contents of the oral cavity, through the complex olfactory organ and the Jacobson's organ.

Discharge orifice: The end opening of the venom duct in the fang of a venomous snake, lying near the sharp point, through which the venom flows into the tissues of a victim.

Distal: Toward the tip of an extremity, appendage, or body part, i.e., most distant from the body.

Diurnal: Active during daytime hours.

Dorsal: Pertaining to the back or upper surface of the body.

Dorsolateral: Pertaining to the area at the juncture of the back and the side.

Dorsum: The top or upper surface of an animal.

Ecdysis: Process of shedding or losing the dead, *keratinous,* outer layer of skin, called the stratum corneum. In snakes the old skin usually comes off in one piece. Other words used to describe this process are: casting; desquamation; exuviation; molting; shedding, and sloughing.

Ectoparasite: Parasites that attack the outside or external body such as mites, ticks, and fleas.

Ectotherm: An animal that regulates its temperature behaviorally by means of outside sources of heat. It moves to warmer or colder areas of its habitat to change its temperature. Other words used to describe this process are: cold-blooded; heterotherm; and poikilotherm.

edwardsi: A proper name, G. Edwards.

Elaphe: Deer-like.

Egg tooth: A structure on the tip of the snout of hatchlings which is used to cut through the leathery egg shell, and is lost a short time after hatching.

Endemic: Confined to, or indigenous in, a certain region.

Envenomation: The introduction of a venom into the tissues of an animal. Different degrees of envenomation have been established in snakebite: including Grade 0: with no venom introduced, often referred to as a dry bite; Grade I, *minimal envenomation*, in which the patient has been clearly bitten and shows puncture wounds, plus localized signs of poison effects; Grade II, *moderate envenomation* in which there is severe and widely spread pain plus marked swelling or edema; Grade III, *severe envenomation,* in which the progress of the venom effects is rapid, and the patient is either in or close to shock. Also referred to as veneation, ophidiasis, and toxemia.

Erythrophore: A lipophore in which the alcohol soluble oil droplets have a red or reddish hue. It is one of the two subtypes of lipophore; the other one being *xanthophore*.

Estivation, aestivation: A state of inactivity during prolonged periods of drought or high temperature.

Facial pit: Depression between the eye and nostril in pit vipers such as the Northern Copperhead and Timber Rattlesnake.

Fang: Enlarged tooth with hollow canal opening near the tip through which venom flows in Northern Copperhead and Timber Rattlesnake.

Fang succession: The functional fang in a venomous snake is regularly replaced by replacement fangs in an orderly sequence. There are two adjoining sockets for fangs on each side of the head, but only one is occupied by a functional fang at any one time. Both fangs are functional and active, and are alternately occupied by a fang, with other replacement fangs moving up to the sockets in turn. Once a fang occupies a socket, it remains in the socket until it is lost.

Fecund: A female with developing follicles capable of producing eggs.

Fossorial: Adapted for living underground; not all fossorial animals are borrowers but rather may use preexisting holes and cavities in the earth.

Foveals: The small scales surrounding the outside of the pit on the Timber Rattlesnake and other species of rattlesnake.

Frontal plate: An unpaired enlarged plate in the middle top of the head between the eyes of snakes.

Geneial, or genial: Refers to chin shield.

Gestation: The period of time that young develop within the body of the female before birth.

Glottis: Refers to the opening of the windpipe.

Granular scales: Very small, tiny grainlike scales that do not overlap one another.

Gravid: Bearing eggs or young, pregnant.

Ground color: The background color between blotches, stripes, bars, chevrons, and other markings.

Gulars: Small scales on the chin, between the lower labials, and the chin shields and the ventral scales.

Habitat: The place where an animal normally lives.

Hatchling: An animal recently hatched from an egg.

Head plates or shields: Large scales on the top of the head.

Haemotoxin: A toxin that affects the blood.

Heterodon: Variable teeth.

Heliophilic: Sun-loving.

Heliothermic: Deriving heat from the sun.

Hemipenes: The copulatory (sexual) organs of male snakes and lizards. snakes and

Herpetofauna: The amphibians and/or reptiles inhabiting a certain area.

Hibernation: Reduction of biological activity, or dormancy during winter.

Home range: An area to which an animal conducts most of its normal activities.

Horizontal undulatory locomotion: A form of movement in which a snake glides forward in a series of uninterrupted waves created by pushing its sides against irregularities in the surface upon which it moves.

horridus: Horrid.

Iridescence: The rainbow sheen created by cells, iridocytes, in the skin that contain light diffracting crystals which produce a variety of iridescence effects, as opposed to color produced by a pigment. It changes in color as the angle of viewing is changed, and in snakes skins is usually an indication of good health.

Insectivorous: Feeding on insects.

Intergenial: Any scale lying between the large, paired *chin shileds* of snakes.

Internasal: Head plate(s), located between the *nasal*, or nostril scales.

Interorbital, or **intersupraocular:** Small scales on the top of the head of some rattlesnakes.

Interstitial: Between the scales.

Jacobson's organ: A sensory structure located in the roof of the mouth in snakes and other reptiles. It is used to identify chemicals in the environment involving taste and/or smell.

Keel: A ridge on individual dorsal scales of some snakes.

Keratin: A hard, tough, fibrous, non-soluble protein produced in the epidermis, or upper layer of skin, which forms scales in snakes.

Labial: Pertaining to the lips, or area around the lips. The upper labials are separated in the front by the *rostral* scale, and the lower labials are separated in the front by the *mental* scale.

Lacunals: Large scales that form the inner border of the pit in pit vipers. Sometimes they extend onto the exterior surface of the pit. If they lie completely on the outside surface as in the Timber Rattlesnake, they are referred to as *foveals.*

Lampropeltis: Shiny shield.

Lateral: Pertaining to the side of an animal.

Lipophore: A chromatophore with the presence of lipids in the form of oil droplets in which naturally occurring pigments are dissolved. They lie on the outermost layers of the dermis, or second layer of skin, and generally appear either yellow (*xanthrophores*), or red (*erythrophores*).

Lobe: Part of the rattle segment. The anterior lobe is always visible, whereas the posterior lobe is hidden by the rattle that follows.

Loreal, or **loral:** A scale on the side of the head between the *nasals*, or nostril scales, and the *preocular* or scale in front of the eye.

Mandible: The bone of the lower jaw.

Matrix: The fleshy end of the tail of rattlesnakes upon which each new segment is formed.

Maxilla: Either of the two dermal bones of the upper jaw in reptiles, separated in the front by the *premaxillaries.*

Maxillary: Pertaining to the upper jaw.

Melanin: The dark-brown to black pigment granules found in *melanophores.*

Melanophore: A chromatophore with the pigment *melanin,* a granular, dark brown to black pigment. It is often characterized by its many branching processes.

Melanistic: Abundance of black pigment, sometimes resulting in an all black, or nearly all-black animal.

Mental: The single scale at the front of the lower jaw in snakes, bordered on both sides by the first lower *labials.*

Mesic: Habitat with moderate moisture level.

Middorsal: Pertaining to the center of the back of an animal.

Midventral: Pertaining to the center of the belly or abdomen of an animal.

mokeson: Moccassin.

Morph: A body form or colored group of individuals. Often used in discussion of polymorphism, or many variations of individual characteristics, such as color, within a population of the same species.

Morphology: The study of an animal's form or shape.

Nasal: Scale containing or next to the nostril.

Neonates: Newborn, newly born.

Nerodia: Wet-like.

Neurotoxin: A toxin that affects the nervous system.

Nocturnal: Active at night.

obsoleta: Dim, obsolete.

Ocular: A scale covering the eye and is visible when the skin is shed as a clear eye shield.

Occipitomaculata: Occipit, spotted.

Oculars: Scales that border the eye such as the *preocular, postocular* and *supraolulars*.

Opheodrys: Snake, oak.

Ophidian: A snake, or relating to a snake.

Ophiophagous: Snake-eating.

Opisthoglyphous: Rear-fanged snakes.

Orbit: The eye opening.

Oviduct: The tubules that carry the egg from the ovary to the *cloaca*.

Oviparity:.The production of young by means of fertilized eggs which are released from the ovary, form a shell, and almost immediately expelled from the body. The entire embryonic development takes place outside the female, inside the deposited egg.

Oviposition: The deposition or laying of eggs.

Ovovivipararity: The production of young by means of eggs that are surrounded by a membrane after release from the ovary, but are not released immediately to the outside. The eggs remain in the female, usually in the oviducts, and undergo much of their fetal period there. This is contrasted with *vivparity* in that no nourishment is derived by the embryo from the mother during ovoviviparity, and no placenta or placenta-like membrane is formed. More recent research has indicated that the eggs in most snakes retained in this manner have some form of maternal-fetal exchange of materials, and therefore the term ovoviviparity is less often applied to the description of reproduction in snakes.

Parietals: A pair of dermal bones in the roof of the skull, located between the *frontals* and *occipitals*. The large scales directly above these bones are referred to as parietal plates and form the last pair of plates and lead into the smaller body scales of the snake.

Parotoid gland: An internal gland of the head, located on the side of the head behind the eye. In most snakes it is a salivary gland, but in the venomous snakes this gland is modified for the production of poison.

Pheromone: A chemical signal secreted by one animal that sends specific information to another animal, often related to mating.

Pit: A deep depression on the side of the head of pit vipers behind and below the nostril, hollowed out of the maxillary bone. It consists of two chambers separated by the pit membrane. It is an infra-red detector, used to determine the accurate direction of the snake's strike even when the snake is visionless. It is the external opening to the heat-sensitive, sensory organ.

Pit membrane: A thin sheet of tissue separating the inner and outer chamber of the pit in pit vipers. It is supplied by ophthalmic (sight), and supramaxillary branches of the trigeminal (5th cranial) nerve, and is sensitive to infra-red radiations.

Plate: A large *scale.* Usually referring to the large scales on the belly of the snake, called ventral plates or scutes, sometimes also used to describe the large head scales.

platyrhinos: Flat snout.

Posterior: The rear or tail end of an animal.

Postnasal: A scale or scales lying behind the nasal *scale* and infront of the *loreal* scale.

Postocular: A scale or scales bordering the posterior portion of the orbit of the eye.

Postrostral: Scale behind the *rostral* scale, *azygous.*

Prefrontals: A pair of plates in front of the frontal plate.

Prehensile: Adapted for grasping or wrapping around.

Prenasal: The front *nasal* scale, when the nasal scale is divided.

Preocular: A scale or scales bordering the front portion of the orbit of the eye.

Proteroglyphous: The presence of fixed, non-erectile venom conducting teeth, fangs, in the front of the mouth.

Proximal: Toward the beginning of or origin of an appendage, extremity, or body part, i.e., closest to the body.

punctatus: Dotted.

Rattle: *Keratinized,* sound-producing terminal (end) appendage on the tail of rattlesnakes. The proximal rattle closest to the tail and is the one most recently added to the string. The *button* is the first permanent rattle acquired by a young snake, which remains as the last part of the rattle, giving it the tapered look, until it is lost due to breakage. The rattle present at birth, the *prebutton* is lost with the first shedding of skin after birth.

Rectilinear locomotion: A form of limbless (no legs), movement upon which a wavelike pattern of rib movement propels the animal forward in a straight line, with no   lateral or sideways movements, often referred to as the caterpillar crawl created by back and forth movements between the snake's skin and the body within the skin. The skin and related ventral belly plates are pulled forward, anchored against some friction point on the ground, and then the body is pulled forward.

Replacement fang: Any one of a series of grooved teeth that lie in back of the functional *fang,* within a sheath of tissue, and which slowly moves forward as it develops, eventually replacing the lost fang.

Resting coil: Klauber, *Rattlesnakes,* 1956, p.444, description of the pancake-like position of the body in rattlesnakes at rest, with most of the body on the ground or resting on other loops of the body, and the head resting on the outer edge of the coil. This can be applied to all snakes.

Rostral: A plate in the middle of the upper lip on the tip of the snout bordering the mouth, separating the *labial* rows.

Saddle: A *blotch* with a general shape resembling a horse saddle, extending down the sides but wider on the back than on the sides.

sauritus: Lizard-like.

Scale: A general term referring to the horny epidermal outgrowths that cover reptiles.
.
Scale pits: Tiny depressions on the back portions of the dorsal scales in some snakes.

Scale rows: Dorsal scales counted diagonally around the body of the snake, beginning and ending at the ventral scales. There is a count around the neck area and around the middle of the body, and near the tail. For example, a scale row formula of 17-19-15, means 17 scales in the row at the front end, 19 scales in the middle row and 15 scales at the posterior end of the snake.

Sclerotic ring: Acomplete ring of ocular scales, with subocular scales present as in the Eastern Hognose Snake.

Scutellum: Refers to a small scale.

Scutellation: Study of the arrangement of scales.

Scutes: Enlarged scale on a reptile; sometimes-called shield or plate.

Serum: In general, the watery part of blood, which remains after coagulation or clotting, has taken place.

Sex: Physical determination of in snakes, refers to the shape of the base of the tail, which is wide in the male, and narrow and more quickly tapering in the female.

Sexually mature: Fully developed and able to reproduce.

Sheath: The protective membrane partially surrounding the base of the fang in snakes with retractile fangs.

Shield: An enlarged scale on snakes restricted to the head plates in snakes.

Shed: A cast off skin, or molt.

Sidewinding locomotion: A form of specialized movement when a snake moves sideways or laterally with a looping motion in which each part of the body is lifted and rolled sideways to a new position, beginning at the head and flowing smoothly to the tail.

sepidon: A siren (water nymph).

sirtalis: Garter-like.

Slough: The cast or shed skin of a snake. It also refers to the tissue lost near a venomous snake bite, as a result of necrotic, or tissue death activity, which leaves an ulcer which takes a long time to heal.

Snakestone: A porous object which, when placed at the site of a snake bite, is supposed to draw the poison out of the wound.

Snout: The front or anterior part of the head, usually including the area around the nostrils.

Solenoglyphous: The presence of movable or erectile, venom conducting hollow teeth, *fangs,* at the front of the mouth as in the Northern Copperhead and Timber Rattlesnake.

Spread: To flatten the neck region, usually by drawing the ribs of the neck region upward and outward such as seen in the hog-nosed snake.

Strike: A single, rapid movement, usually of the head and neck only, made by a snake when attempting to bite either prey or tormentor. In many snakes the strike is made from an S-coil of the front part of the body by straightening the coil suddenly, resembling the punch of a boxer.

Stiking coil: Klauber, *Rattlesnakes,* 1956, 9.444, describes the position of an excited or agitated rattlesnakes body, with the front or anterior third or more of the body raised off the ground, ending with an S-shaped loop of the head and neck. The loop of body on the ground is inflated and spread to increase the anchoring. This coil applies to all snakes.

Storeria: A proper name, David Humphreys Storer.

Subcaudals: Enlarged scales beneath the tail; in a double row in most snakes, but in single rows in others.

Subocular: A scale or scales lying directly below the eye.

Substrate: The surface upon which an animal lives.

Supraocular: A scale lying directly above the eye.

Sympatric: Two species sharing the same habitat.

Suture: A seam; the space between scales or scutes.

Tail: The part of the snake past the anus or vent.

Tail waving: The writhing and wriggling of the tip of the tail as a lure to prey observed in juveniles of many species of snakes, especially evident in yellow-tipped tail of young Northern Copperheads.

Taxon: The technical term for a unit or category, plural: taxa.

Taxonomy: The science of the classification of animals or plants.

Temporals: One or two elongated scales arranged one above the other located behind the ***postoculars***, below the ***parietals*** and above the upper ***labials***, or upper lip scales.

Thamnophis: Bush snake.

Thermoreceptor: An organ sensitive to heat or changes in temperature.

triangulum: Triangle.

Venom: A substance capable of producing toxic reactions when introduced into the tissues of an animal. In snakes is refers to the product of specialized glands used either as a mechanism for immobilizing prey or as a defensive device. The "ordinary way" to collect venom is to permit the snake to bite through a parchment or rubber covered collecting cup along with gentle massage of the parotid gland region.

Venom gland: A gland evolved in reptiles from salivary glands. There are two kinds of glands relating to Connecticut snakes. The first consists of a moderately well developed lobed labial (lip) salivary gland, which discharges a mildly toxic saliva at the base of several teeth, known from some nonfanged snakes and well developed in rear-fanged snakes.

The second type is referred to as a ***parotid gland***, differing from the labial salivary gland by the occurrence of a fascial sheath, and a single duct leading the venom to a specialized, groove fang.

Vent: Opening of the *cloaca* to the outside of the body, anal opening.

Venter: The underside or lower surface of an animal.

Ventral: Pertaining to the underside or lower surface of the body.

Ventrals: Large scales or plates on the under surface, or belly, of the body, from the head to the anal plate.

vernalis: Spring.

Viviparity: The production of young, by means of eggs that are implanted in some form of placenta, permitting exchange of materials between mother and embryo. The.distinctions between this and ***ovoviviparity***, at one time clear-cut, has broken down with recent research, and the distinction is now academic.

BIBLIOGRAPHY

Aldridge, Robert D., and Angelo P. Bufalino. (2003). "Reproductive Female Common Watersnakes (*Nerodia sipedon sipedon*) Are Not Anorexic in the Wild." *Journal of Herpetology,* 37 (2): 416-419.

Bartels, Cathy L., and Danielle L. Dauenhauer. (Eds.) (2001). "CroFab For Snake Bites." *SPAHS Drug Information Service,* The University of Montana.

Barbour, R. W., M. J. Harvey, and J. W. Hardin. (1969). "Home range, movements and activity of the Eastern Worm Snakes, *Carphophis amoenus amoenus.*" *Ecology* 50: 470-476.

Behler, John L., and F. W. King. (1979). *The Audubon Society Field Guide to North American Reptiles and Amphibians.* New York: Alfred A. Knopf, Inc.

Blanchard, F.N. (1942). "The Ring-neck Snakes, genus *Diadophis.*" *Bull. Chicago Acad. Sci.* 7:1-144.

Borrow, Donald J. (1960). *Dictionary of Word Roots and Combining Forms.* California: Mayfield Publishing Company.

Bowen, Kenneth D. (2003). "Ontogenetic Changes in the Coloration of the Northern Watersnake, (*Nerodia sipedon sipedon*)." Journal of Herpetology, 37 (4): 729-731.

Brennan, C.E. (1995). *Rattler Tales from Northcentral Pennsylvania.* Pittsburgh, Pennsylvania: University of Pittsburgh Press.

Brown, William S. (1993). "Biology, Status, and Management of the Timber Rattlesnake (*Crotalus horridus*). A Guide for Conservation." *Society for the Study of Amphibians and Reptiles, Herpetological Circular*, 22: I-vi + 1-78.

Campbell, Johathan A J., and Edmund E. Brodie Jr. (Eds.) (1992). *Biology of the Pitvipers.* Texas: The University of Texas at Arlington.

Clark, A. M., P. E. Moler, E. E. Possardt, A. H. Savitzky, W. S.Brown, and B. W. Bowen. (2003). "Phylogeography of the Timber Rattlesnake *(Crotalus horridus)* Based on mtDNA Sequences." *Journal of Herpetology,* 37 (1): 145-154.

Clark, Rulon W. (2002). "Diet of the Timber Rattlesnake, *Crotalus horridus. Journal of Herpetology*, Vol. 36, No. 3, 494-499."

Cochran, P. A. (1987). "Life History Notes: *Opheodrys aestivus* (Smooth Green Snake)." *Herpetol. Rev*. 18 (2): 36-37.

Conant, Roger. (1951). *The Reptiles of Ohio.* 2nd ed. Univ. Notre Dame Press, Notre Dame, Ind.

Conant, Roger. (1957). *Reptiles and Amphibians of the Northeastern States.* 3rd ed. Philadelphia: Zoological Society of Philadelphia.

Conant, Roger. (1958). *A Field Guide to Reptiles and Amphibians of Eastern/Central North America.* 2nd ed. Boston: Houghton Mifflin Company.

Conant, Roger, and Joseph T.Collins. (1998). *A Field Guide to Reptiles & Amphibians: Eastern and Central North America.* 3rd ed., expanded. New York: Houghton Mifflin Company.

Convention on International Trade in Endangered Species of Wild Fauna and Flora. Amendments to appendices I and II of CITES. *Eleventh Meeting of the Conference of the Parties Nairobe (Kenya)*, April 10-20, 2000.

DeGraaf, R. M., and D. D. Rudis. (1983). *Amphibians and Reptiles of New England: Habitat and Natural History.* Amherst: The University of Massachusetts Press.

Ditmars, Raymond L. (1931). *Snakes of the World.* New York: The Macmillan Company.

Ditmars, Raymond L. (1933). *Reptiles of the World.* New York: The Macmillan Company.

Ditmars, Raymond L. (1935). *Thrills of a Naturalist's Quest.* New York: The Macmillan Company.

Ditmars, Raymond L. (1935). *Serpents of the Northeastern States.* New Ed. New York Zool. Soc.

Ditmars, Raymond L. (1936). *The Reptiles of North America.* New York: Doubleday, Doran & Company, Inc.

Ditmars, Raymond L. (1939). *A Field Book of North American Snakes.* New York: Doubleday & Company, Inc.

Erichsen-Brown, Charlotte. (1979). *Medicinal and Other Uses of North American Plants. A Historical Survey with Special Reference to the Eastern Indian Tribes.* New York: Dover Publications, Inc.

Ernst, Carl. H. and Roger W. Barbour. (1989). *Snakes of Eastern North America.* Virginia: George Mason University Press.

Ernst, Carl H. and G. R. Zug. (1996). *Snakes in Question: The Smithsonian Answer Book.* Washington: Smithsonian Institution Press.

Fitch, H. S. (1960). "Autecology of the Copperhead*." Univ. Kansas Mus. Natur. Hist. Publ.* 13: 85-288.

Fitch, H. S. (1963). "Natural History of the Racer, *Coluber constrictor." Univ. Kansas. Mus. Natur. Hist. Publ.* 15: 351-468.

Fitch, H. S. (1975). "A Demographic Study of the Ringneck Snake *(Diadophis punctatus)* in Kansas*." Univ. Kansas Mus. Natur. Hist. Publ.* (62): 1-53.

Fitch, H.S. (1985). "Observations on Rattle Size and Demography of Prairie Rattlesnakes *(Crotalus viridis)* and Timber Rattlesnakes *(Crotalus horridus)* in Kansas." *Univ. Kansas Mus. Natur. Hist. Occasional Papers.*(118): 1-11.

Fitch, H. S. (2003). "Tail Loss in Garter Snakes." Society for the Study of Amphibians and Reptiles. *Herpetological Review*, 34 (3): 212-213.

Foster, Steven, and James A. Duke. (2000). *Peterson Field Guide, to Medicinal Plants and Herbs of Eastern and Central North America.* 2nd ed. Houghton Mifflin Co., New York.

Gillingham, J. C. (1979). "Reproduction Behavior of the Rat Snakes of Eastern North America, genus *Elaphe." Copeia* 1979: 319-331.

Gillingham, J. C. (1980). "Communication and Combat Behavior in the Black Rat Snake *(Elaphe obsoleta obsoleta)*". *Herpetologica* 36:120-127.

Gloyd, Howard K., and R. Conant. (1990). *Snakes of the Agkistrodon Complex: A Monographic Review.* Soc. Study Amphibians and Reptiles, Ithaca, New York.

Greene, Harry W. (1997). *Snakes. The Evolution of Mystery in Nature.* Berkeley: Univ. California Press.

Halliday, Tim R., and K. Adler. (Ed.) (1987). *The Encyclopedia of Reptiles and Amphibians.* New York: Fact On File Inc.

Henshaw, J. (1904). "Fauna of New England. List of the Reptilia." *Occ. Pap. Boston Soc. Nat. Hist. 7(1):1-13.*

Klauber, M. Laurence. (1972). *Rattlesnakes: Their Habits, Life Histories, and Influence on Mankind.* 2nd ed. 2 vols. Berkeley and Los Angeles: Univ. California Press.

Klemens, W. Michael. (1993). *Amphibians and Reptiles of Connecticut and Adjacent Regions.* State Geolog. Nat. Hist. Survey Connecticut, Bull. 112.

Klemens, W. Michael. (2000). *Amphibians and Reptiles in Connecticut.* Connecticut DEP Bulletin 32.

Lavies, Bianca. (1991). *The Secretive Timber Rattlesnake.* New York: Dutton Children's Books.

Martin, W. H. (1992b). "Phenology of the Timber Rattlesnake, *Crotalus horridus*, in an Unglaciated Section of the Appalachian Mountains." J. A. Campbell and E. D. Brodie Jr., Eds. *Biology of the Pitvipers.* Selva Press, Tyler, Texas. pp. 259-277.

Minton, Sherman. A., Jr., and M. R.Minton. (1980). *Venomous Reptiles.* Rev. ed. New York: Charles Scribner's Sons.

Minton, Sherman A., Jr. (2001). *Life, Love, and Reptiles: An Autobiography of Sherman A Minton, Jr., M.D.* Malabar, Florida: Krieger Publishing Company.

Noble, G. K., and H. J.Clausen. (1936). "The Aggregation Behavior of *Storeria dekayi* and Other Snakes with Special Reference to the Sense Organs Involved." *Ecol. Monogr.,* 6:269-316.

Noble, G. K. (1937). "The Sense Organs Involved in the Courtship of *Storeria, Thamnophis* and other Snakes". *Bull. .American Mus. Nat. Hist.,* 73: 673-725.

Peters, James A. (1964). *Dictionary of Herpetology.* New York: Hafner Publishing Company.

Petersen, R. C. (1970). *Connecticut's Venomous Snakes.* Connecticut St. Geol. Natur. Hist. Surv. Bull. 103: 1-39.

Petersen, R. C., and R. W. Fritsch II. (1986). *Connecticut's Venomous Snakes.* 2nd ed. Connecticut St. Geol. Natur. Hist. Surv. Bull. 111:1-48.

Platt, D. R. (1969). "Natural history of the hognose snakes *Heterodon platyrhinos* and *Heterodon nasicus*." Univ. Kansas Publ. Mus. Nat. Hist. 18 (4): 253-420.

Pope, Clifford H. (1937). *Snakes Alive and How They Live.* New York: Viking Press.

Pope, Clifford H. (1946). *Snakes of the Northeastern United States.* New York: New York Zool. Soc.

Reinert, Howard K., and D. Cundall. (1982). "An Improved Surgical Implantation Method for Radio-tracking Snakes." *Copeia,* 1982: 702-705.

Reinert, Howard K. (1984a). "Habitat Separation Between Sympatric Snake Populations." *Ecology* 65 (2): 478-86.

Reinert, Howard K. (1984b). "Habitat Variation Within Sympatric Snake Populations." *Ecology* 65 (5): 1673-82.

Reinert, Howard K., with David Cundall and Lauretta M. (1984). "Foraging Behavior of the Timber Rattlesnake." *Copeia* (4): 976-981.

Reinert, Howard K., and Robert J. T. Zappalorti. (1988a). Timber Rattlesnakes (*Crotalus horridus*) of the Pine Barrens: Their Movement Patterns and Habitat Preference." *Copeia* (4): 964-978.

Reinert, Howard K., and Robert J. T. Zappalorti. (1988b). "Field Observation of the Association of Adult and Neonatal Timber Rattlesnakes, *Crotalus horridus*, with Possible Evidence for Conspecific Trailing." *Copeia* (4): 1057-1059.

Reinert, Howard K. (1990). "A Prolile and Impact Assessment of Organized Rattlesnake Hunts in Pennsylvania." *Journal of the Pennsylvania Academy of Science* 64 (3): 136-144.

Reinhert, Howard K. (1992). "Radiotelemetric Field Studies of Pitvipers: Data Acquisition and Analysis." 185-197 in *The Biology of Pitvipers,* edited by J. Campbelle and E. D. Brodie, Jr. Tyler, Texas: Selva Press.

Ricciuti, Edward. (2001). *The Snake Almanac*. New York: The Lyons Press. Romer, Alfred S. (1962). *The Vertebrate Body*. Philadelphia: W. B. Saunders Company.Schmidt,

Rossman, D. A., and P. A. Meyers. (1990). "Behavioral and Morphological Adaptations for Snail Extraction in the North American Brown Snakes (genus *Storeria).*" *J. Herpetol.* 24 (4): 434-438.

Schuett, G. W., and J. C. Gillingham. (1986). "Sperm Storage and Multiple Paternity in the Copperhead, *Agkistrodon contortrix*." *Copeia,* (3): 807-811.

Schuett, G. W., and J. C. Gillingham. (1988). "Courtship and Mating of the Copperhead, *Agkistrodon contortrix*." *Copeia,* (2): 374-381.

Schuett, G. W., and J. C. Gillingham. (1989). "Male-male Agnostic behavior of the Copperhead, *Agkistrodon contortrix.*" *Amphibia-Reptilia,* (10): 243-266.

Schmidt, Karl P., and D. D. Davis. (1941). *Field Book of Snakes of the United States and Canada*. New York: G. P. Putman's Sons.

Schmidt, Karl P. (1953). *A Check List of North American Amphibians and Reptiles..* 6th ed. Chicago: Ameri. Soc. Ichthyol. Herpetol.

Schmidt, Karl P. (1953). "Herpetology." Reprinted from *A Century of Progress in the Natural Sciences: 1853-1953*: 591-627. Chicago Nat. Hist. Mus.

Seigel, Richard A., Joseph T. Collins, and Susan J. S.Novak. (Eds.) (2001). *Snakes, Ecology, and Evolutionary Biology*. New Jersey: The Blackburn Press.

Seigel, Richard, and Joseph T. Collins. (Eds.) (2001). *Snakes, Ecology and Behavior*. New Jersey: The Blackburn Press.

Shine, Richard. (2001). "Sexual Dimorphism in Snakes", in *Snakes, Ecology and Behavior*. (Seigel, Collins, eds). New Jersey: The Blackburn Press.

Smith, Charles. (2002-2004). Department of Ecology and Evolutionary Biology, The University of Connecticut. Personal communication.

Tyning, Thomas F. (1990). *A Guide to Amphibians and Reptiles*. New York: Little, Brown and Company.

Vogt, Richard C. (1981). *Natural History of Amphibians and Reptiles of Wisconsin*. Wisconsin: Milwaukee Public Mus.

Werler, John E., and James R. Dixon. (2000). *Texas Snakes. Identification, Distribution, and Natural History*. Austin: University of Texas Press.

Wright, A. H., and A. A. Wright (1957). *Handbook of Snakes of the United States and Canada*. 2 vols. Ithica, New York: Comstock Publishing Associates.

Zimmermann, Arnold A., and C. H. Pope. (1948) "Development and Growth of the Rattle of Rattlesnakes." *Fieldiana: Zool.* 32: 355-413.

Zug, George R., L. J. Vitt, and J. P. Caldwell. (2001). *Herpetology: An Introductory Biology of Amphibians and Reptiles*. 2nd ed. California: Academic Press.

INDEX